CELLULAR AND MOLECULAR PHARMACOLOGY

DR. P BADHE | MRS A BADHE | MS N JADHAV | MS S VEER | MS S MURKAR AND MR S CHAVAN

Made with ♥ on the Notion Press Platform
www.notionpress.com

We would like to dedicate this work to my late grandmother Mrs Chhabubai Shankar Jadhav, my late aunty Mrs Gangubai Hanuman Shevkar and Mrs Usha Kailas Badhe.

We would like to thank our friends and family for their support, encouragement and faith in us.

Contents

Foreword

Dr Pravin Dattatraya Badhe and Mrs Ashwini Pravin Badhe have started working with the same aim of solving the skills issue in Pharmacy students. And after reading this work, I'm highly delighted to say this is definitely going to help the M. pharm students of Pharmacology. These working Principles of Drug Discovery will open the doors for new opportunities for the Master's students.

Dr J D White.
Professor
Brunel University

Foreword

Preface

I realize that this book will help first-year Master's students in Pharmacology. I have spent 15 years in the field of drug discovery, cell biology, life science and pharmacy. I have got two provisional patents and tech transfer about fifteen products. I have published about 10 papers and a couple of preprints. I feel obliged to share my knowledge, analyses, and conclusions.

The reason to write the book was to help first-year Mpharm pharmacology students. The book is written in simple English to get the basics clear to the students and get the idea clear.

The chapters are designed in such as way that students will get the content as per the syllabus and then we have added the updates for more information. This will help the student to understand the recent updates in the field that will help in their project.

Chapter 1 is a general introduction to cell and molecular pharmacology and a content overview of all the areas covered in the syllabus. Chapter 2 presents cell biology with recent updates. Chapter 3 introduces cell signalling with recent updates. Chapter 4 introduces the "Principles and applications of genomic and proteomic tools" with recent updates. Chapter 5 introduces "Pharmacogenomics" along with recent updates. Chapter 6 introduces "Cell culture techniques" along with ongoing recent updates.

Acknowledgements

Mrs Badhe Ashwini Pravin M.sc in Biotechnology

She completed her B. Pharmacy from S.V.P.Ms college of Pharmacy Malegaon (Bk) Baramati and her Masters from Sunrise University Rajashthan. After completing her pharmacy degree she worked at Niramaya Ethicals Pvt Limited Pune. After marriage she moved to London where she was part of Dr Sundus Tewfik's team and work as a Research Assistant at Londonmeteropolitan university London U.K. Simultaneously is completed her pharmacy dispensing at Rowland Pharmacy and worked there till 2016.

Her research was focused on small molecules from plants, plant and animal cell cultures, insilico studies, machine learning, and DNA damage response pathways in breast and skin cancer. She is the founder and director at Swalife healthcare LLP and also works as Chief scientific officer at Swalife biotech Ltd Ireland.

MS. Murkar Sayali Mahesh. M. Pharmacy (Pharmacology)

She is a Member of the Center for Drug Discovery and Development and also a Vice-president of The Sinhgad Cancer Biology Society.

Her research focused on small molecules targeting DNA damage response pathways in Breast Cancer. Her interest is in developing bio tools (like the SwaDeep tool) and also in CADD. In her post-graduation, she developed and optimized various toxicological and bioactivity assays. Currently, she is working on small molecules for the prevention of Cancer.

She completed her B. Pharmacy from GNCOP, Sawarde.

MS. Veer Snehal Dhanaji. M. Pharmacy (Pharmacology)

She is a Member of the Center for Drug Discovery and Development and also a Secretary, of the Sinhgad Cancer Biology Society.

Her research focused on small molecules targeting DNA damage response pathways in Breast Cancer. Her interest is in developing bio tools (like the SwaDeep tool) and also in CADD. In her post-graduation, she developed and optimized various toxicological and bioactivity assays. Currently, she is working on small molecules for the prevention of Cancer.

She completed her B. Pharmacy from the College of Pharmacy, Akluj.

MS. Jadhav Nishigandha Shahaji. M. Pharmacy (Pharmacology)

She completed her B. Pharmacy from Vishal Institute of Pharmaceutical Education and Research, Ale. She is a Member of the Center for Drug Discovery and Development and also the President of the Sinhgad Cancer Biology Society. She is a team member of Developing Bio tools.

Her research focused on targeting DNA damage response pathways in Breast Cancer using herbal drugs. In her post-graduation, she is working the various toxicological and bioactivity assays like Brine shrimp, anti-bacterial and CAM assay and also zebrafish and C. elegans animal models. She is also working on CADD techniques like network pharmacology, and molecular docking for drug discovery. Currently, she is working on small molecules for the treatment of Cancer.

Mr Chavan Sujit Tukaram M Pharmacy (Pharmacology)

He graduated from R.P. College Of Pharmacy Gadpati, Osmanabad. His research centred on employing herbal medications to target DNA damage response pathways in breast cancer. Working on several assays like brine shrimp assay, chicken eye irritation test, zebrafish and animal models. He also works with molecular docking for drug discovery.

Acknowledgements

CHAPTER ONE

Cellular and Molecular Pharmacology

Dr Pravin Badhe and Mrs Ashwini Badhe

Introduction

Cells are the basic unit of life in all living organisms. They are the smallest unit of an organism that can perform all the functions of life, such as metabolism, growth, and reproduction. There are two main types of cells: prokaryotic cells, which do not have a distinct nucleus, and eukaryotic cells, which do have a distinct nucleus. All living organisms are made up of one or more cells.

Cells are incredibly diverse and come in many different shapes and sizes, but all have certain basic structures and functions in common. These include a cell membrane, which acts as a barrier between the cell and its environment, and a cytoskeleton, which provides structural support and helps the cell move. Most cells also contain a variety of organelles, which are specialized structures that perform specific functions. Examples of organelles include the mitochondria, which produce energy for the cell, and the ribosomes, which synthesize proteins.

Eukaryotic cells have a true nucleus, which contains the cell's genetic material, DNA. Prokaryotic cells, on the other hand, do not have a distinct nucleus and their genetic material is scattered throughout the cytoplasm. Additionally, Eukaryotic cells are generally larger and more complex than prokaryotic cells, and they can be found in organisms such as plants and animals. Prokaryotic cells are found in organisms such as bacteria and archaea.

Cells are able to carry out all the processes needed to sustain life through the use of various chemical reactions and by communicating with other cells. Cells also have the ability to replicate and divide, which allows for the growth and repair of the organism. In addition, the cell is able to respond to its environment through the use of receptors on its surface and through communication with other cells.

In short, cells are the fundamental building blocks of all living organisms. They carry out all the necessary functions of life and are diverse in shape and function, but have common structures and abilities that allow for the continuation of life.

Cellular and Molecular Pharmacology

Cellular and molecular pharmacology is a branch of pharmacology that focuses on the study of how drugs interact with cells and molecular targets at the cellular and molecular level. It aims to understand the mechanisms of drug action, the interactions between drugs and receptors, and the ways in which drugs can be used to treat diseases.

One of the key concepts in cellular and molecular pharmacology is the study of drug receptors. These are molecules on the surface of cells that bind to specific drugs and mediate their effects. By understanding the structure and function of these receptors, researchers can develop new drugs that target them more effectively.

Another important area of study in cellular and molecular pharmacology is the study of signal transduction pathways. These are the series of molecular events that occur inside a cell after a drug binds to its receptor. By understanding these pathways, researchers can develop drugs that target specific steps in the pathway and enhance or inhibit the response.

The use of molecular biology techniques such as genomics, proteomics and metabolomics have also become important tools in cellular and molecular pharmacology. With these techniques, researchers can identify new targets and pathways for drug development, and also understand the mechanisms of resistance to drugs.

In short, cellular and molecular pharmacology is a field that aims to understand the mechanisms of drug action at the cellular and molecular level, with the ultimate goal of developing more effective drugs to treat diseases.

Cellular and molecular pharmacology is a rapidly evolving field that is essential for the development of new drugs and therapies. By understanding the mechanisms of drug action at the cellular and molecular level, researchers can identify new targets for drug development, design more effective drugs, and predict potential side effects.

One of the key areas of study in cellular and molecular pharmacology is the identification of new drug targets. This can be achieved through the use of various techniques such as genomics, proteomics, and metabolomics, which allow researchers to identify new proteins, enzymes, and metabolic pathways that are involved in disease. By targeting these new targets, researchers can develop drugs that are more selective and have fewer side effects.

Another important area of study in cellular and molecular pharmacology is the mechanism of drug resistance. Many diseases, including cancer and bacterial infections, have developed resistance to existing drugs. By understanding the molecular mechanisms of resistance, researchers can develop new drugs or strategies to overcome this resistance and improve treatment outcomes.

Another area of study is pharmacokinetics and pharmacodynamics, which deals with the study of how drugs are absorbed, distributed, metabolized, and eliminated by the body, as well as the relationship between drug concentration and the effect. Understanding these processes can help to optimize drug dosing and improve drug efficacy.

Finally, cellular and molecular pharmacology also involves studying the interactions between drugs and other molecules, such as other drugs or nutrients, which can affect the efficacy or safety of a drug.

Overall, cellular and molecular pharmacology is a multidisciplinary field that combines the knowledge of biology, chemistry, and medicine to understand the mechanisms of drug action and develop new and effective therapies for the treatment of diseases.

Another important area of study in cellular and molecular pharmacology is the use of stem cells to study drug effects and develop new therapies. Stem cells, which have the ability to differentiate into various types of cells, can be used to create models of human diseases and test the effects of drugs on these cells. This allows researchers to study the effects of drugs on specific cell types and identify new targets for drug development.

In addition, stem cells can also be used to repair or replace damaged or diseased cells in the body. This is a promising area of research known as regenerative medicine. Stem cells have the potential to be used in the treatment of various diseases such as cancer, diabetes, and heart disease.

The use of animal models is also an important aspect of cellular and molecular pharmacology. Researchers use animal models to study the effects of drugs on living organisms and to identify potential side effects before drugs are tested in human clinical trials. Animal models can also be used to study the mechanism of drug action and to identify new drug targets.

Finally, cellular and molecular pharmacology also involves the study of how drugs are delivered to the body. This is an important aspect of drug development, as it can affect the efficacy and safety of a drug. Researchers are developing new drug delivery systems, such as nanoparticles and liposomes, which can improve the delivery of drugs to specific cells or tissues in the body.

Overall, cellular and molecular pharmacology is a multidisciplinary field that combines the knowledge of biology, chemistry, and medicine to understand the mechanisms of drug action and develop new and effective therapies for the treatment of diseases. It encompasses a wide range of research areas including drug discovery, drug development, drug delivery, and regenerative medicine.

Another area of research in cellular and molecular pharmacology is the study of drug metabolism. This is the process by which drugs are broken down and eliminated by the body. Understanding drug metabolism is important as it can affect the efficacy and safety of a drug. For example, if a drug is metabolized too quickly, it may not be effective, and if it is metabolized too slowly, it can accumulate in the body and cause toxicity. Researchers use techniques such as mass spectrometry, and enzyme activity assays to study the metabolism of drugs.

Pharmacogenetics and pharmacogenomics are other areas of cellular and molecular pharmacology that deals with the study of how genetic variations affect the response to drugs. Genetic variations in drug receptors, enzymes involved in drug metabolism, and other proteins that interact with drugs can affect the efficacy and safety of a drug. By understanding these genetic variations, researchers can develop personalized medicine, where drugs are tailored to the specific genetic makeup of an individual.

Another important area is the study of drug interactions. Drugs can interact with other drugs, supplements, and foods, and these interactions can affect the efficacy and safety of a drug. For example, two drugs can interact and increase or decrease the activity of one another. Researchers use in-vitro, in-vivo and clinical studies to understand the interactions between drugs.

Finally, cellular and molecular pharmacology also involves the study of drug toxicity. This is the study of the harmful effects of drugs on the body. Researchers use various techniques such as cell culture and animal models to study the toxicity of drugs and to identify potential side effects. This information is used to improve the safety of drugs before they are tested in human clinical trials.

In summary, cellular and molecular pharmacology is a complex field that encompasses many different areas of research. It is focused on the study of the interactions between drugs and cells at the molecular level, with the ultimate goal of developing new and effective therapies for the treatment of diseases. It encompasses a wide range of areas including drug discovery, drug development, drug delivery, regenerative medicine, pharmacogenetics, pharmacogenomics, drug interactions and drug toxicity.

One of the most important areas of cellular and molecular pharmacology is the study of drug delivery systems. These are methods used to deliver drugs to the body in a targeted and controlled manner. This can greatly improve the efficacy of drugs and reduce side effects. Some examples of drug delivery systems include nanoparticles, liposomes, and polymeric micelle. These systems can be designed to target specific cells or tissues in the body and to release drugs at a controlled rate over time.

Another important area of research in cellular and molecular pharmacology is the use of imaging techniques to study the distribution and pharmacokinetics of drugs in the body. This can be used to understand how drugs are absorbed, distributed, metabolized, and eliminated by the body. Imaging techniques such as Magnetic Resonance Imaging (MRI), Positron Emission Tomography (PET), and Computed Tomography (CT) can be used to study the distribution of drugs in the body and to identify potential areas of toxicity.

The field of pharmacometrics is also closely related to cellular and molecular pharmacology. It deals with the quantitative analysis of the data generated in pharmacology studies. By using mathematical models and computer simulations, researchers can predict the pharmacokinetics and pharmacodynamics of drugs, and optimize the dosing regimens.

The use of in-silico tools and computational models is also becoming increasingly important in cellular and molecular pharmacology. These tools allow researchers to predict the interactions between drugs and receptors, and to understand the mechanisms of drug action. They can also be used to design new drugs and to identify potential side effects before drugs are tested in human clinical trials.

In conclusion, cellular and molecular pharmacology is a multidisciplinary field that encompasses many different areas of research. It is focused on the study of the interactions between drugs and cells at the molecular level, with the ultimate goal of developing new and effective therapies for the treatment of diseases. It encompasses a wide range of areas including drug delivery, imaging, pharmacometrics, in-silico tools and computational models.

Another important aspect of cellular and molecular pharmacology is the study of drug resistance. This can occur when bacteria, viruses, or cancer cells develop mechanisms to survive exposure to drugs. For example, bacteria can develop enzymes that can inactivate antibiotics, or cancer cells can develop mutations in drug receptors that make them less responsive to drugs. Understanding the mechanisms of drug resistance can help researchers develop new drugs or strategies to overcome this resistance and improve treatment outcomes.

Another area of research in cellular and molecular pharmacology is the use of gene therapy and genetic engineering to treat diseases. This involves the use of genetic material, such as DNA or RNA, to correct genetic mutations or to introduce new genes into cells. This can be used to treat genetic disorders, cancer, and other diseases.

The field of pharmacovigilance is also closely related to cellular and molecular pharmacology. It deals with the monitoring of the safety of drugs once they have been approved and made available to the public. This includes the monitoring of adverse drug reactions, and the identification of potential drug interactions.

Finally, the field of pharmacology is also closely related to the field of toxicology. Toxicology deals with the study of the harmful effects of chemicals and drugs on living organisms. This includes the study of the mechanisms of toxicity, the identification of potential toxicants, and the development of strategies to reduce toxicity.

In conclusion, cellular and molecular pharmacology is a multidisciplinary field that encompasses many different areas of research. It is focused on the study of the interactions between drugs and cells at the molecular level, with the ultimate goal of developing new and effective therapies for the treatment of diseases. It encompasses a wide range of areas including drug resistance, gene therapy, genetic engineering, pharmacovigilance and toxicology.

Another important area of research in cellular and molecular pharmacology is the use of immunotherapies to treat diseases. Immunotherapies are treatments that use the body's immune system to fight diseases such as cancer. These include therapies that target specific immune cells, such as T cells, and therapies that target specific proteins on cancer cells, such as PD-1. Immunotherapies have shown promising results in the treatment of cancer, and researchers are continuing to develop new immunotherapies to improve treatment outcomes.

Another area of research in cellular and molecular pharmacology is the use of CRISPR-based therapies to treat diseases. CRISPR is a powerful tool that can be used to precisely edit genes in living organisms. Researchers are using CRISPR to correct genetic mutations that cause diseases, and to introduce new genes into cells to treat diseases such as cancer.

Pharmacogenetics and pharmacogenomics are other areas of cellular and molecular pharmacology that deals with the study of how genetic variations affect the response to drugs. Genetic variations in drug receptors, enzymes involved in drug metabolism, and other proteins that interact with drugs can affect the efficacy and safety of a drug. By understanding these genetic variations, researchers can develop personalized medicine, where drugs are tailored to the specific genetic makeup of an individual.

Finally, the field of pharmacology is also closely related to the field of nanotechnology. Nanotechnology is the study of the manipulation of materials on a very small scale, typically at the scale of atoms and molecules. Researchers are using nanotechnology to develop new drug delivery systems, such as nanoparticles and liposomes, which can improve the delivery of drugs to specific cells or tissues in the body.

In conclusion, cellular and molecular pharmacology is a multidisciplinary field that encompasses many different areas of research. It is focused on the study of the interactions between drugs and cells at the molecular level, with the ultimate goal of developing new and effective therapies for the treatment of diseases. It encompasses a wide range of areas including immunotherapies, CRISPR-based therapies, pharmacogenetics, pharmacogenomics, and nanotechnology.

One important area of research in cellular and molecular pharmacology is the use of artificial intelligence (AI) and machine learning (ML) in drug discovery and development. AI and ML can be used to analyze large amounts of data, such as genetic data and drug efficacy data, to identify new drug targets, predict drug interactions, and design new drugs. This can greatly speed up the drug development process and improve the chances of success in clinical trials.

Another important area of research in cellular and molecular pharmacology is the use of organoids and organ-on-a-chip technology. Organoids are small, three-dimensional structures that mimic the structure and function of specific organs, such as the brain, lung, or liver. Organ-on-a-chip technology is a method of creating microfabricated devices that can mimic the functions of entire organs, such as the heart or kidney. These technologies can be used to study the effects of drugs on specific organs, and to identify potential side effects before drugs are tested in human clinical trials.

Another important area of research in cellular and molecular pharmacology is the use of computational models and simulations to predict the pharmacokinetics and pharmacodynamics of drugs. These models can be used to predict the absorption, distribution, metabolism, and elimination of drugs in the body, and to optimize dosing regimens. They can also be used to predict the interactions between drugs and receptors, and to understand the mechanisms of drug action.

Finally, the field of pharmacology is also closely related to the field of synthetic biology. Synthetic biology is the design and construction of new biological parts, devices, and systems that do not exist in the natural world. Researchers are using synthetic biology to create new drugs and drug delivery systems and to engineer cells to produce specific proteins.

In conclusion, cellular and molecular pharmacology is a multidisciplinary field that encompasses many different areas of research. It is focused on the study of the interactions between drugs and cells at the molecular level, with the ultimate goal of developing new and effective therapies for the treatment of diseases. It encompasses a wide range of areas including AI/ML, organoids, organ-on-a-chip, computational models and simulations and synthetic biology.

Another important area of research in cellular and molecular pharmacology is the use of RNA-based therapies to treat diseases. RNA-based therapies include small interfering RNAs (siRNAs), messenger RNAs (mRNAs), and microRNAs. These therapies can be used to silence or activate specific genes, and can be used to treat a wide range of diseases including cancer, genetic disorders, and viral infections.

Another important area of research in cellular and molecular pharmacology is the use of cell-based therapies to treat diseases. Cell-based therapies involve the use of living cells to treat diseases such as cancer, genetic disorders, and immune disorders. Examples of cell-based therapies include CAR-T cell therapy and stem cell therapy.

Another important area of research in cellular and molecular pharmacology is the use of pharmacometrics to optimize the dosing regimens of drugs. Pharmacometrics is the use of mathematical models and computer simulations to predict the pharmacokinetics and pharmacodynamics of drugs, and to optimize dosing regimens based on the patient's characteristics such as age, weight, genetics, and other factors.

Finally, the field of pharmacology is also closely related to the field of pharmacoproteomics. Pharmacoproteomics is the study of the effects of drugs on the proteome, which is the complete set of proteins in a cell. Researchers are using pharmacoproteomics to identify new drug targets and to understand the mechanisms of drug action.

In conclusion, cellular and molecular pharmacology is a multidisciplinary field that encompasses many different areas of research. It is focused on the study of the interactions between drugs and cells at the molecular level, with the ultimate goal of developing new and effective therapies for the treatment of diseases. It encompasses a wide range of areas including RNA-based therapies, cell-based therapies, pharmacometrics, and pharmacoproteomics.

Another important area of research in cellular and molecular pharmacology is the use of natural products as a source of new drugs. Natural products are compounds found in plants, animals, and microorganisms that have medicinal properties. Researchers are using natural products as a source of new drugs for the treatment of various diseases, such as cancer, infectious diseases, and neurological disorders. Some examples of natural products that have been used as drugs include paclitaxel, which is derived from the Pacific yew tree, and artemisinin, which is derived from the sweet wormwood plant.

Another important area of research in cellular and molecular pharmacology is the use of pharmacogenetics to personalize medicine. Pharmacogenetics is the study of how genetic variations affect the response to drugs. Genetic variations in drug receptors, enzymes involved in drug metabolism, and other proteins that interact with drugs can affect the efficacy and safety of a drug. By understanding these genetic variations, researchers can develop personalized medicine, where drugs are tailored to the specific genetic makeup of an individual.

Another important area of research in cellular and molecular pharmacology is the use of gene editing tools, such as CRISPR-Cas9, to treat diseases. Gene editing is a powerful tool that can be used to precisely edit genes in living organisms. Researchers are using gene editing to correct genetic mutations that cause diseases, and to introduce new genes into cells to treat diseases such as cancer.

Finally, the field of pharmacology is also closely related to the field of synthetic biology. Synthetic biology is the design and construction of new biological parts, devices, and systems that do not exist in the natural world.

Researchers are using synthetic biology to create new drugs and drug delivery systems and to engineer cells to produce specific proteins.

In conclusion, cellular and molecular pharmacology is a multidisciplinary field that encompasses many different areas of research. It is focused on the study of the interactions between drugs and cells at the molecular level, with the ultimate goal of developing new and effective therapies for the treatment of diseases. It encompasses a wide range of areas including natural products, pharmacogenetics, gene editing, and synthetic biology.

Additionally, another important area of research in cellular and molecular pharmacology is the use of systems biology approaches. Systems biology is an interdisciplinary field that aims to understand the complex interactions and networks within biological systems. It can be applied to the study of drug-cell interactions to better understand the mechanisms of drug action and predict potential side effects.

Furthermore, the field of pharmacology is closely related to the field of bioinformatics. Bioinformatics is the application of computational techniques to the analysis of biological data such as DNA, RNA and protein sequences, as well as functional genomics and epigenomics data. This can be used to identify new drug targets, predict drug interactions, and design new drugs.

In conclusion, cellular and molecular pharmacology is a multidisciplinary field that encompasses many different areas of research. It is focused on the study of the interactions between drugs and cells at the molecular level, with the ultimate goal of developing new and effective therapies for the treatment of diseases. It encompasses a wide range of areas including natural products, pharmacogenetics, gene editing, synthetic biology, systems biology, bioinformatics and many more.

Another important area of research in cellular and molecular pharmacology is the use of gene therapy and genetic engineering to treat diseases. This involves the use of genetic material, such as DNA or RNA, to correct genetic mutations or to introduce new genes into cells. This can be used to treat genetic disorders, cancer, and other diseases.

Additionally, the field of pharmacology is closely related to the field of biotechnology. Biotechnology is the use of living organisms, cells, and their derivatives to produce products for human use. Biotechnology can be used to produce drugs, vaccines, and diagnostic tools. This includes recombinant proteins and monoclonal antibodies, which are used to treat various diseases.

Furthermore, the field of pharmacology is closely related to the field of pharmacometabolomics. Metabolomics is the study of the quantitative measurement of metabolites in a biological system. By using metabolomics, researchers can identify metabolic pathways that are affected by drugs and understand the mechanisms of drug action.

In conclusion, cellular and molecular pharmacology is a multidisciplinary field that encompasses many different areas of research. It is focused on the study of the interactions between drugs and cells at the molecular level, with the ultimate goal of developing new and effective therapies for the treatment of diseases. It encompasses a wide range of areas including gene therapy, genetic engineering, biotechnology, pharmacometabolomics and many more.

Another important area of research in cellular and molecular pharmacology is the use of repurposing existing drugs for new indications. Repurposing existing drugs refers to identifying new therapeutic uses for drugs that have already been approved for other indications. This can be a faster and more cost-effective approach to developing new drugs, as the safety and efficacy of the drug have already been established. Researchers use various techniques such as systems biology, bioinformatics, and computational models to identify new indications for existing drugs.

Another area of research in cellular and molecular pharmacology is the use of personalized medicine to optimize drug therapy. Personalized medicine is an approach to healthcare that takes into account an individual's unique genetic makeup, lifestyle, and environmental factors to optimize treatment decisions. By understanding the genetic and molecular basis of disease, researchers can design drugs and treatment plans that are tailored to the specific needs of an individual.

Another important area of research in cellular and molecular pharmacology is the use of pharmacogenetics and pharmacogenomics to identify genetic markers that predict drug efficacy and toxicity. By identifying genetic markers that predict drug efficacy and toxicity, researchers can develop more effective and safer drugs and optimize treatment regimens for individual patients.

In conclusion, cellular and molecular pharmacology is a multidisciplinary field that encompasses many different areas of research. It is focused on the study of the interactions between drugs and cells at the molecular level, with the ultimate goal of developing new and effective therapies for the treatment of diseases. It encompasses a wide range of areas including drug repurposing, personalized medicine, pharmacogenetics and pharmacogenomics, and many more.

Another important area of research in cellular and molecular pharmacology is the use of pharmacokinetics and pharmacodynamics (PK-PD) to optimize drug therapy. PK-PD is the study of how the body absorbs, distributes, metabolizes, and eliminates drugs. By understanding the PK-PD of a drug, researchers can optimize dosing regimens and improve treatment outcomes.

Another area of research in cellular and molecular pharmacology is the use of pharmacometrics to optimize drug therapy. Pharmacometrics is the use of mathematical models and computer simulations to predict the pharmacokinetics and pharmacodynamics of drugs, and to optimize dosing regimens based on the patient's characteristics such as age, weight, genetics, and other factors.

Another important area of research in cellular and molecular pharmacology is the use of drug combination therapy to treat diseases. Drug combination therapy is the use of multiple drugs to treat a disease. This can be used to improve treatment outcomes and reduce the risk of drug resistance. Researchers use various techniques such as systems biology, bioinformatics, and computational models to identify potential drug combinations.

In conclusion, cellular and molecular pharmacology is a multidisciplinary field that encompasses many different areas of research. It is focused on the study of the interactions between drugs and cells at the molecular level, with the ultimate goal of developing new and effective therapies for the treatment of diseases. It encompasses a wide range of areas including PK-PD, pharmacometrics, drug combination therapy, and many more.

Another important area of research in cellular and molecular pharmacology is the use of drug discovery and development. This involves identifying new drug targets, designing and synthesizing new drugs, and testing the safety and efficacy of these drugs in preclinical and clinical studies. This process can be time-consuming and expensive, but it is crucial in identifying new treatments for diseases.

Another area of research in cellular and molecular pharmacology is the use of drug delivery systems to improve the effectiveness of drugs. Drug delivery systems are methods of delivering drugs to specific cells or tissues in the body. Examples include nanoparticles, liposomes, and targeted delivery systems. These systems can improve the effectiveness of drugs and reduce side effects.

Another important area of research in cellular and molecular pharmacology is the use of pharmacological chaperones to treat diseases. Pharmacological chaperones are drugs that bind to and stabilize misfolded proteins, which can be the cause of many diseases such as genetic disorders and cancer. By stabilizing these misfolded proteins, pharmacological chaperones can prevent the proteins from aggregating and causing damage to cells.

In conclusion, cellular and molecular pharmacology is a multidisciplinary field that encompasses many different areas of research. It is focused on the study of the interactions between drugs and cells at the molecular level, with the ultimate goal of developing new and effective therapies for the treatment of diseases. It encompasses a wide range of areas including drug discovery and development, drug delivery systems, and pharmacological chaperones.

Another important area of research in cellular and molecular pharmacology is the use of in vitro and in vivo models to study drug-cell interactions. In vitro models involve the use of cell cultures, while in vivo models involve the use of animal models. These models can be used to study the pharmacokinetics and pharmacodynamics of drugs, as well as the mechanisms of drug action and potential side effects.

Another area of research in cellular and molecular pharmacology is the use of pharmacological imaging to study drug-cell interactions. Pharmacological imaging involves the use of various imaging techniques such as MRI, CT, and PET to visualize the distribution and metabolism of drugs in the body. This can be used to study the pharmacokinetics and pharmacodynamics of drugs, as well as the mechanisms of drug action and potential side effects.

Another important area of research in cellular and molecular pharmacology is the use of pharmacological proteomics to study drug-cell interactions. Pharmacological proteomics involves the use of mass spectrometry and other techniques to study the effects of drugs on the proteome, which is the complete set of proteins in a cell. By understanding how drugs interact with proteins, researchers can identify new drug targets and understand the mechanisms of drug action.

In conclusion, cellular and molecular pharmacology is a multidisciplinary field that encompasses many different areas of research. It is focused on the study of the interactions between drugs and cells at the molecular level, with the ultimate goal of developing new and effective therapies for the treatment of diseases. It encompasses a wide range of areas including in vitro and in vivo models, pharmacological imaging, pharmacological proteomics, and many more.

CHAPTER TWO

Cell Biology

Mr Sujit Chavan, Mrs Ashwini Badhe and Dr Pravin Badhe

Introduction

Cell biology is the study of cells, including their physiological properties, their structure, the organelles they contain, interactions with their environment, and their life cycle. It is a subfield of biology that deals specifically with the biology of cells, including their function, structure, growth, and division. This field of study is essential for understanding the basic building blocks of living organisms and the processes that sustain life.

Cell biology also encompasses the study of cell processes such as metabolism, cell signaling, and cell-cell interactions. Additionally, it includes the study of genetic material within cells, including DNA replication, transcription, and protein synthesis.

Cell biologists use a variety of techniques to study cells, including microscopy, biochemistry, genetics, and molecular biology. Advances in these techniques have allowed scientists to study cells at the molecular level, leading to a greater understanding of the inner workings of cells and the processes that regulate them.

Research in cell biology has important implications for many areas of science and medicine, including the development of new therapies for diseases, the understanding of cancer, and the development of new agricultural technologies.

The study of cell biology is interdisciplinary and it is studied by many different fields including biochemistry, genetics, microbiology, physics, and medicine. This field is continuously growing with new discoveries and technologies, and many scientists are actively working in this field to uncover new knowledge and improve our understanding of the biological world.

Some key areas of research in cell biology include:

The study of cell structure, including the cytoskeleton, cell membrane, and various organelles. Researchers study the structure and functions of these components, and how they interact with each other to maintain the cell's shape and integrity.

The study of cell division and growth, including mitosis and meiosis. Researchers study how cells divide and replicate to form new cells, and how this process is regulated.

The study of cell signaling, including how cells communicate with each other and respond to signals from their environment. This research can help us understand how cells respond to different stimuli and how they coordinate their activities with other cells.

The study of cell metabolism, including how cells use energy, produce energy, and store energy. This research can help us understand how cells use energy to grow and divide, and how they respond to changes in their environment.

The study of cell development, including how cells differentiate and specialize to form different types of cells. This research can help us understand how cells become different types of cells, and how they develop into the various tissues and organs of the body.

Overall, cell biology is an extremely vast and dynamic field that plays a crucial role in understanding the fundamental principles of life, and the way cells interact, communicate, and function. It has numerous applications in medicine, biotechnology, and the understanding of complex biological systems.

Structure and functions of the cell and its organelles

Cells are the basic unit of life and are essential for the functioning of all living organisms. All cells have a number of features in common, including a cell membrane, cytoplasm, and genetic material.

A cell is the basic unit of life in all living organisms. It is the smallest unit of an organism that can carry out all of the processes of life. There are two main types of cells: prokaryotic and eukaryotic.

Prokaryotic cells are smaller and simpler in structure and do not have a defined nucleus. They are typically found in single-celled organisms such as bacteria.

Eukaryotic cells are larger and more complex in structure and have a defined nucleus. They are typically found in multicellular organisms such as plants and animals.

The main structures of a eukaryotic cell include:

Cell membrane: a thin, flexible barrier that surrounds the cell and regulates the movement of molecules in and out of the cell.

Nucleus: the "control center" of the cell, containing the cell's DNA and controlling the cell's functions.

Cytoskeleton: a network of protein fibers that gives the cell its shape and helps it move.

Mitochondria: the "powerhouses" of the cell, responsible for generating energy for the cell.

Endoplasmic reticulum and Golgi apparatus: involved in the transport and modification of molecules within the cell.

Ribosomes: the site of protein synthesis in the cell.

The main functions of a cell include:

- Metabolism: the chemical reactions that occur within the cell to maintain life.
- Growth and reproduction: the ability to grow and divide to form new cells.
- Response to the environment: the ability to sense and respond to changes in the environment.
- Homeostasis: the ability to maintain a stable internal environment.
- Excretion of waste products: the ability to remove waste products from the cell.

The cell membrane, also known as the plasma membrane, is made up of a double layer of phospholipid molecules. It acts as a barrier, controlling what enters and exits the cell. It also contains various proteins, such as receptors and transport proteins, which help the cell communicate with its environment.

The nucleus is the largest organelle in the cell and is surrounded by a double membrane called the nuclear envelope. Inside the nucleus is the genetic material, DNA, which is organized into structures called chromosomes. The nucleus also contains small organelles called nucleoli, which are involved in the production of ribosomes.

The cytoskeleton is a network of protein fibers that gives the cell its shape and helps it move. It is made up of microfilaments, intermediate filaments, and microtubules. Microfilaments and intermediate filaments provide mechanical strength, while microtubules provide support and help the cell move.

Mitochondria are organelles that are responsible for generating energy for the cell. They are known as the "powerhouses" of the cell because they produce energy in the form of ATP through a process called cellular respiration.

The endoplasmic reticulum and Golgi apparatus are organelles that are involved in the transport and modification of molecules within the cell. The endoplasmic reticulum is a network of membranes that is involved in the synthesis, folding, and transport of proteins and lipids. The Golgi apparatus is a stack of flattened membrane-bound sacs that modifies, sorts, and directs the transport of these molecules to their final destinations.

Ribosomes are the site of protein synthesis in the cell. They are small organelles that are made up of RNA and protein and are responsible for translating the genetic information in the DNA into functional proteins.

In terms of functions, the cell carries out a variety of metabolic reactions to maintain life, such as the process of cellular respiration, which produces energy. It can also grow and reproduce through the process of cell division. Cells can also respond to changes in their environment through mechanisms such as cell signaling. Homeostasis is the maintenance of a stable internal environment, in which cells can regulate their internal environment through various mechanisms such as osmoregulation. Finally, cells have the ability to excrete waste products through processes such as exocytosis.

In addition to these common features, cells also contain a variety of specialized organelles that perform specific functions.

Cell organelles

Cell organelles are specialized structures within a cell that perform specific functions. Some common cell organelles include:

-The nucleus: contains the cell's genetic material and controls the cell's activities.

-Mitochondria: the "powerhouses" of the cell, they generate energy for the cell through cellular respiration.

-Endoplasmic reticulum (ER): a network of membranes involved in protein and lipid synthesis.

-Golgi apparatus: modifies, sorts, and packages proteins and lipids for transport to other parts of the cell or outside of the cell.

-Lysosomes: contain enzymes that break down waste materials and cellular debris.

-Ribosomes: responsible for protein synthesis.

-Vacuoles: storage organelles that hold materials such as water, salts, and enzymes.

-Chloroplasts: only found in plant cells, they convert light energy into chemical energy through photosynthesis.

-Cytoskeleton: a network of protein fibers that provides support and shape to the cell, and helps with movement.

Some of the organelles I mentioned earlier:

-The nucleus: it is typically the largest organelle in a cell and is surrounded by a double membrane called the nuclear envelope. The inner membrane is selectively permeable, allowing certain molecules to pass in and out while keeping the cell's DNA safe inside. The nucleus also contains small, dense structures called nucleoli, which are involved in the production of ribosomes.

-Mitochondria: they are often referred to as the "powerhouses" of the cell because they produce the majority of the cell's energy in the form of ATP through a process called cellular respiration. Mitochondria have their own DNA and are thought to have originated as symbiotic bacteria.

-Endoplasmic reticulum (ER): it is a network of flattened, stacked membranes that is involved in protein and lipid synthesis. The ER is divided into two regions: the rough endoplasmic reticulum (RER) and the smooth endoplasmic reticulum (SER). The RER is studded with ribosomes, which are responsible for protein synthesis. The SER is involved in the synthesis and metabolism of lipids.

-Golgi apparatus: it is made up of a series of flattened, stacked membranes that are responsible for modifying, sorting, and packaging proteins and lipids for transport to other parts of the cell or outside of the cell. The Golgi is divided into three regions: the cis-Golgi, medial-Golgi, and trans-Golgi. Proteins and lipids enter the cis-Golgi and are modified and sorted as they move through the medial-Golgi and trans-Golgi.

-Lysosomes: they are small, spherical organelles that contain enzymes that break down waste materials and cellular debris. Lysosomes are formed in the Golgi apparatus and then transported to the cell's cytoplasm. They play an important role in the cell's recycling process, breaking down and recycling old or damaged cellular components.

-Ribosomes: they are small, dense structures that are responsible for protein synthesis. They are composed of two subunits, one made of RNA and the other made of protein. Ribosomes can be found in the cytoplasm or attached to the endoplasmic reticulum.

-Chloroplasts: They are only found in plant cells and some algae. They convert light energy into chemical energy through photosynthesis, by which the plant produce their own food. Chloroplasts have their own DNA and are thought to have originated as symbiotic bacteria.

-Cytoskeleton: it is a network of protein fibers that provides support and shape to the cell, and helps with movement. It is composed of three main types of protein fibers: microfilaments, intermediate filaments, and microtubules. Microfilaments and microtubules play important roles in cell division and cell movement, while intermediate filaments provide structural support.

-Plasma membrane (or cell membrane): it is a thin, flexible barrier that surrounds the cell, separating the internal environment of the cell from its external environment. The plasma membrane is made up of a lipid bilayer and is selectively permeable, allowing certain molecules to pass in and out of the cell while preventing others from entering. It also plays an important role in cell communication and cell recognition.

-Peroxisomes: they are similar to lysosomes in that they are involved in the breakdown of specific molecules, but they are specialized in breaking down fatty acids and detoxifying certain toxins. They contain enzymes that generate hydrogen peroxide as a byproduct, which is then broken down by other enzymes into water and oxygen.

-Cilia and flagella: they are small, hair-like structures that extend from the cell surface and are used for movement. Cilia are usually shorter and more numerous than flagella and are used for movement of fluids or particles over the cell surface. Flagella are longer and fewer in number and are used for propulsion of the cell through a liquid environment.

-Centrioles: they are small, cylindrical structures that are made up of microtubules and are found in animal cells. Centrioles play an important role in cell division, helping to organize the chromosomes and pull them apart during cell division.

-Microvilli: they are small, finger-like projections that extend from the cell surface and increase the surface area of the cell. Microvilli are found on the surface of cells that are involved in absorption, such as the lining of the small intestine.

-This is not an exhaustive list of all the organelles found in cells but it covers the main ones that are found in most cells, depending on the cell type and its function, some organelles may not be present or may have different specializations.

-The cytoskeleton also includes microtubules which are cylindrical structures that provide support and shape to the cell, and help with cell movement, for example, in cell division and cell migration. They also function as a "highway" for intracellular transport.

-Nucleolus, a small and dense structure inside the nucleus, is responsible for the production of ribosomes, which are the cellular structures that synthesize proteins. The nucleolus is composed of DNA, RNA, and proteins and is formed during cell division.

-The mitochondria also known as the "powerhouse of the cell" has its own DNA and protein synthetic machinery. They are responsible for generating energy in the form of ATP through cellular respiration, a process that occurs in the inner membrane of the mitochondria.

-The secretory pathway, which begins in the rough endoplasmic reticulum (RER) and ends in the Golgi apparatus, is responsible for the synthesis, folding, modification, and transport of proteins and lipids.

-The endoplasmic reticulum (ER) and the Golgi apparatus also play a role in the process of protein folding, quality control, and protein maturation. Proteins that are not properly folded are directed to the lysosomes for degradation.

-The cytoskeleton also includes microfilaments which are made of actin, a protein that gives the cell its shape and enables it to move. Microfilaments also play a role in cell division, cell migration and intracellular transport.

-The extracellular matrix (ECM) is a network of molecules that surrounds the cells and provides support and organization to the tissue. It is composed of proteins such as collagen, elastin, and glycosaminoglycans.

-Peroxisomes, lysosomes and the proteasome are all organelles that play a role in the degradation of macromolecules, such as proteins and lipids, by hydrolysis. They are sometimes referred to as the "degradative organelles"

-Exosomes are small, membrane-bound vesicles that are secreted by cells and play a role in intercellular communication. They can contain a variety of molecules such as proteins, lipids, and nucleic acids and can be involved in processes such as cell signaling, waste disposal, and immune response.

-The cytosol, also known as the cytoplasmic matrix, is the fluid that fills the cell and surrounds the organelles. It contains enzymes and other molecules that are important for cellular metabolism.

-The mitochondria also have a role in regulating the cell's response to stress, programmed cell death (apoptosis) and cell growth.

There are also other organelles that are found in specific cell types such as the chloroplasts in plant cells and the mitochondria in animal cells which carry out specific functions such as photosynthesis and respiration respectively.

In summary, cell organelles are specialized structures that perform specific functions to keep the cell alive and functioning. They are essential to the cell's survival and allow the cell to carry out its specific functions. Understanding the structure and function of these organelles can help us understand how cells work and how they communicate with each other.

It's important to note that the organelles' functions are not always fixed, and they can change depending on the cell's needs and the specific situation. For example, the mitochondria can play a role in cell death if they are damaged and release harmful molecules, but they also play a role in cell growth and division when they are healthy.

Moreover, the structure and function of organelles can vary depending on the type of cell and its stage in the life cycle. The presence or absence of certain organelles can distinguish one type of cell from another.

It's important to remember that cells are complex systems and the organelles' functions are not always independent of each other. They often work together in coordination to perform various cellular functions. Understanding the structure and function of organelles can give us insight into the underlying mechanisms of cellular processes.

Genome organization

Genome organization refers to the way in which the genetic material in an organism's genome is structured and arranged. This includes the number and arrangement of chromosomes, as well as the organization of the DNA within those chromosomes.

Chromosomes are long, linear structures made up of DNA and proteins that contain the genetic information necessary for an organism's development and functioning. In most organisms, the genome is organized into multiple chromosomes, which are present in pairs in the cells of sexually reproducing organisms. The number of chromosomes in an organism's genome can vary widely, with some species having just a few chromosomes and others having many.

Within each chromosome, the DNA is organized into genes, which are the functional units of heredity. Genes contain the instructions for making proteins, which perform a wide range of functions in the body. The genome also contains non-coding DNA, which does not contain instructions for making proteins but may have other functions, such as regulating the activity of genes.

Genome organization plays a crucial role in the functioning of the cell and the organism as a whole. Some of the key roles of genome organization include:

1. Gene expression: The organization of the genome can influence the expression of genes. For example, genes that are located near each other on the same chromosome are often co-regulated and tend to be transcribed together. Similarly, the distance between a gene and its regulatory elements, such as promoter or enhancer sequences, can affect gene expression.
2. Chromosome structure and function: Chromosomes are organized in a specific way to allow for the efficient expression of genes. For example, genes that are actively being transcribed are often located in the more accessible parts of the chromosome, while inactive genes are often found in the more condensed and inaccessible parts.

3. Genetic stability: The organization of the genome plays a role in maintaining the stability of the genome. For example, DNA repair mechanisms are often more efficient at repairing DNA damage in the more accessible parts of the chromosome. In addition, the organization of the genome can influence the occurrence of chromosomal rearrangements, which can lead to genetic disorders.
4. Adaptation and evolution: The organization of the genome can influence an organism's ability to adapt to its environment and evolve over time. For example, the rearrangement of genes on chromosomes can lead to the creation of new gene combinations, which can provide a selective advantage in certain environments.

Overall, the organization of the genome plays a crucial role in the functioning of the cell and the organism as a whole. Understanding the structure and organization of the genome is important for understanding how genes are expressed and how they contribute to an organism's characteristics and traits.

Genome organization refers to the structure and arrangement of genetic material in an organism's genome, including the number and arrangement of chromosomes, as well as the organization of DNA within those chromosomes. The organization of the genome plays a crucial role in gene expression, chromosome structure and function, genetic stability, and adaptation and evolution. Understanding the structure and organization of the genome is important for understanding the underlying mechanisms of an organism's characteristics and traits.

One key aspect is the concept of linkage and recombination. Linkage refers to the physical proximity of genes on a chromosome, and the likelihood that they will be inherited together. Recombination refers to the process by which genetic material is shuffled between chromosomes during sexual reproduction, leading to new combinations of genes. These processes can lead to genetic variation within a population and can have important implications for evolution and adaptation.

Another important aspect of genome organization is the concept of epigenetics. Epigenetics refers to the modifications to the genome that do not change the underlying DNA sequence, but can affect gene expression and chromatin structure. These modifications can be passed on to future generations and play a role in regulating gene expression and development.

In addition to these concepts, there are also a variety of techniques and tools used to study genome organization, such as genome mapping and sequencing, which allow scientists to study the structure and organization of the genome at the molecular level.

Overall, genome organization is a complex and multifaceted field that continues to be an active area of research. Advances in this field have important implications for understanding the underlying mechanisms of genetic diseases, as well as for the development of new medical treatments and therapies.

Another important aspect of genome organization is the concept of genome architecture. Genome architecture refers to the 3D structure of the genome, and how it is organized within the cell nucleus. Recent studies have shown that the genome is not randomly organized within the nucleus, but rather is organized into specific domains, called A/B compartments, which have different properties and functions. A compartments are enriched in active genes and are more accessible to the transcriptional machinery, while B compartments are enriched in inactive genes and are less accessible. This organization of the genome into specific domains is thought to play a role in gene regulation and in the maintenance of the genome's stability.

In addition, the genome organization also plays a role in the regulation of gene expression through the use of regulatory elements such as enhancers and silencers, which are non-coding regions of the genome that control the activity of genes. These elements are often located far away from the gene they regulate, but through the use of long-range chromatin interactions, they can still influence the expression of the gene.

In conclusion, genome organization plays a crucial role in the functioning of the cell and the organism as a whole. It encompasses the number and arrangement of chromosomes, the organization of DNA within those chromosomes, the concept of linkage and recombination, epigenetics, genome architecture, and the use of regulatory elements. Understanding the structure and organization of the genome is important for understanding the underlying mechanisms of an organism's characteristics and traits and for understanding the role of the genome in disease and in response to environmental changes.

Another important aspect of genome organization is the concept of repetitive DNA. Repetitive DNA refers to sequences of DNA that are repeated multiple times within the genome. These sequences can take various forms such as tandem repeats, satellite DNA, and transposable elements. Tandem repeats are sequences that are repeated in a head-to-tail fashion, while satellite DNA is composed of highly repetitive, non-coding sequences. Transposable elements are mobile genetic elements that can move around within the genome and can affect gene expression and genome stability.

Repetitive DNA plays an important role in genome organization, as it can make up a significant portion of the genome. In some cases, repetitive DNA can be associated with genetic disorders, such as fragile X syndrome, which is caused by the expansion of a trinucleotide repeat in the FMR1 gene. However, repetitive DNA also plays a role in the evolution of the genome, as it can act as a source of genetic variation and can affect the structure and function of chromosomes.

In addition, repetitive DNA also plays a role in the regulation of gene expression through the formation of chromatin domains that can act as barriers to the transcriptional machinery, and can also act as scaffolds for the formation of specific chromatin structures.

In summary, genome organization is a complex and multifaceted concept that encompasses various aspects of the structure and arrangement of genetic material in an organism's genome. It includes the number and arrangement of chromosomes, the organization of DNA within those chromosomes, linkage and recombination, epigenetics, genome architecture, the use of regulatory elements, and repetitive DNA. Understanding the structure and organization of the genome is important for understanding the underlying mechanisms of an organism's characteristics and traits, and for understanding the role of the genome in disease and in response to environmental changes.

Continuing on, one important aspect of genome organization that is related to repetitive DNA is telomeres. Telomeres are repetitive DNA sequences that are found at the ends of chromosomes and play a crucial role in the stability of the genome. The function of telomeres is to protect the ends of chromosomes from degradation and from being recognized as DNA damage. Telomeres shorten with each cell division, and when they become too short, the cell can no longer divide and becomes senescent.

In addition, telomeres also play a role in aging and cancer. In normal cells, telomere shortening can trigger senescence and cell death, which helps to prevent the accumulation of damaged cells. However, in cancer cells, telomerase, an enzyme that can add telomeric repeats to the ends of chromosomes, is often reactivated, allowing the cancer cells to continue to divide and evade senescence. As such, telomerase and telomeres are the focus of much research in the field of cancer therapy.

Another important aspect of genome organization is centromeres. Centromeres are regions of the genome that are necessary for the proper separation of chromosomes during cell division. Centromeres are typically composed of repetitive DNA sequences and are often associated with a specific protein called centromere protein A (CENP-A). The organization of centromeres is important for the proper segregation of chromosomes during cell division and for the stability of the genome.

In conclusion, genome organization is a complex and multifaceted concept that encompasses various aspects of the structure and arrangement of genetic material in an organism's genome. The organization of the genome plays a crucial role in gene expression, chromosome structure and function, genetic stability, and adaptation and evolution. Key aspects of genome organization include linkage and recombination, epigenetics, genome architecture, the use of regulatory elements, repetitive DNA, telomeres and centromeres. Understanding the structure and organization of the genome is important for understanding the underlying mechanisms of an organism's characteristics and traits, and for understanding the role of the genome in disease and in response to environmental changes.

Another important aspect of genome organization is the concept of genomic imprinting. Genomic imprinting refers to the phenomenon where certain genes are expressed differently depending on whether they are inherited from the mother or the father. This is due to epigenetic marks, such as DNA methylation, that are established on certain genes during the formation of the egg or sperm, and are maintained through cell division. These marks result in the parent-of-origin-specific expression of certain genes.

Genomic imprinting plays an important role in the regulation of gene expression and can have wide-ranging effects on an organism's development, physiology and physiology. For example, certain genes that are imprinted can control growth and development, and their abnormal expression can lead to certain disorders such as Beckwith-Wiedemann syndrome or Prader-Willi syndrome.

In addition, Genomic Imprinting is also involved in the regulation of the placenta and fetal development. Imprinted genes play a critical role in the growth and development of the placenta, and their abnormal expression can lead to certain pregnancy disorders such as pre-eclampsia, as well as developmental disorders in the offspring.

Another important aspect of genome organization is the concept of the non-coding genome. The non-coding genome refers to the portion of the genome that does not contain instructions for making proteins. This non-coding genome, also called the "dark matter" of the genome, was long thought to be "junk DNA," but recent research has shown that it plays important roles in gene regulation and other processes.

One important role of the non-coding genome is in the regulation of gene expression through the use of non-coding RNAs (ncRNAs). These small RNA molecules, such as miRNA and siRNA, can bind to specific regions of the genome and regulate the expression of genes by either silencing or activating them.

Another important role of the non-coding genome is in the organization of the genome. Studies have shown that certain non-coding regions of the genome, such as CTCF-binding sites, can act as barriers to the transcriptional machinery and can also act as scaffolds for the formation of specific chromatin structures.

In addition, non-coding genome also plays a role in the evolution of the genome. For example, transposable elements, which are mobile genetic elements that can move around within the genome, can affect the structure and function of chromosomes.

Another important aspect of genome organization is the concept of genome size. Genome size refers to the total amount of DNA present in an organism's genome, and it can vary widely among different species. For example, some species, such as the amoeba, have a genome size of several billion base pairs, while others, such as the E. coli bacteria, have a genome size of around 4.6 million base pairs.

Genome size can have an effect on an organism's biology and evolution. For example, larger genomes tend to have more repetitive DNA and transposable elements, which can affect the stability of the genome and the expression of genes. In addition, larger genomes tend to have a higher number of genes, which can provide an organism with a greater capacity for adaptation and evolution.

However, larger genomes also come with a cost. They require more energy to maintain and can also lead to longer cell division times, which can affect an organism's growth and development.

In addition, genome size can also affect the evolution of a species. For example, some species have experienced genome reduction, which is the loss of genetic material from their genome over time. This process can be driven by natural selection, as it can provide an organism with a selective advantage in certain environments.

Another important aspect of genome organization is the concept of genome duplication or polyploidy. Genome duplication refers to the duplication of an organism's genome, resulting in more than two sets of chromosomes. This process can occur through a variety of mechanisms, such as errors during cell division or the fusion of different genomes from different organisms.

Polyploidy can have a significant effect on an organism's biology and evolution. For example, polyploid organisms can have larger cells, which can provide a selective advantage in certain environments. In addition, polyploidy can also lead to increased genetic variation, as the extra sets of chromosomes can result in new combinations of genes.

Polyploidy can also have a positive effect on crop plants. Many crop plants are polyploid, which can result in increased yield, improved stress tolerance, and increased resistance to pests and diseases.

However, polyploidy can also have negative effects. For example, polyploid organisms can have difficulty reproducing with diploid organisms, which can limit their ability to adapt and evolve. In addition, polyploidy can also lead to increased genetic variation, which can result in new combinations of genes that can be harmful.

Another important aspect of genome organization is the concept of genome compaction. Genome compaction refers to the process by which the genome is packaged into a more compact form in order to fit into the limited space of the cell nucleus. This is achieved through the action of various proteins, such as histones, that interact with the

DNA to form higher-order structures called chromatin.

Genome compaction plays an important role in the regulation of gene expression. For example, chromatin can be remodeled to make certain regions of the genome more or less accessible to the transcriptional machinery, which can affect the expression of genes. In addition, chromatin can also be remodeled to form specific structures, such as heterochromatin and euchromatin, which can have different properties and functions.

In addition, genome compaction also plays a role in the stability of the genome. For example, the formation of heterochromatin, which is a tightly packed form of chromatin, can help to prevent the activation of transposable elements and other potentially harmful sequences.

In addition to these key aspects, genome organization also includes several other important concepts such as chromatin remodeling, nuclear organization, and genome architecture. Chromatin remodeling, the process by which chromatin is modified to change its properties and functions, is an important mechanism for regulating gene expression and genome stability. Nuclear organization, the spatial arrangement of the genome within the cell nucleus, plays an important role in the regulation of gene expression and the stability of the genome. Genome architecture, the three-dimensional structure of the genome, plays an important role in the regulation of gene expression and the stability of the genome.

Another important aspect of genome organization is the concept of structural variations. Structural variations refer to changes in the genome that involve the gain or loss of genetic material such as deletion, duplication, inversion, or translocation. These variations can range from small changes involving a few base pairs to large changes involving entire chromosomes.

Structural variations can have a significant effect on an organism's biology and evolution. For example, structural variations can lead to the formation of new genes or the loss of existing genes, which can affect an organism's adaptation and evolution. In addition, structural variations can also lead to the formation of new combinations of genes, which can provide a selective advantage in certain environments.

Structural variations can also have a significant effect on human health. For example, structural variations can lead to the formation of new diseases or the loss of existing diseases. Structural variations can also lead to the formation of new combinations of genes, which can provide a selective advantage in certain environments.

Gene expression and its regulation

Gene expression is the process by which the information contained in a gene is used to produce a specific protein or RNA molecule. This process begins when a gene is activated, or "expressed," and the genetic information it contains is transcribed into a complementary RNA molecule. This RNA molecule is then translated into a protein, which performs a specific function in the cell.

Gene expression is regulated at various stages, including transcription and translation. This regulation can occur at the level of DNA, RNA, and proteins and is essential for ensuring that the right proteins are produced at the right time and place in the cell.

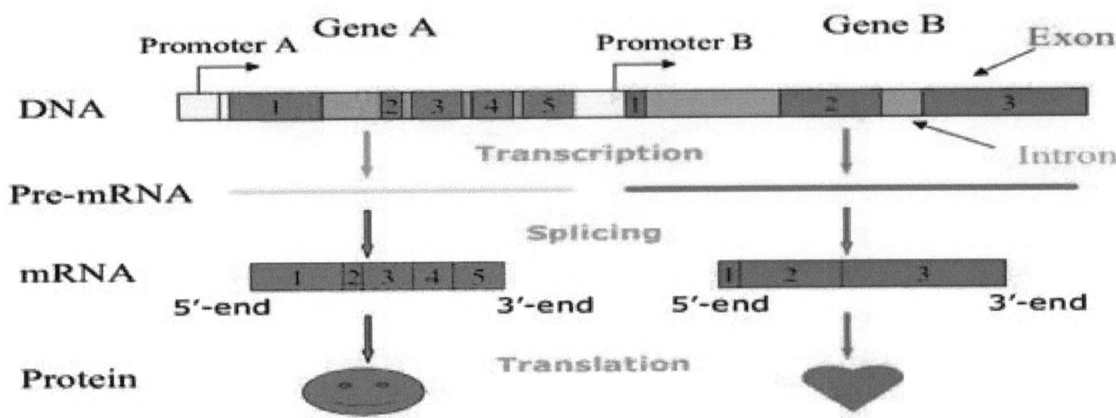

Fig.1 Gene expression [1]

There are many different mechanisms by which gene expression is regulated. One common mechanism is through the use of regulatory proteins called transcription factors, which bind to specific sequences of DNA near a gene and control whether or not it is transcribed. Other regulatory mechanisms include the use of small RNA molecules, which can bind to and inhibit the expression of specific genes, and the modification of histones, which are proteins that help package DNA into a compact structure.

Gene expression is important because it allows cells to produce the proteins that they need to function and carry out their specific roles. Proteins are important because they perform many functions in the cell, including structural support, catalyzing chemical reactions, and carrying out specific tasks. Different cells in the body have different functions, and they produce different sets of proteins to carry out those functions. For example, muscle cells produce proteins that are necessary for contraction, while nerve cells produce proteins that are necessary for transmitting signals.

Gene expression is also important because it allows cells to respond to changes in their environment and to signals from other cells. For example, gene expression can be regulated in response to changes in the cell's nutrient availability, temperature, or other conditions. In addition, gene expression can be regulated by signaling pathways that are activated by signaling molecules produced by other cells.

Overall, gene expression is important because it allows cells to produce the proteins that they need to function and carry out their specific roles, and it allows cells to respond to changes in their environment and signals from other cells.

Gene Regulation

Gene regulation is the process by which the expression of genes is controlled in order to produce the appropriate proteins at the appropriate time and place. Gene regulation is important because it allows cells to produce the proteins that they need to function and carry out their specific roles, and it allows cells to respond to changes in their environment and signals from other cells.

Gene regulation occurs at various levels, including transcriptional regulation (the control of gene transcription), post-transcriptional regulation (the control of mRNA processing and stability), translational regulation (the control of protein synthesis), and post-translational regulation (the control of protein activity and stability).

Gene regulation is important because it allows cells to produce the right proteins at the right time and in the right place. For example, gene regulation allows cells to respond to changes in their environment and to signals from other cells. It also allows cells to differentiate into different cell types and to carry out different functions. Dysregulation of gene expression has been linked to a variety of diseases, including cancer, developmental disorders, and immune disorders.

Overall, the regulation of gene expression is a complex process that plays a critical role in the development and functioning of cells and organisms. Understanding the regulation of gene expression is important for understanding how genes are turned on and off and how they contribute to an organism's traits and characteristics.

Gene expression is the process by which genetic information is used to produce specific proteins or RNA molecules. Gene regulation controls this process to ensure that the right proteins are produced at the right time and place in the cell. This regulation occurs at various levels, including transcription, post-transcription, translation, and post-translation. Gene regulation is important for cell function, response to changes in the environment, and differentiation into different cell types. Dysregulation of gene expression has been linked to various diseases. Understanding the regulation of gene expression is critical for understanding the role of genes in an organism's traits and characteristics.

In addition to the mechanisms mentioned earlier, there are also other ways that gene expression can be regulated. One is through the process of alternative splicing, where different regions of the RNA molecule are included or excluded, leading to the production of different protein variants. Another way is through the use of miRNA, small non-coding RNA molecules that can bind to and regulate the expression of specific target genes by inhibiting translation or promoting degradation of the mRNA.

Epigenetics is also another important aspect of gene regulation. Epigenetics refers to changes in gene activity that occur without changes to the underlying DNA sequence. These changes can include modifications to the DNA molecule itself or to the proteins with which DNA interacts. These modifications can turn genes on or off, and can affect how cells interpret the genetic information.

Lastly, gene regulation also plays a role in the development of organisms. During development, cells differentiate into various types and eventually form the different tissues and organs that make up the body. Gene regulation allows for this process by turning on and off specific genes at different stages of development.

In conclusion, gene regulation is a complex process that plays a critical role in the development and functioning of cells and organisms. It allows cells to produce the right proteins at the right time and in the right place, respond to changes in their environment, differentiate into different cell types, and contribute to the development of organisms. Understanding the mechanisms and regulation of gene expression is essential for understanding the underlying causes of various diseases and for developing treatments.

Another important aspect of gene regulation is the role of the genome environment, this includes the spatial organization of the chromosomes and the interactions of the chromatin with the nuclear architecture. The spatial organization of the chromosomes is known as the 3D genome, and it plays a key role in gene regulation. Chromosomes are not randomly organized within the nucleus, but rather they are organized in a specific way, with some regions being more accessible to the transcription machinery and others being less accessible. This organization is mediated by the chromatin structure, which can be modified by various mechanisms such as the addition or removal of chemical groups on the histones or the binding of specific proteins, which can affect the accessibility of the DNA and the regulation of gene expression.

Another important aspect of gene regulation is the role of non-coding RNAs (ncRNAs). These are a diverse group of RNA molecules that do not code for proteins, but rather play a role in regulating gene expression. Some examples of ncRNAs include miRNAs and lncRNAs. miRNAs are small non-coding RNAs that can bind to and regulate the expression of specific target genes by inhibiting translation or promoting degradation of the mRNA. lncRNAs are long non-coding RNAs that can also modulate gene expression through various mechanisms, such as by recruiting chromatin-modifying enzymes or by acting as decoys for regulatory proteins.

Overall, gene regulation is a complex and dynamic process that involves multiple layers of control and interactions between different factors. Understanding the mechanisms and regulation of gene expression is essential for understanding the underlying causes of various diseases, such as cancer, and for developing treatments.

Another important aspect of gene regulation is the role of the immune system. The immune system plays a critical role in regulating gene expression by recognizing and responding to pathogens, and also by regulating the expression of genes involved in inflammation, tissue repair and cell death.

For instance, the activation of immune cells like T cells and B cells, leads to the expression of specific genes that are necessary for their function. Also, the immune cells secrete various signaling molecules known as cytokines that can activate or repress gene expression in other cells of the body. Furthermore, genetic variations in the genes that regulate the immune response have been linked to various autoimmune and inflammatory diseases.

In addition, the gut microbiome also plays a role in regulating gene expression. The gut microbiome is made up of the microorganisms that live in the gut and it has been shown to regulate gene expression in the host cells through various mechanisms, such as by producing signaling molecules or by modulating the immune response.

To sum up, gene regulation is a complex process that is tightly controlled by various mechanisms, including transcription factors, epigenetic modifications, non-coding RNAs, and the interactions between the genome and the environment. The immune system and gut microbiome also play a role in regulating gene expression. Understanding these mechanisms is essential for understanding the underlying causes of various diseases and for developing treatments.

Another important aspect of gene regulation is the role of environmental factors. Environmental factors such as diet, toxins, radiation, and stress can all affect gene expression. For example, diet can affect gene expression through the action of nutrients and other dietary compounds on specific signaling pathways, while toxins and radiation can affect gene expression through their ability to cause DNA damage and epigenetic modifications.

Stress also plays a role in gene regulation, as it can activate specific signaling pathways that lead to changes in gene expression. The stress response can lead to the activation of genes involved in the regulation of inflammation, cell death, and tissue repair. Chronic stress can also lead to long-term changes in gene expression that are associated with various diseases such as depression and cardiovascular disease.

In summary, gene regulation is a complex and dynamic process that is controlled by various mechanisms and factors, including transcription factors, epigenetic modifications, non-coding RNAs, the interactions between the genome and the environment, the immune system, gut microbiome and environmental factors. Understanding these mechanisms and factors is essential for understanding the underlying causes of various diseases and for developing treatments.

Another important aspect of gene regulation is the use of genetic engineering techniques. Genetic engineering is the manipulation of the genetic material of an organism in order to alter its characteristics. It involves the use of recombinant DNA technology, which allows scientists to isolate, modify, and introduce specific genes into cells or organisms. Genetic engineering has applications in various fields, such as medicine, agriculture, and biotechnology.

One of the most common applications of genetic engineering in medicine is the development of gene therapies. Gene therapies involve the introduction of a normal copy of a gene into cells in order to correct a genetic disorder caused by a mutation in the original gene. This can be done using various methods, such as viral vectors, non-viral vectors, or genome editing techniques.

Genetic engineering also has applications in agriculture, where it is used to improve crop yields, resistance to pests and diseases, and tolerance to environmental stress. Genetic engineering has also led to the development of genetically modified organisms (GMOs) which are organisms whose genetic material has been altered in a way that does not occur naturally.

In summary, genetic engineering is the manipulation of the genetic material of an organism in order to alter its characteristics. It has applications in various fields, such as medicine, agriculture, and biotechnology. Gene therapies, GMOs and other forms of genetic engineering have the potential to help improve human health and agriculture, but they also raise ethical and social concerns. Therefore, further research and regulation is needed to ensure that these techniques are used responsibly and safely.

Importance of siRNA and micro RNA

Small interfering RNA (siRNA) and microRNA (miRNA) are small RNA molecules that play important roles in the regulation of gene expression. Both types of RNA molecules are involved in the process of RNA interference (RNAi), which is a mechanism that cells use to silence specific genes by inhibiting their expression. siRNA and miRNA have many important roles in the regulation of gene expression and play a key role in many biological processes, including the development of cells and tissues, the immune response, and the regulation of cell growth and division.

siRNA molecules are usually around 21 nucleotides in length and are composed of two strands of RNA that are complementary to each other. They are designed to specifically target a particular mRNA molecule based on sequence complementarity. Once the siRNA is bound to the RNA-induced silencing complex (RISC), it uses the complementary base pairing to locate the mRNA molecule that it needs to target. The RISC then cuts the mRNA molecule, leading to its degradation and the silencing of the corresponding gene.

miRNA molecules are also small RNA molecules, typically around 22 nucleotides in length, that bind to specific mRNA molecules and inhibit their translation into proteins. They also play a role in post-transcriptional gene silencing. miRNA molecules are typically transcribed from non-coding regions of the genome and are usually single-stranded. They bind to target mRNA molecules through complementary base-pairing.

Dysregulation of siRNA and miRNA pathways has been implicated in a variety of diseases, including cancer, and the use of these molecules as therapeutic agents is an active area of research. Overall, siRNA and miRNA are important regulators of gene expression that play crucial roles in many aspects of biology and have the potential to be used as therapeutic agents for the treatment of a variety of diseases.

In addition to their potential as therapeutic agents, siRNA and miRNA are also important tools for research. They are commonly used to knock down the expression of specific genes in order to study their function or to test the effects of silencing the gene. This is a powerful tool for understanding the role of specific genes in various biological processes and can be used to study the effects of genetic mutations or to identify new drug targets.

siRNA and miRNA are also being explored as potential diagnostic markers for diseases. The levels of specific siRNA and miRNA molecules can be used to detect the presence of certain diseases or to monitor the progression of the disease.

Furthermore, siRNA and miRNA are also being used in the field of biotechnology for the development of genetically modified organisms. The ability to silence specific genes can be used to create organisms with specific desired characteristics.

In summary, siRNA and miRNA are small RNA molecules that play crucial roles in the regulation of gene expression and are involved in many biological processes. They have the potential to be used as therapeutic agents for the treatment of a variety of diseases and are important tools for research and biotechnology. The ongoing research in this field is expected to reveal more about the molecular mechanisms and potential applications of siRNA and miRNA.

Small interfering RNA (siRNAs)

Small interfering RNAs (siRNAs) are short, double-stranded RNA molecules that play a key role in the process of RNA interference (RNAi). RNAi is a cellular process that silences specific genes by degrading the corresponding mRNA molecules, which prevents the mRNA from being translated into protein. SiRNAs are involved in the initiation of the RNAi process and guide the RNA-induced silencing complex (RISC) to the mRNA molecule that needs to be silenced.

SiRNAs are usually around 21 nucleotides in length and are composed of two strands of RNA that are complementary to each other. They are designed to specifically target a particular mRNA molecule based on sequence complementarity. The two strands of siRNA, known as the sense strand and the antisense strand, are separated by an enzyme called Dicer, and the antisense strand is then incorporated into the RISC.

Once the siRNA is bound to the RISC, it uses the complementary base pairing to locate the mRNA molecule that it needs to target. The RISC then cuts the mRNA molecule, leading to its degradation and the silencing of the corresponding gene. This process is known as post-transcriptional gene silencing.

SiRNAs are important because they play a key role in the process of RNA interference (RNAi), which is a cellular process that silences specific genes. RNAi is an important mechanism for regulating gene expression in cells, and it plays a role in a variety of biological processes, including development, immunity, and response to stress.

The ability of siRNAs to specifically target and silence specific genes has made them a valuable tool in research and medicine. They are commonly used to knock down the expression of specific genes in order to study their function or to test the effects of silencing the gene. They have also been explored as a potential treatment for a variety of diseases, including cancer, viral infections, and genetic disorders.

Overall, SiRNAs are small double-stranded RNA molecules that are involved in the initiation of RNA interference process, they are designed to specifically target a particular mRNA molecule based on sequence complementarity and they are involved in post-transcriptional gene silencing. They are valuable tools in research and medicine, and they have a wide range of applications in different fields.

In addition to their use in research and medicine, siRNAs also have potential applications in agriculture and biotechnology. For example, siRNAs can be used to silence genes in plants that are responsible for causing diseases or for reducing crop yields. This can lead to the development of more resilient and productive crops.

Another potential application of siRNAs is in the field of gene therapy. SiRNAs can be used to specifically silence disease-causing genes in cells, which could be a powerful tool for treating genetic disorders. Researchers are also exploring the use of siRNAs as a way to treat viral infections. By specifically targeting and silencing genes that are essential for the virus to replicate, siRNAs could be used to inhibit the replication of the virus and prevent the spread of the infection.

The siRNA technology is advancing, and new methods of siRNA delivery are being developed. For example, lipid nanoparticles, polymeric nanoparticles, and viral vectors have been used to deliver siRNAs to cells. These delivery methods have improved the efficiency and specificity of siRNA delivery, and they are expected to play an important role in the development of siRNA-based therapeutics.

In conclusion, siRNAs are small double-stranded RNA molecules that play a key role in the process of RNA interference (RNAi) and are used to silence specific genes. They have a wide range of applications in research and medicine, including gene knockdown, disease treatment, drug development, and biotechnology. Their ability to specifically target and silence genes makes them a powerful tool in many areas of science and technology. Ongoing research is expected to reveal new applications and to improve the delivery methods of siRNA to increase its efficiency and specificity.

Applications of SiRNAs

SiRNAs have a variety of applications in research and medicine. They are commonly used to knock down the expression of specific genes in order to study their function or to test the effects of silencing the gene. They have also been explored as a potential treatment for a variety of diseases, including cancer, viral infections, and genetic disorders.

Small interfering RNAs (siRNAs) have a wide range of applications in research and medicine due to their ability to specifically silence the expression of specific genes.

Some of the main applications of siRNAs include:

1. Gene knockdown: SiRNAs are commonly used to knock down the expression of specific genes in order to study their function or to test the effects of silencing the gene. This is often done in cell culture or animal models.
2. Drug discovery: SiRNAs can be used to identify new drug targets by silencing specific genes and observing the effects on disease-related pathways.
3. Gene therapy: SiRNAs have been explored as a potential treatment for a variety of diseases, including cancer, viral infections, and genetic disorders. They can be used to target and silence specific genes that are involved in the disease process.
4. Pesticides: SiRNAs have been developed as a method for controlling pest populations. They can be used to target specific genes in pests, leading to their death or reduced fertility.
5. Industrial and environmental applications: SiRNAs have been explored as a means of controlling microorganisms in industrial processes and in environmental remediation efforts. They can be used to target specific genes in microbes that are involved in processes such as oil degradation or the production of biofuels.
6. Biotechnology: siRNA technology can be used to create genetically modified organisms with specific desired characteristics.

7. Agriculture: siRNAs have potential applications in agriculture and have been used to silence genes in plants that are responsible for causing diseases or for reducing crop yields.
8. Diagnostics: siRNAs are also being explored as potential diagnostic markers for diseases. The levels of specific siRNA molecules can be used to detect the presence of certain diseases or to monitor the progression of the disease.
9. Drug delivery: siRNA delivery methods are being developed to improve the efficiency and specificity of siRNA delivery. Lipid nanoparticles, polymeric nanoparticles, and viral vectors have been used to deliver siRNA to cells.
10. Biomedical research: siRNAs are also used in biomedical research to study the function of specific genes in different biological processes and to understand the underlying mechanisms of diseases.
11. Personalized medicine: siRNAs can be used in personalized medicine by targeting and silencing specific genes that are involved in the disease process and unique to the individual patient.
12. Gene editing: siRNAs can also be used as a tool for gene editing, as they can be designed to target specific sequences in the genome and trigger the cell's own repair mechanisms to make precise changes to the DNA.
13. Biomanufacturing: siRNAs can be used in biomanufacturing to control the expression of specific genes in microorganisms or cells to improve the yield of desired products such as enzymes, proteins or biopharmaceuticals.
14. Tissue engineering: siRNAs can be used to regulate specific genes during tissue engineering to promote the growth of specific cell types, or to prevent the formation of unwanted cells, such as cancer cells.
15. Cosmetics: siRNAs can also be used in the cosmetics industry to regulate specific genes in cells to improve the appearance of skin or hair.

These are some of the main applications of siRNAs, but research in this field is ongoing, and new applications are likely to be discovered in the future. Due to the specificity and efficiency of siRNAs in silencing specific genes, they are expected to play an important role in many areas of science and technology, and to have a significant impact on human health and the environment.

Overall, siRNAs have a wide range of applications in research and medicine due to their ability to specifically silence the expression of specific genes. This has led to many exciting possibilities for understanding the underlying causes of diseases and for developing new therapies to treat them. The ongoing research in this field is expected to reveal more about the molecular mechanisms and potential applications of siRNAs.

MicroRNAs (miRNAs)

MicroRNAs (miRNAs) are small, non-coding RNA molecules that play a key role in the regulation of gene expression in cells. They are transcribed from non-coding regions of the genome, usually from intergenic regions or introns, and are usually around 22 nucleotides in length. MiRNA molecules are processed by the enzyme Dicer, which cuts them into shorter pieces and then they are incorporated into the RNA-induced silencing complex (RISC), which targets specific mRNA molecules for degradation or translation repression.

MiRNAs are important because they play a role in a wide range of biological processes, including cell growth and differentiation, development, immunity, and response to stress. They have been implicated in the regulation of many different genes, including oncogenes, tumor suppressor genes, and genes involved in development and disease.

MiRNAs have been linked to a variety of diseases, including cancer, cardiovascular disease, and neurodegenerative disorders. They are also involved in the regulation of developmental processes and have been found to be essential for normal embryonic development.

Because of their critical role in regulation of gene expression and their association with diseases, miRNAs are an active area of research and have the potential to be developed as therapeutic targets or as diagnostic biomarkers. The development of methods for identifying and quantifying miRNAs in biological samples has enabled the discovery of new miRNAs and their targets, and has provided insights into the biological roles of miRNAs. The ongoing research on miRNA is expected to reveal more about their molecular mechanisms and potential applications in the future.

One of the most promising areas of research on miRNAs is in the field of cancer research. MiRNAs have been found to be involved in the regulation of oncogenes and tumor suppressor genes, and their dysregulation has been linked to the development and progression of many different types of cancer. As a result, miRNAs are being studied as potential diagnostic markers and therapeutic targets for cancer.

Another area of research on miRNAs is in the field of cardiovascular disease. MiRNAs have been found to be involved in the regulation of genes that are associated with cardiovascular disease, such as those involved in inflammation, lipid metabolism, and blood vessel formation. As a result, miRNAs are being studied as potential diagnostic markers and therapeutic targets for cardiovascular disease.

Similarly, miRNAs are also being studied in the field of neurodegenerative disorders. MiRNAs have been found to be involved in the regulation of genes that are associated with neurodegenerative disorders, such as those involved in cell death, inflammation, and protein aggregation.

Another promising area of research is the development of miRNA-based therapeutics. This is being done by the development of synthetic miRNA molecules or by the delivery of miRNA mimics, which are synthetic molecules that mimic the action of natural miRNAs.

Overall, miRNAs are small non-coding RNA molecules that play a key role in the regulation of gene expression in cells and have a wide range of biological processes. They are associated with a variety of diseases including cancer, cardiovascular disease, and neurodegenerative disorders, making them an active area of research and have the potential to be developed as therapeutic targets or as diagnostic biomarkers. The ongoing research on miRNA is expected to reveal more about their molecular mechanisms and potential applications in the future.

Applications of MicroRNA (miRNA)

MicroRNAs (miRNAs) have a variety of applications in research and medicine due to their ability to regulate gene expression in a precise and widespread manner.

Some of the main applications of miRNAs include:

1. Biomarkers: MiRNAs are stable in various biofluids and tissues, and their expression levels can be used as diagnostic or prognostic biomarkers for various diseases.
2. Drug development: MiRNAs can be targeted as therapeutic agents to treat diseases by restoring the expression of specific genes or by inhibiting the expression of disease-associated genes.
3. Gene therapy: MiRNAs can be used as gene therapies to treat diseases by silencing specific genes that are involved in the disease process.
4. Diagnostics: MiRNAs can be used to develop diagnostic tests for a variety of diseases by detecting specific miRNA signatures in biofluids or tissues.
5. Research: MiRNAs are widely used as tools in basic research to study the function of specific genes and to understand the role of miRNAs in normal biology and disease.
6. Personalized medicine: MiRNAs can be used in personalized medicine by targeting specific miRNA signatures unique to the individual patient.
7. Tissue engineering: MiRNAs can be used to regulate specific genes during tissue engineering to promote the growth of specific cell types, or to prevent the formation of unwanted cells, such as cancer cells.
8. Cosmetics: MiRNAs can also be used in the cosmetics industry to regulate specific genes in cells to improve the appearance of skin or hair.
9. Agriculture: miRNAs have potential applications in agriculture and have been used to silence genes in plants that are responsible for causing diseases or for reducing crop yields.
10. Biomanufacturing: miRNAs can be used in biomanufacturing to control the expression of specific genes in microorganisms or cells to improve the yield of desired products such as enzymes, proteins or biopharmaceuticals.
11. Cancer therapy: MiRNAs have been found to be involved in the regulation of oncogenes and tumor suppressor genes, and their dysregulation has been linked to the development and progression of many different types of cancer. MiRNAs are being studied as potential diagnostic markers and therapeutic targets for cancer.
12. Cardiovascular disease therapy: MiRNAs have been found to be involved in the regulation of genes that are associated with cardiovascular disease, such as those involved in inflammation, lipid metabolism, and blood vessel

formation. MiRNAs are being studied as potential diagnostic markers and therapeutic targets for cardiovascular disease.

13. Neurodegenerative disorders therapy: MiRNAs have been found to be involved in the regulation of genes that are associated with neurodegenerative disorders, such as those involved in cell death, inflammation, and protein aggregation. miRNAs are being studied as potential diagnostic markers and therapeutic targets for neurodegenerative disorders.
14. Aging research: MiRNAs have been found to be involved in the regulation of genes that are associated with aging, such as those involved in the regulation of cell proliferation and cell death. miRNAs are being studied as potential therapeutic targets for age-related diseases.
15. Biotechnology: miRNA technology can be used to create genetically modified organisms with specific desired characteristics.

miRNAs have a wide range of applications in research and medicine due to their ability to specifically regulate gene expression. This has led to many exciting possibilities for understanding the underlying causes of diseases and for developing new therapies to treat them. The ongoing research in this field is expected to reveal more about the molecular mechanisms and potential applications of miRNAs.

Overall, miRNAs are important regulators of gene expression that play crucial roles in many aspects of biology and have the potential to be used as therapeutic agents for the treatment of a variety of diseases. The versatility and potency of miRNAs make them valuable tools in a wide range of applications in research and medicine. Ongoing research is expected to reveal new applications and to improve the delivery methods of miRNA to increase its efficiency and specificity.

Overall, the versatility and potency of miRNAs make them valuable tools in a wide range of applications in research and medicine.

Gene Mapping

Gene mapping is the process of determining the location of a gene on a chromosome. It involves identifying the relative position of a gene in relation to other genetic markers on a chromosome. This information is used to create a genetic map, which shows the approximate location of each marker on a chromosome. There are several different methods that can be used for gene mapping, including linkage mapping, physical mapping, and comparative genomics.

- Linkage mapping is the most commonly used method for gene mapping. It involves analyzing the inheritance patterns of multiple genetic markers in families to determine which markers are inherited together more frequently than expected by chance. By analyzing the inheritance patterns of many different markers, researchers can create a genetic map that shows the approximate location of each marker on a chromosome. Linkage mapping is particularly useful for studying complex traits and diseases that are likely to be influenced by multiple genes.
- Physical mapping is another method that can be used for gene mapping. It involves determining the physical location of a gene on a chromosome using techniques such as restriction fragment length polymorphism (RFLP) analysis or fluorescence in situ hybridization (FISH). Physical mapping is particularly useful for studying the organization of the genome and for identifying specific genes that are associated with a particular trait or disease.
- Comparative genomics is a newer method that has been used for gene mapping. It involves comparing the genomes of different organisms to identify conserved regions that are likely to contain important genes. This method is particularly useful for studying the evolution of different species and for identifying genes that have been conserved across different organisms.

Gene mapping has many applications in research and medicine, including understanding the genetic basis of traits and diseases, identifying genetic risk factors, developing diagnostic tests, and discovering potential targets for gene therapy. The continued advancement of gene mapping technologies will continue to provide new insights and opportunities in genetics and medicine.

In addition to the methods mentioned earlier, there are a few more methods that are used for gene mapping. These include:

Cytogenetics: This method uses traditional microscope techniques to identify and study the structure of chromosomes, such as their size, shape and location of the genes. This method is useful for identifying chromosomal abnormalities, such as those that can lead to genetic disorders.

Genome-wide association studies (GWAS): This method involves analyzing the genetic variations of large groups of people, to identify genetic variations that are associated with a particular trait or disease. This method is useful for identifying genetic risk factors for complex diseases such as cancer, heart disease, and diabetes.

Genome-wide linkage analysis: This method is used to study the inheritance patterns of genetic markers in large families, to identify the chromosomal regions that are likely to contain the genes that are associated with a particular trait or disease.

Next-generation sequencing (NGS): This method uses high-throughput DNA sequencing to quickly and cheaply sequence the genomes of many organisms. This method can be used for gene mapping as well as for whole genome sequencing, transcriptome sequencing, and epigenetic analyses.

CRISPR-Cas: CRISPR-Cas is a method for editing genes, it allows for the precise modification of genes and can be used to correct genetic mutations that cause inherited diseases or to introduce desirable traits.

mRNA sequencing: mRNA sequencing, also known as transcriptome sequencing, is a method that allows to measure the amount of mRNA molecules present in a given cell type or tissue. This method can be used to identify genes that are expressed in different cell types or at different stages of development.

Gene mapping has been an important tool in genetics research and has helped researchers to understand the genetic basis of many different traits and diseases. It has also been useful for developing diagnostic tests and for identifying potential targets for gene therapy.

Some of the key importance of gene mapping include:

1. Understanding the genetic basis of traits and diseases: Gene mapping has helped researchers to identify the genetic basis of many different traits and diseases, including inherited disorders, cancer, and complex traits such as height and intelligence. This knowledge has allowed researchers to develop diagnostic tests and to identify potential targets for gene therapy.
2. Identifying genetic risk factors: Gene mapping has helped researchers to identify genetic risk factors for a variety of diseases, including cardiovascular disease, diabetes, and mental health disorders. This information can be used to develop risk prediction models and to design interventions to prevent or mitigate the risk of these diseases.
3. Developing diagnostic tests: Gene mapping has been used to develop diagnostic tests for a variety of inherited disorders, including genetic disorders and cancer. These tests can be used to diagnose these conditions early, which can allow for earlier treatment and better outcomes.
4. Gene therapy: Gene mapping has helped researchers to identify potential targets for gene therapy, which is a type of treatment that involves the delivery of functional copies of genes to cells in order to correct genetic defects.
5. Agricultural and environmental applications: Gene mapping has also been used to study the genetics of crops and livestock in order to improve agriculture and to understand the genetics of microorganisms in environmental samples.

Overall, gene mapping is a powerful tool that has been used to advance our understanding of genetics and has many applications in research and medicine. With the continued development of new technologies and techniques, gene mapping will continue to provide new insights and opportunities in genetics and medicine.

Gene Sequencing

Gene sequencing is the process of determining the precise order of nucleotides (A, C, G, and T) in a DNA molecule. This information is used to study the genetic makeup of an organism and to understand the function of specific genes. There are several different methods that can be used for gene sequencing, including:

Sanger sequencing: This is the traditional method of DNA sequencing, which was developed by Frederick Sanger in the 1970s. It involves using a chain-termination method to determine the order of nucleotides in a DNA molecule.

Next-generation sequencing (NGS): This is a newer method of DNA sequencing that uses high-throughput technologies to quickly and cheaply sequence the genomes of many organisms. NGS technologies include Illumina sequencing, PacBio sequencing, and Nanopore sequencing.

PCR-based sequencing: This method involves amplifying a specific region of DNA using polymerase chain reaction (PCR) and then sequencing the amplified DNA. This method is useful for sequencing specific regions of the genome that are of interest.

Single-molecule sequencing: This method involves sequencing individual DNA molecules, rather than a mixture of DNA molecules. This method can be used to sequence long DNA molecules and to study the genomic structure of chromosomes.

Gene sequencing has many applications in research and medicine, including identifying genetic variations that are associated with a particular trait or disease, studying the evolution of different species, and identifying potential targets for gene therapy. It also plays a critical role in personalised medicine, allowing doctors to provide tailored treatment plans to patients based on their specific genetic makeup. With the continued development of new technologies and techniques, gene sequencing will continue to provide new insights and opportunities in genetics and medicine.

In addition to the methods mentioned earlier, there are a few more methods that are used for gene sequencing:

Massively parallel sequencing (MPS): This method uses microfabrication technology to simultaneously sequence millions of DNA molecules at once. This method is highly efficient, fast and cost-effective and can be used to generate large amounts of sequencing data.

Targeted sequencing: This method allows researchers to sequence specific regions of the genome that are of interest, such as genes associated with a particular trait or disease. This method can be used to identify genetic variations that are associated with a particular trait or disease, and to study the genomic structure of chromosomes.

Exome sequencing: This method involves sequencing only the exome, the part of the genome that codes for proteins. This is a cost-effective method to study the genetic basis of inherited diseases, as most disease-causing mutations are located in the exome.

Transcriptome sequencing: This method involves sequencing all the RNA molecules present in a given cell type or tissue. This method can be used to identify genes that are expressed in different cell types or at different stages of development, and to study the regulation of gene expression.

Epigenetics sequencing: This method involves sequencing the chemical modifications on the DNA and Histone proteins, these modifications can change the way the DNA is packaged in the cell and thus affect the expression of the genes, this method can be used to study the regulation of gene expression and the development of diseases.

Long-read sequencing: This method allows to sequence the genome in a single read, which can span several kilobases or even a megabase. This method can be used to study the genomic structure of chromosomes, including the identification of structural variations and the analysis of repetitive regions that are challenging to sequence with short-read technologies.

Overall, gene sequencing is a powerful tool that has been used to advance our understanding of genetics and has many applications in research and medicine. With the continued development of new technologies and techniques, gene sequencing will continue to provide new insights and opportunities in genetics and medicine.

Gene sequencing is the process of determining the precise order of nucleotides in a DNA molecule. DNA is made up of four nucleotide bases: adenine (A), guanine (G), cytosine (C), and thymine (T). The order of these nucleotide bases determines the genetic information that is stored in a DNA molecule.

Gene sequencing is the process of determining the order of nucleotides in a DNA molecule. It is a fundamental technique in molecular biology and has a wide range of applications in fields such as genetics, evolution, and medicine.

One of the main uses of gene sequencing is in the field of genetics, where it is used to identify genetic variations or mutations that may be associated with certain inherited diseases or traits. For example, gene sequencing can be used to identify genetic mutations that are associated with conditions such as cystic fibrosis or sickle cell anemia. This knowledge can help doctors diagnose and treat these conditions more effectively.

Gene sequencing is also important for the study of evolution, as it allows scientists to compare the DNA of different organisms and understand how they are related and how they have evolved over time. In addition, gene sequencing is used in the field of personalized medicine, where it is used to tailor treatments to an individual's unique genetic makeup.

Overall, gene sequencing is a powerful tool that has revolutionized our understanding of genetics and has had a significant impact on many areas of science and medicine.

Gene sequencing is an important tool in genetics research and has a variety of applications, including:

1. Identifying genetic mutations: Gene sequencing can be used to identify genetic mutations, which are changes in the DNA sequence that can have a variety of consequences, including changes in protein function or the development of diseases.
2. Genetic diagnosis: Gene sequencing can be used to diagnose genetic disorders by identifying changes in the DNA sequence that are associated with specific conditions.
3. Gene therapy: Gene sequencing can be used to design gene therapies, which are treatments that involve the delivery of functional copies of genes to cells in order to correct genetic defects.
4. Evolutionary studies: Gene sequencing can be used to study the evolution of different species by comparing the DNA sequences of different organisms.
5. Drug development: Gene sequencing can be used to identify genetic variations that might influence the effectiveness or side effects of drugs, which can help to optimize drug treatment.

Overall, gene sequencing is an important tool that has a wide range of applications in genetics research and medicine.

Cell cycle and its Regulation

The cell cycle is the process by which a cell grows and divides to produce two daughter cells. It is essential for the growth and development of all living organisms and is tightly regulated to ensure that cells divide at the appropriate times and in the correct ways.

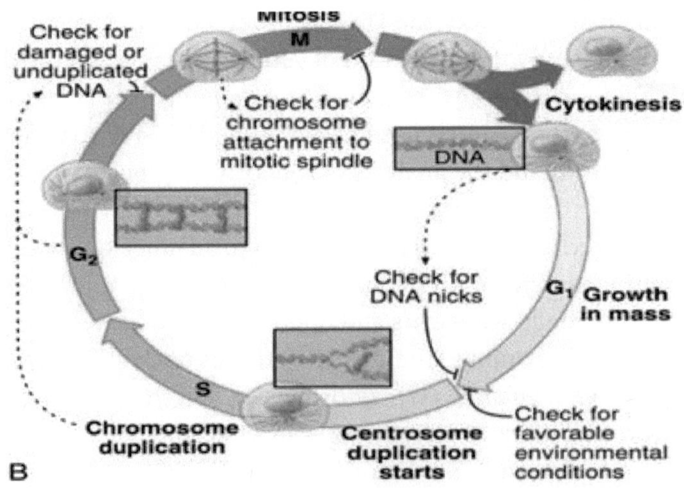

Fig. 2 Cell cycle [2]

The cell cycle can be divided into two main phases: interphase and cell division.

- **Interphase is further divided into three phases:**

1. **G1 phase:** The G1 phase, also known as the "gap 1" phase, is the first phase of the cell cycle. It occurs during interphase, the period between cell divisions. During the G1 phase, the cell grows and carries out its normal functions.During this phase, the cell synthesizes proteins and other cellular components, as well as repairing any damage to its DNA. The G1 phase is also a time for the cell to check that everything is in order before proceeding to the next phase of the cell cycle.If the cell is not ready to divide, it may enter a state called G0, in which it is no longer actively cycling through the cell cycle. This can occur when the cell is damaged, stressed, or not receiving the necessary signals to divide.The length of the G1 phase can vary depending on the type of cell and its environment. For example, cells in rapidly dividing tissues, such as the bone marrow or the lining of the intestine, may have a shorter G1 phase than cells in more stable tissues.Understanding the G1 phase is important for understanding the regulation of the cell cycle and how cells grow and divide. Dysregulation of the G1 phase can lead to problems such as uncontrolled cell growth, which can lead to cancer.

1. **S phase:** Also known as the synthesis phase, this is when the cell's DNA is replicated, preparing for cell division. The S phase, also known as the synthesis phase, is the second phase of the cell cycle. It occurs during interphase, the period between cell divisions. During the S phase, the cell's DNA is replicated, preparing for cell division.During DNA replication, the cell's genome is copied so that each daughter cell will receive an exact copy of the parent cell's DNA. This is a complex process that involves unwinding the DNA double helix, separating the two strands, and synthesizing new strands using the existing strands as templates.The S phase is a crucial part of the cell cycle, as it ensures that each daughter cell receives a complete and accurate copy of the parent cell's genetic material.The length of the S phase can vary depending on the type of cell and its environment. For example, cells in rapidly dividing tissues, such as the bone marrow or the lining of the intestine, may have a shorter S phase than cells in more stable tissues.Understanding the S phase is important for understanding the regulation of the cell cycle and how cells grow and divide. Dysregulation of the S phase can lead to problems such as DNA damage, which can lead to genetic mutations and potentially to cancer.
2. G2 phase: This is a period of preparation for cell division, during which the cell makes sure that everything is ready for mitosis, the process of cell division. The G2 phase, also known as the "gap 2" phase, is the third phase of the cell cycle. It occurs during interphase, the period between cell divisions. During the G2 phase, the cell makes sure that everything is ready for mitosis, the process of cell division.During the G2 phase, the cell synthesizes proteins and other cellular components, as well as repairing any damage to its DNA. The cell also checks that its DNA is correctly replicated and that all the necessary proteins and structures are in place for mitosis.If the cell is not ready to divide, it may enter a state called G0, in which it is no longer actively cycling through the cell cycle. This can occur when the cell is damaged, stressed, or not receiving the necessary signals to divide. The length of the G2 phase can vary depending on the type of cell and its environment. For example, cells in rapidly dividing tissues, such as the bone marrow or the lining of the intestine, may have a shorter G2 phase than cells in more stable tissues.

Understanding the G2 phase is important for understanding the regulation of the cell cycle and how cells grow and divide. Dysregulation of the G2 phase can lead to problems such as uncontrolled cell growth, which can lead to cancer.

- **Cell division is divided into two main phases:**

1. Mitosis: During this phase, the cell's chromosomes are separated and the cell divides into two daughter cells. Mitosis is the process of cell division that occurs during the cell cycle. It is the process by which a single cell divides into two daughter cells, each with an identical set of chromosomes.Mitosis is divided into four main stages: prophase, metaphase, anaphase, and telophase.During prophase, the cell's nucleus becomes visible and the chromatin, or DNA, condenses into chromosomes. The nucleolus disappears and the nucleolus disappears.During metaphase, the chromosomes line up in the center of the cell. During anaphase, the chromosomes are separated and move to opposite poles of the cell.During telophase, two new nuclei form at opposite poles of the cell and a new cell wall forms between the two daughter cells, completing the process of cell division.

Mitosis is a critical process for the growth and development of all living organisms, as it allows cells to replicate and produce new cells. Dysregulation of mitosis can lead to problems such as uncontrolled cell growth, which can lead to cancer. Understanding mitosis is therefore important for understanding and treating a range of diseases

2. Cytokinesis: This is the process by which the cell's cytoplasm is divided into the two daughter cells.

Cytokines are small proteins that are involved in cell communication and play a crucial role in the immune system. They are produced by a wide variety of cells, including immune cells, and act on nearby cells to regulate a range of functions, including immune responses, inflammation, and tissue repair.There are many different types of cytokines, including interleukins, chemokines, and growth factors. Each cytokine has a specific function and acts on specific target cells, often in a complex and coordinated manner.

Cytokines are important for the normal functioning of the immune system and are involved in a wide range of processes, including activating immune cells, regulating inflammation, and promoting tissue repair. Dysregulation of cytokine production or signaling can lead to a range of immune disorders, including autoimmune diseases and chronic inflammation. Cytokines are also important in cancer, as they can promote the growth and survival of cancer cells, as well as modulate the immune response to cancer. Understanding the role of cytokines in health and disease is therefore an active area of research, with the goal of developing targeted therapies for a range of conditions

- **Cell cycle regulation**

The cell cycle is regulated by a number of mechanisms, including cell cycle proteins and signaling pathways. Dysregulation of the cell cycle can lead to problems such as uncontrolled cell growth, which can lead to cancer. Understanding the cell cycle and how it is regulated is therefore important for understanding and treating a range of diseases.

- **Cell cycle proteins**

There are several proteins involved in the regulation of the cell cycle. Some of the key proteins and their roles in the cell cycle are described below:

- Cyclin-dependent kinases (CDKs): CDKs are a group of proteins that bind to and activate other proteins involved in the cell cycle. They are regulated by cyclins, which are proteins that bind to and activate CDKs.
- Cyclins: Cyclins are proteins that bind to and activate CDKs. Different cyclins are expressed at different stages of the cell cycle, and they regulate the activity of CDKs during different phases of the cell cycle.
- Cyclin-dependent kinase inhibitors (CDKIs): CDKIs are proteins that inhibit the activity of CDKs and help to regulate the cell cycle.
- Checkpoint proteins: Checkpoint proteins are proteins that help to ensure that the cell cycle proceeds correctly. They help to ensure that the cell cycle is paused at certain points until certain conditions are met, such as the completion of DNA replication or the repair of DNA damage.

- APC/C: The anaphase-promoting complex (APC/C) is a large protein complex that is responsible for the degradation of proteins that inhibit the progression of the cell cycle. This allows the cell cycle to proceed from one phase to the next.
- Retinoblastoma protein (Rb): The Rb protein is a tumor suppressor protein that helps to regulate the cell cycle by inhibiting the activity of CDKs.
- p53: p53 is a tumor suppressor protein that helps to regulate the cell cycle by inducing cell cycle arrest or apoptosis in response to DNA damage.

These proteins and their interactions play important roles in the regulation of the cell cycle and the maintenance of normal cell growth and division. Dysregulation of these proteins can lead to cancer and other diseases.

- **Signaling pathways**

Signaling pathways are series of molecular events that transmit signals from outside the cell to the inside of the cell. These signals can come from a variety of sources, including hormones, growth factors, and other signaling molecules. Signaling pathways play important roles in many cellular processes, including cell growth, proliferation, differentiation, and death.

There are many different signaling pathways, and they can be classified based on the type of signaling molecules involved and the type of response they elicit. Some common types of signaling pathways include:

- Growth factor signaling pathways: These pathways transmit signals from growth factors, which are proteins that stimulate cell proliferation and survival. They are often activated by receptors on the cell surface, which bind to the growth factor and transmit the signal into the cell.
- Hormone signaling pathways: These pathways transmit signals from hormones, which are signaling molecules produced by glands and secreted into the bloodstream. They are often activated by receptors on the cell surface, which bind to the hormone and transmit the signal into the cell.
- Second messenger signaling pathways: These pathways transmit signals from receptors on the cell surface to intracellular signaling proteins. They often involve the use of second messengers, which are small signaling molecules that are produced inside the cell in response to the activation of the receptor.
- G protein-coupled signaling pathways: These pathways transmit signals from receptors on the cell surface to intracellular signaling proteins. They involve the use of G proteins, which are proteins that are activated by the receptor and transmit the signal into the cell.
- Enzyme-linked signaling pathways: These pathways transmit signals from receptors on the cell surface to intracellular signaling proteins. They involve the activation of enzymes, which are proteins that catalyze chemical reactions inside the cell.
- Signaling pathways play important roles in the regulation of many cellular processes, including the cell cycle. Dysregulation of signaling pathways can lead to diseases such as cancer.

The cell cycle is the process by which a cell grows and divides to produce two daughter cells. It is divided into two main phases: interphase and cell division. Interphase is further divided into three phases: G1, S, and G2. The G1 phase is when the cell grows and carries out its normal functions. During the S phase, the cell's DNA is replicated, preparing for cell division. The G2 phase is a period of preparation for cell division, during which the cell makes sure that everything is ready for mitosis. Understanding the cell cycle and its regulation is important as dysregulation can lead to problems such as uncontrolled cell growth and cancer.

After the G2 phase, the cell enters the final stage of the cell cycle, known as mitosis (M phase). During mitosis, the cell physically divides into two daughter cells, each with an identical copy of the parent cell's genetic material. Mitosis is divided into four main stages: prophase, prometaphase, metaphase, and anaphase. In prophase, the chromatin condenses into visible chromosomes, each consisting of two identical sister chromatids. In prometaphase, the nuclear envelope breaks down and the spindle apparatus forms. In metaphase, the chromosomes align at the center of the cell. In anaphase, the chromatids are separated and pulled towards opposite poles of the cell. Finally, in telophase, the chromosomes reach the poles and the nuclear envelope reforms around them, and the cell will divide into two daughter cells during cytokinesis.

The cell cycle is regulated by a number of internal and external signals, including the presence of growth factors, nutrient availability, and DNA damage. The most well-known regulators of the cell cycle are cyclin-dependent kinases (CDKs), which are activated by binding to specific cyclins. These CDKs control the progression of the cell cycle by phosphorylating specific target proteins, leading to changes in their activity or localization. Other proteins, such as tumor protein p53 and retinoblastoma protein (Rb), act as checkpoint proteins that monitor the cell for DNA damage or other problems and can halt the cell cycle if necessary.

Overall, the cell cycle is a tightly regulated process that is essential for the growth and development of all living organisms. Understanding the cell cycle and its regulation is important for understanding how cells grow and divide, and can provide insight into the development of diseases such as cancer.

Another important checkpoint in the cell cycle is the G1/S checkpoint, which ensures that the cell has enough nutrients and energy to proceed with DNA replication and cell division. This checkpoint is controlled by a protein called Rb, which can inhibit the activity of CDKs by binding to them. When Rb is phosphorylated by CDKs, it releases its inhibitory effect on the CDKs, allowing the cell to proceed through the G1 phase and enter the S phase.

Another important checkpoint in the cell cycle is the G2/M checkpoint, which ensures that the cell's DNA has been replicated correctly and that all necessary proteins and structures are in place for mitosis. This checkpoint is controlled by a protein called checkpoint kinase (CHK) which can halt the cell cycle if DNA damage is detected.

The cell cycle is also regulated by external signals, such as growth factors. Growth factors are molecules that bind to receptors on the cell surface and send signals into the cell that promote cell growth and division. These signals are transduced through intracellular signaling pathways and ultimately activate CDKs, allowing the cell to enter the next stage of the cell cycle.

Cancer is a disease caused by the uncontrolled growth of cells, and one of the hallmarks of cancer is the deregulation of the cell cycle. Cancer cells can evade the normal regulatory mechanisms of the cell cycle, leading to uncontrolled cell growth and division. This can occur through mutations in genes that control the cell cycle, such as Rb or p53, or through the overexpression of growth factors or their receptors. Targeting the cell cycle with drugs that inhibit the activity of CDKs or other cell cycle regulators has been an important strategy in the treatment of cancer.

Understanding the cell cycle and its regulation is a crucial aspect in the study of cell biology and the development of new therapies for cancer and other diseases.

Another important aspect of the cell cycle regulation is the control of telomeres, which are the protective structures at the ends of chromosomes that shorten with each cell division. Telomeres act as a "timekeeper" for the cell cycle, and when they become too short, the cell will enter senescence, a state of permanent cell cycle arrest, and will no longer divide. This mechanism, known as the "Hayflick limit", helps to prevent the development of cancer by limiting the number of times a cell can divide.

However, some cancer cells can bypass this mechanism by activating an enzyme called telomerase which can add telomeric repeats to the telomeres and allow the cells to divide indefinitely. This is one of the reasons why telomerase is considered a promising target for cancer therapy.

Another important aspect of the cell cycle is the regulation of apoptosis, a process of programmed cell death that is responsible for the removal of damaged or unnecessary cells. Apoptosis is controlled by a balance of pro- and anti-apoptotic signals, and it is important for maintaining tissue homeostasis and preventing the development of cancer.

In summary, the cell cycle is a tightly regulated process that is essential for the growth and development of all living organisms. Understanding the cell cycle and its regulation can provide insight into the development of diseases such as cancer, and has been a target for the development of new therapies. The regulation of telomeres, telomerase, and apoptosis are important aspects of the cell cycle regulation and are also involved in the development of cancer.

Another important aspect of the cell cycle regulation is the control of the mitotic spindle, a structure composed of microtubules that forms during mitosis and is responsible for the proper segregation of chromosomes to the daughter cells. The mitotic spindle is assembled by microtubules growing out from opposite poles of the cell, called the poles, and the chromosomes align at the center of the cell, called the metaphase plate. The chromosomes are then pulled to the poles by the microtubules, and the cell physically divides during telophase. The proper formation and function of the mitotic spindle is crucial for the accurate segregation of chromosomes and the avoidance of aneuploidy (abnormal chromosome numbers) which can lead to cancer and other genetic disorders.

Another important aspect of the cell cycle regulation is the control of the centrosome, the microtubule-organizing center of the cell. The centrosome is composed of two centrioles and is responsible for the formation of the mitotic spindle. The centrosome duplicates during the S phase and the two centrioles separate during prophase and move to opposite poles of the cell. The centrosome and centrioles play important roles in the regulation of the cell cycle and their deregulation can lead to cancer and other genetic disorders.

In summary, the cell cycle is a tightly regulated process that is essential for the growth and development of all living organisms. Understanding the cell cycle and its regulation can provide insight into the development of diseases such as cancer, and has been a target for the development of new therapies. The regulation of telomeres, telomerase, apoptosis, mitotic spindle, and centrosome are important aspects of the cell cycle regulation and are also involved in the development of cancer.

Another important aspect of the cell cycle regulation is the control of the cytoskeleton, a network of protein fibers that provides structural support to the cell, and also plays a role in cell division and cell migration. The cytoskeleton is composed of microfilaments, intermediate filaments, and microtubules, and its dynamics are regulated by various cytoskeleton-associated proteins. Microfilaments, composed of actin, are involved in cell movement and shape changes, while intermediate filaments, composed of various proteins such as vimentin and keratin, provide mechanical strength and stability to the cell. Microtubules, composed of tubulin, are involved in cell division and intracellular transport.

The cytoskeleton also plays an important role in cell migration and metastasis, which is the spread of cancer cells from the primary tumor to distant sites in the body. Cancer cells can remodel their cytoskeleton to acquire a more invasive and migratory phenotype, which enables them to escape from the primary tumor and colonize other organs. Targeting the cytoskeleton and its associated proteins has been considered as a promising strategy for cancer therapy.

In summary, the cell cycle is a tightly regulated process that is essential for the growth and development of all living organisms. Understanding the cell cycle and its regulation can provide insight into the development of diseases such as cancer, and has been a target for the development of new therapies. The regulation of telomeres, telomerase, apoptosis, mitotic spindle, centrosome, and cytoskeleton are important aspects of the cell cycle regulation and are also involved in the development of cancer. The cytoskeleton also plays an important role in cell migration and metastasis, which is a crucial aspect in cancer progression.

Another important aspect of the cell cycle regulation is the control of the extracellular matrix (ECM), a complex network of proteins and carbohydrates that surrounds and supports cells in the body. The ECM provides structural support and mechanical cues to cells, and also plays a role in cell signaling, cell migration and cell proliferation. The ECM is composed of various proteins such as collagen, laminin and fibronectin, and its composition and organization can be regulated by various enzymes such as matrix metalloproteinases (MMPs) and tissue inhibitors of metalloproteinases (TIMPs).

Cancer cells can remodel the ECM to acquire a more invasive and migratory phenotype, which enables them to escape from the primary tumor and colonize other organs. Cancer cells can produce enzymes that degrade the ECM and promote cell invasion, and can also produce growth factors that promote cell proliferation and survival. Targeting the ECM and its associated proteins and enzymes has been considered as a promising strategy for cancer therapy.

In summary, the cell cycle is a tightly regulated process that is essential for the growth and development of all living organisms. Understanding the cell cycle and its regulation can provide insight into the development of diseases such as cancer, and has been a target for the development of new therapies. The regulation of telomeres, telomerase, apoptosis, mitotic spindle, centrosome, cytoskeleton, and extracellular matrix are important aspects of the cell cycle regulation and are also involved in the development of cancer. Cancer cells can remodel the extracellular matrix to acquire a more invasive and migratory phenotype, which enables them to escape from the primary tumor and colonize other organs. Targeting the extracellular matrix and its associated proteins and enzymes has been considered as a promising strategy for cancer therapy.

Another important aspect of the cell cycle regulation is the control of epigenetics, which refers to the heritable changes in gene expression and function that do not involve changes in the underlying DNA sequence. Epigenetic modifications, such as DNA methylation, histone modification, and microRNA regulation, can control the activation or repression of genes and play a crucial role in the regulation of the cell cycle.

Epigenetic modifications can also play an important role in the development of cancer. For example, hypermethylation of the promoter regions of tumor suppressor genes is a common event in cancer, which leads to the repression of these genes and the loss of their tumor suppressor function. Similarly, histone modifications can also lead to the repression of tumor suppressor genes and the activation of oncogenes.

Targeting epigenetic modifications has been considered as a promising strategy for cancer therapy. For example, drugs that inhibit DNA methylation, such as azacytidine and decitabine, have been used to treat certain types of cancer. Similarly, drugs that inhibit histone deacetylases (HDACs), such as vorinostat and romidepsin, have been used to treat certain types of cancer.

In summary, the cell cycle is a tightly regulated process that is essential for the growth and development of all living organisms. Understanding the cell cycle and its regulation can provide insight into the development of diseases such as cancer, and has been a target for the development of new therapies. The regulation of telomeres, telomerase, apoptosis, mitotic spindle, centrosome, cytoskeleton, extracellular matrix, and epigenetics are important aspects of the cell cycle regulation and are also involved in the development of cancer. Epigenetic modifications can also play an important role in the development of cancer and targeting these modifications has been considered as a promising strategy for cancer therapy.

Another important aspect of the cell cycle regulation is the control of the immune system, which is responsible for recognizing and eliminating abnormal cells, including cancer cells. The immune system can recognize cancer cells through various mechanisms such as the expression of abnormal antigens, the loss of immune-inhibitory molecules, or the expression of danger signals.

The immune system can eliminate cancer cells through various mechanisms such as cytotoxic T-cells, natural killer cells, and antibody-dependent cellular cytotoxicity. The immune system can also recruit other cells such as macrophages and dendritic cells to the tumor site to help in the elimination of cancer cells.

Cancer cells can evade the immune system through various mechanisms such as the expression of immune-inhibitory molecules, the recruitment of immune-suppressive cells, or the alteration of the tumor microenvironment. These mechanisms can lead to the suppression of the immune response against cancer cells, and contribute to the development and progression of cancer.

Targeting the immune system has been considered as a promising strategy for cancer therapy. For example, immunotherapy, which is the use of the immune system to treat cancer, has been used to treat various types of cancer. Examples of immunotherapy include checkpoint inhibitors, which block the inhibitory signals that cancer cells use to evade the immune system, and cancer vaccines, which help the immune system recognize and attack cancer cells.

In summary, the cell cycle is a tightly regulated process that is essential for the growth and development of all living organisms. Understanding the cell cycle and its regulation can provide insight into the development of diseases such as cancer, and has been a target for the development of new therapies. The regulation of the cell cycle is controlled by a variety of molecular mechanisms, including checkpoints that ensure proper progression through the different stages, and cell cycle regulatory proteins that control the activity of key enzymes. Dysregulation of these mechanisms can lead to uncontrolled cell growth and division, which can ultimately result in the development of cancer. Research in this field is ongoing, with a focus on identifying new targets for therapeutic intervention and developing new treatments for cancer and other diseases associated with cell cycle deregulation.

The cell cycle is divided into two main stages: interphase (G1, S, and G2) and the mitotic phase (M).

During interphase, the cell grows and replicates its DNA in preparation for cell division. The G1 phase is the period of growth and metabolic activity. The S phase is when DNA replication occurs. The G2 phase is a check point for the cell to ensure that DNA replication is complete and correct before proceeding to mitosis.

During the mitotic phase, the cell physically divides into two daughter cells. Mitosis is divided into four subphases: prophase, metaphase, anaphase, and telophase. In prophase, the chromosomes condense and become visible. In metaphase, the chromosomes align in the middle of the cell. In anaphase, the chromosomes are separated and pulled towards opposite poles of the cell. In telophase, the chromosomes decondense and the cell divides.

The cell cycle is regulated by a variety of molecular mechanisms, including checkpoint pathways that monitor the progression of the cell cycle and ensure that it proceeds correctly. Key regulatory proteins, such as cyclins and cyclin-dependent kinases (CDKs), control the activity of enzymes that drive the cell cycle forward.

Dysregulation of the cell cycle, such as mutations in genes that control cell cycle progression or the activation of oncogenes, can lead to uncontrolled cell growth and division, ultimately resulting in the development of cancer. Understanding the molecular mechanisms that regulate the cell cycle has led to the development of new therapies for cancer, such as drugs that target specific cell cycle regulatory proteins or checkpoint pathways.

Research in this field is ongoing, with a focus on identifying new targets for therapeutic intervention and developing new treatments for cancer and other diseases associated with cell cycle deregulation.

The cell cycle is a tightly regulated process, and any disruption to this regulation can lead to uncontrolled cell growth and division, ultimately resulting in the development of cancer. The cell cycle is controlled by a complex interplay of molecular mechanisms, including checkpoint pathways that monitor the progression of the cell cycle, and cell cycle regulatory proteins such as cyclins and cyclin-dependent kinases (CDKs) that control the activity of enzymes that drive the cell cycle forward.

Checkpoint pathways are critical for ensuring that the cell cycle proceeds correctly, and they act as a quality control mechanism to ensure that DNA replication is complete and accurate before the cell proceeds to mitosis. There are several checkpoint pathways, including the G1 checkpoint, the G2 checkpoint, and the M checkpoint. Dysregulation of these checkpoint pathways can lead to the development of cancer.

Cyclins and CDKs are key cell cycle regulatory proteins that control the activity of enzymes that drive the cell cycle forward. Cyclins are proteins that are synthesized and degraded in a cyclic manner, and their levels oscillate during the cell cycle. CDKs are enzymes that are activated by binding to cyclins. Together, cyclins and CDKs control the progression of the cell cycle by phosphorylating target proteins.

Oncogenes are genes that, when activated, can cause cells to divide and grow in an uncontrolled manner. Oncogenes can be activated through mutations, chromosomal translocations, or overexpression. Tumor suppressor genes, on the other hand, are genes that inhibit cell growth and division. When these genes are inactivated or lost, cells can divide and grow uncontrollably, leading to the development of cancer.

Research in this field is ongoing, with a focus on identifying new targets for therapeutic intervention and developing new treatments for cancer and other diseases associated with cell cycle deregulation. New therapies are being developed that target specific cell cycle regulatory proteins or checkpoint pathways, as well as therapies that target oncogenes and tumor suppressor genes.

Also, the use of stem cells and regenerative medicine has been a promising field that aims to use the cell cycle regulation to repair or replace damaged cells or tissues in the body.

One of the most promising areas of research in the field of cell cycle regulation is the development of targeted therapies for cancer. These therapies are designed to specifically target and inhibit the activity of key cell cycle regulatory proteins or checkpoint pathways that are dysregulated in cancer cells. For example, drugs such as cyclin-dependent kinase inhibitors (CDKIs) have been developed that can inhibit the activity of CDKs and slow or halt the progression of the cell cycle in cancer cells. Similarly, drugs that target checkpoint pathways, such as the checkpoint kinase inhibitors, have been developed to inhibit the activity of enzymes that are critical for the proper regulation of the cell cycle.

Another area of research is focused on the use of stem cells and regenerative medicine. Stem cells are undifferentiated cells that have the ability to self-renew and differentiate into multiple cell types. By harnessing the power of stem cells, scientists hope to use the cell cycle regulation to repair or replace damaged cells or tissues in the body. For example, stem cells can be used to regenerate damaged or diseased tissue, such as the heart muscle after a heart attack, or to repair the damage caused by cancer.

Another promising area of research is the use of gene therapy to treat cancer. Gene therapy involves the delivery of genetic material, such as a gene or a piece of DNA, to a cell in order to treat a disease. This can be done by introducing healthy copies of tumor suppressor genes into cancer cells or by introducing genes that inhibit the activity of oncogenes. This approach has the potential to be a highly targeted and effective treatment for cancer.

Overall, the field of cell cycle regulation and cancer research is rapidly advancing, and new therapies are being developed that target specific cell cycle regulatory proteins or checkpoint pathways, as well as therapies that target oncogenes and tumor suppressor genes, stem cells, gene therapy and other approaches.

Another promising area of research in cell cycle regulation is the study of non-coding RNAs (ncRNAs). ncRNAs are RNA molecules that do not code for proteins, but instead play important regulatory roles in the cell. There are several types of ncRNAs, including microRNAs (miRNAs), long non-coding RNAs (lncRNAs) and small interfering RNAs (siRNAs). These ncRNAs have been shown to play a critical role in regulating the cell cycle, as well as many other cellular processes.

miRNAs are small non-coding RNAs that can bind to specific target messenger RNAs (mRNAs) and inhibit their translation, thus reducing the expression of specific proteins. miRNAs have been found to be involved in the regulation of the cell cycle, and have been shown to be differentially expressed in many types of cancer.

lncRNAs are non-coding RNAs that are more than 200 nucleotides long. lncRNAs have been found to be involved in various cellular processes, including the regulation of the cell cycle. They have been shown to act as transcriptional regulators, epigenetic modulators, and scaffolds for protein complexes, among other functions.

siRNAs are small non-coding RNAs that play a critical role in the RNA interference (RNAi) pathway, which is a natural mechanism for controlling gene expression. siRNAs can target specific mRNAs for degradation, thereby reducing the expression of specific proteins. siRNAs have been shown to be involved in the regulation of the cell cycle and have been used as a promising approach in cancer therapy.

Researchers are actively studying the role of ncRNAs in cell cycle regulation and their potential as therapeutic targets for cancer treatment. By better understanding the mechanisms by which ncRNAs regulate the cell cycle, scientists may be able to develop new therapies that target these molecules and halt the progression of cancer.

The field of cell cycle regulation and cancer research is complex, multi-disciplinary and constantly evolving, and new discoveries and therapies continue to emerge. As more research is conducted and new technologies developed, the understanding of the cell cycle regulation, and its disruption in cancer, will continue to grow, leading to new and more effective therapies for cancer and other diseases.

Another area of research that is gaining attention in the field of cell cycle regulation is the study of epigenetics. Epigenetics refers to the heritable changes in gene function that occur without a change in the underlying DNA sequence. These changes can include modifications to the DNA molecule itself or to the proteins with which DNA interacts. Epigenetic modifications can have a profound effect on gene expression and cellular behavior, including the regulation of the cell cycle.

One of the most well-known epigenetic modifications is the methylation of DNA. DNA methylation is the addition of a methyl group to the cytosine residue of the DNA molecule, and it can silence the expression of a gene by preventing the binding of the transcriptional machinery. Hypermethylation of tumor suppressor genes is a common feature of cancer and it is a reason why these genes are not able to perform their role in cell cycle regulation.

Another important epigenetic modification is the modification of histones, which are the proteins that DNA wraps around. Histone modifications can have a profound effect on gene expression and can either activate or silence the expression of genes. Histone modifications that are associated with the cell cycle regulation include acetylation and phosphorylation, among others.

Researchers are actively studying the role of epigenetics in cell cycle regulation and its involvement in cancer. By better understanding the mechanisms by which epigenetics regulate the cell cycle, scientists may be able to develop new therapies that target these modifications and halt the progression of cancer.

In summary, the cell cycle is a tightly regulated process that is essential for the growth and development of all living organisms. Understanding the cell cycle and its regulation can provide insight into the development of diseases such as cancer. The regulation of the cell cycle is controlled by a variety of molecular mechanisms, including checkpoints, cell cycle regulatory proteins, oncogenes, and tumor suppressor genes, non-coding RNAs, and epigenetics. Dysregulation of these mechanisms can lead to uncontrolled cell growth and division, which can ultimately result in the development of cancer. Research in this field is ongoing, with a focus on identifying new targets for therapeutic intervention and developing new treatments for cancer and other diseases associated with cell cycle deregulation.

Cell Death

Cell death is the process by which cells are eliminated from the body. There are two main types of cell death: programmed cell death and necrosis.

Programmed cell death, also known as apoptosis, is a regulated process that occurs during development and tissue homeostasis. It involves the activation of specific genes and the activation of specific enzymes that cause the cell to self-destruct in a controlled manner. Apoptosis is characterized by several morphological changes, including cell shrinkage, chromatin condensation, and the formation of apoptotic bodies.

Necrosis is a type of cell death that occurs as a result of injury or stress. It is an uncontrolled process that occurs when the cell is damaged beyond repair. Necrosis is characterized by the swelling and rupture of the cell, the release of intracellular contents, and inflammation.

Cell death is an important process in the body, as it helps to maintain tissue homeostasis and prevent the accumulation of damaged or unnecessary cells. Dysregulation of cell death can lead to diseases such as cancer, where cells fail to undergo programmed cell death and continue to grow and divide uncontrollably.

Cell death refers to the process by which cells are eliminated from the body. There are two main types of cell death: programmed cell death (apoptosis) and necrosis. Apoptosis is a regulated process that occurs during development and tissue homeostasis and is characterized by morphological changes such as cell shrinkage and chromatin condensation. Necrosis is an uncontrolled process that occurs when a cell is damaged beyond repair, characterized by swelling and rupture of the cell and the release of intracellular contents. Cell death is important for maintaining tissue homeostasis and preventing the accumulation of damaged or unnecessary cells, but dysregulation of cell death can lead to diseases such as cancer.

Programmed cell death, or apoptosis, is a highly regulated process that is essential for proper development and tissue homeostasis. It is initiated by a variety of internal and external signals, and is characterized by a series of morphological changes, including cell shrinkage, chromatin condensation, and the formation of apoptotic bodies. The process is mediated by a family of enzymes called caspases, which cleave specific proteins within the cell, leading to its self-destruction. Apoptosis is a tightly controlled process that helps to ensure the proper development of the organism, and also helps to remove damaged or unnecessary cells.

Necrosis, on the other hand, is an uncontrolled form of cell death that occurs as a result of injury or stress to the cell. It is characterized by the swelling and rupture of the cell, the release of intracellular contents, and inflammation. Necrosis can occur as a result of a variety of insults, including trauma, infection, ischemia, or exposure to toxins. Unlike apoptosis, necrosis is not a regulated process and can lead to inflammation and tissue damage.

Cell death is an important process that helps to maintain tissue homeostasis and prevent the accumulation of damaged or unnecessary cells. However, dysregulation of cell death can lead to a number of diseases, including cancer. Cancer cells are characterized by their ability to evade programmed cell death, allowing them to continue to grow and divide uncontrollably. Inhibiting the process of cell death is an important target in the treatment of cancer.

In addition to apoptosis and necrosis, there is another type of cell death called autophagy. Autophagy is a self-digestion process that cells use to degrade and recycle their own components. This process is important for maintaining cellular homeostasis and can also be activated in response to stress. Autophagy can be categorized into three main types: macroautophagy, microautophagy and chaperone-mediated autophagy. Each type of autophagy has its own mechanism and function.

Macroautophagy is the most well-known type of autophagy, in which the cell forms a double-membrane structure called an autophagosome, which encloses the cytosolic content to be degraded. Microautophagy is similar to macroautophagy but the cytosolic content is directly engulfed by the lysosome. Chaperone-mediated autophagy is a selective type of autophagy in which specific proteins are targeted for degradation by binding to chaperone molecules.

Autophagy plays important roles in many physiological and pathological processes, such as development, aging, and cancer. Autophagy can act as a tumor suppressor by eliminating damaged or abnormal cells, but it can also promote tumor growth by providing energy and nutrients to cancer cells.

Overall, cell death is a complex process that includes multiple types of cell death, each with its own characteristics, mechanisms and functions. Apoptosis, necrosis and autophagy are all important for maintaining tissue homeostasis and preventing the accumulation of damaged or unnecessary cells. Dysregulation of cell death can lead to a number of diseases, including cancer, and understanding the mechanisms of cell death is essential for the development of new therapeutic strategies to treat these diseases.

Another type of cell death that is less well-known is called programmed necrosis, also known as necroptosis. It is a form of programmed cell death that shares some features of both apoptosis and necrosis. It is characterized by the activation of specific receptors, such as TNF receptor 1, and the activation of specific enzymes, such as receptor-interacting protein kinase-3 (RIPK3) and mixed-lineage kinase domain-like protein (MLKL), which leads to the formation of a necrotic-like cell death. Like necrosis, necroptosis is characterized by the swelling and rupture of the cell, the release of intracellular contents, and inflammation.

Programmed necrosis is a regulated process that is activated by specific signals in response to stress, such as hypoxia, starvation, and viral infection. It plays important roles in host defense, tissue repair, and inflammation. However, over activation of programmed necrosis can lead to tissue damage, and contribute to the development of chronic inflammation and degenerative diseases.

Another form of cell death is called ferroptosis, which is a form of cell death that is mediated by the accumulation of lipid peroxides, leading to cell membrane damage and ferroptotic cell death. This type of cell death is characterized by the accumulation of iron, and the activation of specific enzymes such as GPX4 and aconitase. Ferroptosis was discovered relatively recently, and it is still not well understood yet.

In summary, cell death is a complex process that includes multiple types of cell death, each with its own characteristics, mechanisms and functions. Apoptosis, necrosis, autophagy, programmed necrosis, and ferroptosis are all examples of different types of cell death, and each one plays a specific role in maintaining tissue homeostasis and preventing the accumulation of damaged or unnecessary cells. Further research on these different types of cell death may lead to new insights and therapeutic strategies for treating diseases caused by the dysregulation of cell death.

Another type of cell death that is gaining more attention in recent years is called pyroptosis. It is a form of inflammatory programmed cell death that is mediated by a family of enzymes called caspase-1. Pyroptosis is activated by specific signals, such as bacterial or viral infections, and is characterized by the release of pro-inflammatory cytokines and the formation of a specialized type of apoptotic body called a "pyropoptosome".

Pyroptosis is an important mechanism of host defense against pathogens, as it helps to eliminate infected cells and prevent the spread of infection. However, overactivation of pyroptosis can lead to excessive inflammation and tissue damage, and contribute to the development of chronic inflammatory diseases such as autoimmune disorders and certain types of cancer.

Another type of cell death is parthanatos, which is a form of cell death that is mediated by the accumulation of a small molecule called poly(ADP-ribose) (PAR). Parthanatos is activated by specific signals, such as DNA damage, and is characterized by the activation of specific enzymes such as poly(ADP-ribose) polymerase (PARP) and the formation of a specialized type of apoptotic body called a "PAR-body".

Parthanatos is an important mechanism of host defense against DNA damage, as it helps to eliminate damaged cells and prevent the formation of cancer. However, overactivation of parthanatos can lead to excessive DNA damage, and contribute to the development of certain types of cancer.

Overall, cell death is a highly complex and multi-faceted process that includes multiple types of cell death, each with its own characteristics, mechanisms, and functions. Recent research has led to the discovery of new types of cell death such as pyroptosis, ferroptosis, parthanatos and many more, and further research on these different types of cell death may lead to new insights and therapeutic strategies for treating diseases caused by the dysregulation of cell death.

It is worth noting that some of these types of cell death are not mutually exclusive and can overlap in certain cases. For example, in some instances, cells may initiate apoptosis but fail to complete it, resulting in a necrotic-like death. Similarly, cells may initiate autophagy but fail to complete it, resulting in necrosis.

Another important aspect to consider is that cell death can also be classified based on the location of the cell, such as apoptosis in the immune system, which is called immunological apoptosis or peripheral apoptosis, which is the type of apoptosis that occurs outside the central nervous system.

Furthermore, there are also different pathways to activate different types of cell death, for example, intrinsic pathway and extrinsic pathway for apoptosis, and receptor-mediated pathway and mitochondrial pathway for necrosis.

In conclusion, cell death is a highly complex and multi-faceted process that includes multiple types of cell death, each with its own characteristics, mechanisms and functions. Each type of cell death plays a specific role in maintaining tissue homeostasis and preventing the accumulation of damaged or unnecessary cells. However, dysregulation of cell death can lead to a number of diseases, including cancer. Understanding the different types of cell death and the mechanisms that regulate them is essential for the development of new therapeutic strategies to treat these diseases.th events

Cell death is a normal and essential process that occurs in all living organisms. There are several types of cell death, including:

1. Apoptosis: This is a programmed cell death that occurs in a controlled and orderly manner. Apoptosis is important for maintaining tissue homeostasis and eliminating damaged or unnecessary cells.
2. Necrosis: This is an uncontrolled and destructive form of cell death that occurs as a result of physical injury, infection, or other forms of stress. Necrosis can lead to inflammation and tissue damage.
3. Autophagy: This is a process of cellular self-degradation in which cells break down and recycle their own components. Autophagy is important for maintaining cellular homeostasis and can also play a role in cell death under certain conditions.
4. Anoikis: This is a form of cell death that occurs when cells are detached from the extracellular matrix or other supportive structures. Anoikis is important for maintaining tissue architecture and preventing the spread of cancer cells.
5. Senescence: This is a state of permanent cell cycle arrest that occurs in response to DNA damage or other stress signals. Senescent cells do not divide, but they can secrete signaling molecules that can influence the behavior of surrounding cells.

Each of these cell death events plays a specific role in the development and maintenance of living organisms. Dysregulation of cell death can lead to various diseases, including cancer, neurodegeneration, and autoimmune disorders.

Cell death is a normal and essential process that occurs in all living organisms. There are several types of cell death, including apoptosis, necrosis, autophagy, anoikis, and senescence. Each plays a specific role in the development and maintenance of living organisms. Dysregulation of cell death can lead to various diseases, including cancer, neurodegeneration, and autoimmune disorders.

Apoptosis is a type of cell death that is regulated by specific genetic and biochemical pathways. It is characterized by the activation of caspases, a family of proteases that cleave specific target proteins and lead to the fragmentation of the cell's DNA, the condensation of chromatin, and the formation of apoptotic bodies. Apoptosis is important for the development and maintenance of tissues, as it allows for the removal of damaged or unnecessary cells without triggering an inflammatory response. Apoptosis is also important in the immune system, as it allows for the removal of infected or cancerous cells without causing tissue damage.

Necrosis, on the other hand, is an uncontrolled and destructive form of cell death that occurs as a result of physical injury, infection, or other forms of stress. Necrosis is characterized by the loss of plasma membrane integrity, the swelling of the cell, and the release of intracellular contents into the extracellular space. Necrosis can lead to inflammation and tissue damage.

Autophagy is a process of cellular self-degradation in which cells break down and recycle their own components. Autophagy is important for maintaining cellular homeostasis and can also play a role in cell death under certain conditions. Autophagy is activated in response to various stress signals, such as starvation, oxidative stress, and DNA damage.

Anoikis is a form of cell death that occurs when cells are detached from the extracellular matrix or other supportive structures. Anoikis is important for maintaining tissue architecture and preventing the spread of cancer cells. It is activated by the loss of cell-matrix interactions and signaling pathways that lead to the activation of pro-apoptotic proteins.

Senescence is a state of permanent cell cycle arrest that occurs in response to DNA damage or other stress signals. Senescent cells do not divide, but they can secrete signaling molecules that can influence the behavior of surrounding cells. Senescence is thought to play a role in aging and the development of certain diseases, such as cancer.

In summary, cell death is a complex process that is regulated by multiple genetic and biochemical pathways. Each type of cell death plays a specific role in the development and maintenance of living organisms, and dysregulation of cell death can lead to various diseases.

Cell death regulators

Cell death is regulated by a balance of pro-death and anti-death signals. Pro-death signals promote cell death, while anti-death signals inhibit cell death. Some key regulators of cell death include:

- Apoptotic proteins: These proteins, such as caspases and Bcl-2 family proteins, play a central role in the regulation of apoptosis.
- Necrotic proteins: These proteins, such as RIPK1 and RIPK3, play a central role in the regulation of necrosis.
- Autophagic proteins: These proteins, such as ATG5 and LC3, play a central role in the regulation of autophagy.
- Anoikis proteins: These proteins, such as E-cadherin and vinculin, play a central role in the regulation of anoikis.
- Senescence proteins: These proteins, such as p16INK4a and p53, play a central role in the regulation of senescence.

In addition to these specific regulators of cell death, many other signaling pathways, transcription factors, and epigenetic modifications also play a role in the regulation of cell death. Dysregulation of these pathways and factors can lead to the abnormal activation or inhibition of cell death, which can contribute to the development of various diseases.

Cell death is a complex process that is regulated by multiple genetic and biochemical pathways. The different types of cell death, including apoptosis, necrosis, autophagy, anoikis, and senescence, each have distinct characteristics and triggers.

Apoptosis is a tightly regulated process that is triggered by various internal and external signals, including DNA damage, viral infections, and cytokines. This form of cell death is characterized by the activation of caspases, a family of proteases that cleave specific target proteins and lead to the fragmentation of the cell's DNA, the condensation of chromatin, and the formation of apoptotic bodies. Apoptosis is important for the development and maintenance of tissues, as it allows for the removal of damaged or unnecessary cells without triggering an inflammatory response.

Necrosis, on the other hand, is an uncontrolled and destructive form of cell death that occurs as a result of physical injury, infection, or other forms of stress. Necrosis is characterized by the loss of plasma membrane integrity, the swelling of the cell, and the release of intracellular contents into the extracellular space. This can lead to inflammation and tissue damage, which can be harmful to the organism.

Autophagy is a process of cellular self-degradation in which cells break down and recycle their own components. Autophagy is activated in response to various stress signals, such as starvation, oxidative stress, and DNA damage. It plays an important role in maintaining cellular homeostasis and can also play a role in cell death under certain conditions.

Anoikis is a form of cell death that occurs when cells are detached from the extracellular matrix or other supportive structures. Anoikis is activated by the loss of cell-matrix interactions and signaling pathways that lead to the activation of pro-apoptotic proteins. It is important for maintaining tissue architecture and preventing the spread of cancer cells.

Senescence is a state of permanent cell cycle arrest that occurs in response to DNA damage or other stress signals. Senescent cells do not divide, but they can secrete signaling molecules that can influence the behavior of surrounding cells. Senescence is thought to play a role in aging and the development of certain diseases, such as cancer.

In summary, cell death is a complex process that is regulated by multiple genetic and biochemical pathways. Each type of cell death plays a specific role in the development and maintenance of living organisms, and dysregulation of cell death can lead to various diseases. Understanding the molecular mechanisms and signaling pathways that regulate cell death can provide insight into the development and treatment of diseases. Additionally, targeting specific cell death pathways may provide therapeutic options for treating diseases associated with abnormal cell death such as cancer, neurodegenerative diseases, and autoimmune disorders. It's also important to note that in cancer research, the ability to induce cancer cell death selectively is an attractive strategy for cancer treatment.

Apoptosis

Apoptosis, or programmed cell death, is a normal and essential process that occurs in all living organisms. It plays a critical role in development, tissue homeostasis, and immune defense. Apoptosis can be triggered by both intrinsic and extrinsic signals.

Regulators of apoptosis:

Apoptosis is regulated by a balance of pro-apoptotic and anti-apoptotic signals. Pro-apoptotic signals promote cell death, while anti-apoptotic signals inhibit cell death. Some key regulators of apoptosis include:

- Bcl-2 family proteins: These proteins regulate the intrinsic pathway of apoptosis by controlling the release of cytochrome c from the mitochondria.
- Caspases: These proteases cleave and degrade specific cellular proteins and are key mediators of the apoptotic process.
- Death receptors: These receptors, such as Fas and TNF-R1, bind to ligands on the surface of other cells and trigger the extrinsic pathway of apoptosis.
- Tumor suppressor genes: These genes, such as TP53 and BRCA1, play a critical role in the regulation of apoptosis and the maintenance of genomic stability. Dysregulation of tumor suppressor genes can lead to the development of cancer.

Intrinsic pathway of apoptosis:

The intrinsic pathway of apoptosis, also known as the mitochondrial pathway, is activated by signals that originate from within the cell, such as DNA damage or oxidative stress. It involves the activation of caspases, a family of proteases that cleave and degrade specific cellular proteins. The intrinsic pathway is initiated by the release of cytochrome c from the mitochondria, which activates the caspase cascade.

The intrinsic pathway of apoptosis is regulated by a balance of pro-apoptotic and anti-apoptotic signals. Pro-apoptotic signals, such as Bax and Bak, promote the release of cytochrome c from the mitochondria, while anti-apoptotic signals, such as Bcl-2 and Bcl-xL, inhibit the release of cytochrome c.

Once activated, the caspase cascade leads to the cleavage and degradation of a variety of cellular proteins, including structural proteins, enzymes, and transcription factors. This leads to the characteristic morphological changes of apoptosis, such as cell shrinkage, membrane blebbing, and chromatin condensation.

The intrinsic pathway of apoptosis plays a critical role in the maintenance of tissue homeostasis and the elimination of damaged or unnecessary cells. Dysregulation of the intrinsic pathway can lead to various diseases, including cancer, neurodegeneration, and autoimmune disorders.

Extrinsic pathway of apoptosis:

The extrinsic pathway of apoptosis is activated by signals that originate from outside the cell, such as growth factor withdrawal or immune attack. It involves the activation of death receptors on the cell surface, which trigger the caspase cascade.

The extrinsic pathway of apoptosis, also known as the death receptor pathway, is activated by signals that originate from outside the cell, such as growth factor withdrawal or immune attack. It involves the activation of death receptors on the cell surface, which trigger the caspase cascade.

The extrinsic pathway of apoptosis is initiated by the binding of ligands, such as TNF-alpha or FasL, to their respective death receptors on the cell surface. This leads to the recruitment and activation of the adaptor protein FADD, which in turn activates the initiator caspase-8. Activated caspase-8 then cleaves and activates downstream effector caspases, leading to the characteristic morphological changes of apoptosis.

The extrinsic pathway of apoptosis is regulated by a balance of pro-apoptotic and anti-apoptotic signals. Pro-apoptotic signals, such as TRADD and FADD, promote the activation of caspase-8, while anti-apoptotic signals, such as c-FLIP and XIAP, inhibit the activation of caspase-8.

The extrinsic pathway of apoptosis plays a critical role in immune defense and the regulation of immune responses. Dysregulation of the extrinsic pathway can lead to various diseases, including cancer, autoimmune disorders, and inflammatory diseases.

Apoptosis is a normal and essential process that occurs in all living organisms, playing a critical role in development, tissue homeostasis, and immune defense. It can be triggered by both intrinsic and extrinsic signals.

The intrinsic pathway of apoptosis, also known as the mitochondrial pathway, is activated by signals that originate from within the cell, such as DNA damage or oxidative stress. It involves the activation of caspases, a family of proteases that cleave and degrade specific cellular proteins. The intrinsic pathway is initiated by the release of cytochrome c from the mitochondria, which activates the caspase cascade.

The extrinsic pathway of apoptosis is activated by signals that originate from outside the cell, such as growth factor withdrawal or immune attack. It involves the activation of death receptors on the cell surface, which trigger the caspase cascade. The extrinsic pathway is initiated by the binding of ligands, such as TNF-alpha or FasL, to their respective death receptors on the cell surface.

Both intrinsic and extrinsic pathways are regulated by a balance of pro-apoptotic and anti-apoptotic signals and play critical roles in maintaining tissue homeostasis and regulating immune responses. Dysregulation of apoptosis can lead to various diseases, including cancer, neurodegeneration, autoimmune disorders, and inflammatory diseases.

Apoptosis is a highly regulated process that is crucial for the maintenance of tissue homeostasis and the elimination of damaged or unnecessary cells. One of the key features of apoptosis is the activation of a family of proteases called caspases, which cleave and degrade specific cellular proteins. This leads to the characteristic morphological changes of apoptosis, such as cell shrinkage, membrane blebbing, and chromatin condensation.

Apoptosis can be triggered by both intrinsic and extrinsic signals. The intrinsic pathway is activated by signals that originate from within the cell, such as DNA damage or oxidative stress. It involves the release of cytochrome c from the mitochondria, which activates the caspase cascade. The extrinsic pathway is activated by signals that originate from outside the cell, such as growth factor withdrawal or immune attack. It involves the activation of death receptors on the cell surface, which trigger the caspase cascade.

The intrinsic and extrinsic pathways are regulated by a balance of pro-apoptotic and anti-apoptotic signals. Pro-apoptotic signals promote cell death, while anti-apoptotic signals inhibit cell death. Some key regulators of apoptosis include:

Bcl-2 family proteins, which regulate the intrinsic pathway of apoptosis by controlling the release of cytochrome c from the mitochondria. Caspases, which are key mediators of the apoptotic process.

Death receptors, such as Fas and TNF-R1, which bind to ligands on the surface of other cells and trigger the extrinsic pathway of apoptosis.

Tumor suppressor genes, such as TP53 and BRCA1, which play a critical role in the regulation of apoptosis and the maintenance of genomic stability.

Dysregulation of apoptosis can lead to various diseases, including cancer, neurodegeneration, autoimmune disorders, and inflammatory diseases. In cancer, for example, the process of apoptosis is often disrupted, leading to the accumulation of abnormal cells and the development of tumors. Similarly, in autoimmune disorders, the immune system may attack healthy cells due to a malfunction in the apoptotic process.

Research on apoptosis has led to the development of new therapeutic strategies for treating cancer, autoimmune disorders, and other diseases. For example, drugs that target pro-survival proteins like Bcl-2 and inhibit the intrinsic pathway of apoptosis are being developed and tested as potential cancer treatments. Similarly, drugs that target death receptors or ligands that activate the extrinsic pathway of apoptosis are being developed to treat autoimmune disorders.

There are several different pathways that can lead to the initiation of the intrinsic apoptotic pathway. One of the main pathways involves the activation of the p53 tumor suppressor gene, which is often mutated in cancer cells. When DNA is damaged, p53 is activated and can then induce the expression of pro-apoptotic genes such as Bax and Bak. These genes in turn promote the release of cytochrome c from the mitochondria, leading to the activation of the caspase cascade.

Another pathway that can lead to the initiation of the intrinsic apoptotic pathway is the intrinsic DNA damage response pathway. This pathway is activated by DNA damage and leads to the activation of the ATM and ATR kinases. These kinases then phosphorylate and activate pro-apoptotic proteins such as Bax and Bak, leading to the release of cytochrome c from the mitochondria.

In addition to these pathways, there are also several other pathways that can lead to the initiation of the intrinsic apoptotic pathway. These include the endoplasmic reticulum stress response pathway, the oxidative stress response pathway, and the mitochondrial permeability transition pore pathway. Each of these pathways involves the activation of different signaling molecules and transcription factors that ultimately lead to the release of cytochrome c from the mitochondria and the activation of the caspase cascade.

Once the caspase cascade is activated, the caspases cleave and degrade a variety of cellular proteins, leading to the characteristic morphological changes of apoptosis. Some of the key proteins that are targeted by the caspases include structural proteins such as actin and tubulin, enzymes such as DNases and proteases, and transcription factors such as c-Myc and E2F1.

In addition to the morphological changes, apoptosis also leads to a number of biochemical changes. For example, during the early stages of apoptosis, the cell's membrane potential is lost, leading to the release of ATP and other molecules. Additionally, the cell's cytoskeleton is disassembled, leading to the loss of cell shape and the formation of membrane blebs. Finally, chromatin condenses and fragments, leading to the formation of apoptotic bodies. These apoptotic bodies are then recognized and engulfed by phagocytes.

Overall, apoptosis is a complex and highly regulated process that plays a critical role in development, tissue homeostasis, and immune defense. Dysregulation of the apoptotic process can lead to various diseases, including cancer, neurodegeneration, and autoimmune disorders.

Another important aspect of apoptosis is the process of phagocytosis, which is the engulfment and degradation of apoptotic cells by phagocytes. This process is critical for the removal of apoptotic cells and the maintenance of tissue homeostasis. Proper phagocytosis of apoptotic cells is also essential for preventing inflammation and the development of autoimmune disorders.

Phagocytes, such as macrophages and dendritic cells, recognize and engulf apoptotic cells through a process known as "efferocytosis". During efferocytosis, phagocytes bind to specific surface molecules on the apoptotic cells, such as phosphatidylserine, and then engulf the cells. Once engulfed, the apoptotic cells are degraded in a process that is similar to autophagy.

Another important aspect of apoptosis is the role it plays in cancer development and treatment. Cancer cells often evade apoptosis by mutating or inactivating key regulators of the apoptotic process, such as p53 and Bcl-2 family proteins. Therefore, targeting the apoptotic pathways in cancer cells is a promising strategy for the development of cancer therapies.

There are several different types of drugs that target the apoptotic pathways in cancer cells. One type of drug is known as a "Bcl-2 inhibitor", which targets anti-apoptotic Bcl-2 family proteins and promotes the intrinsic apoptotic pathway. Another type of drug is a "caspase inhibitor", which targets the caspase cascade and blocks the execution of the apoptotic process.

Overall, apoptosis is a complex and highly regulated process that plays a critical role in development, tissue homeostasis, and immune defense. A deeper understanding of the molecular mechanisms that regulate apoptosis can lead to the development of new therapies for diseases such as cancer, neurodegeneration, and autoimmune disorders.

Another important aspect of apoptosis is the role it plays in developmental biology. Apoptosis plays a critical role in the formation of various organs and structures during embryonic development, such as the nervous system, the heart, and the limbs. Apoptosis also plays a role in the formation and maintenance of the immune system, the removal of unwanted cells, and the formation of the blood-brain barrier.

Apoptosis also plays a role in the aging process. As cells age, they become less responsive to growth signals and eventually enter a state of permanent growth arrest known as senescence. However, senescent cells can still cause damage to the surrounding tissue and promote chronic inflammation. Apoptosis can help to remove senescent cells, preventing this damage and inflammation.

In addition, Apoptosis plays a critical role in the maintenance of tissue homeostasis, the balance between cell proliferation and cell death. Apoptosis helps to remove damaged or unnecessary cells, preventing the accumulation of mutations and the development of cancer. Apoptosis also helps to maintain the appropriate number of cells in a tissue, preventing overgrowth and the formation of tumors.

In summary, Apoptosis plays a critical role in various physiological processes such as, development, tissue homeostasis, aging, and cancer. Apoptosis is a complex process that is regulated by a balance of pro-apoptotic and anti-apoptotic signals. Dysregulation of the apoptotic process can lead to various diseases such as cancer, neurodegeneration, and autoimmune disorders. New therapies that target the apoptotic pathways in cancer cells are currently under development.

Another important aspect of apoptosis is the role it plays in the response of cells to DNA damage. DNA damage can occur due to a variety of factors, such as radiation, chemicals, and free radicals. If DNA damage is not repaired, it can lead to mutations and the development of cancer. Apoptosis plays a critical role in the response to DNA damage by eliminating cells that are irreparably damaged and cannot be repaired.

The intrinsic apoptotic pathway is activated by DNA damage through the activation of the tumor suppressor protein p53. p53 is activated by DNA damage and then induces the transcription of pro-apoptotic genes, such as BAX and PUMA. These genes promote the release of cytochrome c from the mitochondria and the activation of the caspase cascade.

Another important aspect of the intrinsic pathway of apoptosis is the role of the protein, known as "ATM" (ataxia telangiectasia mutated) kinase. ATM is activated by DNA double-strand breaks, and it phosphorylates a number of key proteins, including p53, which leads to the activation of the intrinsic apoptotic pathway. The intrinsic pathway of apoptosis is also activated by other DNA damage-response proteins such as ATR, and the DNA damage checkpoint kinase 1 (CHK1).

In addition, the extrinsic pathway of apoptosis is also activated by DNA damage through the activation of death receptors on the cell surface. For example, the receptor TNF-R1 can be activated by DNA damage and trigger the extrinsic pathway of apoptosis. This pathway is mediated by the adaptor protein FADD, which in turn activates the initiator caspase-8. Activated caspase-8 then cleaves and activates downstream effector caspases, leading to the characteristic morphological changes of apoptosis.

It is worth noting that the intrinsic and extrinsic pathways of apoptosis can also interact with each other. For example, the extrinsic pathway can activate the intrinsic pathway through the recruitment of adaptor proteins such as FADD to the mitochondria. Conversely, the intrinsic pathway can activate the extrinsic pathway through the release of death ligands such as SMAC/DIABLO.

Another important aspect of apoptosis is the role of autophagy in the clearance of apoptotic cells. Autophagy is a process of cellular self-digestion that allows cells to degrade and recycle their own components. Once the cell undergoes apoptosis, the autophagy process is activated to clear the apoptotic cell and prevent inflammation.

In summary, Apoptosis plays a critical role in various physiological processes such as, developmental biology, tissue homeostasis, aging, and cancer. Apoptosis is a complex process that is regulated by a balance of pro-apoptotic and anti-apoptotic signals. Dysregulation of the apoptotic process can lead to various diseases such as cancer, neurodegeneration, and autoimmune disorders. New therapies that target the apoptotic pathways in cancer cells are currently under development.

Another important aspect of apoptosis is the role of the ubiquitin-proteasome system (UPS) in the degradation of apoptotic proteins. The UPS is a system that targets proteins for degradation by attaching ubiquitin molecules to them. This process is mediated by a family of enzymes called E3 ubiquitin ligases, which target specific proteins for degradation by the proteasome.

During apoptosis, the UPS is activated to degrade specific proteins that are involved in the apoptotic process. For example, the protein BID, which is a pro-apoptotic protein, is targeted for degradation by the UPS during the intrinsic pathway of apoptosis. This process is mediated by the E3 ubiquitin ligase called SCF-beta-TrCP, which targets BID for degradation by the proteasome.

Another example is the protein caspase-3, which is a key mediator of the apoptotic process. Caspase-3 is targeted for degradation by the UPS during the intrinsic pathway of apoptosis. This process is mediated by the E3 ubiquitin ligase called ITCH, which targets caspase-3 for degradation by the proteasome.

The UPS plays an important role in the regulation of the apoptotic process by controlling the levels of specific proteins that are involved in the process. By targeting these proteins for degradation, the UPS helps to fine-tune the apoptotic response and prevent excessive cell death.

In addition, recent research has shown that the regulation of the UPS can also play a role in cancer development, as some cancer cells can evade apoptosis by altering the UPS. For example, cancer cells can overexpress anti-apopttic proteins, such as Bcl-2, which can prevent the activation of the intrinsic pathway of apoptosis. Cancer cells can also inhibit the activity of E3 ubiquitin ligases, which can prevent the degradation of pro-apoptotic proteins, such as BID, and thus allow cancer cells to evade apoptosis.

In summary, apoptosis is a complex process that is regulated by a balance of pro-apoptotic and anti-apoptotic signals through intrinsic and extrinsic pathways. The intrinsic pathway is activated by signals that originate from within the cell, such as DNA damage or oxidative stress, while the extrinsic pathway is activated by signals that originate from outside the cell, such as growth factor withdrawal or immune attack. Both pathways involve the activation of caspases, which cleave and degrade specific cellular proteins, leading to the characteristic morphological changes of apoptosis. The ubiquitin-proteasome system also plays a role in the degradation of apoptotic proteins, which helps to fine-tune the apoptotic response and prevent excessive cell death. Dysregulation of apoptosis can lead to various diseases, including cancer, neurodegeneration, autoimmune disorders, and inflammatory diseases.

Another important aspect of apoptosis is the role of the autophagy in the clearance of apoptotic cells. Autophagy is a process by which cells degrade and recycle their own cellular components, including damaged or unnecessary organelles and proteins. During apoptosis, autophagy is activated to clear the apoptotic cells and prevent the release of potentially harmful intracellular contents.

Autophagy is mediated by a series of complex molecular mechanisms that involve the formation of autophagosomes, which are double-membrane vesicles that engulf cellular components and deliver them to lysosomes for degradation. The process is regulated by a set of autophagy-related genes (ATG) and proteins, such as ATG5, ATG7, and ATG12, which are essential for the formation of autophagosomes.

Recent research has shown that autophagy plays a role in the clearance of apoptotic cells in various tissues and organs, including the liver, lungs, heart, and brain. Autophagy helps to prevent the release of potentially harmful intracellular contents, such as DNA and proteins, which could trigger inflammatory responses and tissue damage.

In addition, autophagy has also been shown to play a role in cancer development and progression. Cancer cells often have altered autophagy, which can help them to evade apoptosis and survive in harsh environments. Cancer cells can also use autophagy to obtain energy and nutrients, which can promote their growth and survival.

In summary, apoptosis is a complex process that is regulated by a balance of pro-apoptotic and anti-apoptotic signals, and is also regulated by autophagy, which helps to clear the apoptotic cells and prevent the release of potentially harmful intraceellular contents. Autophagy also plays a role in cancer development and progression, as cancer cells can use autophagy to evade apoptosis and obtain energy and nutrients.

Another important aspect of apoptosis is the role of the immune system in the recognition and clearance of apoptotic cells. Apoptotic cells are recognized by specialized receptors on the surface of immune cells, such as phagocytes, which engulf and clear the apoptotic cells. This process is known as efferocytosis, and it helps to prevent the release of potentially harmful intracellular contents and to avoid the development of inflammation and tissue damage.

Immune cells also produce anti-inflammatory cytokines and chemokines, which help to promote the resolution of inflammation and tissue repair. Furthermore, the recognition and clearance of apoptotic cells by the immune system also plays a role in the regulation of immune tolerance and the development of immune memory.

In summary, apoptosis is a complex process that is regulated by a balance of pro-apoptotic and anti-apoptotic signals, and also involves the clearance of apoptotic cells by autophagy and the immune system. The recognition and clearance of apoptotic cells by the immune system, known as efferocytosis, plays a role in the regulation of inflammation and tissue repair, and also in the regulation of immune tolerance and the development of immune memory. Dysregulation of apoptosis and the clearance of apoptotic cells can lead to various diseases, including cancer, neurodegeneration, autoimmune disorders, and inflammatory diseases.

Another important aspect of apoptosis is the role of the mitochondria, which are the powerhouses of the cell. The mitochondria play a central role in the intrinsic pathway of apoptosis by releasing pro-apoptotic molecules, such as cytochrome c, into the cytosol. These molecules activate the caspase cascade and lead to the characteristic morphological changes of apoptosis.

Mitochondria also play a role in the regulation of the intrinsic pathway of apoptosis. The Bcl-2 family proteins, which are key regulators of the intrinsic pathway, are localized on the outer membrane of the mitochondria. These proteins can be divided into pro-apoptotic and anti-apoptotic members, which balance the release of cytochrome c from the mitochondria. The pro-apoptotic members, such as Bax and Bak, promote the release of cytochrome c, while the anti-apoptotic members, such as Bcl-2 and Bcl-xL, inhibit the release of cytochrome c.

Mitochondria also play a role in the regulation of the extrinsic pathway of apoptosis. The death receptors, such as Fas and TNF-R1, can directly activate the intrinsic pathway by recruiting the pro-apoptotic Bcl-2 family member, Bid, to the mitochondria. Bid then promotes the release of cytochrome c, which activates the caspase cascade.

Mitochondria also play a role in the regulation of autophagy, which is another process that is important in the clearance of apoptotic cells. Autophagy is the process by which cells degrade and recycle their own cellular contents, including damaged or unnecessary organelles. Autophagy can also be induced by stress signals, such as nutrient starvation, and it helps to maintain the integrity and function of the cell.

In summary, the mitochondria play a central role in the regulation of apoptosis, by controlling the release of pro-apoptotic molecules, such as cytochrome c, into the cytosol, and also by regulating the intrinsic and extrinsic pathways of apoptosis. Mitochondria also play a role in the regulation of autophagy, which is important in the clearance of apoptotic cells. Dysregulation of the mitochondria can lead to various diseases, including cancer, neurodegeneration, and autoimmune disorders.

Another important aspect of apoptosis is the role of the cytoskeleton, which provides structural support and organization to the cell. The cytoskeleton is composed of microfilaments, intermediate filaments, and microtubules, which are composed of various types of protein subunits.

During apoptosis, the cytoskeleton is rapidly disassembled, which leads to the characteristic morphological changes of apoptosis, such as cell shrinkage, membrane blebbing, and chromatin condensation. The cytoskeleton is also involved in the formation of the apoptotic bleb, which is a protrusion of the plasma membrane that forms during the early stages of apoptosis. The apoptotic bleb is important in the engulfment of apoptotic cells by neighboring cells or phagocytes.

The cytoskeleton is also involved in the regulation of the intrinsic and extrinsic pathways of apoptosis. For example, the pro-apoptotic Bcl-2 family member, Bax, can bind to and disrupt the cytoskeleton, which promotes the release of cytochrome c from the mitochondria. The death receptors, such as Fas and TNF-R1, can also recruit cytoskeletal proteins, such as actin, to the plasma membrane, which is important in the formation of the death-inducing signaling complex (DISC).

In summary, the cytoskeleton plays a critical role in the regulation of apoptosis by providing structural support and organization to the cell, and by disassembling during the early stages of apoptosis. The cytoskeleton is also involved in the formation of the apoptotic bleb, which is important in the engulfment of apoptotic cells, and it is also involved in the regulation of the intrinsic and extrinsic pathways of apoptosis. Dysregulation of the cytoskeleton can lead to various diseases, including cancer, neurodegeneration, and autoimmune disorders.

Another important aspect of apoptosis is the role of autophagy, which is a process by which cells degrade and recycle their own components. Autophagy is activated in response to various stressors, such as nutrient deprivation, oxidative stress, and DNA damage.

Autophagy can also act as a pro-survival mechanism, as it can help cells to maintain energy and nutrient levels during periods of stress. However, autophagy can also lead to cell death in certain conditions, particularly when the stress is severe or prolonged. In this case, autophagy can act as a pro-death mechanism, known as autophagic cell death or type II programmed cell death.

Autophagy can also interact with apoptosis in various ways. For example, autophagy can act as a pro-survival mechanism by removing damaged organelles and preventing the release of pro-apoptotic factors, such as cytochrome c. Autophagy can also act as a pro-death mechanism by augmenting the intrinsic pathway of apoptosis. For example, autophagy can promote the activation of caspase-9 and caspase-3, and can also enhance the formation of the apoptotic bleb.

In summary, autophagy is a process by which cells degrade and recycle their own components. Autophagy can act as a pro-survival or pro-death mechanism, depending on the type and severity of the stress. Autophagy can also interact with apoptosis in various ways, by promoting or inhibiting the intrinsic and extrinsic pathways of apoptosis. Dysregulation of autophagy can lead to various diseases, including cancer, neurodegeneration, and autoimmune disorders.

Necrotic proteins

Necrotic proteins are proteins that have been damaged or degraded due to cellular necrosis, a type of cell death in which cells die due to injury or disease. Necrosis is characterized by the collapse of the cell membrane, the release of cellular contents into the extracellular space, and the eventual removal of the dead cells by the immune system. Necrotic proteins can be harmful to the body and contribute to the progression of diseases such as cancer and neurodegeneration.

Necrotic proteins can be generated by a variety of mechanisms, including oxidative stress, inflammation, and exposure to toxins or other harmful agents. They can also be generated by mutations or other genetic defects that lead to abnormal protein folding or degradation. These proteins can then accumulate in cells and tissues, causing damage to healthy cells and contributing to the development of diseases such as cancer and neurodegeneration.

In cancer, necrotic proteins can contribute to the formation of tumor necrosis factor (TNF), a protein that promotes inflammation and cell death in cancer cells. In neurodegenerative diseases such as Alzheimer's and Parkinson's disease, necrotic proteins can accumulate in the brain and contribute to the formation of neurofibrillary tangles and amyloid plaques, which are associated with the progressive degeneration of nerve cells.

The accumulation of necrotic proteins in cells and tissues can be reduced by a number of different mechanisms, including the use of antioxidants and other molecules that protect against oxidative stress, the use of anti-inflammatory drugs, and the use of drugs that promote the clearance of damaged proteins. Additionally, research into the underlying mechanisms of protein damage and degradation is ongoing, with the goal of developing new treatments and therapies for diseases associated with necrotic proteins.

Another way to remove necrotic proteins is through the process of autophagy, a self-degradation process in which cells recycle their own components, including damaged proteins. Autophagy is a complex process that involves the formation of a double-membraned vesicle called an autophagosome, which encloses the damaged proteins and other cellular components. The autophagosome then fuses with a lysosome, which contains enzymes that degrade the enclosed materials.

Autophagy is a natural process that occurs in cells in response to stress, such as starvation or exposure to toxins. However, as cells age or become damaged, the process of autophagy may become less efficient, which can lead to the accumulation of necrotic proteins and other cellular debris.

There are also some drugs that can stimulate autophagy like rapamycin, which can be used in cancer treatment, neurodegenerative diseases, and other age-related disorders.

In conclusion, necrotic proteins are damaged proteins that are generated by a variety of mechanisms, including oxidative stress, inflammation, and exposure to toxins or other harmful agents. They can accumulate in cells and tissues and contribute to the progression of diseases such as cancer and neurodegeneration. The removal of necrotic proteins through autophagy and other processes can be an important strategy for reducing the damage caused by these proteins and preventing the development of diseases.

In addition to autophagy, the body has other mechanisms to remove necrotic proteins, including the ubiquitin-proteasome system (UPS) and the lysosomal degradation system. The UPS is a complex system that marks damaged proteins with a small protein called ubiquitin, which signals the proteasome, a large protein complex, to degrade the marked proteins. The lysosomal degradation system, on the other hand, involves the degradation of proteins by lysosomal enzymes within the lysosomes, which are organelles that are similar to the autophagosomes in their function.

Both the UPS and the lysosomal degradation system are important for the degradation of damaged proteins and their removal from the cell. However, in some cases, the accumulation of necrotic proteins can overwhelm these systems and lead to their dysfunction, which can contribute to the development of diseases such as cancer and neurodegenerative diseases.

In addition to targeting necrotic proteins through autophagy, the UPS and the lysosomal degradation system, there are other strategies that have been proposed to reduce the damage caused by necrotic proteins, including the use of drugs that promote the clearance of damaged proteins, gene therapy, and dietary interventions. Some scientists are also looking into the possibility of using nanoparticles to target necrotic proteins and remove them from the body.

In conclusion, necrotic proteins are damaged proteins that are generated by a variety of mechanisms, including oxidative stress, inflammation, and exposure to toxins or other harmful agents. They can accumulate in cells and tissues, contributing to the progression of diseases such as cancer and neurodegeneration. The body has several mechanisms to remove necrotic proteins, including autophagy, the ubiquitin-proteasome system, and the lysosomal degradation system. However, in some cases, the accumulation of necrotic proteins can overwhelm these systems and lead to their dysfunction, which can contribute to the development of diseases.

Another mechanism by which necrotic proteins can be removed is through the process of phagocytosis. Phagocytosis is the process by which cells, such as immune cells, engulf and degrade foreign particles, including necrotic proteins. For example, macrophages, a type of immune cell, can recognize and engulf necrotic cells and proteins through a process called efferocytosis. This process plays an important role in the removal of necrotic cells and proteins and the maintenance of tissue homeostasis.

It's also worth mentioning that accumulation of necrotic proteins can lead to cell death via necrosis and apoptosis. Necrosis is a type of cell death that is characterized by the loss of membrane integrity and the release of cellular contents into the extracellular space. Apoptosis, on the other hand, is a programmed form of cell death that is characterized by the activation of specific enzymes that degrade the cell from within.

Research on necrotic proteins is ongoing, and scientists are working to better understand the underlying mechanisms of protein damage and degradation. This research could lead to the development of new treatments and therapies for diseases associated with necrotic proteins. For example, scientists are studying the potential of drugs that can promote autophagy or the UPS and lysosomal degradation system to clear necrotic proteins and prevent the development of diseases.

In conclusion, necrotic proteins are damaged proteins that are generated by a variety of mechanisms, including oxidative stress, inflammation, and exposure to toxins or other harmful agents. They can accumulate in cells and tissues, contributing to the progression of diseases such as cancer and neurodegeneration. The body has several mechanisms to remove necrotic proteins, including autophagy, the ubiquitin-proteasome system, lysosomal degradation system and phagocytosis. These mechanisms play important roles in the removal of necrotic proteins and the maintenance of tissue homeostasis. However, in some cases, the accumulation of necrotic proteins can overwhelm these systems and lead to dysfunction, which can contribute to the development of diseases.

Another important aspect to consider is that the accumulation of necrotic proteins can also activate the immune system, leading to inflammation and an immune response. This can occur through the release of danger-associated molecular patterns (DAMPs) from necrotic cells and proteins. These DAMPs can activate cells of the innate immune system, such as macrophages and dendritic cells, which in turn can produce pro-inflammatory cytokines and recruit other immune cells to the site of injury. This process can lead to the resolution of the necrotic tissue and the removal of necrotic proteins, but if prolonged or excessive, it can also lead to chronic inflammation and tissue damage.

Additionally, the accumulation of necrotic proteins can also lead to the formation of senescence-associated secretory phenotype (SASP), which is a set of pro-inflammatory cytokines and other molecules that are secreted by senescent cells. These senescent cells are cells that have stopped dividing, due to DNA damage or other reasons, and they have been linked to aging and age-related diseases. The SASP can contribute to the chronic inflammation and tissue damage associated with aging and age-related diseases.

In summary, necrotic proteins are damaged proteins that are generated by a variety of mechanisms, including oxidative stress, inflammation, and exposure to toxins or other harmful agents. They can accumulate in cells and tissues, contributing to the progression of diseases such as cancer and neurodegeneration, and activating the immune system. The body has several mechanisms to remove necrotic proteins, including autophagy, the ubiquitin-proteasome system, lysosomal degradation system, phagocytosis and the immune response. However, in some cases, the accumulation of necrotic proteins can overwhelm these systems and lead to dysfunction, chronic inflammation, tissue damage and the development of diseases.

Another way that necrotic proteins can contribute to the development of diseases is through the formation of protein aggregates. These aggregates are formed when multiple proteins come together and form large, insoluble structures. These aggregates can be composed of a variety of different proteins, including necrotic proteins.

Protein aggregates can form in a number of different ways, including through the misfolding of proteins, through the formation of cross-links between proteins, or through the accumulation of damaged proteins. These aggregates can have a variety of different effects on cells and tissues, including the disruption of normal cellular functions, the inhibition of protein degradation, and the activation of the immune system.

Protein aggregates are associated with a number of different diseases, including neurodegenerative diseases such as Alzheimer's disease, Huntington's disease, and Parkinson's disease, as well as other diseases such as amyloidosis and prion diseases.

Research on the formation and clearance of protein aggregates is ongoing, and scientists are working to better understand the underlying mechanisms and develop new treatments and therapies for diseases associated with protein aggregates. For example, scientists are studying the potential of drugs that can promote the clearance of protein aggregates through the use of chaperones or other molecules that can disrupt the formation of aggregates.

In conclusion, necrotic proteins are damaged proteins that are generated by a variety of mechanisms, including oxidative stress, inflammation, and exposure to toxins or other harmful agents. They can accumulate in cells and tissues, contributing to the progression of diseases such as cancer and neurodegeneration, activating the immune system, and forming protein aggregates. These protein aggregates are associated with a number of different diseases, including neurodegenerative diseases, amyloidosis and prion diseases. The body has several mechanisms to remove necrotic proteins and protein aggregates, including autophagy, the ubiquitin-proteasome system, lysosomal degradation system, phagocytosis, the immune response and chaperone-mediated clearance. However, in some cases, the accumulation of necrotic proteins and protein aggregates can overwhelm these systems and lead to dysfunction, chronic inflammation, tissue damage and the development of diseases.

It's also worth noting that the accumulation of necrotic proteins and protein aggregates can lead to the formation of reactive oxygen species (ROS) and oxidative stress. ROS are highly reactive molecules that can damage proteins, lipids, and DNA, leading to cellular dysfunction and death. This can further contribute to the development of diseases associated with necrotic proteins and protein aggregates.

Additionally, the accumulation of necrotic proteins and protein aggregates can also lead to the inhibition of the autophagic and lysosomal degradation pathways, which can further contribute to their accumulation and the development of diseases.

Research on necrotic proteins and protein aggregates is ongoing, and scientists are working to better understand the underlying mechanisms of protein damage and degradation, and the development of new treatments and therapies for diseases associated with necrotic proteins and protein aggregates.

In conclusion, necrotic proteins are damaged proteins that are generated by a variety of mechanisms and can accumulate in cells and tissues, contributing to the progression of various diseases such as cancer, neurodegeneration and other age-related disease. They can also form protein aggregates, which can further exacerbate the pathology. The body has several mechanisms to remove necrotic proteins and protein aggregates, including autophagy, the ubiquitin-proteasome system, lysosomal degradation system, phagocytosis, the immune response and chaperone-mediated clearance. However, in some cases, the accumulation of necrotic proteins and protein aggregates can overwhelm these systems and lead to dysfunction, chronic inflammation, tissue damage, oxidative stress and the development of diseases. The research on necrotic proteins and protein aggregates is ongoing and scientists are working to better understand the underlying mechanisms and develop new treatments and therapies for diseases associated with necrotic proteins and protein aggregates.

Another important point to consider is that necrotic proteins and protein aggregates can also have an impact on other cellular processes. For example, they can disrupt the normal function of intracellular signaling pathways, leading to changes in gene expression and cellular behavior. They can also disrupt the normal function of the endoplasmic reticulum (ER) and the mitochondria, leading to changes in protein folding and energy metabolism. This can further contribute to the development of diseases associated with necrotic proteins and protein aggregates.

Additionally, necrotic proteins and protein aggregates can also impact the function of the extracellular matrix (ECM). The ECM is a complex network of proteins and other molecules that provides structural support to cells and tissues. Disruptions to the ECM can lead to changes in cell adhesion, migration, and differentiation, which can further contribute to the development of diseases associated with necrotic proteins and protein aggregates.

Research on the interactions between necrotic proteins, protein aggregates and cellular processes is ongoing, and scientists are working to better understand the underlying mechanisms and develop new treatments and therapies for diseases associated with necrotic proteins and protein aggregates.

In conclusion, necrotic proteins are damaged proteins that are generated by a variety of mechanisms and can accumulate in cells and tissues, contributing to the progression of various diseases such as cancer, neurodegeneration and other age-related disease. They can also form protein aggregates, which can further exacerbate the pathology. The body has several mechanisms to remove necrotic proteins and protein aggregates but in some cases, the accumulation of necrotic proteins and protein aggregates can overwhelm these systems and lead to dysfunction, chronic inflammation, tissue damage, oxidative stress, disruption of intracellular signaling pathways, endoplasmic reticulum, mitochondria and extracellular matrix and the development of diseases. The research on necrotic proteins and protein aggregates is ongoing and scientists are working to better understand the underlying mechanisms and develop new treatments and therapies for diseases associated with necrotic proteins and protein aggregates.

Another important point to consider is the role of necrotic proteins and protein aggregates in aging. As we age, our cells and tissues are exposed to a variety of stressors that can lead to the accumulation of necrotic proteins and protein aggregates. This can contribute to the development of age-related diseases such as Alzheimer's disease, Parkinson's disease, and cancer. Additionally, the accumulation of necrotic proteins and protein aggregates can also contribute to the decline in cellular and tissue function that is associated with aging.

Moreover, there are some studies showing that some of the necrotic proteins and protein aggregates can act as damage-associated molecular patterns (DAMPs), which can activate the innate immune system through pattern recognition receptors (PRRs) and contribute to chronic inflammation, which is associated with aging and age-related diseases.

Scientists are currently investigating ways to prevent or reduce the accumulation of necrotic proteins and protein aggregates in order to slow the aging process and prevent age-related diseases. For example, some studies have suggested that caloric restriction or intermittent fasting may help to reduce the accumulation of necrotic proteins and protein aggregates in cells and tissues, while other studies have suggested that certain drugs or supplements may have a similar effect.

In summary, necrotic proteins are damaged proteins that are generated by a variety of mechanisms and can accumulate in cells and tissues, contributing to the progression of various diseases such as cancer, neurodegeneration and other age-related disease. They can also form protein aggregates, which can further exacerbate the pathology. The body has several mechanisms to remove necrotic proteins and protein aggregates but in some cases, the accumulation of necrotic proteins and protein aggregates can overwhelm these systems, lead to dysfunction, chronic inflammation, tissue damage, oxidative stress, disruption of intracellular signaling pathways, endoplasmic reticulum, mitochondria, extracellular matrix and the development of diseases. The accumulation of necrotic proteins and protein aggregates can also be associated with aging and age-related diseases, and scientists are working to better understand the underlying mechanisms and develop new treatments and therapies for diseases associated with necrotic proteins and protein aggregates.

Another important aspect to consider is the potential therapeutic applications of targeting necrotic proteins and protein aggregates. Several strategies are currently being developed to target necrotic proteins and protein aggregates in order to prevent or treat diseases associated with their accumulation.

One approach is to develop drugs that can inhibit the formation of necrotic proteins and protein aggregates. For example, some researchers are developing drugs that can inhibit the formation of amyloid-beta plaques in Alzheimer's disease, or α-synuclein aggregates in Parkinson's disease.

Another approach is to develop drugs that can promote the clearance of necrotic proteins and protein aggregates. For example, some researchers are developing drugs that can activate autophagy, the ubiquitin-proteasome system, or lysosomal degradation, in order to promote the clearance of necrotic proteins and protein aggregates.

Additionally, scientists are also investigating the use of antibodies or other molecules that can bind to necrotic proteins and protein aggregates and promote their clearance by phagocytosis or the immune system.

It's worth noting that these approaches are still in the early stages of development and more research is needed to fully understand the underlying mechanisms and evaluate the safety and efficacy of these strategies in humans.

In conclusion, necrotic proteins are damaged proteins that are generated by a variety of mechanisms and can accumulate in cells and tissues, contributing to the progression of various diseases such as cancer, neurodegeneration and other age-related disease. They can also form protein aggregates, which can further exacerbate the pathology. The body has several mechanisms to remove necrotic proteins and protein aggregates but in some cases, the accumulation of necrotic proteins and protein aggregates can overwhelm these systems, lead to dysfunction, chronic inflammation, tissue damage, oxidative stress, disruption of intracellular signaling pathways, endoplasmic reticulum, mitochondria, extracellular matrix and the development of diseases. The accumulation of necrotic proteins and protein aggregates can also be associated with aging and age-related diseases. Scientists are working to better understand the underlying mechanisms and develop new treatments and therapies for diseases associated with necrotic proteins and protein aggregates, including developing drugs that can inhibit the formation of necrotic proteins and protein aggregates, promote the clearance of necrotic proteins and protein aggregates, and using antibodies or other molecules that can bind to necrotic proteins and protein aggregates to promote their clearance by the immune system or phagocytosis.

Another potential therapeutic strategy is the use of small molecules or natural compounds that can modulate the activity of specific enzymes or proteins involved in the formation or clearance of necrotic proteins and protein aggregates. For example, some studies have shown that compounds such as curcumin, resveratrol, and quercetin can modulate the activity of enzymes involved in the formation of amyloid-beta plaques in Alzheimer's disease.

Another strategy is to use gene therapy to target the underlying genetic causes of diseases associated with necrotic proteins and protein aggregates. For example, some researchers are developing gene therapies that can correct mutations in genes that cause inherited forms of neurodegenerative diseases such as Huntington's disease.

It is worth noting that these therapies are still in the early stages of development and more research is needed to fully understand the underlying mechanisms and evaluate the safety and efficacy of these strategies in humans.

In summary, necrotic proteins are damaged proteins that are generated by a variety of mechanisms and can accumulate in cells and tissues, contributing to the progression of various diseases such as cancer, neurodegeneration and other age-related disease. There are several mechanisms to remove necrotic proteins and protein aggregates but in some cases, the accumulation of necrotic proteins and protein aggregates can overwhelm these systems, lead to dysfunction, chronic inflammation, tissue damage, oxidative stress, disruption of intracellular signaling pathways, endoplasmic reticulum, mitochondria, extracellular matrix and the development of diseases. Scientists are working to better understand the underlying mechanisms and develop new treatments and therapies for diseases associated with necrotic proteins and protein aggregates, including developing drugs that can inhibit the formation of necrotic proteins and protein aggregates, promote the clearance of necrotic proteins and protein aggregates, using antibodies or other molecules that can bind to necrotic proteins and protein aggregates to promote their clearance by the immune system or phagocytosis, using small molecules or natural compounds that can modulate the activity of specific enzymes or proteins involved in the formation or clearance of necrotic proteins and protein aggregates, and using gene therapy to target the underlying genetic causes of diseases associated with necrotic proteins and protein aggregates.

Another strategy that is being studied is the use of nanoparticles to target necrotic proteins and protein aggregates. Researchers are developing nanoparticles that can specifically bind to necrotic proteins and protein aggregates and deliver therapeutic molecules such as drugs or enzymes to the site of accumulation. This approach can increase the specificity and efficiency of therapy, and potentially reduce the side effects associated with traditional drug delivery methods.

Furthermore, researchers are also studying the use of stem cells to target necrotic proteins and protein aggregates. Some studies have shown that stem cells can migrate to the site of necrotic proteins and protein aggregates, and induce the clearance of these proteins through the release of enzymes or other molecules. Additionally, some studies have suggested that stem cells may be able to differentiate into specific cell types that can replace the cells that have been lost due to necrotic proteins and protein aggregate accumulation.

It's important to note that these strategies are still in the early stages of development and more research is needed to fully understand the underlying mechanisms and evaluate the safety and efficacy of these strategies in humans.

In summary, necrotic proteins are damaged proteins that are generated by a variety of mechanisms and can accumulate in cells and tissues, contributing to the progression of various diseases such as cancer, neurodegeneration and other age-related disease. Scientists are working to better understand the underlying mechanisms and develop new treatments and therapies for diseases associated with necrotic proteins and protein aggregates, including developing drugs that can inhibit the formation of necrotic proteins and protein aggregates, promote the clearance of necrotic proteins and protein aggregates, using antibodies or other molecules that can bind to necrotic proteins and protein aggregates to promote their clearance by the immune system or phagocytosis, using small molecules or natural compounds that can modulate the activity of specific enzymes or proteins involved in the formation or clearance of necrotic proteins and protein aggregates, using gene therapy to target the underlying genetic causes of diseases associated with necrotic proteins and protein aggregates, using nanoparticles to target necrotic proteins and protein aggregates, and using stem cells to target necrotic proteins and protein aggregates.

It's also worth noting that there are ongoing studies to investigate the effects of lifestyle changes such as diet, exercise, and stress management on the accumulation of necrotic proteins and protein aggregates. Studies have shown that a diet rich in antioxidants, omega-3 fatty acids, and other nutrients can help reduce oxidative stress, inflammation, and the accumulation of necrotic proteins and protein aggregates. Regular exercise has also been shown to improve overall health and reduce the accumulation of necrotic proteins and protein aggregates. Stress management techniques such as meditation, yoga, and cognitive behavioral therapy can also help reduce chronic inflammation, which is a contributing factor in the accumulation of necrotic proteins and protein aggregates.

In conclusion, necrotic proteins are damaged proteins that are generated by a variety of mechanisms and can accumulate in cells and tissues, contributing to the progression of various diseases such as cancer, neurodegeneration and other age-related disease. Scientists are working to better understand the underlying mechanisms and develop new treatments and therapies for diseases associated with necrotic proteins and protein aggregates. Lifestyle changes such as diet, exercise, and stress management are also being studied as potential ways to reduce the accumulation of necrotic proteins and protein aggregates. It's important to note that these strategies and treatments are still in the early stages of development and more research is needed to fully understand the underlying mechanisms and evaluate the safety and efficacy of these strategies in humans.

Another approach to targeting necrotic proteins and protein aggregates is to use CRISPR-based genome editing techniques. CRISPR-based genome editing is a powerful tool that can be used to correct or delete specific genes that contribute to the formation or accumulation of necrotic proteins and protein aggregates. This approach is being studied in the context of several diseases associated with necrotic proteins and protein aggregates, such as Alzheimer's disease, Huntington's disease, and other neurodegenerative disorders.

Additionally, researchers are also investigating the use of small interfering RNAs (siRNAs) as a way to target necrotic proteins and protein aggregates. siRNAs are small pieces of RNA that can be designed to bind to specific genes and inhibit their expression. This approach can be used to reduce the formation or accumulation of necrotic proteins and protein aggregates, and is being studied in the context of several diseases such as Alzheimer's disease and Huntington's disease.

Another strategy that is being studied is the use of chaperone proteins to target necrotic proteins and protein aggregates. Chaperone proteins are a class of proteins that can interact with other proteins and help to maintain their proper folding and function. Some chaperone proteins can bind to and stabilize specific necrotic proteins and protein aggregates, preventing their further aggregation and accumulation, which can slow down or stop the progression of disease.

It's important to note that all of these strategies are still in the early stages of development and more research is needed to fully understand the underlying mechanisms and evaluate the safety and efficacy of these strategies in humans.

In summary, necrotic proteins are damaged proteins that are generated by a variety of mechanisms and can accumulate in cells and tissues, contributing to the progression of various diseases such as cancer, neurodegeneration and other age-related disease. Scientists are working to better understand the underlying mechanisms and develop new treatments and therapies for diseases associated with necrotic proteins and protein aggregates, including developing drugs that can inhibit the formation of necrotic proteins and protein aggregates, promoting the clearance of necrotic proteins and protein aggregates, using antibodies or other molecules that can bind to necrotic proteins and protein aggregates, using small molecules or natural compounds that can modulate the activity of specific enzymes or proteins, using gene therapy, using nanoparticles, using stem cells, using CRISPR-based genome editing techniques, using small interfering RNAs (siRNAs), using chaperone proteins and lifestyle changes.

Autophagic proteins

Autophagic proteins are a group of proteins that play a role in the process of autophagy, a cellular mechanism that allows cells to degrade and recycle their own components. These proteins are responsible for recognizing and marking specific molecules or organelles within the cell for degradation, as well as for the formation and fusion of the autophagosome, the membrane-bound structure that encloses the targeted materials for degradation. Examples of autophagic proteins include Atg5, Atg7, Atg8, and LC3. Dysregulation of autophagic proteins has been linked to several diseases, including cancer and neurodegeneration.

Autophagy is a process that helps cells to remove and recycle damaged or unnecessary components, such as damaged proteins, organelles, and pathogens. This process is essential for maintaining cellular homeostasis and is also involved in various physiological processes, including cell growth, differentiation, and survival.

The process of autophagy is divided into three stages: initiation, elongation, and maturation. Autophagic proteins play a crucial role in each of these stages.

Initiation: Autophagic proteins, such as Atg1, Atg13, and FIP200, are responsible for the formation of the phagophore, a small membrane-bound structure that will eventually give rise to the autophagosome.

Elongation: Autophagic proteins, such as Atg3, Atg4, Atg7, Atg9, and WIPI, are responsible for expanding the phagophore into a mature autophagosome.

Maturation: Autophagic proteins, such as Atg5, Atg7, Atg8, and LC3, are responsible for the final maturation of the autophagosome, which includes the closing of the autophagosomal membrane and the fusion of the autophagosome with lysosomes.

Dysregulation of autophagic proteins has been linked to several diseases. For example, mutations in genes that encode autophagic proteins have been linked to neurodegenerative diseases such as Parkinson's disease and Alzheimer's disease. Similarly, cancer cells often have abnormal levels of autophagic proteins, which can help them to evade cell death and promote their survival. Therefore, understanding the role of autophagic proteins in disease is an active area of research, with the goal of developing new therapies that target these proteins.

There are different types of autophagy, including macroautophagy, microautophagy, and chaperone-mediated autophagy (CMA).

Macroautophagy (also known as "autophagy") is the most well-studied type of autophagy, and it is the type I described in my previous answer. In macroautophagy, the cell recognizes and marks specific molecules or organelles for degradation, and then forms a double-membrane structure called the autophagosome around them. The autophagosome then fuses with a lysosome, which contains enzymes that can degrade the contents of the autophagosome.

Microautophagy is a process by which the cell's lysosomal membrane directly engulfs and degrades small molecules or organelles.

Chaperone-mediated autophagy (CMA) is a selective form of autophagy that specifically targets proteins. In CMA, a chaperone protein binds to a specific protein and then delivers it to the lysosome for degradation.

Autophagic proteins are involved in all types of autophagy, and they play different roles depending on the type of autophagy. For example, in macroautophagy, autophagic proteins are involved in the formation and maturation of the autophagosome, while in CMA, autophagic proteins are involved in the recognition and delivery of specific proteins to the lysosome.

Autophagy has a critical role in maintaining homeostasis in the cell and it's tightly regulated by different pathways and molecules. The regulation of autophagy is a complex process that involves a variety of signaling pathways, including the mammalian target of rapamycin (mTOR) pathway, the AMP-activated protein kinase (AMPK) pathway, and the unfolded protein response (UPR) pathway, among others.

Research on autophagic proteins and autophagy is still ongoing, it's a dynamic and growing field, with the potential to identify new targets for the treatment of various diseases.

In addition to their role in the maintenance of cellular homeostasis, autophagy also plays a role in various physiological processes, including:

Development and differentiation: Autophagy has been shown to play a role in the development of various organs, such as the brain, liver, and heart, as well as in the differentiation of stem cells.

Cancer: Autophagy can have both pro- and anti-tumorigenic effects, depending on the context. In some cases, autophagy can promote cancer cell survival by enabling cells to remove damaged proteins and organelles, while in other cases, it can promote cell death by removing vital components of the cell.

Inflammation and immunity: Autophagy plays an important role in the innate immune response by helping to remove pathogens and damaged cells. In addition, autophagy has been shown to play a role in regulating inflammation.

Aging: Autophagy is known to decline with age, and this decline has been linked to the accumulation of damaged proteins and organelles, as well as to the development of age-related diseases.

Autophagic proteins can be targeted for therapeutic intervention for a variety of diseases, by modulating their expression or activity. For example, drugs that inhibit the mTOR pathway, such as rapamycin, have been shown to increase autophagy and have been used in the treatment of certain cancers. Similarly, drugs that activate the AMPK pathway, such as metformin, have been shown to increase autophagy and have been used in the treatment of diabetes and other diseases.

It's worth to mention that autophagy is a complex process, and it's not fully understood yet. There are still many questions to be answered, such as how autophagic proteins are regulated, how they interact with other proteins and pathways, and how they contribute to disease. Understanding the details of the autophagic process is critical to fully harness its therapeutic potential.

Autophagy-related (Atg) proteins: These proteins are essential for the initiation, elongation, and maturation of the autophagosome. They include Atg1, Atg3, Atg4, Atg5, Atg7, Atg8, Atg9, and Atg12.

Autophagosome-associated proteins: These proteins are involved in the formation and maturation of the autophagosome. They include LC3, GABARAP, and GATE16.

Autophagosome-lysosome fusion proteins: These proteins are involved in the fusion of the autophagosome with the lysosome. They include SNARE proteins, such as VAMP8 and VAMP7, and Rab GTPases, such as Rab7.

Autophagic receptors: These proteins act as receptors that recognize and mark specific molecules or organelles for degradation by autophagy. They include p62/SQSTM1, NBR1, and OPTN.

Chaperone-mediated autophagy (CMA) proteins: These proteins are responsible for the recognition and delivery of specific proteins to the lysosome for degradation. They include HSPA8 and HSPA5 (also known as BiP)

It's worth noting that the autophagic process is a complex and dynamic process that is still not fully understood. The field is continuously growing with new discoveries and findings about the mechanisms, pathways, and proteins involved in the process, and how they are related to different diseases and conditions.

Also, the modulation of autophagic proteins can have different effects depending on the cell type, the stage of the disease, and the context. Therefore, it's important to consider the specific context and the cells/tissues targeted when developing new therapeutic strategies that modulate autophagic proteins.

It's also important to mention that autophagy is not only a process that removes damaged or unnecessary components, but it also plays a role in the cellular response to stress, including nutrient deprivation, hypoxia, and oxidative stress. Autophagy can help cells to adapt to these stressful conditions by providing an alternative source of energy by breaking down and recycling intracellular components, and by removing damaged molecules and organelles that could potentially be harmful.

Autophagy can also be induced by certain types of drugs, such as rapamycin and metformin, which target specific signaling pathways that regulate the process. This has led to the development of new therapeutic strategies that aim to modulate autophagy as a way to treat diseases.

For example, in cancer, autophagy can act as a pro-survival mechanism by removing damaged organelles and proteins and by providing a source of energy. However, in some cases, autophagy can also promote cell death, depending on the context. Therefore, targeting autophagic proteins and pathways can have different effects depending on the stage of the disease and the type of cancer.

In neurodegenerative diseases, such as Alzheimer's and Parkinson's diseases, autophagy plays a critical role in the clearance of abnormal proteins that accumulate in the brain. Therefore, targeting autophagic proteins and pathways could be a promising strategy to slow down the progression of these diseases. For example, increasing autophagy by activating the AMPK pathway or inhibiting mTOR has been shown to be beneficial in animal models of these diseases.

In addition, autophagy has also been linked to other diseases such as diabetes, heart disease, and liver disease. For example, in diabetes, autophagy plays a role in the regulation of insulin sensitivity and glucose metabolism, and a decline in autophagic activity has been linked to the development of diabetes. Similarly, in heart disease, autophagy is important for maintaining the integrity of the heart muscle, and a decline in autophagic activity has been linked to the development of heart disease.

Overall, autophagic proteins and pathways are emerging as important therapeutic targets for a variety of diseases. However, it's important to note that the regulation of autophagy is complex and context-dependent, and further research is needed to fully understand the mechanisms underlying autophagic processes and to develop effective therapeutic strategies.

Anoikis proteins

Anoikis is a type of programmed cell death that occurs in cells that have detached from the extracellular matrix (ECM) or basement membrane, the structures that provide mechanical and biochemical support to cells. Anoikis proteins are proteins that play a role in the process of anoikis. Examples of Anoikis-related proteins include the E-cadherin, Rho GTPases, and caspases. These proteins can be involved in signaling pathways that lead to cell detachment, as well as pathways that trigger cell death once detachment has occurred.

Anoikis is an important mechanism for maintaining tissue integrity and preventing the proliferation of detached cells, which can lead to the development of cancer and other diseases. The process of anoikis is initiated by the loss of cell-matrix adhesion, which disrupts the signaling pathways that regulate cell survival and proliferation. The loss of adhesion can be caused by a variety of factors, including changes in the ECM, mutations in adhesion molecules, and alterations in the signaling pathways that regulate cell-matrix interactions.

One of the key proteins involved in anoikis is E-cadherin, an adhesion molecule that helps to hold cells together. When E-cadherin is lost, cells can detach from the ECM and become susceptible to anoikis. Rho GTPases, a family of signaling molecules, also play a critical role in anoikis by regulating the actin cytoskeleton, which is necessary for cell adhesion. In addition, caspases, a group of proteases that play a key role in programmed cell death, are activated in response to cell detachment, leading to the death of detached cells.

In summary, Anoikis is a process of programmed cell death that occurs in cells that have detached from the extracellular matrix or basement membrane, and Anoikis-related proteins include the E-cadherin, Rho GTPases, and caspases which are involved in signaling pathways that lead to cell detachment, as well as pathways that trigger cell death once detachment has occurred.

In addition to E-cadherin, Rho GTPases, and caspases, other proteins have also been identified as playing a role in anoikis. For example, the protein p53 is known to be involved in the process of anoikis and has been shown to induce cell death in response to cell detachment. Similarly, the protein Bax has been shown to play a role in the induction of anoikis.

Another protein that has been shown to play a role in anoikis is integrin, a protein that helps to anchor cells to the extracellular matrix. Integrin is composed of alpha and beta subunits and different combination of subunits can lead to different cell behaviors. When integrin is activated, it can help to protect cells from anoikis by promoting cell-matrix adhesion.

Finally, recent research has also highlighted the importance of microRNAs (miRNAs) in the regulation of anoikis. MiRNAs are small non-coding RNAs that can bind to specific target mRNAs, thereby modulating their translation and stability. MiRNAs have been shown to play a role in regulating cell adhesion and proliferation and have been linked to the regulation of anoikis.

In conclusion, anoikis is a complex process that is regulated by a variety of proteins, including E-cadherin, Rho GTPases, caspases, p53, Bax, integrin and miRNAs. Understanding the molecular mechanisms that underlie anoikis may provide insight into the development of cancer and other diseases and could potentially lead to the development of new therapeutic strategies for preventing the proliferation of detached cells.

In addition to the proteins and miRNAs I've mentioned earlier, other signaling pathways and molecules also play a role in anoikis. For example, the signaling pathways of MAPKs(mitogen-activated protein kinases) and PI3K(phosphatidylinositol 3-kinase)/Akt are known to be involved in anoikis. The MAPK pathways are activated when cells detach from the ECM, leading to the activation of caspases and the induction of anoikis. Similarly, the PI3K/Akt pathway plays a role in regulating cell survival and proliferation and its inactivation can lead to anoikis.

Another molecule that plays a role in anoikis is the protein Apaf1 (apoptotic protease activating factor 1), which is known to be involved in the regulation of the caspase cascade that leads to cell death. Research has shown that Apaf1 is required for the induction of anoikis in response to cell detachment.

Another important aspect of anoikis is the role of the cytoskeleton. The cytoskeleton is composed of microtubules, intermediate filaments, and microfilaments. The cytoskeleton plays a crucial role in maintaining cell shape and integrity, and disruptions to the cytoskeleton can lead to anoikis. In particular, the actin cytoskeleton is known to be involved in anoikis, with studies showing that the loss of actin stress fibers can lead to anoikis.

In summary, anoikis is a complex process that is regulated by a variety of proteins, miRNAs, signaling pathways, and molecules. The MAPKs, PI3K/Akt, Apaf1, cytoskeleton and other signaling pathways and molecules are also involved in the regulation of anoikis. Understanding the molecular mechanisms that underlie anoikis may provide insight into the development of cancer and other diseases and could potentially lead to the development of new therapeutic strategies for preventing the proliferation of detached cells.

Another important aspect of anoikis is the role of signaling pathways that involve the transcription factor NF-kB (nuclear factor kappa-light-chain-enhancer of activated B cells). The NF-kB pathway is activated in response to cell detachment and can promote cell survival by inhibiting the activation of caspases. This pathway plays a critical role in protecting cells from anoikis and can also promote cell proliferation in detached cells.

In addition, the Wnt signaling pathway is also known to play a role in anoikis. This pathway is activated in response to cell detachment and can promote cell survival by inhibiting the activation of caspases. Wnt signaling can also promote cell proliferation in detached cells.

Another important aspect is the role of autophagy in anoikis. Autophagy is a process by which cells degrade and recycle their own components, including proteins and organelles. Autophagy can play a protective role in anoikis by reducing the accumulation of damaged proteins and organelles, which can lead to cell death.

Finally, it is also worth noting that the mechanism of anoikis can vary depending on the type of cell and the tissue in which it is located. For example, anoikis in epithelial cells may involve the activation of different signaling pathways and proteins than anoikis in mesenchymal cells.

In conclusion, anoikis is a complex process that is regulated by a variety of proteins, miRNAs, signaling pathways, and molecules. The MAPKs, PI3K/Akt, Apaf1, cytoskeleton, NF-kB, Wnt signaling pathways, autophagy and other signaling pathways and molecules are also involved in the regulation of anoikis. Understanding the molecular mechanisms that underlie anoikis may provide insight into the development of cancer and other diseases and could potentially lead to the development of new therapeutic strategies for preventing the proliferation of detached cells.

Senescence proteins

Senescence proteins are a group of proteins that are involved in the process of cellular senescence, which is the state of a cell that has stopped dividing and will no longer replicate. Some examples of senescence proteins include p16INK4a, p21WAF1, and p53. These proteins act as tumor suppressors and play a role in aging and age-related diseases. They are activated in response to various types of cellular stress, such as DNA damage, and cause the cell to enter a permanent state of growth arrest, preventing it from becoming cancerous.

Cellular senescence is a complex process that is triggered by various internal and external factors, such as DNA damage, oxidative stress, and telomere shortening. When a cell enters senescence, it undergoes a number of changes, including an increase in the expression of senescence-associated biomarkers, such as senescence-associated beta-galactosidase (SA-beta-gal) and p16INK4a.

The p16INK4a protein is a cyclin-dependent kinase inhibitor that prevents the cell cycle from progressing. When activated, it binds to and inactivates cyclin-dependent kinases 4 and 6, preventing the cell from entering the S-phase of the cell cycle.

p21WAF1 is a cyclin-dependent kinase inhibitor that works in a similar way to p16INK4a, but it can also inhibit other kinases, such as DNA-dependent protein kinase.

p53 is a transcription factor that plays a central role in the response to DNA damage. When activated, it can cause the cell to enter a temporary growth arrest, allowing time for DNA repair, or it can trigger apoptosis (cell death) if the damage is too severe. It also upregulates the expression of genes that promote DNA repair and cell cycle arrest, like p16INK4a and p21WAF1.

These senescence proteins are important in preventing the formation of cancer, as they inhibit the growth of damaged cells that could otherwise become cancerous. However, the accumulation of senescent cells in tissues with aging is associated with the decline in tissue function, and senescence-associated secretory phenotype(SASP) produces inflammatory cytokines, matrix metalloproteinases, and growth factors that can promote chronic inflammation, tissue remodeling, and cancer, which are known as "senescence-associated diseases"

In short, senescence proteins play a critical role in the regulation of cell growth and division and are important in preventing cancer, but their accumulation with aging can lead to age-related diseases.

In addition to their role in preventing cancer, senescence proteins have also been implicated in a wide range of age-related diseases. For example, the accumulation of senescent cells in various tissues has been linked to the development of conditions such as osteoarthritis, cardiovascular disease, and frailty.

One of the key mechanisms by which senescent cells contribute to these diseases is through the senescence-associated secretory phenotype (SASP). SASP refers to the release of a wide range of inflammatory cytokines, matrix metalloproteinases, and growth factors by senescent cells. These molecules can promote chronic inflammation and tissue remodeling, which can lead to the development of various diseases.

In recent years, there has been a growing interest in the potential therapeutic use of senescence proteins in the treatment of age-related diseases. For example, some studies have suggested that targeting senescence proteins, such as p16INK4a and p53, could be a promising approach for the treatment of cancer, while others have suggested that targeting senescence proteins could be a way to slow down the aging process and delay the onset of age-related diseases.

However, it is important to note that senescence proteins play critical roles in preventing cancer and that targeting senescence proteins could have unintended consequences, such as promoting the growth of damaged cells. Therefore, more research is needed to fully understand the potential therapeutic use of senescence proteins and to develop safe and effective treatments that target these proteins.

In conclusion, senescence proteins are a group of proteins that are involved in the process of cellular senescence. They play a critical role in the regulation of cell growth and division, and are important in preventing cancer, but their accumulation with aging can lead to age-related diseases. Targeting senescence proteins is an active area of research in the field of aging, but more research is needed to fully understand their potential therapeutic use and to develop safe and effective treatments that target these proteins.

Recent research has also shown that senescence proteins play a role in the development of metabolic disorders such as obesity, diabetes, and metabolic syndrome. The accumulation of senescent cells in adipose tissue and liver has been linked to the development of insulin resistance and glucose intolerance. The SASP factors produced by senescent cells can also lead to inflammation and fibrosis in these tissues, which can further contribute to metabolic dysfunction.

Additionally, senescence proteins have also been found to play a role in the development of neurological disorders such as Alzheimer's disease. The accumulation of senescent cells in the brain has been linked to the development of neurodegeneration and cognitive decline. The SASP factors produced by senescent cells can also contribute to inflammation and oxidative stress in the brain, which can further contribute to the development of neurological disorders.

In terms of the therapeutic potential of targeting senescence proteins, researchers are currently exploring various strategies such as senolytic drugs that selectively eliminate senescent cells, and senomorphics drugs that inhibit the SASP and pro-inflammatory pathways.

While there is still much to learn about the role of senescence proteins in aging and age-related diseases, the growing body of research in this field highlights the potential therapeutic value of targeting senescence proteins in the treatment of a wide range of diseases.

It's also worth noting that senescence proteins are not only being studied in the context of aging and age-related diseases but also in cancer, as well as in other diseases where cellular senescence plays a role, like fibrosis, and autoimmune diseases.

In summary, senescence proteins play a critical role in the regulation of cell growth and division, and are important in preventing cancer, but their accumulation with aging can lead to age-related diseases. Targeting senescence proteins is an active area of research in the field of aging and various diseases, and various strategies such as senolytic drugs and senomorphics drugs are being explored as a potential therapeutic approach to target senescence proteins.

As the research in this field continues to evolve, it is becoming increasingly clear that senescence proteins play a complex and multifaceted role in the aging process and in the development of age-related diseases.

One area of active research is the interplay between senescence proteins and the immune system. Studies have shown that senescent cells can affect the function of immune cells, and that the accumulation of senescent cells can lead to a decline in immune function, which can further contribute to the development of age-related diseases. Additionally, the SASP factors produced by senescent cells can also recruit and activate immune cells, which can further contribute to inflammation and tissue remodeling.

Another area of active research is the relationship between senescence proteins and epigenetics. Epigenetic modifications, such as DNA methylation and histone modifications, can influence the expression of senescence proteins and have been found to play a role in the regulation of cellular senescence.

Additionally, recent studies have also shown that the senescence proteins have the potential to be used as biomarkers to identify individuals at risk of age-related diseases. For example, the presence of senescent cells in blood has been found to be associated with an increased risk of mortality, and senescence-associated biomarkers have been found to be elevated in individuals with age-related diseases such as Alzheimer's disease and type 2 diabetes.

In conclusion, senescence proteins play a complex and multifaceted role in the aging process and in the development of age-related diseases. Research in this field is ongoing and continues to reveal new insights into the role of senescence proteins in health and disease, and the potential therapeutic value of targeting senescence proteins. Additionally, the senescence proteins are also being studied as biomarkers to identify individuals at risk of age-related diseases.

Another area of active research in senescence proteins is the relationship between senescence and stem cells. Stem cells are a special type of cell that have the ability to self-renew and to differentiate into various specialized cell types. They play a critical role in tissue repair and regeneration. However, as we age, the function of stem cells declines, and this can contribute to the decline in tissue function. Recent studies have shown that senescence proteins can play a role in regulating the function of stem cells, both positively and negatively. For example, some studies have shown that senescence proteins can promote the differentiation of stem cells, while others have shown that senescence proteins can inhibit the self-renewal of stem cells.

Another area of research is the role of senescence proteins in the development of cancer. Cancer is a disease characterized by the uncontrolled growth and proliferation of cells. Senescence proteins play a critical role in preventing the formation of cancer, as they inhibit the growth of damaged cells that could otherwise become cancerous. However, some cancer cells have found ways to evade senescence and continue to proliferate. For example, cancer cells can mutate or lose the function of senescence proteins, or they can develop resistance to the senescence-inducing signals.

Finally, another area of active research in senescence proteins is the relationship between senescence and the extracellular matrix (ECM). The ECM is the network of proteins and carbohydrates that surrounds and supports cells in tissues. Senescent cells can modify the ECM by releasing enzymes that break down the matrix and by secreting new ECM components. This can lead to changes in tissue architecture and stiffness, and can affect the behavior of neighboring cells. For example, the ECM can influence the migration and proliferation of cells, and can also modulate the immune response.

It is important to note that while senescence proteins play a critical role in preventing cancer and promoting tissue repair, their accumulation in tissues with aging can lead to age-related diseases and dysfunction. Therefore, the targeting of senescence proteins is an active area of research in the field of aging and age-related diseases, with the goal of developing safe and effective therapies that can eliminate senescent cells or inhibit the SASP without disrupting the normal functions of senescence proteins.

In summary, senescence proteins play a complex and multifaceted role in the aging process and in the development of age-related diseases. Research in this field continues to reveal new insights into the role of senescence proteins in health and disease, and the potential therapeutic value of targeting senescence proteins. Additionally, senescence proteins are also being studied in the context of stem cells, cancer and the extracellular matrix.

Another area of research in senescence proteins is the relationship between senescence and the gut microbiome. The gut microbiome is the collection of microorganisms that live in the gastrointestinal tract. Recent studies have shown that the gut microbiome can influence the development of age-related diseases, and that senescence proteins can also affect the gut microbiome. For example, senescent cells can alter the composition and function of the gut microbiome, which can further contribute to inflammation and metabolic dysfunction. Additionally, the gut microbiome can also influence the development of senescence in cells, by modulating the expression of senescence proteins and by affecting the immune response.

Another area of research is the relationship between senescence proteins and environmental factors. Environmental factors such as diet, physical activity, and exposure to toxins and pollutants can affect the development of senescence in cells. For example, a diet high in sugar and fat can increase the accumulation of senescent cells in tissues, and exposure to pollutants can also promote the development of senescence. Additionally, physical activity and calorie restriction have been shown to decrease the accumulation of senescent cells and to improve the function of senescent cells.

It's also worth noting that senescence is not only a feature of aging but also a protective mechanism against cancer and other diseases, senescence can be triggered by various types of stress like DNA damage, telomere shortening and oncogenic mutations, among others.

In conclusion, senescence proteins play a complex and multifaceted role in the aging process and in the development of age-related diseases. Research in this field continues to reveal new insights into the role of senescence proteins in health and disease, and the potential therapeutic value of targeting senescence proteins. Additionally, senescence proteins are also being studied in the context of the gut microbiome, environmental factors and the different types of stress that can trigger senescence.

Another area of research in senescence proteins is the relationship between senescence and metabolism. Metabolism is the set of chemical reactions that occur in the body to maintain life and support growth and development. As we age, metabolism can become disrupted, leading to the development of metabolic disorders such as type 2 diabetes. Recent studies have shown that senescence proteins can affect metabolism, both positively and negatively. For example, some senescence proteins can promote insulin sensitivity and glucose uptake, while others can inhibit these processes. Additionally, the SASP factors produced by senescent cells can also influence metabolism, by modulating the expression of metabolic genes and by affecting the function of metabolic tissues such as the liver and adipose tissue.

Another area of research is the relationship between senescence proteins and aging interventions. As we age, we accumulate a large number of senescent cells in our tissues, which can contribute to the development of age-related diseases. Various interventions have been proposed to target senescent cells with the goal of extending healthspan and lifespan. For example, senolytic drugs, which selectively eliminate senescent cells, have been shown to improve the health and lifespan of mice. Additionally, genetic interventions that target senescence proteins have also been shown to extend healthspan and lifespan in animal models.

Finally, it's also worth mentioning that senescence proteins can also be used as therapeutic targets for different types of cancer. For instance, senescence proteins can be targeted with drugs that inhibit the activity of the protein or its downstream signaling pathways, leading to the inhibition of cancer cell growth and proliferation.

In conclusion, senescence proteins play a complex and multifaceted role in the aging process and in the development of age-related diseases. Research in this field continues to reveal new insights into the role of senescence proteins in health and disease, and the potential therapeutic value of targeting senescence proteins, not only for aging but also for cancer. Additionally, senescence proteins are also being studied in the context of metabolism, aging interventions, and cancer therapy.

Another area of research in senescence proteins is the relationship between senescence and the immune system. The immune system plays a critical role in protecting the body from infection and disease, and also plays a key role in the clearance of senescent cells. As we age, the immune system becomes less effective, which can contribute to the accumulation of senescent cells in tissues. Recent studies have shown that senescence proteins can affect the immune system, both positively and negatively. For example, some senescence proteins can promote the activation of immune cells, while others can inhibit the activation of immune cells. Additionally, the SASP factors produced by senescent cells can also influence the immune system, by modulating the expression of immune genes and by affecting the function of immune cells.

Another area of research is the relationship between senescence proteins and the gut-brain axis. The gut-brain axis refers to the communication between the gut and the brain, which plays a critical role in maintaining health and well-being. Recent studies have shown that the gut-brain axis can be affected by senescence proteins, both positively and negatively. For example, some senescence proteins can promote the communication between the gut and the brain, while others can inhibit the communication between the gut and the brain. Additionally, the SASP factors produced by senescent cells can also influence the gut-brain axis, by modulating the expression of gut-brain genes and by affecting the function of gut-brain cells.

In conclusion, senescence proteins play a complex and multifaceted role in the aging process and in the development of age-related diseases. Research in this field continues to reveal new insights into the role of senescence proteins in health and disease, and the potential therapeutic value of targeting senescence proteins. Additionally, senescence proteins are also being studied in the context of the immune system, gut-brain axis, and other physiological systems that play a role in health and aging.

Another area of research in senescence proteins is the relationship between senescence and the cardiovascular system. The cardiovascular system, which includes the heart and blood vessels, plays a critical role in maintaining overall health and well-being. As we age, the cardiovascular system can become compromised, leading to the development of conditions such as hypertension and atherosclerosis. Recent studies have shown that senescence proteins can affect the cardiovascular system, both positively and negatively. For example, some senescence proteins can promote the function of the cardiovascular system, while others can inhibit the function of the cardiovascular system. Additionally, the SASP factors produced by senescent cells can also influence the cardiovascular system, by modulating the expression of cardiovascular genes and by affecting the function of cardiovascular cells.

Another area of research is the relationship between senescence proteins and the nervous system. The nervous system, which includes the brain and spinal cord, plays a critical role in maintaining overall health and well-being. As we age, the nervous system can become compromised, leading to the development of conditions such as neurodegeneration. Recent studies have shown that senescence proteins can affect the nervous system, both positively and negatively. For example, some senescence proteins can promote the function of the nervous system, while others can inhibit the function of the nervous system. Additionally, the SASP factors produced by senescent cells can also influence the nervous system, by modulating the expression of nervous system genes and by affecting the function of nervous system cells.

In conclusion, senescence proteins play a complex and multifaceted role in the aging process and in the development of age-related diseases. Research in this field continues to reveal new insights into the role of senescence proteins in health and disease, and the potential therapeutic value of targeting senescence proteins. Additionally, senescence proteins are also being studied in the context of various physiological systems such as the cardiovascular and nervous system that play a key role in maintaining overall health and well-being.

Another area of research is the relationship between senescence proteins and stem cells. Stem cells are undifferentiated cells that have the ability to differentiate into a variety of different cell types. As we age, the number and function of stem cells decline, leading to the development of age-related diseases. Recent studies have shown that senescence proteins can affect stem cells, both positively and negatively. For example, some senescence proteins can promote the function and self-renewal of stem cells, while others can inhibit the function and self-renewal of stem cells. Additionally, the SASP factors produced by senescent cells can also influence stem cells, by modulating the expression of stem cell genes and by affecting the function of stem cells.

In conclusion, senescence proteins play a complex and multifaceted role in the aging process and in the development of age-related diseases. Research in this field continues to reveal new insights into the role of senescence proteins in health and disease, and the potential therapeutic value of targeting senescence proteins. Additionally, senescence proteins are also being studied in the context of stem cells, which play a crucial role in tissue regeneration and repair.

Another area of research is the relationship between senescence proteins and epigenetics. Epigenetics refers to the changes in gene expression that occur without changes to the underlying DNA sequence. These changes can be caused by a variety of factors, including aging. Recent studies have shown that senescence proteins can affect epigenetics, both positively and negatively. For example, some senescence proteins can promote the regulation of gene expression, while others can inhibit the regulation of gene expression. Additionally, the SASP factors produced by senescent cells can also influence epigenetics, by modulating the expression of epigenetic genes and by affecting the function of epigenetic cells.

In conclusion, senescence proteins play a complex and multifaceted role in the aging process and in the development of age-related diseases. Research in this field continues to reveal new insights into the role of senescence proteins in health and disease, and the potential therapeutic value of targeting senescence proteins. Additionally, senescence proteins are also being studied in the context of epigenetics, which play a crucial role in understanding the underlying mechanisms of aging and age-related diseases.

Recent updates:

The retinal pigment epithelium-1 (RPE1) cell line underwent 31 CRISPR-Cas9 tests against 27 genotoxic substances, according to Michele Olivieri et al. These tests located 890 genes whose deletion affects sensitivity to or tolerance to chemicals that damage DNA. Through the analysis of this dataset, it was found that the gene ERCC6L2 (which is mutated in a bone-marrow failure syndrome) codes for a canonical non-homologous end-joining pathway factor, that the RNA polymerase II component ELOF1 modulates the response to transcription-blocking agents, and that the G-quadruplex ligand pyridostatin's cytotoxicity is caused by its ability to trap topoisomerase This map of the DNA damage response offers a wealth of information for research into this crucial biological mechanism and has implications for the creation and application of genotoxic drugs in the treatment of cancer. [3].

Idris, Adi, et al. describe a novel lipid nanoparticle (LNP) delivery strategy for a highly efficient small interfering RNA (siRNA) therapy against SARS-CoV-2 infection. Three potential siRNAs that successfully inhibit the SARS-CoV-2 virus by more than 90% either alone or in combination identified after a large number of siRNAs targeting highly conserved areas of the virus were examined. For the delivery of these potential siRNA therapies to the lungs, an organ that suffers significant damage during SARS-CoV-2 infection, they concurrently created and screened two novel LNP formulations. [4].

The genetic regulatory code governing the amount of mRNA in seven model organisms, spanning from bacteria to humans, is examined by Zrimec, Jan, et al. using deep learning on more than 20,000 mRNA datasets. Since up to 82% of the diversity in transcript levels is encoded in the gene regulatory structure, it is possible to predict the abundance of mRNA in all organisms just from the DNA sequence. We find that motif interactions could account for the entire dynamic range of mRNA levels by looking for DNA regulatory motifs throughout the gene regulatory structure. Co-evolution between coding and non-coding areas shows that gene expression levels are determined by a complex network of regulatory components rather than by a single motif or region. [5].

Organelles of the cell play a role in several illnesses. Given that the Golgi complex helps normal urothelial cells build the blood-urine barrier and that it may be responsible for cancer cells losing the blood-urine barrier.[6].

Deregulation of miRNA is a common feature of several illnesses. As a result, a wide variety of research fields concentrate on the creation of miRNA therapies for the treatment of a variety of human illnesses. The first-ever miRNA therapy is undergoing phase II clinical trials for the treatment of hepatitis C virus (HCV) infection. The miR-122 medication miravirsen is a short locked nucleic acid (LNA) that is moving quickly from the bench to the clinic. [7].

References :-

1. Xie, H. (2003). IDENTIFICATION OF CpG ISLANDS AND POTENTIAL PROMOTERS IN HUMAN GENOME (Doctoral dissertation, The University of Iowa).

2. Pollard, T. D., Earnshaw, W. C., Lippincott-Schwartz, J., & Johnson, G. (2016). Cell biology E-book.

3. Olivieri, M., Cho, T., Álvarez-Quilón, A., Li, K., Schellenberg, M. J., Zimmermann, M., ... & Durocher, D. (2020). A genetic map of the response to DNA damage in human cells. Cell, 182(2), 481-496.

4. Idris, A., Davis, A., Supramaniam, A., Acharya, D., Kelly, G., Tayyar, Y., ... & Morris, K. V. (2021). A SARS-CoV-2 targeted siRNA-nanoparticle therapy for COVID-19. Molecular Therapy, 29(7), 2219-2226.

5. Zrimec, J., Börlin, C. S., Buric, F., Muhammad, A. S., Chen, R., Siewers, V., ... & Zelezniak, A. (2020). Deep learning suggests that gene expression is encoded in all parts of a co-evolving interacting gene regulatory structure. Nature communications, 11(1), 1-16.

6. Kreft, M. E., Mironov, A. A., & Hudoklin, S. (2022). The Golgi complex: An organelle that determines urothelial cell biology in health and disease. Histochemistry and Cell Biology, 158(3), 229-240.

7. Chakraborty, C., Sharma, A. R., Sharma, G., & Lee, S. S. (2021). Therapeutic advances of miRNAs: A preclinical and clinical update. Journal of advanced research, 28, 127-138.

CHAPTER THREE

Cell signalling

Mrs Ashwini Badhe and Dr Pravin Badhe

Introduction-

Cell signalling is the process by which cells communicate with each other and coordinate their functions. It is essential for the proper functioning of all living organisms and plays a critical role in many biological processes, including development, immune response, and tissue repair.

There are several different types of cell signalling, including electrical, chemical, and mechanical signalling. Electrical signalling involves the transmission of electrical signals through gap junctions, which are channels that allow ions to flow between cells. Chemical signalling involves the release and detection of signalling molecules, such as hormones and neurotransmitters, which bind to specific receptors on the surface of cells or within their cytoplasm. Mechanical signalling involves the physical interaction of cells through contact or the transmission of mechanical forces through the extracellular matrix.

Cell signaling involves a series of complex and highly regulated steps, including signal transduction, which is the process by which a signaling molecule activates a specific pathway within the cell. This activation can lead to a variety of responses, such as the transcription of genes, the modification of proteins, or the activation of ion channels.

Overall, cell signaling is a fundamental aspect of cell biology and is essential for the proper functioning and coordination of cells within an organism.

Another important aspect of cell signaling is the regulation of these signals. This can occur at various levels, such as the production and release of signaling molecules, the expression and distribution of receptors, and the downstream signaling pathways activated by these receptors. Additionally, cells also have mechanisms to inactivate or degrade signaling molecules once they have fulfilled their function.

Another important aspect of cell signaling is the specificity of the signals. Signaling molecules and receptors have evolved to be specific to certain cells or groups of cells, allowing for precise communication and coordination within an organism. This specificity also plays a role in the immune system, where specific signaling molecules and receptors help to identify and target invading pathogens while leaving healthy cells unharmed.

In summary, cell signaling is a complex process that plays a vital role in the proper functioning of living organisms. It involves the transmission, detection, and regulation of signals, which can lead to a variety of responses within cells. The specificity of these signals allows for precise communication and coordination among cells, and is essential for many biological processes, including development, immune response, and tissue repair.

Cell signaling can be divided into two main categories: intracellular signaling and intercellular signaling. Intracellular signaling refers to the communication that occurs within a single cell, and can involve signaling molecules that bind to receptors on the cell's surface or within the cytoplasm. These signals can activate intracellular signaling pathways that lead to changes in gene expression or protein activity.

Intercellular signaling, on the other hand, refers to the communication that occurs between cells. This can include chemical signaling, in which signaling molecules are released by one cell and bind to receptors on other cells. It can also include mechanical signaling, in which cells physically interact with each other through contact or the transmission of mechanical forces through the extracellular matrix.

Chemical signaling can be further divided into paracrine signaling, autocrine signaling, and endocrine signaling. Paracrine signaling involves the release of signaling molecules that act on nearby cells, while autocrine signaling involves a cell releasing a signaling molecule that binds to receptors on the same cell. Endocrine signaling involves the release of signaling molecules, called hormones, into the bloodstream, which can act on cells throughout the body.

There are also different types of receptors that cells use to detect signaling molecules. These can include G protein-coupled receptors, which activate intracellular signaling pathways in response to a ligand binding, and ion channels which can be activated or inhibited by ligand binding.

Overall, cell signaling is a highly regulated and complex process that plays a critical role in the proper functioning of living organisms. It involves the transmission, detection, and regulation of signals, and can lead to a variety of responses within cells, including changes in gene expression, protein activity, and cell division. Understanding the mechanisms and regulation of cell signaling is important for understanding many biological processes and diseases, including cancer, immune disorders, and neurological disorders.

Another important aspect of cell signaling is the role of second messengers. Second messengers are molecules that are produced or activated within the cell in response to the binding of a signaling molecule to a receptor. They act as intermediates in intracellular signaling pathways, amplifying the initial signal and allowing it to reach different parts of the cell. Some examples of second messengers include cyclic AMP (cAMP), inositol triphosphate (IP3), and calcium ions ($Ca2+$).

Signal transduction pathways are the series of reactions by which a cell converts a signal on its surface into an appropriate response. The receptors on the cell surface act as a sensor, detecting the presence of the signaling molecule and transmitting the signal to the intracellular machinery. Signal transduction pathways can be divided into two main categories: cascade pathways and phosphorylation-dependent pathways. The cascade pathways are a series of enzymes that amplify the signal and the phosphorylation-dependent pathways involve the transfer of a phosphate group from ATP to a protein, which can lead to changes in the protein's activity or localization.

Another important aspect of cell signaling is the role of signaling proteins. Signaling proteins are molecules that act as intermediates in intracellular signaling pathways. They can act as enzymes, scaffolds, and adaptors, and can help to transmit the signal and modify the activity of other proteins.

In addition to the intracellular signaling, there are also other important mechanisms of cell signaling, such as epigenetics. Epigenetics refers to heritable changes in gene function that do not involve changes to the underlying DNA sequence. These changes can be caused by modifications to the DNA itself, such as methylation, or to the proteins with which DNA interacts, such as histones. Epigenetic mechanisms can play a role in the regulation of gene expression and cell signaling.

In conclusion, cell signaling is a complex and highly regulated process that plays a critical role in the proper functioning of living organisms. It involves the transmission, detection, and regulation of signals, and can lead to a variety of responses within cells. Understanding the mechanisms and regulation of cell signaling is important for understanding many biological processes and diseases.

Intercellular signalling pathway

An intercellular signaling pathway is a series of events that occurs when a signaling molecule is transmitted from one cell to another and leads to a specific cellular response. This process is essential for communication between cells and coordination of their functions within an organism.

There are several different types of intercellular signaling pathways, including paracrine signaling, endocrine signaling, and autocrine signaling.

In paracrine signaling, a signaling molecule is released by one cell and acts on nearby cells. This type of signaling is common in tissues where cells are in close proximity to each other, such as the immune system and the endocrine system.

In endocrine signaling, a signaling molecule is released into the bloodstream and travels to distant cells or tissues to elicit a response. This type of signaling is common in the endocrine system, which is responsible for the production and release of hormones.

In autocrine signaling, a signaling molecule acts on the same cell that released it. This type of signaling is involved in various cellular processes, including cell growth and survival.

Overall, intercellular signaling pathways are essential for communication between cells and coordination of their functions within an organism. Dysregulation of these pathways can lead to various diseases and disorders.

Intercellular signaling pathways are mediated by various signaling molecules, such as hormones, growth factors, and neurotransmitters. These molecules bind to specific receptors on the target cell, which initiates a cascade of events leading to a specific cellular response.

One important aspect of intercellular signaling is signal transduction, which refers to the process by which a signaling molecule is converted into a cellular response. This process involves the activation of intracellular signaling pathways, such as the MAPK/ERK pathway, the PI3K/Akt pathway, and the JAK/STAT pathway.

Another important aspect of intercellular signaling is feedback regulation, which helps to maintain homeostasis within the organism. For example, after a hormone binds to its receptor, it may activate an intracellular signaling pathway that ultimately leads to the inhibition of the hormone's own production or release.

Intercellular signaling pathways play important roles in various physiological processes, such as growth and development, immunity, and metabolism. Dysregulation of these pathways can lead to various diseases and disorders, including cancer, diabetes, and autoimmune diseases. Therefore, understanding the mechanisms of intercellular signaling pathways is crucial for the development of new therapies for these diseases.

Intercellular signaling pathways involve a complex series of molecular interactions and can be divided into several steps.

Receptor activation: Signaling molecules bind to specific receptors on the target cell membrane, leading to the activation or inhibition of the receptor.

Second messenger system: The activated receptor then triggers a cascade of intracellular events, such as the production of second messengers, which amplify the signal and lead to further downstream effects.

Intracellular signaling pathways: Second messengers activate intracellular signaling pathways, such as the MAPK/ERK pathway, the PI3K/Akt pathway, and the JAK/STAT pathway, which lead to the initiation of various cellular responses.

Gene regulation: Intracellular signaling pathways can also lead to the regulation of gene expression, which can result in changes in protein synthesis, cell growth, and differentiation.

Feedback regulation: Once a cellular response has been initiated, feedback mechanisms are activated to regulate the intensity and duration of the response. This can include the inhibition of receptor activation, the degradation of signaling molecules, and the inhibition of second messenger production.

Intercellular signaling pathways are highly regulated and can be modulated by various mechanisms, such as receptor desensitization, receptor internalization, and regulation of signaling molecules and intracellular signaling pathways.

Intercellular signaling pathways are also interconnected, and the activation of one pathway can lead to the activation or inhibition of other pathways. This allows for the coordination of multiple cellular responses and the integration of multiple signals, which is essential for the proper functioning of an organism.

Understanding the mechanisms of intercellular signaling pathways is crucial for the development of new therapies for diseases, such as cancer, diabetes, and autoimmune diseases. Targeting specific signaling molecules, receptors, or intracellular signaling pathways can lead to the inhibition of disease-causing pathways and the activation of protective pathways.

Intercellular signaling pathways are highly complex and dynamic systems that involve a wide range of molecular interactions. Some of the key molecules and structures involved in intercellular signaling pathways include:

Receptors: These are proteins that are located on the cell membrane and are responsible for detecting signaling molecules. Receptors can be classified into several different types, such as G protein-coupled receptors, receptor tyrosine kinases, and nuclear receptors.

G proteins: These are intracellular proteins that act as molecular switches and are activated by G protein-coupled receptors. G proteins activate intracellular signaling pathways and second messengers, such as cyclic AMP (cAMP) and inositol triphosphate (IP3).

Second messengers: These are small, water-soluble molecules that are produced in response to receptor activation and amplify the signal. Second messengers can include cyclic nucleotides, such as cAMP and cyclic GMP (cGMP), as well as inositol phosphates, such as IP3 and diacylglycerol (DAG).

Protein kinases: These are enzymes that transfer a phosphate group from ATP to target proteins, thereby activating or inhibiting them. Protein kinases are key players in intracellular signaling pathways and can include receptor tyrosine kinases, serine/threonine kinases, and protein kinase C (PKC).

Transcription factors: These are proteins that bind to specific DNA sequences and regulate gene expression. Transcription factors can be activated or inhibited by intracellular signaling pathways and can lead to changes in protein synthesis, cell growth, and differentiation.

Signaling molecules: These are the molecules that are responsible for transmitting the signal between cells. Signaling molecules can include hormones, growth factors, neurotransmitters, and cytokines.

Intercellular signaling pathways are tightly regulated by various mechanisms to ensure proper functioning of the organism. These mechanisms can include receptor desensitization, receptor internalization, and regulation of signaling molecules and intracellular signaling pathways.

Dysregulation of intercellular signaling pathways can lead to various diseases and disorders, such as cancer, diabetes, and autoimmune diseases. Targeting specific signaling molecules, receptors, or intracellular signaling pathways can lead to the inhibition of disease-causing pathways and the activation of protective pathways.

Understanding the mechanisms of intercellular signaling pathways is crucial for the development of new therapies for diseases, and researchers continue to work on identifying new signaling molecules and receptors, as well as developing new drugs that can target these pathways.

The study of intercellular signaling pathways is a rapidly evolving field that is essential for understanding the mechanisms that control cell behavior and the development of new therapies for diseases. There are several key approaches and techniques that are used to study intercellular signaling pathways:

Biochemical techniques: These techniques are used to analyze the components of intercellular signaling pathways, such as receptors, signaling molecules, and intracellular signaling pathways. Techniques include western blotting, which is used to detect proteins, and ELISA, which is used to detect the presence of specific signaling molecules.

Cell-based assays: These assays are used to study the effects of signaling molecules on cells in culture. Techniques include measuring changes in cell proliferation, cell death, and gene expression.

Genetic techniques: These techniques are used to study the function of specific signaling molecules, receptors, and intracellular signaling pathways. Techniques include RNA interference (RNAi), which is used to knock down specific genes, and CRISPR-Cas9, which is used to edit specific genes.

Systems biology: This approach uses a combination of computational and experimental techniques to study the complex interactions between signaling molecules, receptors, and intracellular signaling pathways. Systems biology can help to identify new signaling pathways and potential drug targets.

Animal models: These models are used to study the effects of intercellular signaling pathways in vivo. Animal models can include genetically modified mice and zebrafish, which can be used to study the effects of specific signaling molecules and receptors on development and disease.

Overall, the study of intercellular signaling pathways is a multidisciplinary field that involves the use of various techniques and approaches to understand the complex interactions between signaling molecules, receptors, and intracellular signaling pathways.

By understanding the mechanisms of intercellular signaling pathways, researchers hope to develop new therapies for diseases that are caused by dysregulation of these pathways, such as cancer, diabetes, and autoimmune diseases.

Intracellular signalling pathway

Intracellular signaling pathways are pathways within a single cell that transmit a signal from the cell surface to the nucleus or other intracellular organelles. These pathways play a critical role in many cellular processes, including cell growth, differentiation, and death.

There are several different types of intracellular signaling pathways, including receptor-mediated signaling pathways and second messenger signaling pathways.

Receptor-mediated signaling pathways

In receptor-mediated signaling pathways, a signaling molecule binds to a specific receptor on the cell surface, which activates a signaling cascade within the cell. This cascade involves the sequential activation of various intracellular signaling proteins, such as enzymes, ion channels, and transcription factors. These proteins transmit the signal to the nucleus or other intracellular organelles, leading to a specific cellular response.Receptor-mediated signaling pathways transmit a signal from the cell surface to the nucleus or other intracellular organelles in response to the binding of a signaling molecule to a specific receptor. These pathways play a critical role in many cellular processes, including cell growth, differentiation, and death.

There are several different types of receptors that mediate signaling pathways, including G protein-coupled receptors, ion channel receptors, and enzyme-linked receptors.

- G protein-coupled receptors are a type of receptor that spans the cell membrane and is activated by the binding of a signaling molecule to the extracellular domain. Upon activation, the receptor activates a G protein, which is a signaling protein that is associated with the intracellular domain of the receptor. The activated G protein then activates an intracellular signaling cascade, which involves the sequential activation of various intracellular signaling proteins, such as enzymes, ion channels, and transcription factors. These proteins transmit the signal to the nucleus or other intracellular organelles, leading to a specific cellular response.
- Ion channel receptors are a type of receptor that spans the cell membrane and is activated by the binding of a signaling molecule to the extracellular domain. Upon activation, the receptor opens or closes an ion channel, which allows ions to flow into or out of the cell. This flow of ions leads to a change in the electrical potential of the cell, which can trigger various intracellular signaling pathways.
- Enzyme-linked receptors are a type of receptor that is activated by the binding of a signaling molecule to the extracellular domain. Upon activation, the receptor activates an intracellular enzyme, which can then modify various intracellular signaling proteins, leading to a specific cellular response.

Overall, receptor-mediated signaling pathways are essential for the proper functioning of cells and are involved in many important cellular processes. Dysregulation of these pathways can lead to various diseases and disorders.

Overall, intracellular signaling pathways play a critical role in many cellular processes, including cell growth, differentiation, and death. There are several different types of intracellular signaling pathways, including receptor-mediated signaling pathways and second messenger signaling pathways. Both types of pathways are essential for the proper functioning of cells and are involved in many important cellular processes. Dysregulation of these pathways can lead to various diseases and disorders.

Intracellular signaling pathways are complex networks that allow cells to respond to external and internal stimuli. They involve the activation of specific receptors on the cell surface, which in turn trigger a cascade of intracellular signaling events. These events ultimately lead to a specific cellular response, such as cell growth, differentiation, or death.

One of the key components of intracellular signaling pathways are protein kinases. These enzymes play a critical role in transmitting the signal by phosphorylating specific target proteins, which leads to changes in their activity and function.

Another important component of intracellular signaling pathways is the regulation of gene expression. Many intracellular signaling pathways ultimately lead to changes in gene expression, which is regulated by transcription factors. These proteins bind to specific DNA sequences and regulate the transcription of genes into RNA.

Intracellular signaling pathways are also regulated by negative feedback mechanisms. These mechanisms ensure that the signaling pathways are not activated indefinitely and that the cellular response is appropriate and proportional to the stimulus. Negative feedback mechanisms can include the deactivation of signaling molecules or the inhibition of protein kinases.

Intracellular signaling pathways are also closely connected to other cellular processes such as the cell cycle, cell adhesion and cytoskeleton dynamics. It is through these interactions that intracellular signaling pathways are able to coordinate the different functions of a cell.

Dysregulation of intracellular signaling pathways can lead to various diseases and disorders, including cancer, diabetes, and heart disease. In cancer, for example, mutations in signaling molecules or receptors can lead to uncontrolled cell growth and proliferation. In diabetes, mutations in signaling pathways that regulate insulin production and glucose metabolism can lead to insulin resistance and high blood sugar levels.

Overall, intracellular signaling pathways are essential for the proper functioning of cells and are involved in many important cellular processes. Understanding the mechanisms and regulation of intracellular signaling pathways is crucial for the development of new therapies for various diseases and disorders.

Intracellular signaling pathways are also closely connected to other cellular processes such as cell metabolism and the immune system. Many intracellular signaling pathways are activated in response to changes in the cell's energy status and metabolic state. For example, the insulin signaling pathway is activated in response to high glucose levels and regulates the uptake and utilization of glucose by cells.

The immune system also heavily relies on intracellular signaling pathways. For example, when a cell is infected by a virus or bacteria, it triggers the activation of intracellular signaling pathways that leads to the production of inflammatory molecules and the recruitment of immune cells to the site of infection.

Additionally, intracellular signaling pathways are also regulated by post-translational modifications such as phosphorylation, ubiquitination, and acetylation. These modifications can lead to changes in the activity, localization, and stability of signaling molecules and receptors.

Another aspect of intracellular signaling pathways is the concept of crosstalk between different signaling pathways. Crosstalk refers to the ability of one signaling pathway to influence or modulate the activity of another signaling pathway. Crosstalk can occur through the direct interaction of signaling molecules or through the regulation of common downstream targets. Crosstalk allows cells to integrate and respond to multiple signals simultaneously.

Research on intracellular signaling pathways is ongoing, and new insights and discoveries are continuously being made. Advances in molecular biology and genetics have allowed for the identification and characterization of many signaling molecules and receptors, and the development of new technologies has facilitated the study of intracellular signaling pathways in living cells.

Overall, intracellular signaling pathways are essential for the proper functioning of cells and are involved in many important cellular processes. Understanding the mechanisms and regulation of intracellular signaling pathways is crucial for the development of new therapies for various diseases and disorders. It's also important to note that intracellular signaling pathways are highly interconnected, and many signaling pathways interact and regulate one another, which makes it a complex system that scientists still uncovering the secrets of it.

Another important aspect of intracellular signaling pathways is the concept of signal transduction. Signal transduction refers to the process by which a signal from the cell surface is transmitted and amplified through a cascade of intracellular signaling events, ultimately leading to a specific cellular response. The process of signal transduction involves the activation of receptors on the cell surface, the activation of intracellular signaling molecules, and the regulation of downstream targets such as protein kinases, ion channels, and transcription factors.

One of the key components of signal transduction is the activation of downstream effectors. These are molecules that are activated by the intracellular signaling cascade and ultimately lead to the cellular response. Examples of downstream effectors include protein kinases, which phosphorylate target proteins and alter their activity, and transcription factors, which regulate the expression of genes.

Another important aspect of signal transduction is the regulation of intracellular signaling pathways. This can include the activation or inhibition of signaling molecules, the regulation of protein levels, and the regulation of post-translational modifications.

Research on intracellular signaling pathways has led to the development of new therapies for various diseases and disorders. For example, the development of small molecule inhibitors that target specific signaling molecules or protein kinases has led to the development of new treatments for cancer. The use of monoclonal antibodies that target specific receptors has also led to the development of new therapies for autoimmune diseases and cancer.

Overall, intracellular signaling pathways are complex systems that are essential for the proper functioning of cells. Understanding the mechanisms and regulation of these pathways is crucial for the development of new therapies for various diseases and disorders. Research in this field is ongoing, and new insights and discoveries are continuously being made. Advances in molecular biology and genetics have allowed for the identification and characterization of many signaling molecules and receptors, and the development of new technologies has facilitated the study of intracellular signaling pathways in living cells. Additionally, the concept of signal transduction and the regulation of intracellular signaling pathways play a crucial role in the proper functioning of cells. Understanding these mechanisms can lead to new therapies and treatments for diseases and disorders.

Second messenger signaling pathways

In second messenger signaling pathways, the binding of a signaling molecule to a receptor on the cell surface leads to the activation of an intracellular second messenger, such as cyclic adenosine monophosphate (cAMP) or inositol triphosphate (IP3). The second messenger then activates various intracellular signaling proteins, which transmit the signal to the nucleus or other intracellular organelles.

Second messenger signaling pathways are pathways that transmit a signal from the cell surface to the nucleus or other intracellular organelles in response to the binding of a signaling molecule to a specific receptor. These pathways involve the activation of an intracellular second messenger, which is a small molecule that is produced in response to the activation of a receptor. The second messenger then activates various intracellular signaling proteins, which transmit the signal to the nucleus or other intracellular organelles.

There are several different types of second messengers, including cyclic adenosine monophosphate (cAMP), inositol triphosphate (IP3), and diacylglycerol (DAG). Each of these second messengers is activated by a specific type of receptor and leads to the activation of a specific set of intracellular signaling proteins.

One example of a second messenger signaling pathway is the cAMP pathway, which is activated by the binding of a signaling molecule to a G protein-coupled receptor. Upon activation, the receptor activates a G protein, which in turn activates an enzyme called adenylate cyclase. Adenylate cyclase converts ATP to cAMP, which then activates a protein called protein kinase A (PKA). PKA can then phosphorylate various intracellular signaling proteins, leading to a specific cellular response.

Second messenger signaling pathways are essential for the proper functioning of cells and are involved in many important cellular processes. Dysregulation of these pathways can lead to various diseases and disorders

Overall, intracellular signaling pathways are essential for the proper functioning of cells and are involved in many important cellular processes. Dysregulation of these pathways can lead to various diseases and disorders.

Second messenger signaling pathways are a vital component of cell signaling and are used by cells to respond to various external and internal signals. These pathways are activated by the binding of a signaling molecule to a specific receptor on the cell surface, which leads to the production of an intracellular second messenger. The second messenger then activates various intracellular signaling proteins, which transmit the signal to the nucleus or other intracellular organelles. There are several different types of second messengers, each activated by a specific type of receptor and leading to the activation of a specific set of intracellular signaling proteins. Examples of second messengers include cyclic adenosine monophosphate (cAMP), inositol triphosphate (IP3), and diacylglycerol (DAG). Dysregulation of these pathways can lead to various diseases and disorders, such as cancer, diabetes, and heart disease. Understanding the mechanism of second messenger signaling pathways is crucial for understanding how cells respond to their environment and for the development of new therapeutic strategies for treating diseases.

Second messenger signaling pathways are a complex and dynamic process that involve multiple steps and multiple players. These pathways are activated by the binding of a signaling molecule to a specific receptor on the cell surface, which leads to the production of an intracellular second messenger. The second messenger is a small, highly diffusible molecule that is produced in response to the activation of a receptor. These second messengers act as an intermediary between the cell surface and intracellular signaling proteins, transmitting the signal from the cell surface to the nucleus or other intracellular organelles.

The production of the second messenger is usually controlled by a specific enzyme or protein, which is activated by the receptor. For example, the G protein-coupled receptors activate G proteins, which in turn activate enzymes such as adenylate cyclase, phospholipase C, or phospholipase D. These enzymes then produce the second messenger, such as cAMP, IP3, or DAG.

Once the second messenger is produced, it then activates various intracellular signaling proteins, such as protein kinase A (PKA), protein kinase C (PKC), or mitogen-activated protein kinases (MAPKs). These proteins then phosphorylate specific target proteins, leading to changes in their activity, localization, or stability. These changes in the target proteins then lead to the initiation of a specific cellular response, such as cell growth, differentiation, or apoptosis.

Second messenger signaling pathways are essential for the proper functioning of cells and are involved in many important cellular processes such as cell growth, differentiation, apoptosis, and metabolism. Dysregulation of these pathways can lead to various diseases and disorders such as cancer, diabetes, and heart disease. Understanding the mechanism of second messenger signaling pathways is crucial for understanding how cells respond to their environment and for the development of new therapeutic strategies for treating diseases.

It's worth to mention that second messenger signaling pathways are not the only signaling mechanism inside the cell. There are other signaling pathways such as receptor tyrosine kinase signaling pathway, PI3K/Akt signaling pathway, Wnt signaling pathway, Hedgehog signaling pathway, Notch signaling pathway and many more. Each of them plays a specific role in different cellular processes and are activated by different type of signaling molecules.

Second messenger signaling pathways are also regulated by negative feedback mechanisms, which help to ensure that the signal is transmitted in a precise and controlled manner. These negative feedback mechanisms can occur at various levels of the pathway, including at the level of the receptor, the second messenger, or the intracellular signaling proteins.

One example of a negative feedback mechanism is the phosphorylation of the receptor itself by intracellular signaling proteins. This can lead to the desensitization or internalization of the receptor, which reduces its ability to bind the signaling molecule and thus reduces the production of the second messenger.

Another example is the degradation of the second messenger by specific enzymes, such as phosphodiesterase, which hydrolyzes cAMP to AMP. This decreases the concentration of the second messenger and reduces its ability to activate intracellular signaling proteins.

Finally, negative feedback mechanisms can occur at the level of intracellular signaling proteins, such as protein phosphatases, which dephosphorylate phosphoproteins and thus reduce their activity.

All these negative feedback mechanisms help to ensure that the signal is transmitted in a precise and controlled manner, and that the response of the cell is appropriate to the intensity and duration of the signal. Understanding how these negative feedback mechanisms work is essential for understanding how cells respond to their environment and for the development of new therapeutic strategies for treating diseases.

Overall, second messenger signaling pathways are a complex and dynamic process that involve multiple steps and multiple players, and are regulated by both positive and negative feedback mechanisms. These pathways play a crucial role in the proper functioning of cells and are involved in many important cellular processes such as cell growth, differentiation, apoptosis, and metabolism. Dysregulation of these pathways can lead to various diseases and disorders, thus understanding the mechanism of second messenger signaling pathways is crucial for understanding how cells respond to their environment and for the development of new therapeutic strategies for treating diseases.

Another important aspect of second messenger signaling pathways is the cross-talk between different pathways. This means that different signaling molecules can activate multiple pathways and that different pathways can interact and modulate each other's activity. For example, the cAMP pathway can interact with the phosphoinositide 3-kinase (PI3K) pathway, which is activated by the binding of a signaling molecule to a tyrosine kinase receptor. The PI3K pathway leads to the production of a second messenger called phosphatidylinositol 3,4,5-triphosphate (PIP3), which can activate a protein called AKT. AKT can then phosphorylate and activate other intracellular signaling proteins, leading to a specific cellular response.

Cross-talk between different pathways allows cells to integrate multiple signals and to coordinate their response to different stimuli. This is important for the proper functioning of cells and for the adaptation of cells to their environment.

Another important aspect of second messenger signaling pathways is the spatial and temporal regulation of the signal. The signaling molecules, receptors, second messengers, and intracellular signaling proteins are not uniformly distributed throughout the cell, but are localized in specific compartments and domains. This allows cells to respond differently to signals depending on the location of the signal. For example, signaling molecules can be localized at the cell surface or in the extracellular matrix, which can activate different receptors and lead to different cellular responses.

In addition, the duration and intensity of the signal can also influence the cellular response. A transient and weak signal can lead to a different response than a sustained and strong signal. This allows cells to respond differently to different stimuli and to adapt to their environment.

Overall, second messenger signaling pathways are a complex and dynamic process that involve multiple steps and multiple players, and are regulated by both positive and negative feedback mechanisms, cross-talk between different pathways, and the spatial and temporal regulation of the signal. These pathways play a crucial role in the proper functioning of cells and are involved in many important cellular processes. Dysregulation of these pathways can lead to various diseases and disorders, thus understanding the mechanism of second messenger signaling pathways is crucial for understanding how cells respond to their environment and for the development of new therapeutic strategies for treating diseases.

Another important aspect of second messenger signaling pathways is the regulation of the signaling molecules and receptors. This includes the regulation of the expression and localization of the signaling molecules and receptors, as well as the regulation of the activity and internalization of the receptors.

The expression of signaling molecules and receptors can be regulated at the transcriptional and post-transcriptional levels. For example, the expression of a signaling molecule can be increased or decreased by the activation or repression of its gene. The localization of signaling molecules and receptors can also be regulated, for example, by the formation of specific complexes with other molecules, or by the attachment to the extracellular matrix or the cytoskeleton.

The activity and internalization of receptors can also be regulated. For example, the activity of a receptor can be modulated by the phosphorylation or dephosphorylation of specific residues, by the formation of specific complexes with other molecules, or by the binding of specific ligands. The internalization of a receptor can also be regulated, for example, by the endocytosis or the recycling of the receptor.

Regulation of signaling molecules and receptors is important for the proper functioning of cells and for the adaptation of cells to their environment. It allows cells to respond differently to different stimuli and to adapt to changes in their environment.

In addition, second messenger signaling pathways are also regulated by negative feedback mechanisms. Negative feedback mechanisms are mechanisms that reduce or inhibit the activity of a signaling pathway. For example, the activity of a second messenger can be reduced by the action of specific enzymes that degrade the second messenger, or by the inactivation of the enzymes that produce the second messenger. The activity of a receptor can also be reduced by the internalization or degradation of the receptor, or by the binding of specific ligands that block the activity of the receptor.

Negative feedback mechanisms are important for the proper functioning of cells and for the adaptation of cells to their environment. They allow cells to fine-tune their response to different stimuli and to avoid over-activation of the signaling pathways.

Overall, second messenger signaling pathways are highly regulated and complex process, involving multiple steps and multiple players, and are regulated by both positive and negative feedback mechanisms, cross-talk between different pathways, and the spatial and temporal regulation of the signal and the regulation of the signaling molecules and receptors. Understanding the regulation of these pathways is crucial for understanding how cells respond to their environment and for the development of new therapeutic strategies for treating diseases.

Another important aspect of second messenger signaling pathways is their role in the coordination of multiple cellular processes. These pathways are often interconnected and can interact with each other to regulate a wide range of cellular functions. This can be achieved through a process called cross-talk, where signaling molecules and receptors from one pathway interact with signaling molecules and receptors from another pathway to modulate their activity.

For example, the cAMP pathway can interact with the IP3 pathway to modulate the activity of protein kinase C (PKC). The cAMP pathway can also interact with the MAPK pathway to modulate the activity of transcription factors and to regulate the expression of specific genes.

Another important aspect of second messenger signaling pathways is the spatial and temporal regulation of the signal. Signaling molecules and receptors are often localized in specific regions of the cell or in specific organelles, and the signaling pathway is activated only in the regions or organelles where the signaling molecules and receptors are present.

For example, the cAMP pathway is often localized in the plasma membrane of the cell and is activated only in the regions of the cell where the signaling molecules and receptors are present. The IP3 pathway is often localized in the endoplasmic reticulum and the sarcoplasmic reticulum, and is activated only in these organelles.

Additionally, second messenger signaling pathways are also regulated by the temporal regulation of the signal, which refers to the duration and the frequency of the signal. The duration and the frequency of the signal can be modulated by the activity of enzymes that degrade the second messenger, by the inactivation of the enzymes that produce the second messenger, by the internalization or degradation of the receptor, and by the binding of specific ligands that block the activity of the receptor.

Overall, second messenger signaling pathways play an important role in the coordination of multiple cellular processes and are regulated by both positive and negative feedback mechanisms, cross-talk between different pathways, the spatial and temporal regulation of the signal and the regulation of the signaling molecules and receptors. Understanding the regulation of these pathways is crucial for understanding how cells respond to their environment and for the development of new therapeutic strategies for treating diseases.

Classification of Receptor family

Receptors are proteins that are found on the surface of cells or within the cytoplasm and are responsible for detecting signaling molecules. There are several different ways to classify receptors based on their structure and function.

One way to classify receptors is based on the type of signaling molecule they recognize. There are several different types of signaling molecules, including hormones, neurotransmitters, growth factors, and cytokines. Receptors that recognize these signaling molecules are classified as hormone receptors, neurotransmitter receptors, growth factor receptors, and cytokine receptors, respectively.

Another way to classify receptors is based on their structure and the mechanism by which they transmit the signal. There are several different types of receptors based on structure, including G protein-coupled receptors, ion channel receptors, and enzyme-linked receptors. G protein-coupled receptors are a type of receptor that spans the cell membrane and is activated by the binding of a signaling molecule to the extracellular domain. Upon activation, the receptor activates a G protein, which is a signaling protein that is associated with the intracellular domain of the receptor. Ion channel receptors are a type of receptor that spans the cell membrane and is activated by the binding of a signaling molecule to the extracellular domain. Upon activation, the receptor opens or closes an ion channel, which allows ions to flow into or out of the cell. Enzyme-linked receptors are a type of receptor that is activated by the binding of a signaling molecule to the extracellular domain. Upon activation, the receptor activates an intracellular enzyme, which can then modify various intracellular signaling proteins.

Overall, receptors are an important class of proteins that play a critical role in the transmission of signals within cells and the coordination of their functions within an organism.

G protein-coupled receptor

G protein-coupled receptors (GPCRs) are a type of receptor that is found on the surface of cells and functions to transmit signals from small signaling molecules, such as hormones and neurotransmitters. When a GPCR is activated by a signaling molecule, it initiates a signaling pathway by activating a G protein, which is a type of intracellular signaling protein.

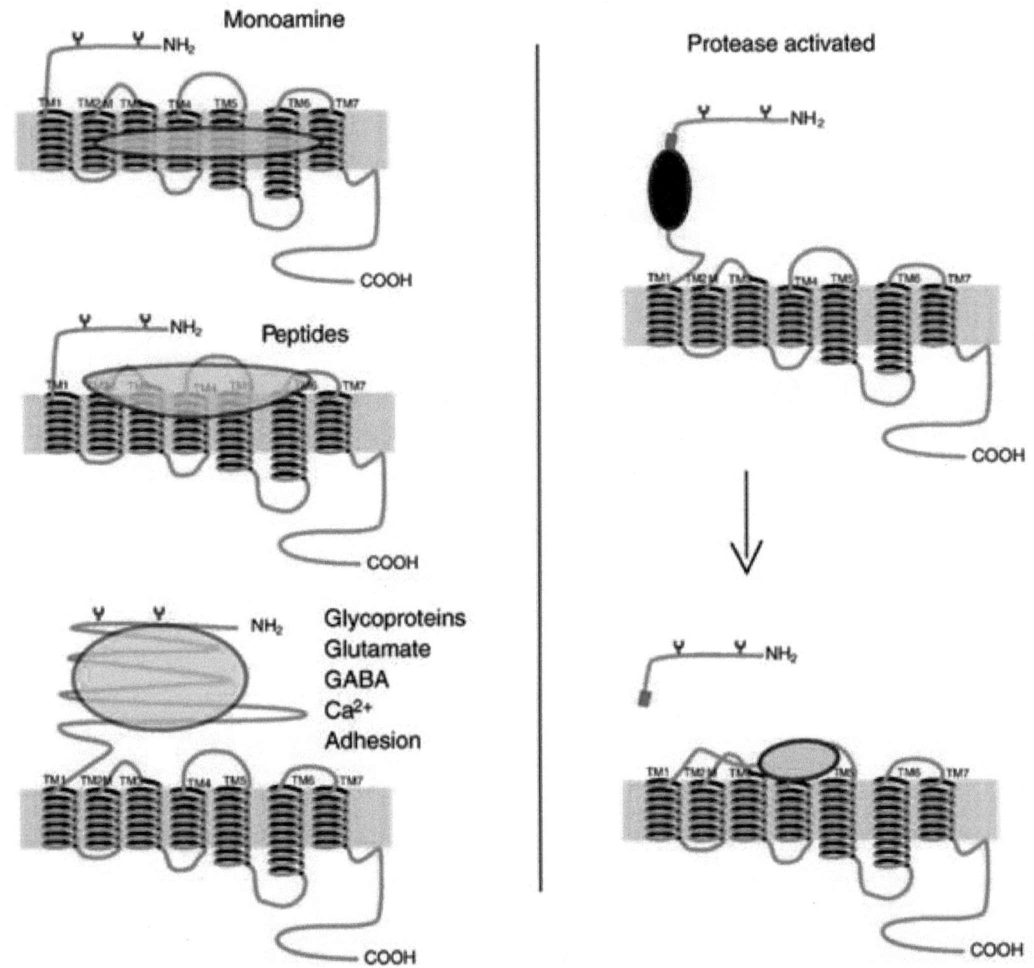

Fig 10:- secondary structure and the location of agonist binding sites for different GPCRs.[1]

GPCRs are transmembrane proteins, meaning they span the cell membrane and have both an extracellular and intracellular domain. The extracellular domain of the GPCR binds to the signaling molecule, while the intracellular domain is linked to the G protein.

Activation of the GPCR leads to a conformational change in the receptor, which in turn activates the G protein. The activated G protein then activates an intracellular signaling pathway, which can lead to a variety of cellular responses, such as the regulation of ion channels, enzyme activity, or gene expression.

G protein-coupled receptors (GPCRs) are a type of transmembrane receptor that are important in many physiological processes. They are activated by a wide variety of signaling molecules, including hormones, neurotransmitters, and sensory stimuli such as light and smell. When activated, GPCRs can initiate a signaling cascade that leads to changes in the activity of various enzymes, ion channels, and other proteins within the cell.

GPCRs are important because they are involved in many essential physiological processes, including immune function, cardiovascular function, and the regulation of mood, appetite, and sleep. Dysregulation of GPCR signaling has been implicated in the development of various diseases, including cancer, diabetes, and mental health disorders.

GPCRs are also important because they are the target of many drugs, including anti-inflammatory agents, cardiovascular drugs, and psychiatric drugs. In fact, around 40% of all drugs on the market are thought to work by targeting GPCRs. This makes GPCRs an important area of research in the development of new therapeutic agents.

Additionally, GPCRs are a very diverse family of receptors, with over 800 members in the human genome. They can be classified into different subfamilies based on their structure and signaling pathways, such as Gs-coupled receptors, Gi/o-coupled receptors, and Gq-coupled receptors. Each subfamily has a unique mechanism of signaling and different downstream effects.

GPCRs are also known for their high degree of plasticity, which allows them to interact with multiple ligands and signal through different pathways. This feature makes them an attractive target for drug development as it increases the chances of finding new drug candidates that can modulate the receptor's activity in different ways.

In summary, G protein-coupled receptors (GPCRs) are a large family of transmembrane receptors that play a critical role in many physiological processes. They are activated by a wide variety of signaling molecules and initiate intracellular signaling pathways that lead to changes in the activity of various enzymes, ion channels, and other proteins within the cell. GPCRs are important targets for drug development and are involved in the development of many diseases. Understanding the structure and function of GPCRs is crucial for the discovery of new therapeutic agents and the development of treatments for various diseases.

One important aspect of GPCR signaling is that it can be modulated by several mechanisms, such as desensitization, internalization, and signaling bias.

Desensitization refers to the process by which GPCRs lose their responsiveness to ligands after prolonged stimulation, which allows the cell to regulate the duration and intensity of the signal. Internalization refers to the process by which GPCRs are endocytosed and brought into the cell, where they can be recycled or degraded. This mechanism can also modulate the duration and intensity of the signal.

Signaling bias refers to the ability of GPCRs to activate different intracellular signaling pathways depending on the ligand that binds to them. This allows GPCRs to have diverse physiological effects by activating different downstream signaling pathways.

Another important aspect of GPCR signaling is that it can be modulated by accessory proteins, such as arrestins, which can bind to the GPCRs and modulate their signaling. Arrestins can act as a "brake" on GPCR signaling by inhibiting the activity of G proteins and promoting the desensitization and internalization of GPCRs.

G protein-coupled receptors also play a critical role in the development of several diseases, such as cancer, diabetes, and mental health disorders. For example, mutations in GPCRs or their signaling pathways have been linked to the development of several types of cancer, such as breast cancer and prostate cancer. Similarly, dysfunction of GPCRs has been linked to the development of diabetes and metabolic disorders. Dysregulation of GPCR signaling in the brain has also been linked to the development of several mental health disorders, including depression and schizophrenia.

To conclude, G protein-coupled receptors are a large and diverse family of transmembrane receptors that play a critical role in many physiological processes. They are activated by a wide variety of signaling molecules and initiate intracellular signaling pathways that lead to changes in the activity of various enzymes, ion channels, and other proteins within the cell. GPCRs are also known for their high degree of plasticity, which allows them to interact with multiple ligands and signal through different pathways. They are important targets for drug development and are involved in the development of many diseases. Understanding the structure and function of GPCRs is crucial for the discovery of new therapeutic agents and the development of treatments for various diseases.

Another key aspect of GPCR signaling is that it can be modulated by post-translational modifications, such as phosphorylation, ubiquitination, and SUMOylation. These modifications can change the activity, localization, or stability of GPCRs and affect their signaling.

Phosphorylation is one of the most common post-translational modifications of GPCRs. It can occur on various residues of GPCRs and can be mediated by different kinases, such as protein kinase A, protein kinase C, and mitogen-activated protein kinases. Phosphorylation can modulate the activity, localization, or stability of GPCRs, and can also affect their interactions with other proteins.

Ubiquitination is another post-translational modification that can affect GPCR signaling. It is a process by which ubiquitin, a small protein, is covalently attached to other proteins. This process can target GPCRs for degradation by the proteasome, a cellular complex that degrades proteins. This can affect the levels and duration of GPCR signaling.

SUMOylation is a similar process to ubiquitination where a small protein called SUMO is covalently attached to other proteins. SUMOylation can also affect the localization, stability, or activity of GPCRs and modulate their signaling.

It is worth noting that these post-translational modifications can also be targeted by drugs. For example, some drugs can block the activity of kinases that phosphorylate GPCRs or deubiquitinating enzymes (DUBs) that remove ubiquitin from GPCRs. Therefore, understanding the role of post-translational modifications in GPCR signaling is important for the development of new drugs that can modulate GPCR activity in a specific and targeted way.

In summary, G protein-coupled receptors are a large and diverse family of transmembrane receptors that play a critical role in many physiological processes. They are activated by a wide variety of signaling molecules and initiate intracellular signaling pathways that lead to changes in the activity of various enzymes, ion channels, and other proteins within the cell. GPCRs are also known for their high degree of plasticity, which allows them to interact with multiple ligands and signal through different pathways. They are important targets for drug development and are involved in the development of many diseases. Understanding the structure and function of GPCRs, their post-translational modifications, and their interactions with accessory proteins is crucial for the discovery of new therapeutic agents and the development of treatments for various diseases.

Another important aspect of GPCR signaling is their ability to form oligomers. Oligomers are clusters of multiple GPCRs that associate together on the cell surface. Oligomerization can affect the activity, localization, and signaling of GPCRs. For example, some GPCRs can form homo-oligomers, which are clusters of the same type of GPCR, while others can form hetero-oligomers, which are clusters of different types of GPCRs. Oligomerization can also affect the specificity and sensitivity of GPCR signaling, as well as the ability of GPCRs to interact with other proteins and modulators.

GPCR oligomers have also been found to play important roles in disease. For example, certain GPCR oligomers have been shown to be involved in cancer and other diseases such as cardiovascular disease, diabetes, and neurological disorders. Understanding the molecular mechanisms of GPCR oligomerization and its role in disease is a promising area of research that could lead to the development of new therapeutic strategies for treating these diseases.

Another important aspect of GPCRs is their ability to interact with accessory proteins, also called scaffold proteins or adaptor proteins. These proteins can modulate the activity of GPCRs by affecting their localization, stability, or signaling. For example, some accessory proteins can act as positive regulators of GPCR signaling by recruiting intracellular signaling molecules to the activated GPCR, while others can act as negative regulators by inhibiting GPCR signaling.

Finally, it is worth noting that GPCRs are also subject to desensitization, which is the process by which GPCRs lose responsiveness to a ligand after prolonged exposure. Desensitization can occur via several mechanisms, such as internalization, phosphorylation, and dephosphorylation. Understanding the mechanisms of desensitization and its role in GPCR signaling is important for the development of drugs that can modulate GPCR activity in a specific and targeted way, as well as for the understanding of how GPCRs function in physiological and pathological conditions.

In summary, G protein-coupled receptors (GPCRs) are a diverse and important class of transmembrane receptors that play a critical role in many physiological processes. They are activated by a wide variety of signaling molecules and initiate intracellular signaling pathways that lead to changes in the activity of various enzymes, ion channels, and other proteins within the cell. GPCRs have a high degree of plasticity, which allows them to interact with multiple ligands and signal through different pathways. They can also form oligomers and interact with accessory proteins, which modulate their activity. Understanding the structure and function of GPCRs, their post-translational modifications, oligomerization, and interactions with accessory proteins is crucial for the discovery of new therapeutic agents and the development of treatments for various diseases.

Another important aspect of GPCRs is their ability to interact with G protein-coupled receptor kinases (GRKs) and arrestins. GRKs are a family of enzymes that phosphorylate GPCRs, leading to their desensitization and internalization. Arrestins are a family of proteins that bind to phosphorylated GPCRs and prevent them from interacting with G proteins. This process is known as "arrestin-mediated desensitization."

GRKs and arrestins play a crucial role in regulating GPCR signaling and are important for the normal functioning of the cell. They are also involved in various disease states, such as cancer, heart disease, and neurological disorders. Understanding the mechanisms of GRK and arrestin-mediated desensitization is important for the development of drugs that can modulate GPCR activity in a specific and targeted way.

Another important aspect of GPCRs is their ability to interact with intracellular signaling pathways. GPCRs can activate multiple intracellular signaling pathways, including the cAMP/PKA pathway, the phospholipase C/IP3 pathway, and the phospholipase A2 pathway. These pathways can lead to a variety of cellular responses, such as the regulation of ion channels, enzyme activity, and gene expression. Understanding the intracellular signaling pathways activated by GPCRs is important for understanding how GPCRs function in physiological and pathological conditions.

GPCRs are also subject to regulation by post-translational modifications, such as phosphorylation, glycosylation, and palmitoylation. These modifications can affect the activity, localization, and signaling of GPCRs. For example, phosphorylation can lead to desensitization, while palmitoylation can affect the localization of GPCRs. Understanding the mechanisms of post-translational modifications and their role in GPCR signaling is important for the development of drugs that can modulate GPCR activity in a specific and targeted way.

In summary, G protein-coupled receptors (GPCRs) are a diverse and important class of transmembrane receptors that play a critical role in many physiological processes. They are activated by a wide variety of signaling molecules, initiate intracellular signaling pathways, and are subject to various forms of regulation, such as desensitization, oligomerization, and interactions with accessory proteins and intracellular signaling pathways. Understanding the structure, function, and regulation of GPCRs is crucial for the discovery of new therapeutic agents and the development of treatments for various diseases.

Another important aspect of GPCRs is their diversity. GPCRs are classified into several different families, including the rhodopsin-like GPCRs, the secretin-like GPCRs, and the metabotropic glutamate receptors. Each family has a unique structure and is activated by different signaling molecules. For example, the rhodopsin-like GPCRs are activated by small molecules such as hormones and neurotransmitters, while the metabotropic glutamate receptors are activated by the neurotransmitter glutamate.

GPCRs can also form oligomers, or clusters of multiple GPCRs, which can lead to the modulation of GPCR activity. For example, GPCR oligomers can lead to the enhancement or inhibition of GPCR signaling, and can also play a role in the formation of signaling complexes. Understanding the mechanisms of GPCR oligomerization and its role in GPCR signaling is important for the development of drugs that can modulate GPCR activity in a specific and targeted way.

Another important aspect of GPCRs is their role in disease. Dysregulation of GPCR signaling has been linked to a wide range of diseases, such as cancer, diabetes, cardiovascular disease, and neurological disorders. For example, mutations in GPCRs have been linked to a number of inherited diseases, such as retinitis pigmentosa and cancer. In addition, GPCRs have been identified as potential therapeutic targets for a wide range of diseases, including cancer, diabetes, and mental health disorders.

Finally, GPCRs are also important for drug discovery. Many drugs currently on the market target GPCRs, and GPCRs continue to be an important area of research for the development of new therapeutic agents. For example, GPCRs are being studied as potential targets for the development of new cancer treatments, and GPCR-targeted drugs have also been identified as potential therapies for a wide range of neurological and psychiatric disorders.

In conclusion, G protein-coupled receptors (GPCRs) are a diverse and important class of transmembrane receptors that play a critical role in many physiological processes. They are activated by a wide variety of signaling molecules, initiate intracellular signaling pathways, and are subject to various forms of regulation, such as desensitization, oligomerization, and interactions with accessory proteins and intracellular signaling pathways. Understanding the structure, function, and regulation of GPCRs is crucial for the discovery of new therapeutic agents and the development of treatments for various diseases.

Another important aspect of GPCRs is their role in drug development. GPCRs are one of the most common targets for drug discovery and development, with approximately 40% of all drugs on the market thought to act through GPCRs. This is because GPCRs are involved in many physiological processes, and their dysregulation has been linked to a wide range of diseases.

Drugs that target GPCRs can work in different ways, such as by activating or inhibiting the receptor, or by modifying the signaling pathways downstream of the receptor. Some examples of drugs that target GPCRs include beta blockers, which are used to treat hypertension and heart disease by blocking the activity of the beta-adrenergic receptors, and selective serotonin reuptake inhibitors (SSRIs), which are used to treat depression by inhibiting the serotonin transporter (SERT) and increasing the availability of serotonin at the serotonin receptors.

The development of drugs that target GPCRs can be challenging, however, due to the diversity and complexity of GPCRs and their signaling pathways. For example, many GPCRs have multiple subtypes, each with unique properties and signaling pathways. Additionally, GPCRs can form oligomers and interact with other proteins, which can modulate their activity. To overcome these challenges, researchers use a variety of techniques, such as X-ray crystallography, computer simulations, and high-throughput screening, to gain a detailed understanding of the structure and function of GPCRs, and to identify new drug targets and potential drug candidates.

In conclusion, G protein-coupled receptors (GPCRs) are a diverse and important class of transmembrane receptors that play a critical role in many physiological processes, and are the target of many drugs. Understanding the structure, function, and regulation of GPCRs is crucial for the discovery of new therapeutic agents, and the development of treatments for various diseases. GPCRs are one of the most common targets for drug discovery and development, with approximately 40% of all drugs on the market thought to act through GPCRs. The development of drugs that target GPCRs can be challenging, but with advances in technology and research, new drugs can be developed to effectively target GPCRs and treat a wide range of diseases.

Another important aspect of GPCRs is the concept of "biased agonism." Biased agonism refers to the ability of different ligands (molecules that bind to a receptor) to selectively activate different signaling pathways downstream of a GPCR. This means that different ligands can have different effects on the cell, even though they bind to the same receptor. Biased agonism can be beneficial because it allows for the development of drugs that selectively target specific signaling pathways, thereby reducing the risk of side effects.

One example of biased agonism is the beta-2 adrenergic receptor (beta-2AR), which is a GPCR that is activated by epinephrine and norepinephrine. Different ligands that bind to the beta-2AR can selectively activate different downstream signaling pathways, such as Gs or Gq. This can lead to different physiological effects, such as the relaxation of smooth muscle or the activation of intracellular enzymes.

Another example of biased agonism is the serotonin 5-HT2A receptor, which is a GPCR that is activated by serotonin. Different ligands that bind to the 5-HT2A receptor can selectively activate different downstream signaling pathways, such as phosphoinositide 3-kinase (PI3K) or mitogen-activated protein kinase (MAPK). This can lead to different physiological effects, such as the regulation of cell growth or the modulation of synaptic transmission.

The concept of biased agonism opens up new opportunities for the development of drugs that selectively target specific signaling pathways, and thereby reduce the risk of side effects. Biased agonism can also help to explain why different drugs that target the same receptor can have different effects, and can help to identify new drug targets and potential drug candidates.

In conclusion, G protein-coupled receptors (GPCRs) are a diverse and important class of transmembrane receptors that play a critical role in many physiological processes, and are the target of many drugs. Understanding the structure, function, and regulation of GPCRs is crucial for the discovery of new therapeutic agents, and the development of treatments for various diseases. GPCRs are one of the most common targets for drug discovery and development, with approximately 40% of all drugs on the market thought to act through GPCRs. The development of drugs that target GPCRs can be challenging, but with advances in technology and research, new drugs can be developed to effectively target GPCRs and treat a wide range of diseases. The concept of biased agonism opens up new opportunities for the development of drugs that selectively target specific signaling pathways, and thereby reduce the risk of side effects.

Tyrosin kinase receptor

Tyrosine kinase receptors are a type of transmembrane receptor that are activated by extracellular signaling molecules, such as growth factors and hormones. When activated, these receptors phosphorylate tyrosine residues on intracellular proteins, which can lead to the activation of downstream signaling pathways.

Tyrosine kinase receptors are important because they play a key role in many physiological processes, including cell growth, differentiation, and survival. Dysregulation of tyrosine kinase receptor signaling has been implicated in the development of various diseases, including cancer, autoimmune disorders, and cardiovascular disease.

There are several different types of tyrosine kinase receptors, including epidermal growth factor receptor (EGFR), insulin receptor, and vascular endothelial growth factor receptor (VEGFR). These receptors are important targets for the development of therapeutic drugs, particularly in the treatment of cancer. Tyrosine kinase inhibitors, which block the activity of these receptors, have been developed and are used as chemotherapy agents in the treatment of various types of cancer.

Tyrosine kinase inhibitors (TKIs) are a class of drugs that target tyrosine kinase receptors, specifically the intracellular tyrosine kinase domains of these receptors. TKIs are used to treat a variety of cancers, including lung, breast, and colon cancer. They work by binding to the tyrosine kinase domain of the receptor, preventing it from phosphorylating tyrosine residues and activating downstream signaling pathways. This can inhibit cell growth and proliferation, ultimately leading to cell death.

There are several different types of TKIs, including small molecule TKIs and monoclonal antibodies. Small molecule TKIs, such as gefitinib and erlotinib, target specific receptors, such as EGFR. Monoclonal antibodies, such as cetuximab and panitumumab, bind to the extracellular domain of the receptor and prevent ligand binding, which is necessary for receptor activation.

While TKIs have been successful in treating cancer, they can also have side effects and may not be effective in all patients. Additionally, some cancers can develop resistance to TKIs through mutations in the tyrosine kinase domain of the receptor or through activation of alternative signaling pathways. Research is ongoing to develop new TKIs and combination therapies to overcome these challenges.

Tyrosine kinase receptors (TKRs) are a large family of transmembrane proteins that are activated by binding of extracellular ligands, such as growth factors, hormones and cytokines. They play a critical role in cell growth, differentiation, and survival, as well as in the development of various diseases including cancer, autoimmune disorders, and cardiovascular disease.

When TKRs are activated, they undergo a conformational change that brings the intracellular tyrosine kinase domains of the receptor into close proximity, allowing them to phosphorylate tyrosine residues on intracellular proteins. These phosphorylated tyrosines act as binding sites for proteins containing SH2 domains, which in turn can activate downstream signaling pathways involved in cell growth, survival, and proliferation.

EGFR, Insulin receptor, and VEGFR are examples of TKRs. EGFR is a receptor for epidermal growth factor and is overexpressed in many types of cancer, including lung, breast, and colon cancer. Insulin receptor is activated by insulin and is involved in glucose metabolism and insulin signaling. VEGF is a growth factor that promotes angiogenesis and is involved in the development of cancer and other diseases.

Tyrosine kinase inhibitors (TKIs) are drugs that target TKRs by binding to the intracellular tyrosine kinase domains of these receptors. TKIs are used to treat a variety of cancers, including lung, breast, and colon cancer. They work by binding to the tyrosine kinase domain of the receptor, preventing it from phosphorylating tyrosine residues and activating downstream signaling pathways. This can inhibit cell growth and proliferation, ultimately leading to cell death.

There are two main types of TKIs: small molecule TKIs and monoclonal antibodies. Small molecule TKIs, such as gefitinib and erlotinib, are orally administered drugs that target specific receptors, such as EGFR. Monoclonal antibodies, such as cetuximab and panitumumab, are injectable drugs that bind to the extracellular domain of the receptor and prevent ligand binding, which is necessary for receptor activation.

While TKIs have been successful in treating cancer, they can also have side effects and may not be effective in all patients. Additionally, some cancers can develop resistance to TKIs through mutations in the tyrosine kinase domain of the receptor or through activation of alternative signaling pathways. Research is ongoing to develop new TKIs and combination therapies to overcome these challenges.

Tyrosine kinase receptors (TKRs) are a large family of transmembrane proteins that are activated by binding of extracellular ligands, such as growth factors, hormones, and cytokines. They play a critical role in cell growth, differentiation, and survival, as well as in the development of various diseases including cancer, autoimmune disorders, and cardiovascular disease.

When TKRs are activated, they undergo a conformational change that brings the intracellular tyrosine kinase domains of the receptor into close proximity, allowing them to phosphorylate tyrosine residues on intracellular proteins. These phosphorylated tyrosines act as binding sites for proteins containing SH2 domains, which in turn can activate downstream signaling pathways involved in cell growth, survival, and proliferation.

EGFR, Insulin receptor, and VEGFR are examples of TKRs. EGFR is a receptor for epidermal growth factor and is overexpressed in many types of cancer, including lung, breast, and colon cancer. Insulin receptor is activated by insulin and is involved in glucose metabolism and insulin signaling. VEGF is a growth factor that promotes angiogenesis and is involved in the development of cancer and other diseases.

Tyrosine kinase inhibitors (TKIs) are drugs that target TKRs by binding to the intracellular tyrosine kinase domains of these receptors. TKIs are used to treat a variety of cancers, including lung, breast, and colon cancer. They work by binding to the tyrosine kinase domain of the receptor, preventing it from phosphorylating tyrosine residues and activating downstream signaling pathways. This can inhibit cell growth and proliferation, ultimately leading to cell death.

There are two main types of TKIs: small molecule TKIs and monoclonal antibodies. Small molecule TKIs, such as gefitinib and erlotinib, are orally administered drugs that target specific receptors, such as EGFR. Monoclonal antibodies, such as cetuximab and panitumumab, are injectable drugs that bind to the extracellular domain of the receptor and prevent ligand binding, which is necessary for receptor activation.

While TKIs have been successful in treating cancer, they can also have side effects and may not be effective in all patients. Additionally, some cancers can develop resistance to TKIs through mutations in the tyrosine kinase domain of the receptor or through activation of alternative signaling pathways. Research is ongoing to develop new TKIs and combination therapies to overcome these challenges. There are also newer therapies like dual inhibitors, allosteric inhibitors, and bispecific antibodies have been developed or are under development as TKI to overcome the resistance and improve the efficacy.

The precise mechanisms of TKR-mediated signaling and the downstream pathways that are activated can vary depending on the specific receptor and the context in which it is activated. However, there are some general principles that are common to most TKRs.

When a TKR is activated by binding of its ligand, the intracellular tyrosine kinase domains of the receptor come into close proximity, allowing them to phosphorylate tyrosine residues on intracellular proteins. These phosphorylated tyrosines act as binding sites for proteins containing SH2 domains, which in turn can activate downstream signaling pathways involved in cell growth, survival, and proliferation.

One of the most well-studied downstream signaling pathways activated by TKRs is the RAS-RAF-MEK-ERK pathway, which is involved in the regulation of cell proliferation and survival. Activation of this pathway leads to the phosphorylation and activation of the RAS protein, which in turn activates the RAF protein. Activated RAF then phosphorylates and activates the MEK protein, which in turn phosphorylates and activates the ERK protein. Activated

ERK can then enter the nucleus and phosphorylate transcription factors, which can lead to the activation of genes involved in cell growth and proliferation.

Another important downstream signaling pathway activated by TKRs is the PI3K-Akt pathway, which is involved in the regulation of cell survival. Activation of this pathway leads to the activation of the PI3K protein, which in turn phosphorylates and activates the Akt protein. Activated Akt can then enter the nucleus and phosphorylate transcription factors, which can lead to the activation of genes involved in cell survival.

Other downstream signaling pathways activated by TKRs include the JAK-STAT pathway, the PLC-γ pathway, and the SRC family kinase pathway.

It's also important to note that TKRs can also recruit other signaling molecules to the receptor to form a signaling complex, which in turn activates downstream signaling pathways. For example, many TKRs recruit and activate the GRB2-SOS complex, which leads to the activation of the RAS-RAF-MEK-ERK pathway.

In addition, TKRs can also be regulated by negative feedback mechanisms that can limit or inhibit their activity. For example, phosphatases can dephosphorylate and inactivate TKRs, or other proteins can bind to and inhibit the activity of TKRs.

Overall, TKRs are involved in a complex web of signaling pathways that are tightly regulated to control cell growth, differentiation, and survival. Dysregulation of these pathways can lead to the development of diseases such as cancer, autoimmune disorders, and cardiovascular disease. In the future, a greater understanding of the signaling pathways activated by TKRs and the mechanisms of resistance to TKIs may lead to the development of more effective therapies for these diseases.

Nuclear Receptor

Nuclear receptors are a class of proteins that act as transcription factors within the cell nucleus. They are activated by ligands, such as hormones, and bind to specific DNA sequences in the promoter region of target genes to regulate their expression.

There are several different types of nuclear receptors, including estrogen receptors, androgen receptors, and thyroid hormone receptors. These receptors are important in the regulation of many physiological processes, including metabolism, development, and the stress response. Dysregulation of nuclear receptor signaling has been implicated in the development of various diseases, including cancer, metabolic disorders, and neurological disorders.

Nuclear receptors are also important because they are the target of many drugs, including hormone replacement therapy drugs and cholesterol-lowering drugs. In fact, around 25% of all drugs on the market are thought to work by targeting nuclear receptors. This makes nuclear receptors an important area of research in the development of new therapeutic agent.

Nuclear receptors are a large family of transcription factors that play an important role in regulating gene expression in response to various physiological signals. These receptors are activated by specific ligands, such as hormones and other small molecules, and bind to specific DNA sequences in the promoter region of target genes to control their expression. Different types of nuclear receptors include estrogen receptors, androgen receptors, and thyroid hormone receptors, each of which plays a key role in different physiological processes such as metabolism, development, and the stress response. Dysregulation of nuclear receptor signaling has been linked to the development of a wide range of diseases including cancer, metabolic disorders, and neurological disorders. Additionally, nuclear receptors are also an important target for drug development, with around 25% of all drugs on the market thought to work by targeting these receptors. Therefore, the study of nuclear receptors continues to be an active area of research with the potential to inform the development of new therapeutic agents.

Nuclear receptors are a diverse family of transcription factors that are activated by specific ligands, such as hormones and other small molecules, to control gene expression. They consist of several structural domains, including a ligand-binding domain, a DNA-binding domain, and a transactivation domain. The ligand-binding domain is responsible for binding to the activating ligand, while the DNA-binding domain binds to specific DNA sequences in the promoter region of target genes. The transactivation domain then regulates the expression of these target genes.

There are several different types of nuclear receptors, including steroid hormone receptors (such as estrogen receptors, androgen receptors, and progesterone receptors), thyroid hormone receptors, retinoic acid receptors, and vitamin D receptors. Each type of nuclear receptor is activated by a specific ligand and regulates the expression of a different set of target genes.

Dysregulation of nuclear receptor signaling has been linked to various diseases, including cancer, metabolic disorders, and neurological disorders. For example, mutations in estrogen receptors have been linked to breast cancer, and mutations in androgen receptors have been linked to prostate cancer. Similarly, mutations in thyroid hormone receptors have been linked to thyroid cancer.

Nuclear receptors are also important drug targets. Many drugs, including hormone replacement therapy drugs and cholesterol-lowering drugs, work by targeting nuclear receptors. Researchers continue to investigate the potential of targeting nuclear receptors as a means of developing new therapeutics for a wide range of diseases.

In addition, since nuclear receptors are activated by specific ligands, it's possible to develop drugs that can mimic or block the action of these ligands, making them useful for treating various disorders. Some examples of drugs that target nuclear receptors include Tamoxifen (an antagonist of estrogen receptor) used to treat breast cancer and Raloxifene (an agonist of estrogen receptor) used to prevent osteoporosis.

Overall, Nuclear receptors play a crucial role in regulating gene expression, and their importance in maintaining normal physiology and their involvement in various diseases make them an important area of research in the field of molecular biology and pharmacology.

In addition to their role in regulating gene expression and their potential as drug targets, nuclear receptors also play a role in various other physiological processes. For example, steroid hormone receptors such as estrogen and androgen receptors are important for the development and maintenance of reproductive tissues and secondary sexual characteristics. Thyroid hormone receptors are crucial for the regulation of metabolism, and vitamin D receptors play a key role in maintaining bone health.

Nuclear receptors also play a role in the body's response to stress. Some nuclear receptors, such as the glucocorticoid receptor, are activated in response to stress and play a role in the body's stress response by regulating the expression of genes involved in inflammation and glucose metabolism.

Moreover, Nuclear receptors are also involved in the maintenance of energy balance and the regulation of body weight. For example, Peroxisome proliferator-activated receptors (PPARs) are activated by fatty acids and play a role in lipid metabolism, glucose homeostasis, and insulin sensitivity.

In conclusion, Nuclear receptors are a diverse family of transcription factors that play a crucial role in regulating gene expression in response to various physiological signals. They are activated by specific ligands and bind to specific DNA sequences in the promoter region of target genes to control their expression. Nuclear receptors are involved in many physiological processes, including metabolism, development, and the stress response. Dysregulation of nuclear receptor signaling has been linked to various diseases, including cancer, metabolic disorders, and neurological disorders. Nuclear receptors are also important drug targets, and the study of these receptors continues to be an active area of research with the potential to inform the development of new therapeutic agents.

Secondary messenger

Secondary messengers are small, diffusible molecules that are produced and used within cells to transmit signals from extracellular signaling molecules to intracellular targets. They are called "secondary" because they are downstream of primary signaling molecules, which can include hormones, neurotransmitters, and growth factors.

Secondary messengers play a key role in signal transduction, the process by which cells receive and respond to signals from their environment. They are involved in many essential physiological processes, including immune function, cardiovascular function, and the regulation of mood, appetite, and sleep. Dysregulation of secondary messenger signaling has been implicated in the development of various diseases, including cancer, diabetes, and mental health disorders.

There are several different types of secondary messengers, including cyclic AMP (cAMP), cyclic GMP (cGMP), and inositol triphosphate (IP3). Each type of secondary messenger is activated by specific signaling pathways and can lead to the activation of specific intracellular targets, such as enzymes, ion channels, and transcription factors

For example, cAMP is activated by the adenylyl cyclase enzyme and leads to the activation of protein kinase A (PKA), which can phosphorylate a variety of intracellular proteins, leading to changes in gene expression and other cellular responses. IP3 is activated by phospholipase C (PLC) and leads to the release of intracellular calcium stores, which can also activate various intracellular targets.

In addition to these well-known secondary messengers, there are also many other small molecules that can act as secondary messengers, including nitric oxide (NO), diacylglycerol (DAG), and sphingosine-1-phosphate (S1P). These messengers are activated by different signaling pathways and can lead to a wide variety of cellular responses, depending on the specific context and the cell type in question. Overall, secondary messengers play a critical role in the complex network of signaling pathways that allow cells to respond to their environment and coordinate their behavior with other cells in the body.

Another important aspect of secondary messenger signaling is that it can be regulated by various means, including the action of enzymes that degrade the secondary messenger or by the action of enzymes that inactivate the signaling pathways that activate them. This allows cells to fine-tune their responses to signaling molecules and limit over-activation of signaling pathways, which can lead to cell damage or disease. Additionally, some secondary messengers can also act in a feedback loop to inhibit the signaling pathways that activated them. This can provide an additional level of control over the cell's response to a signal.

Overall, secondary messengers are a fundamental aspect of cell signaling and play a key role in the regulation of many physiological processes. Understanding the mechanisms of secondary messenger signaling and the ways in which it can be regulated is crucial for understanding the underlying causes of various diseases and for developing effective therapies.

Another important aspect of secondary messenger signaling is that it can be modulated by various means, such as by the action of enzymes that degrade the secondary messenger or by the action of enzymes that inactivate the signaling pathways that activate them. This allows cells to fine-tune their responses to signaling molecules and limit over-activation of signaling pathways, which can lead to cell damage or disease. Additionally, some secondary messengers can also act in a feedback loop to inhibit the signaling pathways that activated them. This can provide an additional level of control over the cell's response to a signal.

Research in the field of secondary messenger signaling has led to the development of drugs that target specific signaling pathways and secondary messengers, which can be used to treat a variety of diseases. For example, drugs that target cAMP-dependent PKA signaling have been developed for the treatment of heart disease, and drugs that target NO signaling have been developed for the treatment of erectile dysfunction.

In summary, secondary messengers play a critical role in the complex network of signaling pathways that allow cells to respond to their environment and coordinate their behavior with other cells in the body. Understanding the mechanisms of secondary messenger signaling and the ways in which it can be regulated is crucial for understanding the underlying causes of various diseases and for developing effective therapies.

Another important aspect of secondary messenger signaling is that it can be modulated by various means, such as by the action of enzymes that degrade the secondary messenger or by the action of enzymes that inactivate the signaling pathways that activate them. This allows cells to fine-tune their responses to signaling molecules and limit over-activation of signaling pathways, which can lead to cell damage or disease. Additionally, some secondary messengers can also act in a feedback loop to inhibit the signaling pathways that activated them. This can provide an additional level of control over the cell's response to a signal.

Research in the field of secondary messenger signaling has led to the development of drugs that target specific signaling pathways and secondary messengers, which can be used to treat a variety of diseases. For example, drugs that target cAMP-dependent PKA signaling have been developed for the treatment of heart disease, and drugs that target NO signaling have been developed for the treatment of erectile dysfunction.

In summary, secondary messengers play a critical role in the complex network of signaling pathways that allow cells to respond to their environment and coordinate their behavior with other cells in the body. Understanding the mechanisms of secondary messenger signaling and the ways in which it can be regulated is crucial for understanding the underlying causes of various diseases and for developing effective therapies. It's also important to mention that the study of these messengers have a wide range of applications in the field of pharmacology, where the manipulation of these messengers can be used to target specific diseases and conditions.

Cyclic AMP (cAMP)

Cyclic AMP (cAMP) is a secondary messenger that is involved in a wide range of physiological processes. It is produced by the enzyme adenylate cyclase, which is activated by signaling molecules such as hormones and neurotransmitters. cAMP acts as a signaling molecule by activating protein kinase A (PKA), which in turn can phosphorylate a variety of intracellular proteins.

cAMP is important in the regulation of many physiological processes, including metabolism, immune function, and cardiovascular function. It is also involved in the regulation of gene expression and plays a role in the development of long-term memories. Dysregulation of cAMP signaling has been implicated in the development of various diseases, including cancer, diabetes, and mental health disorders.

cAMP is also an important target for the development of therapeutic drugs. For example, drugs that increase cAMP levels, such as phosphodiesterase inhibitors, are used to treat cardiovascular disorders and asthma. On the other hand, drugs that decrease cAMP levels, such as adenylate cyclase inhibitors, are used to treat conditions such as hypertension and glaucoma.

In addition to its role in intracellular signaling, cAMP also plays a key role in the regulation of the activity of ion channels. For example, it can activate the opening of potassium channels, leading to hyperpolarization of cells and inhibition of neurotransmitter release. Similarly, cAMP can also activate the opening of chloride channels, leading to inhibition of neurotransmitter release.

cAMP is also involved in the regulation of the activity of enzymes such as phosphodiesterases (PDEs) which help to control the levels of cAMP in cells. PDEs catalyze the hydrolysis of cAMP to 5'-AMP, thereby decreasing the intracellular levels of cAMP.

Overall, cAMP is a versatile and important signaling molecule that plays a crucial role in many physiological processes and is a target for the development of therapeutic drugs. Dysregulation of cAMP signaling can lead to various diseases, highlighting the importance of understanding the mechanisms of cAMP signaling in normal physiology and pathology.

Another interesting aspect of cAMP signaling is its ability to interact with other signaling pathways. For example, cAMP can interact with the phosphoinositide 3-kinase (PI3K) pathway, which is a key signaling pathway involved in cell growth and survival. cAMP can also interact with the mitogen-activated protein kinase (MAPK) pathway, which is involved in cell proliferation, differentiation, and survival.

cAMP can also play a role in the regulation of cell motility and migration. For example, in the case of cancer cells, cAMP signaling can be involved in the regulation of cell migration, invasion and metastasis.

Overall, cAMP is a versatile signaling molecule that plays a crucial role in many physiological processes and its dysregulation can lead to various diseases. Understanding the mechanisms of cAMP signaling in normal physiology and pathology is important for the development of new therapeutic strategies.

It is also worth noting that cAMP is not the only secondary messenger, there are others such as cGMP, IP3, and DAG and they all play important roles in various physiological processes and are also target for therapeutic drug development.

In addition to its intracellular signaling roles, cAMP also plays a role in the regulation of extracellular processes. For example, cAMP can act as a signaling molecule in the regulation of immune responses by modulating the activity of immune cells such as T cells and B cells. cAMP can also play a role in the regulation of inflammation by modulating the activity of inflammatory cells such as macrophages and neutrophils.

cAMP is also involved in the regulation of hormone secretion by cells of the endocrine system such as the pancreas and the adrenal glands. For example, cAMP is involved in the regulation of insulin and glucagon secretion by the pancreas, and adrenaline and noradrenaline secretion by the adrenal glands.

Furthermore, cAMP is also involved in the regulation of smooth muscle contraction and relaxation. For example, cAMP is involved in the regulation of smooth muscle contraction in the airway and blood vessels, and plays a role in the regulation of blood pressure and blood flow.

In summary, cAMP is a versatile signaling molecule that plays a crucial role in the regulation of a wide range of physiological processes, both intracellular and extracellular. Dysregulation of cAMP signaling can lead to various diseases, highlighting the importance of understanding the mechanisms of cAMP signaling in normal physiology and pathology for the development of new therapeutic strategies.

Another important aspect of cAMP signaling is its role in the regulation of cell growth and differentiation. cAMP can promote cell proliferation and differentiation by activating intracellular signaling pathways that regulate cell cycle progression, such as the MAPK pathway and the PI3K pathway.

cAMP can also play a role in the regulation of stem cell differentiation. For example, in the case of neural stem cells, cAMP can promote the differentiation of stem cells into neurons, by activating intracellular signaling pathways that regulate cell cycle progression and gene expression.

cAMP is also involved in the regulation of cell death, or apoptosis. For example, in the case of cancer cells, cAMP can promote apoptosis by activating intracellular signaling pathways that regulate cell death, such as the caspase cascade.

In addition, cAMP is also involved in the regulation of cellular stress responses. For example, cAMP can promote the activation of the heat shock response by activating intracellular signaling pathways that regulate the expression of heat shock proteins.

Overall, cAMP plays a crucial role in the regulation of cell growth, differentiation, cell death and cellular stress response. Understanding the mechanisms of cAMP signaling in these processes can provide new insights into the development of therapeutic strategies for the treatment of diseases related to cell growth and differentiation such as cancer, degenerative diseases and aging.

Cyclic GMP (cGMP)

Cyclic GMP (cGMP) is a secondary messenger that is involved in a wide range of physiological processes. It is produced by the enzyme guanylate cyclase, which is activated by signaling molecules such as hormones and neurotransmitters. cGMP acts as a signaling molecule by activating protein kinase G (PKG), which in turn can phosphorylate a variety of intracellular proteins.

cGMP is important in the regulation of many physiological processes, including blood pressure, smooth muscle relaxation, and platelet aggregation. It is also involved in the regulation of gene expression and plays a role in the development of long-term memories. Dysregulation of cGMP signaling has been implicated in the development of various diseases, including cardiovascular disorders and cancer.

cGMP is also an important target for the development of therapeutic drugs. For example, drugs that increase cGMP levels, such as phosphodiesterase inhibitors, are used to treat cardiovascular disorders and male erectile dysfunction. On the other hand, drugs that decrease cGMP levels, such as guanylate cyclase inhibitors, are used to treat conditions such as hypertension and glaucoma.

cGMP signaling is also involved in the regulation of neurotransmission in the central nervous system. In particular, cGMP is involved in the regulation of the activity of the neurotransmitter, GABA, which is important for the regulation of anxiety and seizure activity.

In addition to its role in physiological processes, cGMP is also involved in the regulation of cell growth and proliferation. Elevated levels of cGMP have been observed in various types of cancer, and it is thought that this may contribute to the development and progression of these diseases.

Overall, cGMP is a critical signaling molecule that plays a key role in regulating various physiological processes in the body. Its dysregulation has been linked to a number of diseases and disorders, making it an important target for the development of therapeutic drugs.

Another important aspect of cGMP is its role in the regulation of cell apoptosis (programmed cell death). Elevated levels of cGMP have been linked to increased cell survival and decreased apoptosis, while decreased levels of cGMP are linked to increased apoptosis. This makes cGMP an important target for the development of drugs for cancer treatment and other diseases where apoptosis plays a role.

cGMP is also involved in the regulation of insulin secretion and glucose metabolism in the pancreas. In particular, cGMP has been shown to stimulate insulin secretion and play a role in the regulation of glucose homeostasis. This makes cGMP an important target for the development of drugs for diabetes treatment.

In conclusion, cGMP is a versatile and critical signaling molecule that plays a role in a wide range of physiological processes, including blood pressure regulation, smooth muscle relaxation, platelet aggregation, gene expression, neurotransmission, cell growth, and apoptosis. Dysregulation of cGMP signaling has been linked to various diseases, making it a promising target for the development of therapeutic drugs.

Another aspect of cGMP is its role in the regulation of the immune system. cGMP has been shown to play a role in the regulation of the activity of immune cells, such as T-lymphocytes and macrophages. This makes cGMP an important target for the development of drugs for immune-related disorders, such as allergies, autoimmune diseases, and cancer immunotherapy.

cGMP also plays a role in the regulation of the circadian rhythm, the internal 24-hour "clock" that regulates many physiological processes in the body. cGMP has been shown to be involved in the regulation of the activity of clock genes, which control the circadian rhythm. This makes cGMP an important target for the development of drugs for circadian rhythm-related disorders, such as insomnia, jet lag, and shift work disorder.

In addition, cGMP is involved in the regulation of the sleep-wake cycle, it has been shown to play a role in the regulation of the activity of neurotransmitters such as dopamine and serotonin, which are involved in the regulation of mood, emotion, and sleep.

In summary, cGMP is a multifaceted signaling molecule with diverse physiological roles in the body such as regulating the immune system, circadian rhythm, sleep-wake cycle, and glucose metabolism, making it a promising target for the development of therapeutic drugs for a wide range of diseases and disorders.

Another area where cGMP plays a role is in the field of neuroscience. cGMP has been shown to be involved in synaptic plasticity, the ability of the brain to change and adapt in response to new information and experiences. It has been found that cGMP is involved in the regulation of long-term potentiation (LTP) and long-term depression (LTD), which are key mechanisms underlying learning and memory. This makes cGMP an important target for the development of drugs for cognitive disorders such as Alzheimer's disease and other forms of dementia.

In the field of ophthalmology, cGMP is also an important target for the treatment of eye diseases. For example, drugs that increase cGMP levels, such as phosphodiesterase inhibitors, are used to treat age-related macular degeneration (AMD) and retinitis pigmentosa (RP). These conditions are caused by the degeneration of the light-sensitive cells in the retina, which leads to progressive vision loss. cGMP is also involved in the regulation of the intraocular pressure and that is why guanylate cyclase inhibitors have been used to treat glaucoma.

In summary, cGMP is a versatile signaling molecule that plays a critical role in regulating a wide range of physiological processes in the body. Its dysregulation has been linked to various diseases, making it an important target for the development of therapeutic drugs for a wide range of diseases and disorders, including cardiovascular disorders, cancer, diabetes, immune-related disorders, circadian rhythm-related disorders, cognitive disorders, and eye diseases.

Another area where cGMP plays a role is in the field of reproductive health. cGMP is involved in the regulation of sperm function and fertilization. For example, cGMP has been shown to be involved in the regulation of sperm motility and the acrosome reaction, which is necessary for sperm to penetrate and fertilize the egg. Drugs that increase cGMP levels, such as phosphodiesterase inhibitors, have been used to treat male infertility caused by low sperm motility.

In the field of sexual health, cGMP is also an important target for the treatment of erectile dysfunction. The drugs that increase cGMP levels, such as phosphodiesterase inhibitors, are used to treat erectile dysfunction by increasing blood flow to the penis. This helps to achieve and maintain an erection during sexual activity.

In the field of women's health, cGMP is also involved in the regulation of the menstrual cycle. cGMP has been shown to be involved in the regulation of ovulation and the contraction of the uterus during childbirth. Dysregulation of cGMP signaling has been linked to various menstrual cycle-related disorders such as polycystic ovary syndrome (PCOS) and endometriosis.

In summary, cGMP plays a critical role in the regulation of many physiological processes related to reproductive health, including sperm function, fertilization, sexual function, ovulation, and menstrual cycle. Its dysregulation has been linked to various reproductive health-related disorders making it an important target for the development of therapeutic drugs.

As a final note, it is worth mentioning that cGMP is an important target for the development of diagnostic tools as well. For example, in the field of cardiovascular disease, cGMP levels can be measured in blood samples to assess the severity of the disease and to monitor the effectiveness of treatment. Similarly, in the field of sexual dysfunction, cGMP levels can be measured in the corpus cavernosum (erectile tissue in the penis) to assess the erectile function.

In conclusion, cGMP is a versatile signaling molecule that plays a critical role in regulating a wide range of physiological processes in the body. Its dysregulation has been linked to various diseases, making it an important target for the development of therapeutic drugs for a wide range of diseases and disorders, including cardiovascular disorders, cancer, diabetes, immune-related disorders, circadian rhythm-related disorders, cognitive disorders, eye diseases, reproductive health-related disorders and diagnostic tools. The research in this field is ongoing and more discoveries are expected in the future.

calcium ion

Calcium ions (Ca2+) are important intracellular signaling molecules that play a role in many physiological processes. They are involved in muscle contraction, nerve impulse transmission, hormone secretion, and the regulation of gene expression.

Calcium ions are stored in the endoplasmic reticulum (ER) and the mitochondria, and their levels are tightly regulated in cells. They can be released from these storage sites in response to various stimuli, including hormones, neurotransmitters, and mechanical stress. The release of calcium ions can then trigger various downstream signaling pathways, such as the activation of protein kinases and transcription factors.

Calcium ions are also important in the regulation of ion channels, which are proteins that allow ions to flow in and out of cells. The activity of many types of ion channels is controlled by the concentration of calcium ions in the cell.

Dysregulation of calcium ion signaling has been implicated in the development of various diseases, including cardiovascular disorders, neurodegenerative diseases, and cancer. Calcium ions are also an important target for the development of therapeutic drugs, particularly in the treatment of hypertension and bone disorders.

Additionally, Calcium ions play a crucial role in bone formation and maintenance. They are essential for the development and mineralization of bone, and are involved in the process of bone remodeling. A deficiency in calcium intake can lead to osteoporosis, a condition characterized by weak and brittle bones. Calcium ions also play a role in blood coagulation, by activating enzymes that lead to the formation of a blood clot.

Also, Calcium ions are important for the proper functioning of the heart. They are involved in the contraction of heart muscle cells, and also play a role in the electrical activity of the heart. Abnormalities in calcium ion signaling have been linked to conditions such as hypertension and arrhythmias.

Overall, Calcium ions are essential for the proper functioning of many physiological processes in the body. They are involved in cell signaling, muscle contraction, hormone secretion, and the regulation of gene expression, and play a crucial role in the development and maintenance of healthy bones and proper heart function. Dysregulation of calcium ion signaling has been linked to various diseases, and calcium ions are an important target for the development of therapeutic drugs.

Calcium ions are also important for the functioning of the immune system. They are involved in the activation of immune cells, such as T-cells and B-cells, and play a role in the process of inflammation. Additionally, calcium ions are essential for the proper functioning of the nervous system. They are involved in the transmission of nerve impulses and are important for the development and function of synapses, the structures that allow nerve cells to communicate with each other.

Calcium ions are also important for the functioning of the digestive system. They play a role in the contraction of smooth muscle cells in the gut, and are necessary for the absorption of nutrients in the small intestine. Calcium ions also have a role in the regulation of blood pressure and blood sugar levels.

In summary, Calcium ions are a key component in many physiological processes, including muscle contraction, nerve impulse transmission, hormone secretion, and the regulation of gene expression. They play a crucial role in the development and maintenance of healthy bones, proper heart function, immune system, nervous system, and digestive system. Dysregulation of calcium ion signaling has been linked to various diseases and are an important target for the development of therapeutic drugs.

Another important role of calcium ions is in the regulation of cell growth and division. Calcium ions act as intracellular messengers to regulate the activity of enzymes and proteins that are involved in cell growth, differentiation and apoptosis. They also play a role in the regulation of cell signaling pathways, such as the MAPK/ERK pathway, which is involved in cell growth and survival.

Calcium ions also have an important role in the process of cell adhesion. They are involved in the binding of cells to the extracellular matrix and other cells, which is important for the formation of tissues and organs.

In addition to their roles in physiological processes, calcium ions also have important industrial and technological applications. Calcium ions are used in the production of cement, glass and ceramics, and are used as a coagulant in the purification of water and the treatment of sewage. They are also used as a dietary supplement for humans and animals, and are added to many foods and beverages to increase their calcium content.

In conclusion, Calcium ions are a versatile and important intracellular messenger that plays a role in many physiological processes, including muscle contraction, nerve impulse transmission, hormone secretion, and the regulation of gene expression. They also play important roles in the regulation of cell growth and division, cell adhesion and have many industrial and technological applications. They are essential for the proper functioning of many physiological processes in the body and their dysregulation has been linked to various diseases.

As you may have noticed, Calcium ions have a wide range of functions in the body and are essential for proper cellular physiology. They play a vital role in the maintenance of healthy bones and teeth, and are important for the proper functioning of the heart, blood vessels, muscles, and nerves. Moreover, Calcium ions are important for the proper functioning of the immune system and the digestive system, and they also play a role in the regulation of blood pressure and blood sugar levels.

It's important to note that, Calcium ions are needed in sufficient amounts in order to perform all these functions. The recommended daily intake of calcium for adults is about 1000-1300 mg per day, depending on age and sex. However, in some cases, as a result of certain medical conditions, dietary deficiencies or other factors, the body may not be able to absorb or retain enough calcium, which can lead to calcium deficiency disorders such as osteoporosis.

In conclusion, Calcium ions are essential for proper cellular physiology and are involved in a wide range of physiological processes. They play a vital role in the maintenance of healthy bones and teeth, and are important for the proper functioning of the heart, blood vessels, muscles, and nerves, immune system and the digestive system, and also play a role in the regulation of blood pressure and blood sugar levels. It's important to have sufficient calcium intake to maintain the balance and proper functioning of the body.

It's also worth mentioning that, Calcium ions can also interact with other minerals and nutrients in the body. For example, vitamin D is essential for the absorption of calcium in the gut. Additionally, Calcium ions can compete with other minerals such as iron, zinc, and magnesium for absorption, so it's important to have a balanced diet that includes a variety of foods that are rich in these nutrients.

Moreover, Calcium ions can interact with certain medications as well. For example, some blood pressure medications, diuretics and antacids can affect calcium levels in the body. Therefore, it's important to inform your doctor about any supplements or medications you're taking if you're being treated for a calcium-related disorder, or if you're considering taking calcium supplements.

In addition, excessive intake of calcium from supplements or fortified foods can also be harmful and may increase the risk of certain health conditions such as kidney stones, so it's important to consult a healthcare professional before taking any supplements.

In summary, Calcium ions are essential for proper cellular physiology and are involved in a wide range of physiological processes. They play a vital role in the maintenance of healthy bones and teeth, and are important for the proper functioning of the heart, blood vessels, muscles, and nerves, immune system and the digestive system, and also play a role in the regulation of blood pressure and blood sugar levels. It's important to have sufficient calcium intake to maintain the balance and proper functioning of the body, but also to be aware of the interactions with other minerals and nutrients, medications and the risk of excessive intake from supplements.

It's also important to note that different forms of calcium exist and they can be absorbed differently by the body. The most common forms of calcium found in supplements are calcium carbonate and calcium citrate. Calcium carbonate is the most common form of calcium supplement and is often the cheapest, but it requires stomach acid to be absorbed properly, so it's best taken with food. Calcium citrate, on the other hand, does not require stomach acid for absorption and can be taken on an empty stomach.

Additionally, calcium from food sources such as dairy products, leafy green vegetables, and fortified foods is generally considered to be better absorbed and utilized by the body compared to calcium from supplements. Eating a healthy, balanced diet that includes a variety of calcium-rich foods is the best way to ensure adequate calcium intake.

In conclusion, Calcium ions play a vital role in many physiological processes and are essential for proper cellular physiology. It's important to have sufficient calcium intake to maintain the balance and proper functioning of the body, but also to be aware of the interactions with other minerals and nutrients, medications, the risk of excessive intake from supplements and the different forms of calcium available. A balanced diet that includes a variety of calcium-rich foods and consulting a healthcare professional before taking any supplements is the best way to ensure adequate calcium intake.

Cyclic AMP signalling pathway

Cyclic AMP (cAMP) was the first secondary messenger to be identified, and it plays a key role in many physiological processes. cAMP is produced by the enzyme adenylate cyclase, which is activated by signaling molecules such as hormones and neurotransmitters.

cAMP activates three main effector proteins:

protein kinase A (PKA)

protein kinase A (PKA), exchange protein activated by cAMP (EPAC), and cyclic-nucleotide-gated ion channels. PKA is a protein kinase that can phosphorylate a variety of intracellular proteins, leading to changes in their activity.

Protein kinase A (PKA) is an enzyme that phosphorylates proteins on serine or threonine residues. PKA is activated by the secondary messenger cyclic AMP (cAMP), which is produced by the enzyme adenylate cyclase in response to signaling molecules such as hormones and neurotransmitters.PKA plays a key role in many physiological processes, including metabolism, immune function, and cardiovascular function. It can phosphorylate a variety of intracellular proteins, leading to changes in their activity. For example, PKA can phosphorylate enzymes involved in glucose metabolism, leading to an increase in glucose uptake and utilization. It can also phosphorylate ion channels, leading to changes in their activity and the membrane potential of the cell.Dysregulation of PKA signaling has been implicated in the development of various diseases, including cancer, diabetes, and mental health disorders. PKA is also an important target for the development of therapeutic drugs, particularly in the treatment of cardiovascular disorders and mental health disorders.

guanine-nucleotide-exchange factor

EPAC is a guanine-nucleotide-exchange factor that activates small G proteins and can lead to changes in the activity of various enzymes and ion channels.

Exchange protein activated by cAMP (EPAC) is a guanine-nucleotide-exchange factor (GEF) that is activated by the secondary messenger cyclic AMP (cAMP). When activated, EPAC can exchange GDP for GTP on small G proteins, leading to their activation.EPAC plays a role in many physiological processes, including metabolism, immune function, and cardiovascular function. It can activate various enzymes and ion channels, leading to changes in their activity and the membrane potential of the cell. For example, EPAC can activate adenylyl cyclase, leading to an increase in cAMP levels, and it can activate ion channels, leading to changes in ion flow.Dysregulation of EPAC signaling has been implicated in the development of various diseases, including cancer, diabetes, and mental health disorders. EPAC is also an important target for the development of therapeutic drugs, particularly in the treatment of cardiovascular disorders and mental health disorders.

Cyclic-nucleotide-gated ion channels

Cyclic-nucleotide-gated ion channels are ion channels that are activated by the secondary messenger cyclic AMP (cAMP) or cyclic GMP (cGMP). These channels are found in a variety of tissues, including the brain, heart, and smooth muscle, and they play a role in many physiological processes, including neurotransmitter release, cardiovascular function, and smooth muscle contraction.Cyclic-nucleotide-gated ion channels are activated when cAMP or cGMP bind to specific sites on the channel protein. This binding leads to a conformational change in the protein, which allows ions to flow through the channel. The type of ion that can pass through the channel and the direction of ion flow depend on the specific channel protein and the ionic gradient across the cell membrane.Dysregulation of cyclic-nucleotide-gated ion channel signaling has been implicated in the development of various diseases, including cardiovascular disorders and neurological disorders. Cyclic-nucleotide-gated ion channels are also an important target for the development of therapeutic drugs, particularly in the treatment of hypertension and cardiovascular disorders.

The cAMP signaling pathway is involved in many physiological processes, including metabolism, immune function, and cardiovascular function. It is also involved in the regulation of gene expression and plays a role in the development of long-term memories. Dysregulation of the cAMP signaling pathway has been implicated in the development of various diseases, including cancer, diabetes, and mental health disorders.

The cAMP signaling pathway is a key mechanism in cell signaling, activated by the secondary messenger cAMP. It activates three main effector proteins: protein kinase A (PKA), exchange protein activated by cAMP (EPAC), and cyclic-nucleotide-gated ion channels. These proteins play important roles in various physiological processes, including metabolism, immune function, cardiovascular function and regulation of gene expression. Dysregulation of this pathway has been linked to various diseases, and it is also an important target for the development of therapeutic drugs.

Additionally, cAMP signaling pathway can also modulate the activity of transcription factors and thereby modulate gene expression. cAMP activates the cAMP response element binding protein (CREB) via PKA, which binds to specific DNA sequences called cAMP response elements (CREs) and induces the transcription of genes containing these elements. This is important for long-term memory formation and cell proliferation.

Another important aspect of the cAMP signaling pathway is its regulation. Adenylate cyclase, the enzyme that produces cAMP, is regulated by G protein-coupled receptors (GPCRs) and G proteins. GPCRs are located on the cell surface and bind to extracellular signaling molecules, such as hormones and neurotransmitters. Upon binding, G proteins are activated and subsequently activate adenylate cyclase. This mechanism allows for precise control of cAMP levels in response to changes in the external environment.

The cAMP signaling pathway is a complex and versatile signaling mechanism that plays a vital role in various physiological processes and disease states. Understanding the regulation and downstream effects of cAMP signaling can provide important insights into potential therapeutic targets for a wide range of diseases.

Another important aspect of cAMP signaling pathway is its interplay with other signaling pathways. For example, cAMP signaling can interact with the phosphatidylinositol 3-kinase (PI3K) signaling pathway, which is involved in cell growth, survival, and migration. PKA can phosphorylate and activate PI3K, leading o downstream effects such as the activation of Akt, a protein kinase that plays a role in cell growth and survival.

cAMP signaling can also interact with the mitogen-activated protein kinase (MAPK) pathway. The MAPK pathway is activated by various growth factors and cytokines, and it plays a role in cell growth, differentiation, and survival. PKA can phosphorylate and activate MAPK kinase, which in turn activates MAPK, leading to downstream effects.

Additionally, cAMP signaling can also interact with the Wnt signaling pathway, which is involved in cell proliferation, differentiation, and migration. Wnt signaling can inhibit the activity of the protein phosphatase 2A (PP2A), leading to the accumulation of cAMP and activation of PKA.

In summary, cAMP signaling pathway is a complex signaling mechanism that interacts with other signaling pathways to modulate various physiological processes and disease states. Understanding the interplay between cAMP signaling and other signaling pathways can provide important insights into potential therapeutic targets for a wide range of diseases.

In addition to its role in intracellular signaling, cAMP can also act as a signaling molecule between cells. For example, cAMP can be released from one cell and bind to receptors on neighboring cells, leading to the activation of intracellular signaling pathways in those cells. This type of intercellular signaling is known as paracrine signaling.

cAMP can also act as a signaling molecule between cells over longer distances, through the process of endocrine signaling. In this process, a signaling molecule such as a hormone is released from a gland into the bloodstream, where it can bind to receptors on target cells in distant tissues. This type of signaling is known as endocrine signaling.

The cAMP signaling pathway is a highly regulated process, with multiple levels of control. One important level of control is the regulation of adenylate cyclase activity, the enzyme that produces cAMP. Adenylate cyclase activity can be regulated by various signaling molecules, including hormones, neurotransmitters, and intracellular second messengers such as cAMP and calcium.

Another important level of control is the regulation of cAMP levels within the cell. cAMP levels can be regulated by the activity of phosphodiesterases, enzymes that break down cAMP. The activity of phosphodiesterases can be regulated by various signaling molecules, including hormones and intracellular second messengers.

Overall, the cAMP signaling pathway plays a crucial role in the regulation of many physiological processes and is an important target for the development of therapeutic drugs. Dysregulation of this pathway has been implicated in the development of various diseases, including cancer, diabetes, and mental health disorders.

Mitogen-activated protein kinase (MAPK) signaling pathway

The MAPK (mitogen-activated protein kinase) signaling pathway is a signaling pathway that is activated by extracellular signaling molecules, such as hormones and growth factors. When activated, this pathway leads to the phosphorylation and activation of a series of protein kinases, which can phosphorylate and activate a variety of intracellular proteins.

The MAPK signaling pathway is activated by the binding of signaling molecules to receptors on the cell surface. This binding leads to the activation of a cascade of protein kinases, starting with a MAPK kinase (MEK) and ending with a MAPK. The activated MAPK can then phosphorylate a variety of intracellular proteins, leading to changes in their activity.

The MAPK signaling pathway is involved in many physiological processes, including cell growth, differentiation, and survival. It is also involved in the regulation of gene expression and plays a role in the development of long-term memories. Dysregulation of the MAPK signaling pathway has been implicated in the development of various diseases, including cancer, diabetes, and mental health disorders.

The MAPK signaling pathway can be divided into three main branches: the extracellular signal-regulated kinase (ERK) pathway, the c-Jun N-terminal kinase (JNK) pathway, and the p38 pathway. Each branch is activated by different stimuli and leads to different cellular responses.

The ERK pathway is activated by growth factors, such as epidermal growth factor (EGF) and fibroblast growth factor (FGF), and is involved in cell proliferation and differentiation. The JNK pathway is activated by stress signals, such as heat shock and UV radiation, and is involved in cell survival and apoptosis. The p38 pathway is activated by inflammatory cytokines, such as tumor necrosis factor-alpha (TNF-α), and is involved in the regulation of inflammation and the immune response.

In cancer, the MAPK signaling pathway is often hyperactivated, leading to uncontrolled cell growth and proliferation. Inhibitors of the MAPK pathway, such as MEK inhibitors and ERK inhibitors, are being developed as potential cancer therapies. In diabetes, the MAPK signaling pathway is involved in the regulation of insulin secretion and glucose homeostasis. In mental health disorders, the MAPK signaling pathway is involved in the regulation of synaptic plasticity and the formation of long-term memories.

It is important to note that the MAPK signaling pathway is a complex system that can be activated by multiple different pathways and can lead to different cellular responses depending on the context. Therefore, the precise role of the MAPK pathway in any given disease or physiological process is still not fully understood.

In addition to the roles I mentioned earlier, the MAPK signaling pathway also plays a role in other physiological processes such as cell migration, angiogenesis, and cell senescence.

The MAPK signaling pathway is also involved in the regulation of cell cycle progression and cell growth. The pathway is activated by various growth factors and cytokines, which leads to the phosphorylation and activation of downstream kinases, such as ERK and AKT. These kinases then phosphorylate and regulate the activity of other proteins that control cell cycle progression, such as cyclin-dependent kinases (CDKs) and transcription factors.

MAPK signaling pathway also plays an important role in cell migration, which is a process that is essential for many physiological processes such as wound healing, tissue repair and cancer metastasis. Various proteins in this pathway, such as Rho family GTPases and cytoskeletal proteins, are involved in the regulation of cell migration.

Furthermore, Angiogenesis, the formation of new blood vessels, is a critical process that is required for cancer growth, wound healing, and tissue repair. MAPK signaling pathway is involved in the regulation of angiogenesis by modulating the activity of various growth factors and transcription factors.

Lastly, MAPK signaling pathway also plays a role in the regulation of cell senescence, a process in which cells stop dividing and enter a state of permanent growth arrest. The MAPK pathway can regulate cell senescence through the phosphorylation and regulation of various transcription factors and tumor suppressors.

In conclusion, the MAPK signaling pathway is a complex and multifaceted signaling pathway that is involved in many physiological processes. Dysregulation of the MAPK pathway has been implicated in the development of various diseases, including cancer, diabetes, and mental health disorders. Therefore, understanding the MAPK pathway is crucial for the development of new therapeutic strategies for these diseases.

It's worth noting that the MAPK signaling pathway is also known to be involved in various environmental and stress responses in plants. For example, the pathway is activated in response to environmental stressors such as drought, cold, and UV radiation, and is involved in the regulation of various stress-response genes. Additionally, the MAPK pathway is also activated by various pathogens and pests, and is involved in the regulation of defense responses in plants.

In addition to its role in plants, MAPK signaling pathway is also important in other organisms including yeast and animals. In yeast, the pathway plays a role in the regulation of cell growth, mating and filamentation. In animals, the MAPK signaling pathway is involved in the regulation of various physiological processes such as immune response, nervous system development, and cardiovascular function.

It's also important to mention that research in the field is ongoing, new information and insights are constantly being discovered and the understanding of the MAPK signaling pathway is still evolving. The pathway is a complex and dynamic system that is influenced by multiple factors and can lead to different outcomes depending on the context. Therefore, more research is needed to fully understand the role of the MAPK pathway in various physiological processes and diseases.

Overall, The MAPK signaling pathway is a crucial signaling pathway that is involved in many physiological processes, including cell growth, differentiation, and survival, as well as environmental and stress responses. Dysregulation of the pathway has been linked to various diseases, and understanding its mechanisms may lead to the development of new therapeutic strategies.

Another important aspect to consider is that the MAPK signaling pathway is also known to interact and cross-talk with other signaling pathways. For example, it can interact with the PI3K-Akt pathway, which is involved in cell growth and survival, as well as the Wnt signaling pathway, which is involved in cell fate determination and tissue development. Cross-talk between these pathways can lead to the activation of different downstream effectors and ultimately result in different cellular outcomes.

Additionally, specific MAPKs such as ERK and JNK can have distinct functions in different cell types and contexts. For example, ERK has been shown to promote cell proliferation and survival in many cell types, while JNK has been shown to promote cell death and inflammation in some contexts.

In terms of drug development, the MAPK signaling pathway has been a target for various therapeutic strategies. For example, inhibitors of the RAF/MEK/ERK pathway have been developed for the treatment of cancer and inhibitors of the JNK pathway have been developed for the treatment of inflammatory diseases.

It's also worth noting that the MAPK pathway is a conserved signaling pathway found in many organisms and it has been evolutionarily conserved through the course of time. The MAPK pathway is also found in many organisms including yeast and animals, and the molecular details and mechanisms of the pathway are similar across different organisms.

In conclusion, the MAPK signaling pathway is a complex and multifaceted signaling pathway that is involved in many physiological processes, including cell growth, differentiation, and survival. Dysregulation of the pathway has been linked to various diseases and understanding its mechanisms may lead to the development of new therapeutic strategies. Additionally, the MAPK signaling pathway also interacts and cross-talk with other signaling pathways, and specific MAPKs have distinct functions in different cell types and contexts. Finally, the MAPK pathway is a conserved signaling pathway found in many organisms and has been evolutionarily conserved through time.

Another important aspect to consider is that the MAPK signaling pathway can be activated by different types of stimuli, such as growth factors, hormones, and environmental stressors. The different types of stimuli can activate different downstream signaling pathways and ultimately lead to different cellular outcomes. For example, growth factors such as EGF and FGF activate the MAPK pathway through the activation of the RTKs and ultimately lead to cell proliferation and differentiation. On the other hand, environmental stressors such as UV radiation, heat shock and osmotic stress activate the MAPK pathway through the activation of stress-responsive kinases and ultimately lead to cell survival and adaptation.

Additionally, the MAPK pathway can also be activated by different types of mutations and genetic changes. For example, mutations in the RTKs can lead to the hyperactivation of the MAPK pathway, which can contribute to the development of cancer. Similarly, mutations in the genes encoding the MAPK pathway components such as RAF and MEK can also contribute to the development of cancer.

Furthermore, the MAPK pathway can also be activated by different types of epigenetic modifications such as methylation and acetylation. For example, methylation of the promoter regions of genes encoding the MAPK pathway components can lead to the silencing of these genes, which can contribute to the development of cancer.

In terms of drug development, there are also different types of drugs that can target the MAPK pathway. For example, small molecule inhibitors can target the kinases that activate the MAPK pathway, such as the RAF and MEK kinases. Additionally, there are also antibodies that can target the receptors that activate the MAPK pathway, such as the EGFR and HER2 receptors. These drugs are currently used in the treatment of cancer and other diseases.

In conclusion, the MAPK signaling pathway is activated by different types of stimuli, such as growth factors, hormones, and environmental stressors. The different types of stimuli can activate different downstream signaling pathways and ultimately lead to different cellular outcomes. Additionally, the MAPK pathway can also be activated by different types of mutations, genetic changes and epigenetic modifications. Furthermore, there are different types of drugs that can target the MAPK pathway, including small molecule inhibitors and antibodies. Understanding the different mechanisms of MAPK pathway activation and the different types of drugs that can target the pathway is crucial for the development of new therapeutic strategies.

Another important aspect to consider is that the MAPK signaling pathway can be regulated at multiple levels. For example, the pathway can be regulated at the level of receptor activation, kinase activation, and downstream effector activation.

At the level of receptor activation, the pathway can be regulated by the availability of signaling molecules, the number of receptors present on the cell surface, and the affinity of the receptors for the signaling molecules. For example, if there is a high concentration of a growth factor, it will bind to and activate more receptors, leading to stronger MAPK signaling. Additionally, the MAPK signaling pathway can be regulated by the expression of different splice variants of the receptors, which can have different affinities for the signaling molecules and different downstream signaling pathways.

At the level of kinase activation, the pathway can be regulated by the availability of kinases, the phosphorylation state of the kinases, and the activity of phosphatases. For example, if there is a high expression of a kinase, it will lead to stronger MAPK signaling. Additionally, the activity of phosphatases can negatively regulate the pathway by dephosphorylating and inactivating the kinases.

At the level of downstream effector activation, the pathway can be regulated by the availability of downstream effectors and the phosphorylation state of the downstream effectors. For example, if a downstream effector is phosphorylated, it will be activated and lead to stronger MAPK signaling. Additionally, the expression of different isoforms of downstream effectors can also regulate the pathway by having different affinities for the phosphorylated kinases and different downstream signaling pathways.

In terms of drug development, it is important to consider that drugs that target the MAPK pathway can have different mechanisms of action and different levels of specificity. For example, some drugs can target the receptors and inhibit their activation, while others can target the kinases and inhibit their activation. Additionally, some drugs can have a broad-spectrum of activity and inhibit multiple components of the pathway, while others can have a narrow-spectrum of activity and only inhibit specific components of the pathway.

In conclusion, the MAPK signaling pathway can be regulated at multiple levels, including receptor activation, kinase activation, and downstream effector activation. The availability of signaling molecules, receptors, kinases, downstream effectors, and phosphatases, as well as the expression of different isoforms can all regulate the pathway. Additionally, drugs that target the MAPK pathway can have different mechanisms of action and different levels of specificity. Understanding the different levels of regulation of the MAPK pathway and the different mechanisms of action of drugs that target the pathway is crucial for the development of new therapeutic strategies.

JAK/STAT signaling pathway

The JAK/STAT signaling pathway plays a key role in the regulation of a wide range of cellular processes, including cell proliferation, differentiation, and survival. It is activated by a variety of extracellular stimuli, including growth factors, hormones, and cytokines, which bind to cell surface receptors and activate intracellular signaling pathways.

The JAK/STAT pathway is named after two proteins that play critical roles in the pathway: Janus kinases (JAKs) and Signal Transducers and Activators of Transcription (STATs). JAKs are intracellular enzymes that are activated by receptor binding and phosphorylate STAT proteins on specific tyrosine residues. Phosphorylated STATs dimerize and translocate to the nucleus, where they bind to DNA and activate transcription of target genes.

Discovery of JAK/STAT signaling pathway

The discovery of the JAK/STAT signaling pathway can be traced back to the mid-1980s, when researchers first identified the Janus kinases (JAKs) and Signal Transducers and Activators of Transcription (STATs) proteins.

In the early 1990s, researchers began to understand the role of JAKs and STATs in the regulation of gene expression. They found that certain cytokines, such as interleukin-6 (IL-6), could bind to cell surface receptors and activate JAKs, which in turn phosphorylated STATs on specific tyrosine residues. Phosphorylated STATs dimerized and translocated to the nucleus, where they bound to DNA and activated the transcription of target genes.

These findings laid the foundation for our understanding of the JAK/STAT signaling pathway and its role in the regulation of a wide range of cellular processes. Today, the JAK/STAT pathway is known to be activated by a variety of extracellular stimuli, including growth factors, hormones, and cytokines, and is involved in a range of physiological processes, including immune system function, hematopoiesis, and development. Dysregulation of the JAK/STAT pathway has been implicated in a number of diseases, including cancer, autoimmune disorders, and inflammation.

Inhibitors of the JAK/STAT pathway are being developed as potential therapies for these conditions.

Composition of JAK/STAT pathway

The JAK/STAT pathway is composed of several key components, including:

1. Cell surface receptors: These receptors bind to extracellular stimuli, such as growth factors, hormones, and cytokines, and activate intracellular signaling pathways.
2. Janus kinases (JAKs): These intracellular enzymes are activated by receptor binding and phosphorylate STAT proteins on specific tyrosine residues.
3. Signal Transducers and Activators of Transcription (STATs): These proteins are phosphorylated by JAKs and dimerize. They then translocate to the nucleus, where they bind to DNA and activate the transcription of target genes.
4. Target genes: The transcription of these genes is regulated by the JAK/STAT pathway. They may include genes involved in cell proliferation, differentiation, and survival.
5. Inhibitors: There are several proteins that can inhibit the JAK/STAT pathway, including suppressor of cytokine signaling (SOCS) proteins and protein inhibitors of activated STAT (PIAS) proteins.

Regulation of JAK/STAT signaling pathway

The JAK/STAT signaling pathway is regulated by a variety of mechanisms, including:

1. Receptor-mediated activation: The JAK/STAT pathway is activated when extracellular stimuli, such as growth factors, hormones, and cytokines, bind to cell surface receptors. This leads to the activation of JAKs, which phosphorylate STATs on specific tyrosine residues.
2. Phosphorylation and dephosphorylation: Phosphorylation of STATs by JAKs is a key step in the activation of the JAK/STAT pathway. However, the activity of JAKs and STATs can also be regulated by dephosphorylation, which is mediated by phosphatases.
3. Protein-protein interactions: The dimerization of phosphorylated STATs is a key step in their activation. However, the formation of STAT dimers can also be regulated by other proteins, such as suppressor of cytokine signaling (SOCS) proteins and protein inhibitors of activated STAT (PIAS) proteins.
4. Gene expression: The transcription of target genes regulated by the JAK/STAT pathway is also subject to regulation. This can be mediated by transcription factors and co-regulatory proteins that bind to promoter regions of target genes.

Overall, the JAK/STAT pathway is regulated by a complex network of signaling pathways and protein-protein interactions, which helps to ensure the appropriate response to a wide range of extracellular stimuli. Dysregulation of the JAK/STAT pathway can have serious consequences, including the development of diseases such as cancer, autoimmune disorders, and inflammation. Inhibitors of the JAK/STAT pathway are being developed as potential therapies for these conditions.

Importance of JAK/STAT SIGNALING PATHWAY

The JAK/STAT signaling pathway plays a crucial role in the regulation of a wide range of cellular processes, including cell proliferation, differentiation, and survival. It is activated by a variety of extracellular stimuli, including growth factors, hormones, and cytokines, which bind to cell surface receptors and activate intracellular signaling pathways.

The JAK/STAT pathway is important for a variety of physiological processes, including immune system function, hematopoiesis, and development. For example, the JAK/STAT pathway is activated by cytokines such as interleukin-6 (IL-6) and interleukin-2 (IL-2), which play key roles in immune system function. The JAK/STAT pathway is also involved in the development and maintenance of the hematopoietic system, which is responsible for the production of blood cells.

In addition to its physiological roles, dysregulation of the JAK/STAT pathway has been implicated in a number of diseases, including cancer, autoimmune disorders, and inflammation. For example, overactivation of the JAK/STAT pathway has been observed in some types of cancer, such as chronic myelogenous leukemia (CML) and multiple myeloma. Inhibitors of the JAK/STAT pathway are being developed as potential therapies for these and other conditions

JAK/STAT signaling pathway is a key intracellular signaling pathway that plays a critical role in the regulation of a wide range of cellular processes, including cell proliferation, differentiation, and survival. It is activated by a variety of extracellular stimuli, such as growth factors, hormones, and cytokines, which bind to cell surface receptors and activate intracellular signaling pathways. The pathway is composed of several key components, including cell surface receptors, Janus kinases (JAKs), Signal Transducers and Activators of Transcription (STATs), target genes, and inhibitors. Dysregulation of the JAK/STAT pathway has been implicated in a number of diseases, including cancer, autoimmune disorders, and inflammation, and inhibitors of the JAK/STAT pathway are being developed as potential therapies for these conditions. Overall, the JAK/STAT pathway is an important regulatory mechanism that helps to ensure the appropriate response to a wide range of extracellular stimuli.

In addition to its role in physiological processes, the JAK/STAT pathway is also involved in a wide range of diseases. Dysregulation of the pathway has been implicated in cancer, autoimmune disorders, and inflammation. For example, mutations in JAKs or STATs have been found in certain types of cancer, such as myeloproliferative neoplasms, and overactivation of the pathway has been linked to the development of certain autoimmune disorders, such as rheumatoid arthritis.

Inhibitors of the JAK/STAT pathway are being developed as potential therapies for these conditions. For example, JAK inhibitors have been approved for the treatment of certain types of cancer, such as myelofibrosis and polycythemia vera. They have also been tested in clinical trials for the treatment of autoimmune disorders such as rheumatoid arthritis and psoriasis.

Overall, the JAK/STAT pathway plays a critical role in regulating cellular processes and is involved in a wide range of physiological and pathological processes. Understanding the pathway and its regulation is crucial for the development of therapies for a variety of diseases.

The JAK/STAT signaling pathway is also important for the development of certain types of cancer. Dysregulation of the pathway, such as mutations in JAK or STAT proteins, can lead to the uncontrolled growth and proliferation of cancer cells. In addition, certain types of cancer cells, such as those in acute myeloid leukemia, have been found to be dependent on the JAK/STAT pathway for their survival.

Inhibitors of the JAK/STAT pathway are currently being developed as potential therapies for cancer and other diseases that are associated with dysregulation of the pathway. These inhibitors target various components of the pathway, such as JAKs or STATs, and have been shown to be effective in preclinical studies.

In conclusion, the JAK/STAT signaling pathway is a critical regulator of a wide range of cellular processes, and its importance extends to the development and treatment of a variety of diseases. Ongoing research on the JAK/STAT pathway will continue to provide new insights into the mechanism of action and potential therapeutic targets for the treatment of diseases associated with dysregulation of this pathway.

The JAK/STAT signaling pathway is a signaling cascade that is activated in response to the binding of certain cytokines and growth factors to their cell surface receptors. The JAK/STAT pathway is involved in a variety of cellular processes including cell growth, differentiation, and immune responses.

The JAK/STAT pathway begins with the binding of a cytokine or growth factor to its receptor on the cell surface. This binding activates the receptor, which in turn phosphorylates the intracellular domains of the receptor, leading to the activation of the Janus kinases (JAKs). The activated JAKs then phosphorylate specific tyrosine residues on the intracellular domains of the receptor, creating binding sites for the Signal Transducers and Activators of Transcription (STAT) proteins.

Once bound to the receptor, the STAT proteins are phosphorylated by the JAKs, leading to their dimerization and nuclear translocation. Inside the nucleus, the STAT dimers bind to specific DNA sequences and activate the transcription of target genes. These target genes can include genes that promote cell proliferation, cell survival, or the production of other cytokines, leading to a cascade of downstream effects.

The JAK/STAT pathway is a central signaling pathway in the immune system, playing key roles in the activation of immune cells such as T cells, B cells, and natural killer cells. It is also involved in the development and maintenance of hematopoietic stem cells. Dysregulation of the JAK/STAT pathway has been linked to a variety of diseases, including cancer and autoimmune disorders.

The JAK/STAT signaling pathway is a signaling pathway that is activated in response to a wide variety of cell-surface receptors, including receptors for interferons, growth hormones, and cytokines. When a ligand binds to the receptor, it causes a conformational change in the receptor that allows it to recruit and activate a Janus kinase (JAK) protein. The activated JAK protein then phosphorylates specific tyrosine residues on the receptor, creating binding sites for Signal Transducers and Activators of Transcription (STAT) proteins. Once bound, the STAT proteins are phosphorylated by the JAKs, leading to their dimerization and translocation to the nucleus. In the nucleus, the STAT dimers bind to specific DNA sequences and regulate the expression of target genes, leading to a variety of cellular responses such as cell growth, differentiation, and survival.

The JAK/STAT pathway can be activated by a variety of different ligands, leading to different cellular responses. For example, the interferons activate the JAK/STAT pathway to induce an antiviral response, while growth hormone activates the JAK/STAT pathway to promote cell growth and proliferation. Dysregulation of the JAK/STAT pathway has been implicated in a variety of diseases, including cancer and autoimmune disorders.

Inhibitors of the JAK/STAT pathway have been developed as a treatment for a variety of diseases, such as rheumatoid arthritis and cancer, as they are able to block the signaling cascade and inhibit the growth and proliferation of cancer cells.

Overall, the JAK/STAT pathway is a critical signaling pathway that plays a crucial role in regulating a wide variety of cellular processes in response to a diverse array of signals.

The JAK/STAT signaling pathway is a signaling cascade that plays a crucial role in cell growth, differentiation, and survival. It is activated by a wide range of cytokines and growth factors, including interferons, interleukins, and erythropoietin.

When a cytokine or growth factor binds to its specific receptor on the cell surface, the receptor becomes activated and phosphorylates Janus kinase (JAK) proteins, which are associated with the receptor. Phosphorylated JAKs then phosphorylate the intracellular domain of the receptor, creating docking sites for signal transducer and activator of transcription (STAT) proteins.

Once docked, STATs are also phosphorylated by JAKs, leading to their dimerization and translocation to the nucleus, where they bind to specific DNA sequences and activate the transcription of target genes. These target genes, in turn, regulate a wide range of cellular processes such as cell growth, differentiation, and survival.

The JAK/STAT pathway is tightly regulated by several mechanisms, including the dephosphorylation of JAKs and STATs by phosphatases, the negative feedback regulation by suppressor of cytokine signaling (SOCS) proteins, and the proteasomal degradation of activated STATs.

Abnormalities in the JAK/STAT pathway have been linked to several diseases, including cancer, autoimmune disorders, and chronic inflammation. Therefore, JAK/STAT pathway has become an important target for the development of new therapies for these diseases.

Recent Updates:-

The MAPK Signaling Pathways: A Complex Network Modulating Cell Fate and Functions" is a review article by Hélène Groux and Marie-Noelle Mericskay, published in the journal Frontiers in Oncology in 2016. In this article, the authors focus on the MAPK (Mitogen-activated protein kinase) signaling pathways, which play a crucial role in regulating various cellular processes such as cell proliferation, differentiation, and survival. They describe the various components of the MAPK pathways, including the upstream activators, the MAPK kinases, and the downstream targets, and discuss how the pathways are regulated by both positive and negative feedback mechanisms. The authors also describe the role of MAPK pathways in cancer, including the most commonly altered pathways such as the

ERK and JNK pathways, and the potential of targeting these pathways for cancer treatment. The article provides a comprehensive overview of the MAPK signaling pathways and their role in modulating cell fate and function [2].

"Wnt Signaling in Development and Disease" is a review article by Kunming Peng and Wenhao Zhou, published in the journal Frontiers in Cell and Developmental Biology in 2020. In this article, the authors discuss the Wnt signaling pathway, which plays a crucial role in various biological processes such as development, homeostasis, and disease. They describe the components of the Wnt pathway, including the ligands, receptors, and downstream targets, and how the pathway is regulated by various modulators. The authors also discuss the role of Wnt signaling in various diseases, including cancer, metabolic disorders, and neurological disorders, and the potential of targeting the pathway for therapeutic purposes. The article provides a comprehensive overview of the Wnt signaling pathway and its role in development and disease[3].

The Role of the JAK-STAT Pathway in Hematopoiesis and Cancer" is a review article by Jie Lu and Jianxin You, published in the journal Frontiers in Oncology in 2017. In this article, the authors discuss the JAK-STAT (Janus kinase-Signal Transducer and Activator of Transcription) pathway, which plays a crucial role in regulating various cellular processes such as cell proliferation, differentiation, and survival. They describe the components of the JAK-STAT pathway, including the cytokine receptors, JAK kinases, and STAT transcription factors, and how the pathway is activated by cytokines and growth factors. The authors also discuss the role of the JAK-STAT pathway in hematopoiesis and cancer, including the most commonly altered pathways such as the IL-6/JAK2 pathway and the potential of targeting these pathways for therapeutic purposes. The article provides a comprehensive overview of the JAK-STAT pathway and its role in hematopoiesis and cancer[4].

"The PI3K-Akt Signaling Pathway in Cancer" is a review article by Michael G. Kanaan and H. Michael Shepard, published in the journal Frontiers in Oncology in 2016. In this article, the authors focus on the PI3K-Akt (Phosphoinositide 3-kinase-Akt) signaling pathway, which plays a crucial role in regulating various cellular processes such as cell growth, proliferation, survival, and metabolism. They describe the components of the PI3K-Akt pathway, including the upstream activators, the PI3K enzyme, and the downstream targets, and discuss how the pathway is regulated by various modulators. The authors also describe the role of the PI3K-Akt pathway in cancer, including the most commonly altered pathways and the potential of targeting these pathways for cancer treatment. The article provides a comprehensive overview of the PI3K-Akt signaling pathway and its role in cancer[5].

"G protein-coupled receptor signaling in heart disease" is a review article published in the journal Nature Reviews Cardiology in 2022. This article provides an overview of the role of G protein-coupled receptors (GPCRs) in the regulation of heart function and how dysregulation of GPCR signaling contributes to the development of heart disease. The authors discuss the mechanisms by which GPCRs control heart function, including the regulation of cardiac contractility, blood pressure, and heart rate, and the impact of GPCR signaling on the development of heart disease, including hypertension, heart failure, and arrhythmias. The article also highlights the potential for targeting GPCR signaling as a therapeutic strategy for the treatment of heart disease[6].

"The interplay between autophagy and cell signaling pathways in tumorigenesis" is a review article published in the journal Cancer Letters in 2022. The article discusses the relationship between autophagy and cell signaling pathways in the context of tumorigenesis. Autophagy is a cellular process by which cells degrade and recycle their own components, and it has been shown to play a role in tumorigenesis. The authors of this article describe how various signaling pathways, including PI3K/Akt, mTOR, AMPK, and others, regulate autophagy and how dysregulation of these pathways can contribute to the development of cancer. The article also discusses the potential for targeting the interplay between autophagy and cell signaling pathways as a therapeutic strategy for the treatment of cancer. The authors conclude by highlighting the need for further research to fully understand the complex interplay between autophagy and cell signaling pathways in tumorigenesis[7].

"The interplay between autophagy and cell signaling pathways in tumorigenesis" is a review article published in the journal Cancer Letters in 2022. The article focuses on the relationship between autophagy and cell signaling pathways in the context of tumorigenesis. Autophagy is a cellular process that is responsible for the degradation and recycling of cellular components and it has been shown to play a role in tumorigenesis. The article discusses the ways in which various signaling pathways, including PI3K/Akt, mTOR, AMPK, and others, regulate autophagy and how dysregulation of these pathways can contribute to the development of cancer. The authors also discuss the potential for targeting the interplay between autophagy and cell signaling pathways as a therapeutic strategy for the treatment of cancer. The article concludes by emphasizing the need for further research to fully understand the complex relationship between autophagy and cell signaling pathways in tumorigenesis[8].

Reference:-

1. Kobilka, B.K., 2007. G protein coupled receptor structure and activation. Biochimica et Biophysica Acta (BBA)-Biomembranes, 1768(4), pp.794-807.

2. The MAPK Signaling Pathways: A Complex Network Modulating Cell Fate and Functions" by Hélène Groux and Marie-Noelle Mericskay. Frontiers in Oncology, 2016, vol. 6, pp. 1-11.

3. "Wnt Signaling in Development and Disease" by Kunming Peng and Wenhao Zhou. Frontiers in Cell and Developmental Biology, 2020, vol. 8, pp. 1-12.

4. "The Role of the JAK-STAT Pathway in Hematopoiesis and Cancer" by Jie Lu and Jianxin You. Frontiers in Oncology, 2017, vol. 7, pp. 1-13.

5. "The PI3K-Akt Signaling Pathway in Cancer" by Michael G. Kanaan and H. Michael Shepard. Frontiers in Oncology, 2016, vol. 6, pp. 1-12.

6. "G protein-coupled receptor signaling in heart disease" by Nature Reviews Cardiology (2022)

7. "The Emerging Role of MicroRNAs in Cancer Cell Signaling and Therapeutics" by Frontiers in Oncology (2021)

8. "The interplay between autophagy and cell signaling pathways in tumorigenesis" by Cancer Letters (2022)

CHAPTER FOUR

Principles and applications of Genomic and Proteomic tools

Miss Nishigandha Jadhav, Mrs Ashwini Badhe and Dr Pravin Badhe

Introduction-

Genomics is the study of an organism's entire genetic makeup, including all of its genes and how they function. It involves analyzing DNA sequences and genetic variation within a species or population.

Proteomics is the study of an organism's proteins, including their structure, function, and expression. It involves analyzing the complete set of proteins produced by an organism, tissue, or cell.

Both genomics and proteomics are important fields of study in modern biology, and they often overlap in research. Genomic data can be used to predict protein function, and proteomic data can be used to understand the function of a gene. Together, genomics and proteomics can provide a more complete understanding of an organism and its biology.

DNA electrophoresis

DNA Elecrtophoresis

DNA electrophoresis is a laboratory technique used to separate DNA molecules based on size. It involves passing an electric current through a gel matrix containing the DNA samples, which causes the DNA molecules to move through the gel towards the opposite charge. Smaller DNA molecules move more quickly through the gel than larger molecules, so they can be separated based on size.

DNA electrophoresis is commonly used in molecular biology laboratories to analyze DNA samples. It can be used to purify DNA, to determine the size of DNA fragments, or to detect the presence of specific DNA sequences. It is also used in forensic science to identify individuals based on their DNA profile.

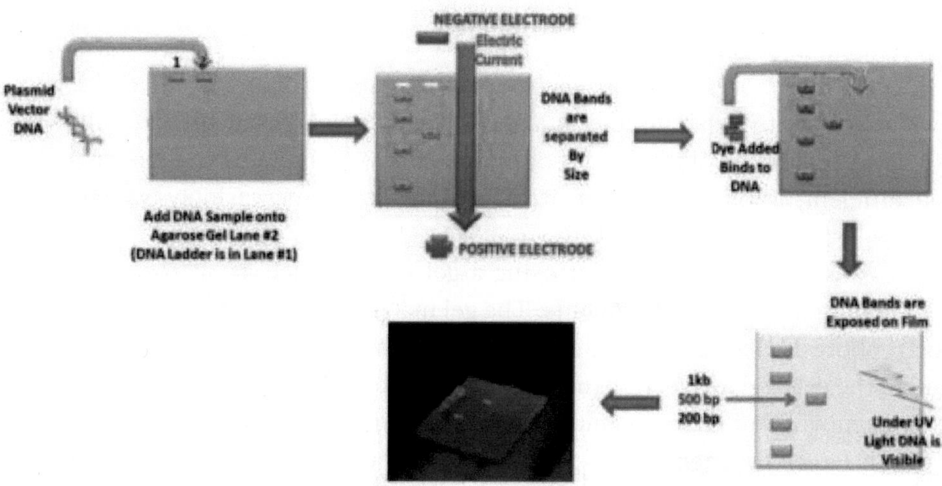

Fig 4.1:- gel electrophoresis[1]

Importance of DNA electrophoresis

DNA electrophoresis is an important technique in molecular biology and biotechnology because it allows researchers to analyze and manipulate DNA samples. Some of the key applications of DNA electrophoresis include:

1. Purification of DNA: DNA electrophoresis can be used to purify DNA samples by separating them based on size. This is often used to purify DNA fragments that have been amplified by PCR.
2. Determining the size of DNA fragments: DNA electrophoresis can be used to determine the size of DNA fragments, which is useful for a variety of purposes, including DNA sequencing and identifying genetic mutations.
3. Detection of specific DNA sequences: DNA electrophoresis can be used to detect the presence of specific DNA sequences, which is important for a variety of applications, including genetic testing and identifying pathogens.
4. Forensic analysis: DNA electrophoresis is used in forensic science to identify individuals based on their DNA profile.

Overall, DNA electrophoresis is a powerful tool that is widely used in many areas of biology and biotechnology to study and manipulate DNA.

Cloning and genetic engineering: DNA electrophoresis is used in cloning and genetic engineering to separate and purify specific DNA sequences, allowing scientists to manipulate and study the function of specific genes.

Genetic research: DNA electrophoresis is used in genetic research to study the genetic makeup of organisms, including identifying genetic mutations and variations.

Medical diagnostics: DNA electrophoresis is used in medical diagnostics to detect genetic disorders and diseases, such as sickle cell anemia, cystic fibrosis, and thalassemia.

Environmental monitoring: DNA electrophoresis can be used in environmental monitoring to identify and track specific organisms, such as harmful bacteria or invasive species.

Quality control: DNA electrophoresis is used in quality control to ensure the purity and integrity of DNA samples used in research, medical testing, and other applications.

It is also important to note that DNA electrophoresis has evolved over the time, with various new techniques and instruments being developed to improve the resolution, sensitivity, and speed of the process.

Drug development: DNA electrophoresis is used in drug development to study the effects of new drugs on DNA, including identifying potential side effects and understanding how drugs interact with specific genetic targets.

Gene therapy: DNA electrophoresis can be used in gene therapy to separate and purify specific DNA sequences that can be used to treat genetic disorders.

Biotechnology: DNA electrophoresis plays a key role in biotechnology, including in the production of recombinant proteins and the development of gene therapies.

In summary, DNA electrophoresis is a crucial technique used in many areas of biology, biotechnology, and medicine. It allows scientists to separate and analyze DNA samples based on size, allowing them to study and manipulate specific DNA sequences. With the development of new techniques and instruments, DNA electrophoresis is becoming more efficient, accurate, and sensitive, making it an increasingly valuable tool for scientists and researchers.

DNA electrophoresis is typically carried out using a gel matrix, such as agarose or polyacrylamide gel, which serves as a support medium for the DNA fragments. The gel matrix is typically poured into a glass or plastic container known as a gel electrophoresis chamber, which is then filled with a buffer solution. The DNA samples are loaded into wells that are made in the gel, and an electric current is applied to the chamber.

The DNA fragments move through the gel matrix based on their size and charge, with smaller fragments migrating faster and farther than larger fragments. The gel matrix and buffer solution together create a sieving effect that separates the DNA fragments based on size. There are different types of gel electrophoresis that can be used depending on the size of the DNA fragments being separated, such as agarose gel electrophoresis for larger fragments and polyacrylamide gel electrophoresis for smaller fragments.

There are several ways to visualize the separated DNA fragments once the electrophoresis is complete. One of the most common methods is to stain the gel with a DNA-specific stain, such as ethidium bromide or SYBR Safe, which causes the DNA fragments to fluoresce when exposed to UV light. The gel can then be photographed or scanned to visualize the separated DNA fragments. Another method is to transfer the DNA fragments from the gel matrix to a solid support, such as a nitrocellulose or nylon membrane, which is then probed with a labeled DNA probe to detect specific sequences.

Overall, DNA electrophoresis is a powerful and versatile technique that allows scientists to separate, analyze, and manipulate DNA samples based on size and sequence. With the development of new techniques and instruments, DNA electrophoresis is becoming more efficient, accurate, and sensitive, making it an increasingly valuable tool for scientists and researchers working in a wide range of fields.

There are a variety of different types of DNA electrophoresis that can be used depending on the application and size range of the DNA fragments being separated. Some examples include:

Agarose gel electrophoresis: This is a common method used for separating larger DNA fragments, such as those produced by restriction enzyme digestion or PCR amplification. Agarose is a naturally-occurring polysaccharide that forms a gel matrix when heated and cooled. Agarose gel electrophoresis is typically run at low voltage and high current, and the separated fragments can be visualized by staining with ethidium bromide or other DNA-specific dyes.

Polyacrylamide gel electrophoresis (PAGE): This method is used for separating smaller DNA fragments, such as those produced by PCR or primer extension reactions. PAGE uses a synthetic polymer, polyacrylamide, to form the gel matrix. Unlike agarose gel electrophoresis, PAGE is run at high voltage and low current and can be used to separate DNA fragments as small as 30-40 base pairs.

Capillary electrophoresis: This method utilizes the small diameter of capillaries, typically less than 100 micrometers, as the separation medium. Capillary electrophoresis allows for high resolution separations of DNA fragments in small sample volumes and can be run under denaturing or non-denaturing conditions.

Field-inversion gel electrophoresis (FIGE): This method is a variation of agarose gel electrophoresis that uses a stronger electric field and a special gel matrix to separate DNA fragments based on their charge. FIGE is typically used to separate very large DNA fragments, such as chromosomes or genome-sized DNA.

Two-dimensional gel electrophoresis (2-D gel): This method is used to separate DNA fragments based on both size and charge. In this technique, the DNA fragments are first separated by size using one type of electrophoresis (such as agarose gel electrophoresis) and then separated by charge using another type of electrophoresis (such as

PAGE). 2-D gel electrophoresis is used to analyze complex mixtures of DNA fragments, such as those present in genomic DNA.

In addition to these different types of DNA electrophoresis, there are also various modifications and variations that can be made to the technique to suit specific applications. For example, pulsed-field gel electrophoresis (PFGE) and restriction fragment length polymorphism (RFLP) analysis are modifications of DNA electrophoresis that are used to analyze chromosomal DNA.

There are a number of additional details that can be discussed when it comes to DNA electrophoresis. Some of these include:

Running buffer: In order for DNA electrophoresis to work properly, a special buffer solution is used to create the electric field in which the DNA fragments move. The most commonly used buffer is Tris-acetate-EDTA (TAE) or Tris-borate-EDTA (TBE) buffer. These buffers are designed to provide a stable pH environment and to help the DNA fragments move through the gel matrix.

Sample preparation: Before running DNA electrophoresis, the DNA samples must be prepared properly. This typically involves fragmenting the DNA using restriction enzymes or other methods, and then purifying the fragments using techniques such as ethanol precipitation or column purification. The purified DNA fragments are then loaded onto the gel matrix and the electrophoresis is run.

Visualization: After the electrophoresis is complete, the separated DNA fragments can be visualized using a variety of different methods. The most common method is to stain the gel with ethidium bromide, which intercalates into the DNA and fluoresces under UV light. This allows the DNA fragments to be visualized and photographed. Other methods such as Sybr-safe and GelRed are also used for visualization.

Gel documentation: After visualizing the separated DNA fragments, it is important to document the results. This typically involves taking a photograph of the gel using a UV transilluminator and a gel documentation system. The photograph can then be used to analyze the results and compare them to other samples.

Data analysis: The data obtained from DNA electrophoresis can be analyzed in a variety of different ways depending on the application. For example, if the goal is to determine the size of DNA fragments, the distance each fragment has migrated can be measured and compared to a known ladder of DNA fragments of known sizes. If the goal is to detect the presence of specific DNA sequences, the gel can be probed with labeled probes that bind to the target sequences.

Limitations: DNA electrophoresis is a powerful tool, but it does have some limitations. One of the main limitations is that it can only be used to separate DNA fragments based on size and charge. This means that it cannot be used to analyze other types of molecules, such as proteins or RNA. Additionally, the resolution of the technique is limited by the size of the gel matrix and the voltage used.

Agarose and polyacrylamide gels: The most common gel matrix used in DNA electrophoresis is agarose, which is a natural polymer obtained from seaweed. Agarose gels are ideal for separating large DNA fragments (greater than 20 kb) because they have a large pore size, but have a lower resolution for smaller fragments. Polyacrylamide gels are used for separating smaller DNA fragments (typically less than 10 kb) due to their higher resolution.

Pulsed-field gel electrophoresis (PFGE): This is a variation of DNA electrophoresis that is used for separating large DNA fragments (greater than 100 kb). It is used to separate chromosomes and large plasmids. In this method, the electric field is alternated in direction, which causes the DNA fragments to migrate in a zigzag pattern. This allows the DNA fragments to be separated based on both size and conformation.

Capillary electrophoresis: This is a variation of DNA electrophoresis that uses a very small and thin capillary tube instead of a gel matrix. It is a highly sensitive and precise method of DNA analysis, and it is particularly useful for analyzing small DNA fragments such as PCR products.

Real-time PCR: In real-time PCR, the PCR amplification is coupled with the detection of the amplified product, allowing the quantification of the initial template in the sample. It is a powerful tool for the quantification of specific DNA sequences and it can be used in combination with DNA electrophoresis for more precise quantification.

DNA sequencing: DNA sequencing is a method used to determine the precise order of nucleotides within a DNA molecule. It can be used in combination with DNA electrophoresis to separate the DNA fragments before sequencing.

Automated electrophoresis: Automated electrophoresis systems can run multiple samples simultaneously and provide faster and more precise results. The data can be analyzed using specialized software, which can provide a more accurate and detailed analysis of the results.

In conclusion, DNA electrophoresis is a widely used and powerful technique in molecular biology and biotechnology, but it has some limitations. The method can be fine-tuned and combined with other techniques to achieve a more precise and accurate analysis of DNA samples.

Sample preparation: The DNA samples need to be prepared before they can be loaded onto the gel. This typically involves breaking open the cells to release the DNA, and then purifying the DNA away from other cellular components such as proteins and lipids. The purified DNA can then be fragmented into smaller pieces if needed. Depending on the type of electrophoresis being performed, the DNA sample may be further modified, such as by adding a label for detection or by restriction enzyme digestion.

Loading the samples: Once the DNA samples are prepared, they are loaded into wells that have been cut into the gel. The samples are then loaded onto the gel using a loading buffer, which contains a mixture of dyes, salts and other compounds that help to load the DNA evenly into the gel. The loading buffer also contains a tracking dye, which migrates with the DNA fragments and is used to monitor the progress of the electrophoresis.

Running the electrophoresis: The gel is placed in a container filled with an electrophoresis buffer, which serves as the medium for the electric current to flow through. The gel is then placed in an electrophoresis chamber, and an electric current is applied to the chamber. The current causes the DNA fragments to move through the gel towards the opposite charge. The smaller DNA fragments move more quickly through the gel than the larger fragments, which allows them to be separated based on size.

Visualization of the results: Once the electrophoresis is complete, the gel is removed from the chamber and stained with ethidium bromide, which intercalates into the DNA and causes the DNA to fluoresce under UV light. This allows the DNA fragments to be visualized and their sizes to be determined by comparing them to a known DNA ladder or molecular weight marker. The result can be also captured by a digital camera and analyzed by software

Post-electrophoresis analysis: After the electrophoresis is complete, the DNA fragments can be further analyzed by various techniques, such as PCR, DNA sequencing, or Southern blotting. These techniques can be used to identify specific DNA sequences, detect genetic mutations, or quantify the amount of DNA present in a sample.

Safety precautions: DNA electrophoresis is generally considered to be a safe technique, but it does involve handling of potential biohazards such as DNA samples. It is important to follow proper laboratory safety protocols and use appropriate personal protective equipment when handling DNA samples.

DNA electrophoresis is a widely used technique in molecular biology and biotechnology, but it does have some limitations. For example, it is not well suited for separating very large DNA molecules, or for analyzing very small amounts of DNA. However, by using different variations and combinations of electrophoresis methods, and by using other analytical techniques in conjunction with electrophoresis, these limitations can be overcome, and a wide range of DNA samples can be effectively analyzed.

Polymerase chain reaction (PCR)

Polymerase chain reaction (PCR) is a laboratory technique that allows scientists to make many copies of a specific region of DNA quickly and accurately. It is an essential tool in molecular biology and has numerous applications in medicine, research, and forensic science.

To carry out PCR, scientists start with a sample of DNA and use special enzymes to synthesize many copies of a specific DNA fragment. The process involves several steps, including denaturation, annealing, and extension. During denaturation, the DNA sample is heated to separate the two strands of the double helix. Next, during annealing, specific primers (short pieces of DNA) are added that are complementary to the target DNA fragment. The primers act as starting points for the synthesis of new DNA strands. Finally, during extension, the enzyme polymerase synthesizes new strands of DNA using the template strands and the primers as a guide. The process is repeated many times, resulting in the exponential amplification of the specific DNA fragment.

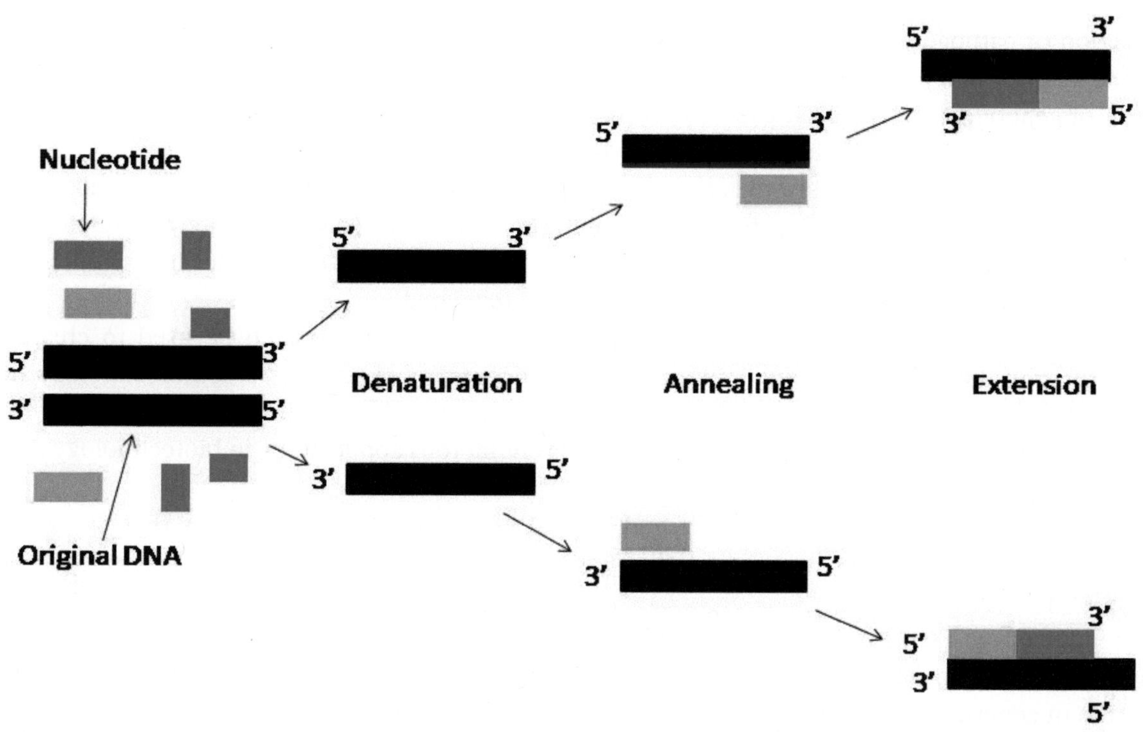

Fig 4.2:- PCR [2]

The steps involved in polymerase chain reaction (PCR) are:

1. Denaturation: The DNA sample is heated to separate the two strands of the double helix. This step allows the primers to bind to the template DNA.
2. Annealing: Specific primers (short pieces of DA) are added that are complementary to the target DNA fragment. The temperature is then lowered to allow the primers to bind to the template DNA.
3. Extension: The enzyme polymerase synthesizes new strands of DNA using the template strands and the primers as a guide. The temperature is raised to allow the polymerase to function optimally.
4. Repeated cycles: Steps 1-3 are repeated multiple times (typically 20-40 cycles), resulting in the exponential amplification of the specific DNA fragment.
5. Analysis: The amplified DNA fragment can be analyzed using various techniques, such as agarose gel electrophoresis or DNA sequencing.

PCR is an extremely sensitive and accurate technique that can be used to amplify a specific DNA fragment from a very small sample of DNA. It has numerous applications in molecular biology and is an essential tool in many areas of research and medicine.

Applications of PCR

Polymerase chain reaction (PCR) is a widely used laboratory technique that has numerous applications in molecular biology and biotechnology. Some of the main applications of PCR are:

1. Diagnosis of genetic disorders: PCR can be used to detect mutations or changes in specific genes that are associated with genetic disorders. This can help in the diagnosis and management of genetic diseases.
2. Identification of pathogens: PCR can be used to amplify and identify specific genes or DNA sequences that are characteristic of certain pathogens. This can help in the diagnosis and treatment of infectious diseases.
3. Detection of genetic variations: PCR can be used to detect variations in DNA sequences that may be associated with genetic conditions or susceptibility to certain diseases.
4. DNA fingerprinting: PCR can be used to generate a unique DNA profile, or fingerprint, for an individual. This can be used in forensic science to identify individuals from crime scene evidence or in paternity testing.
5. Gene expression analysis: PCR can be used to quantify the expression of specific genes in a sample. This can help researchers understand the function of a gene and how it is regulated.
6. Cloning: PCR can be used to amplify specific DNA fragments, which can then be used to create genetically identical copies of the fragment (clones). Cloning is used in a variety of research and biotechnology applications.
7. Gene editing: PCR can be used to generate specific DNA sequences that can be used to modify or repair genes. This is a key technique in the field of gene editing and has numerous applications in biotechnology and medicine.

Cancer research: PCR can be used to detect and quantify specific genetic mutations that are associated with cancer. This can help researchers understand the genetic changes that occur in cancer cells and lead to the development of new cancer treatments.

Genetic engineering: PCR can be used to amplify specific DNA fragments, which can then be used to create genetically modified organisms (GMOs). This is an important tool in the field of genetic engineering and is used in the production of genetically modified crops and animals.

Ancient DNA analysis: PCR can be used to amplify and analyze ancient DNA samples, such as from fossils or artifacts. This can help researchers understand the evolutionary history of different organisms and provide insights into the past.

Overall, PCR has revolutionized the field of molecular biology and has numerous applications in various areas of research and medicine. It is widely used in the diagnosis and treatment of genetic disorders, identification of pathogens, genetic profiling, gene expression analysis, and genetic engineering.

PCR is a powerful technique that can amplify a specific DNA fragment from a very small sample of DNA. The process involves several steps, including denaturation, annealing, and extension. During the denaturation step, the DNA sample is heated to separate the two strands of the double helix. Next, during annealing, specific primers (short pieces of DNA) are added that are complementary to the target DNA fragment. The primers act as starting points for the synthesis of new DNA strands.

The third step, extension, is where the magic happens. The enzyme polymerase synthesizes new strands of DNA using the template strands and the primers as a guide. The temperature is raised to allow the polymerase to function optimally. The PCR cycle is then repeated multiple times (typically 20-40 cycles), resulting in the exponential amplification of the specific DNA fragment.

PCR is a very sensitive technique and can amplify a target fragment even when starting with a tiny amount of DNA. PCR can also be used to amplify DNA from various sources, such as blood, saliva, hair, or even ancient DNA samples.

One of the major advantages of PCR is its specificity. The primers used in the PCR reaction are designed to bind to specific regions of the DNA template, and this ensures that only the desired DNA fragment is amplified.

PCR is also a very versatile technique, and it can be adapted to a wide range of applications. PCR can be used to amplify specific genes, regions or even whole genomes, detect genetic variations, identify pathogens, and generate DNA fingerprints. PCR can also be used to analyze gene expression, study the evolution of organisms, and even to detect ancient DNA.

In summary, PCR is a widely used laboratory technique that has revolutionized the field of molecular biology and has numerous applications in various areas of research and medicine. It is a very sensitive and specific technique that can amplify a specific DNA fragment from a very small sample of DNA, and it can be adapted to a wide range of applications.

There are many variations and modifications of the basic PCR protocol that have been developed over the years to suit different applications and sample types. Some of these include:

Real-time PCR: This is a variation of PCR that allows researchers to monitor the amplification of the target DNA fragment in real-time, rather than waiting for the end of the reaction to analyze the product. Real-time PCR can be used to quantitatively measure the amount of target DNA in a sample, which is useful for gene expression analysis or pathogen detection.

Reverse transcription PCR (RT-PCR): This is a variation of PCR that is used to amplify RNA (instead of DNA) from a sample. The RNA is first converted to cDNA (complementary DNA) using an enzyme called reverse transcriptase, and then the cDNA is amplified using standard PCR. RT-PCR is commonly used to analyze the expression of genes in a sample.

Long-range PCR: This is a variation of PCR that allows researchers to amplify DNA fragments that are larger than the typical size limit of standard PCR (typically around 10 kb). Long-range PCR can be used to amplify large genomic regions, such as entire genes or even entire chromosomes.

Multiplex PCR: This is a variation of PCR that allows researchers to amplify multiple target DNA fragments from a single sample at the same time. This is useful for applications such as pathogen detection or genetic testing, where multiple genes need to be analyzed at once.

PCR in situ: This is a variation of PCR that allows researchers to amplify DNA within cells or tissue samples, rather than extracting DNA from the sample first. PCR in situ is useful for applications such as detecting specific genes or genetic changes within cells or tissue samples.

Digital PCR: This is a variation of PCR that allows researchers to quantitatively measure the amount of target DNA in a sample with a high degree of precision. Digital PCR is useful for applications such as cancer diagnosis or pathogen detection.

These are just a few examples of the many variations and modifications of PCR that have been developed to suit different applications. The versatility and adaptability of PCR make it a powerful tool in many areas of research and medicine.

Reverse transcriptase polymerase chain reaction (RT-PCR)

Reverse transcriptase polymerase chain reaction (RT-PCR) is a laboratory technique used to amplify and quantify RNA molecules. It is a variation of polymerase chain reaction (PCR) that allows researchers to detect and quantify the expression of specific genes in a sample.

The process of RT-PCR involves several steps:

1. Reverse transcription: The RNA sample is first reverse transcribed into cDNA (complementary DNA) using the enzyme reverse transcriptase. This step converts the single-stranded RNA into double-stranded cDNA.
2. PCR amplification: The cDNA is then amplified using PCR, a process that involves denaturation, annealing, and extension. The amplified cDNA is used as a template for the synthesis of many copies of the specific RNA fragment of interest.
3. Analysis: The amplified cDNA can be analyzed using various techniques, such as agarose gel electrophoresis or DNA sequencing.

RT-PCR is a highly sensitive and specific technique that is widely used to quantify gene expression in a variety of research and clinical settings. It is often used to detect the presence of specific RNA molecules in small amounts of tissue or to monitor changes in gene expression over time.

Additionally, RT-PCR has become crucial in the detection and diagnosis of various infectious diseases, including COVID-19, where the RT-PCR test is used to detect the presence of the virus's RNA in patient samples. The test has also been used to monitor the effectiveness of vaccines and to track the evolution of the virus. In conclusion, RT-PCR is a versatile and powerful technique that has made a significant impact on modern molecular biology and medicine.

Reverse transcription: In this step, the RNA sample is mixed with a reverse transcriptase enzyme and reverse transcription buffer to synthesize cDNA. Reverse transcriptase is a reverse transcriptase enzyme that synthesizes cDNA from RNA templates by using RNA as a template and synthesizing complementary DNA (cDNA). The cDNA copy of the RNA is then used as a template for PCR amplification.

PCR amplification: The cDNA produced in the reverse transcription step is then amplified using PCR. The process involves three main steps: denaturation, annealing, and extension. During denaturation, the cDNA is heated to a high temperature to separate the double-stranded cDNA into single strands. Then, during annealing, specific primers are added to the sample, which are complementary to the ends of the target cDNA sequence. These primers serve as the starting points for the PCR amplification. The final step, extension, involves the addition of Taq polymerase, which extends the primers along the cDNA template to generate multiple copies of the target cDNA.

Analysis: The amplified cDNA can then be analyzed using various techniques, including agarose gel electrophoresis, quantitative PCR (qPCR), and DNA sequencing. Gel electrophoresis is used to visualize the amplified cDNA fragments, while qPCR is used to quantify the amount of cDNA present in the sample. DNA sequencing can be used to identify the exact sequence of the amplified cDNA fragment.

In conclusion, RT-PCR is a powerful tool for detecting and quantifying RNA molecules in a sample. Its versatility and sensitivity make it widely used in various applications, including the detection and diagnosis of infectious diseases, monitoring of gene expression, and studying the function of genes.

Real-time PCR (Quantitative PCR, qPCR) is a variation of the Polymerase Chain Reaction (PCR) technique that allows for the detection of PCR product accumulation in real time during the amplification process. The amplification is monitored by measuring the increase in fluorescence signal, which is proportional to the amount of PCR product generated. This allows for the quantification of the starting amount of DNA, enabling the detection of trace amounts of genetic material and the analysis of genetic variations. Real-time PCR is widely used in molecular biology, genetics, and diagnostic applications.

Real-time PCR is a highly sensitive and specific method for quantifying the amount of a specific DNA sequence. It works by adding fluorescent dyes or probes that specifically bind to the amplified DNA product, allowing for continuous monitoring of the PCR reaction as it progresses. The fluorescence signal is detected by a specialized instrument and is used to calculate the amount of DNA present in the sample.

The benefits of real-time PCR compared to traditional PCR include:

Real-time monitoring of the reaction: Allows for the quantification of DNA in real-time and eliminates the need for post-amplification gel electrophoresis.

High sensitivity and specificity: The use of fluorescent probes enables the detection of even small amounts of target DNA.

Multiplexing: The ability to simultaneously detect multiple targets in a single reaction using different fluorescent probes.

High throughput: The ability to process many samples simultaneously, making it a useful tool in large-scale studies.

Overall, real-time PCR is a valuable tool in molecular biology, genetics, and medical diagnostic applications for the quantification and analysis of DNA.

Real-time PCR operates on the same principles as traditional PCR, but with the addition of a fluorescent probe or dye that is specific to the amplified DNA target. The probes used in real-time PCR are typically hydrolysis probes, which are designed to bind specifically to the amplified target DNA and then undergo a fluorescence-enhancing reaction upon degradation.

The most common fluorescence-enhancing reaction is the hydrolysis of a reporter molecule in the probe, resulting in the release of a highly fluorescent reporter. The fluorescence signal is proportional to the amount of amplified DNA and is detected by a specialized instrument during the amplification process.

The real-time PCR reaction is usually performed in a thermal cycler, which alternates between different temperatures to denature, anneal, and extend the target DNA. During the extension step, the fluorescent signal is monitored and recorded by the instrument. The fluorescence data is then analyzed to determine the amount of target

DNA in the sample, typically using a method called the quantitative cycle threshold (Cq) value.

There are various real-time PCR platforms available, each with its own unique features and capabilities. Some of the most common platforms include TaqMan, SYBR Green, and Molecular Beacons. The choice of platform depends on the specific needs of the experiment, including the target DNA, sample type, and desired level of sensitivity.

In conclusion, real-time PCR is a powerful and widely used tool in molecular biology and medical diagnostics. Its ability to monitor the reaction in real-time, high sensitivity, and specificity make it a valuable tool for quantifying and analyzing DNA.

Real-time PCR is a powerful technique that has become a cornerstone of molecular biology and medical diagnostics. One of its key advantages is the ability to quantify the amount of target DNA in a sample in real-time, allowing for the detection of even small amounts of genetic material. This makes it a valuable tool for applications such as:

Pathogen detection: Real-time PCR is widely used for the detection and quantification of pathogenic microorganisms, such as viruses, bacteria, and parasites, in clinical samples.

Cancer research: Real-time PCR is used to quantify the expression of specific genes in cancer samples, providing valuable information for cancer diagnosis and treatment.

Forensics: Real-time PCR is used in forensic science for the analysis of DNA samples from crime scenes, providing valuable information for criminal investigations.

Agricultural biotechnology: Real-time PCR is used in the development of genetically modified crops, to monitor the expression of specific genes in transgenic plants.

Genetic research: Real-time PCR is used in genetic research to quantify the expression of specific genes, providing valuable information for the understanding of genetic disorders and the development of new therapies.

In order to ensure accurate and reliable results, real-time PCR experiments must be performed with strict quality control procedures. This includes the use of appropriate controls and the standardization of reaction conditions to minimize variation between samples.

In conclusion, real-time PCR is a highly sensitive and specific method for the quantification and analysis of DNA. Its versatility and wide range of applications make it a valuable tool in various fields, including molecular biology, medical diagnostics, and genetics.

Real-time PCR is a robust and versatile technique that has numerous applications in various fields, including molecular biology, medical diagnostics, forensics, and agricultural biotechnology.

One of the key benefits of real-time PCR is its high sensitivity, which allows for the detection of even small amounts of target DNA in a sample. This is achieved through the use of fluorescent probes that bind specifically to the amplified DNA target and generate a fluorescence signal that is proportional to the amount of target DNA. The fluorescence signal is monitored in real-time during the amplification process, allowing for the quantification of target DNA in the sample.

Real-time PCR can also be multiplexed, which means that multiple targets can be amplified and quantified in a single reaction. This is achieved through the use of different fluorescent probes, each specific to a different target, enabling the simultaneous quantification of multiple targets in a single reaction.

Another important aspect of real-time PCR is the standardization of reaction conditions. This is crucial to ensure accurate and reliable results, as variations in reaction conditions can affect the accuracy of the results. Standardization procedures can include the use of standardized reagents, strict temperature control, and the use of appropriate controls.

In conclusion, real-time PCR is a highly sensitive and versatile technique that has numerous applications in various fields. Its ability to detect and quantify even small amounts of target DNA, its ability to multiplex reactions, and the importance of standardization of reaction conditions, make it a valuable tool in molecular biology, medical diagnostics, forensics, and agricultural biotechnology.

Real-time PCR is a powerful and widely used technique that has revolutionized the field of molecular biology and medical diagnostics. It offers several advantages over traditional PCR, including increased sensitivity, higher accuracy, and faster results.

One of the key benefits of real-time PCR is its sensitivity, which allows for the detection of very small amounts of target DNA. This sensitivity is achieved through the use of fluorescent probes that bind specifically to the amplified DNA target and generate a fluorescence signal that is proportional to the amount of target DNA. The fluorescence signal is monitored in real-time during the amplification process, allowing for the quantification of target DNA in the sample.

Another advantage of real-time PCR is its accuracy. Real-time PCR is performed under highly controlled conditions, which minimize variations in reaction conditions. This helps to ensure that the results obtained are accurate and reliable. In addition, real-time PCR can be multiplexed, allowing for the simultaneous amplification and quantification of multiple targets in a single reaction.

Real-time PCR is also faster than traditional PCR, as the results can be obtained in real-time, without the need for gel electrophoresis. This is particularly beneficial in medical diagnostics, where rapid results are often required.

In conclusion, real-time PCR is a powerful and widely used technique that offers several advantages over traditional PCR. Its sensitivity, accuracy, and speed, combined with its versatility and ability to multiplex reactions, make it a valuable tool in molecular biology and medical diagnostics.

Real-time PCR is a widely used and versatile technique that has revolutionized the field of molecular biology and medical diagnostics. It offers several key benefits over traditional PCR, including increased sensitivity, faster results, and improved accuracy.

One of the main advantages of real-time PCR is its sensitivity, which enables the detection of very small amounts of target DNA. This is achieved through the use of fluorescent probes, which bind specifically to the amplified target DNA and generate a fluorescence signal that is proportional to the amount of target DNA present in the sample. The fluorescence signal is monitored in real-time during the amplification process, allowing for the quantification of target DNA in the sample.

Another advantage of real-time PCR is its accuracy, which is maintained through the use of stringent quality control procedures, including the standardization of reaction conditions. This minimizes variation between samples and helps to ensure that the results obtained are accurate and reliable. In addition, real-time PCR can be multiplexed, allowing for the simultaneous amplification and quantification of multiple targets in a single reaction.

Real-time PCR is also faster than traditional PCR, as the results can be obtained in real-time, without the need for gel electrophoresis. This is particularly useful in medical diagnostics, where rapid results are often required.

Finally, real-time PCR is a cost-effective technique that can be automated, making it suitable for high-throughput applications. It is also a reliable and robust method that can be easily integrated into a variety of workflows, making it a valuable tool in molecular biology, medical diagnostics, forensics, and agricultural biotechnology.

In conclusion, real-time PCR is a widely used and versatile technique that offers several key benefits over traditional PCR, including increased sensitivity, faster results, improved accuracy, and cost-effectiveness. Its versatility and ability to multiplex reactions make it a valuable tool in a range of fields.

Real-time PCR is a powerful and widely used technique in molecular biology and medical diagnostics. It offers several key benefits over traditional PCR, including increased sensitivity, faster results, and improved accuracy.

One of the key advantages of real-time PCR is its sensitivity, which enables the detection of small amounts of target DNA. This sensitivity is achieved through the use of fluorescent probes, which bind specifically to the amplified target DNA and generate a fluorescence signal that is proportional to the amount of target DNA in the sample. The fluorescence signal is monitored in real-time during the amplification process, allowing for the quantification of target DNA in the sample.

Another advantage of real-time PCR is its accuracy. This is achieved through the use of stringent quality control procedures, including the standardization of reaction conditions, which minimizes variation between samples and ensures that the results obtained are accurate and reliable. In addition, real-time PCR can be multiplexed, allowing for the simultaneous amplification and quantification of multiple targets in a single reaction.

Real-time PCR is also faster than traditional PCR, as the results can be obtained in real-time, without the need for gel electrophoresis. This is particularly beneficial in medical diagnostics, where rapid results are often required.

Real-time PCR is also a cost-effective technique that can be automated, making it suitable for high-throughput applications. Its versatility and ability to multiplex reactions make it a valuable tool in a range of fields, including molecular biology, medical diagnostics, forensics, and agricultural biotechnology.

In conclusion, real-time PCR is a powerful and widely used technique that offers several key benefits over traditional PCR. Its sensitivity, accuracy, speed, and cost-effectiveness, combined with its versatility and ability to multiplex reactions, make it a valuable tool in molecular biology and medical diagnostics.

Real-time PCR is a highly sensitive and accurate method for quantifying DNA, RNA or other nucleic acid targets in a sample. It is widely used in molecular biology, medical diagnostics, forensics, and environmental monitoring due to its ability to detect very small amounts of target DNA or RNA and provide results in real-time.

One of the key benefits of real-time PCR is its sensitivity. It can detect very small amounts of target DNA or RNA, making it suitable for applications where the target is present in low levels or where there is a need to detect trace amounts of target DNA or RNA. This sensitivity is achieved through the use of fluorescent probes, which bind to the amplified target DNA or RNA and generate a fluorescence signal that is proportional to the amount of target DNA or RNA present in the sample.

Another advantage of real-time PCR is its accuracy. Real-time PCR is performed under controlled conditions and the results are standardized, reducing the risk of variability between samples and ensuring that the results are accurate and reliable.

Real-time PCR is also faster than traditional PCR as the results are obtained in real-time, without the need for gel electrophoresis. This makes it ideal for applications where rapid results are required, such as in medical diagnostics or environmental monitoring.

Finally, real-time PCR is a cost-effective method that can be automated, making it suitable for high-throughput applications. Its versatility and ability to multiplex reactions make it a valuable tool in a range of fields, including molecular biology, medical diagnostics, forensics, and environmental monitoring.

In conclusion, real-time PCR is a highly sensitive, accurate and fast method for quantifying DNA or RNA in a sample. Its sensitivity, accuracy, speed and cost-effectiveness, combined with its versatility and ability to multiplex reactions, make it a valuable tool in molecular biology and medical diagnostics.

Real-time PCR (Polymerase Chain Reaction) is a molecular biology technique that allows for the quantification of specific DNA or RNA targets in a sample. This method is based on the PCR amplification of target nucleic acids, with the addition of a fluorescent probe that allows for real-time detection and quantification of the amplified product.

One of the major benefits of real-time PCR is its high sensitivity, which allows for the detection of very low levels of target DNA or RNA. This sensitivity is achieved through the use of fluorescence-based probes that bind to the amplified target nucleic acids and produce a signal that is proportional to the amount of target in the sample.

Another advantage of real-time PCR is its accuracy. The method is performed under controlled conditions and the results are standardized, reducing the risk of variability between samples and ensuring accurate and reliable results.

Real-time PCR is also much faster than traditional PCR, as the results are obtained in real-time without the need for gel electrophoresis. This is particularly beneficial in medical diagnostics where rapid results are often required.

Additionally, real-time PCR is cost-effective and can be automated, making it suitable for high-throughput applications. Its versatility and ability to multiplex reactions, allowing the simultaneous amplification and quantification of multiple targets in a single reaction, make it a valuable tool in a range of fields, including molecular biology, medical diagnostics, forensics, and environmental monitoring.

In conclusion, real-time PCR is a powerful and widely used technique that offers several key benefits over traditional PCR. Its sensitivity, accuracy, speed, and cost-effectiveness, combined with its versatility and ability to multiplex reactions, make it an essential tool in molecular biology and medical diagnostics.

Real-time PCR (Polymerase Chain Reaction) is a laboratory technique that is used to detect and quantify specific DNA or RNA targets in a sample. It is based on the PCR amplification of the target nucleic acids, with the addition of a fluorescent probe that allows for real-time monitoring of the amplification process.

One of the key advantages of real-time PCR is its high sensitivity, which enables the detection of very low levels of target DNA or RNA. This sensitivity is achieved through the use of fluorescence-based probes that bind to the amplified target nucleic acids and produce a signal that is proportional to the amount of target in the sample.

Another important advantage of real-time PCR is its accuracy. The method is performed under controlled conditions and the results are standardized, reducing the risk of variability between samples and ensuring accurate and reliable results.

In addition, real-time PCR is much faster than traditional PCR, as the results are obtained in real-time without the need for gel electrophoresis. This makes it a valuable tool in medical diagnostics where rapid results are often required.

Furthermore, real-time PCR is cost-effective and can be automated, making it suitable for high-throughput applications. Its versatility and ability to multiplex reactions, allowing the simultaneous amplification and quantification of multiple targets in a single reaction, make it a valuable tool in a range of fields, including molecular biology, medical diagnostics, forensics, and environmental monitoring.

To summarize, real-time PCR is a powerful and widely used technique that offers several key benefits over traditional PCR. Its sensitivity, accuracy, speed, and cost-effectiveness, combined with its versatility and ability to multiplex reactions, make it an essential tool in molecular biology and medical diagnostics.

Gene Sequencing

Gene sequencing is a laboratory technique that determines the precise order of nucleotides in a DNA molecule. Nucleotides are the building blocks of DNA, and the specific sequence of nucleotides in a DNA molecule encodes the genetic information that determines the characteristics and traits of an organism. By sequencing the DNA of an organism, scientists can identify the specific genes that are present and learn more about their function. Gene sequencing is an important tool in many areas of biology, including genetics, genomics, and biotechnology. There are several different techniques for gene sequencing, including Sanger sequencing, which is based on the polymerase chain reaction (PCR), and next-generation sequencing (NGS), which uses high-throughput technologies to sequence large amounts of DNA quickly and inexpensively.

There are several different techniques that can be used for gene sequencing, including:

1. Sanger sequencing: This is a traditional method of gene sequencing that is based on the polymerase chain reaction (PCR) and involves the selective incorporation of chain-terminating nucleotides. It is a relatively slow and expensive method, but it is still widely used because of its accuracy and reliability.
2. Next-generation sequencing (NGS): NGS is a high-throughput method that allows scientists to sequence large amounts of DNA quickly and inexpensively. There are several different NGS platforms available, including Illumina, Pacific Biosciences, and Oxford Nanopore Technologies. NGS is often used for large-scale genomic studies and for the rapid identification of genetic variations.
3. Single-molecule sequencing: This method involves sequencing the DNA of a single molecule, rather than amplifying it using PCR. Single-molecule sequencing is a relatively new technology, but it has the potential to be faster and more accurate than other methods.
4. Sequencing by synthesis: This method involves synthesizing a DNA molecule one nucleotide at a time, while simultaneously detecting the nucleotide that has been added. Sequencing by synthesis is used by several different NGS platforms.
5. Pyrosequencing: This method involves measuring the light produced by the enzymes involved in DNA synthesis, which allows scientists to determine the sequence of nucleotides in a DNA molecule. Pyrosequencing is used by some NGS platforms.

Gene sequencing is important for a variety of reasons. Some of the key applications and benefits of gene sequencing include:

- Understanding the function of genes: By sequencing the DNA of an organism, scientists can identify the specific genes that are present and learn more about their function. This can help us to understand how different genes contribute to the development and functioning of an organism.
- Identifying genetic variations: Gene sequencing can be used to identify differences in the DNA sequence between individuals or populations. These differences, known as genetic variations, can affect an individual's traits, susceptibility to certain diseases, and response to medications.
- Studying evolution: By comparing the DNA sequences of different organisms, scientists can learn about their evolutionary relationships and the evolutionary history of life on Earth.
- Diagnosing genetic disorders: Gene sequencing can be used to identify mutations or variations in an individual's DNA that may be associated with a genetic disorder. This information can be used to diagnose and manage genetic conditions, and to develop treatments and therapies.
- Developing personalized medicine: By analyzing an individual's DNA, physicians can tailor medical treatments and therapies to that person's specific genetic makeup, which may improve their effectiveness and reduce the risk of side effects.
- Agricultural and environmental applications: Gene sequencing can be used to improve crops and livestock by identifying genes that are associated with desirable traits, such as resistance to pests or diseases. It can also be used to study the impact of human activities on the environment, such as the impact of pollution on the genetics of different species.

Microarray technique

A microarray is a laboratory technique that is used to analyze the expression levels of many genes simultaneously. It involves the use of a glass slide or a microchip that is coated with a large number of DNA probes, each of which corresponds to a specific gene. Samples of DNA or RNA are then added to the microarray, and the probe molecules bind to the complementary sequences in the sample. The binding of the probe molecules to the sample DNA or RNA can be detected using a variety of techniques, including fluorescent labeling and imaging. Microarray analysis allows researchers to determine which genes are expressed at high levels and which are expressed at low levels in a given sample, which can provide insight into the biological processes that are taking place. Microarray technology is used in a variety of research and clinical settings, including drug development, diagnosis of genetic disorders, and cancer research.

Microarrays are tools that are used to measure the expression levels of thousands of genes simultaneously. They are used in a variety of applications, including gene expression analysis, genotyping, and DNA methylation analysis.

One of the main advantages of microarrays is their ability to simultaneously measure the expression levels of thousands of genes in a single experiment, making them a high-throughput tool for gene expression analysis. This can be useful in identifying genes that are differentially expressed in different conditions or tissues, which can provide insight into the underlying biological processes that are occurring.

Microarrays are also used in genotyping applications, which involve identifying specific genetic variants in an individual's genome. This can be useful in identifying genetic risk factors for certain diseases or in identifying individuals who may be responsive to certain medications.

Overall, microarrays are important tools in modern molecular biology research, as they allow researchers to quickly and efficiently analyze gene expression and genotyping data.

There are a number of applications for microarray techniques in molecular biology and genomics research. Some of the most common applications include:

1. Gene expression analysis: Microarrays can be used to measure the expression levels of thousands of genes simultaneously, allowing researchers to identify which genes are more or less active in a particular tissue or under certain conditions.

2. Genotyping: Microarrays can be used to identify specific genetic variants, such as single nucleotide polymorphisms (SNPs), in an individual's genome. This can be useful in identifying genetic risk factors for certain diseases or in identifying individuals who may be responsive to certain medications.
3. DNA methylation analysis: Microarrays can be used to measure the methylation status of cytosine residues in DNA, which can provide insight into gene regulation and the epigenetic modifications that occur in cells.
4. RNA interference (RNAi) screens: Microarrays can be used to identify genes that are essential for cell viability or that have a specific function in a particular pathway or process. This can be done by knocking down the expression of each gene in the genome individually and measuring the effect on the cell.
5. Drug discovery: Microarrays can be used to identify genes that are affected by a particular drug and to understand how the drug is acting on the cellular level.
6. Diagnostics: Microarrays can be used in diagnostic assays to detect the presence of specific genetic variations or to measure the expression levels of genes that are associated with a particular disease.

SDS page

SDS page is a technique used to separate proteins based on their size. It stands for "sodium dodecyl sulfate polyacrylamide gel electrophoresis." In SDS-PAGE, proteins are denatured and uniformly charged by the detergent sodium dodecyl sulfate (SDS) before being separated on a polyacrylamide gel. The separation is based on the size of the proteins, with smaller proteins migrating more quickly through the gel matrix than larger proteins. The separated proteins can then be visualized by staining with a protein-specific dye or by transferring the proteins to a membrane and detecting them with an appropriate protein-specific antibody. SDS-PAGE is commonly used in molecular biology and biochemistry to analyze the purity and size of proteins.

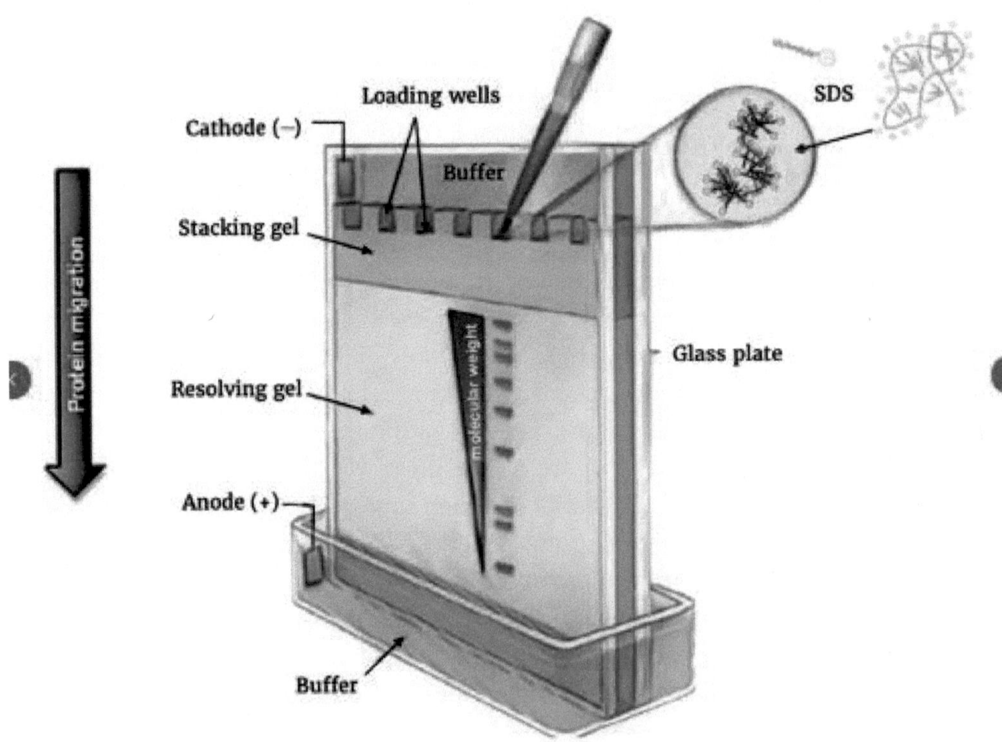

Fig 4.3: SDS page gel electrophoresis [3]

Importance of SDS page

SDS-PAGE is an important technique for analyzing proteins because it allows researchers to separate and identify individual proteins from complex mixtures. This can be useful for a variety of purposes, including:

- Quality control: SDS-PAGE can be used to assess the purity and integrity of a protein sample.
- Characterization: SDS-PAGE can be used to determine the size and molecular weight of a protein, which can be important for understanding its structure and function.
- Comparisons: SDS-PAGE can be used to compare the protein content of different samples, such as to identify changes in protein expression between healthy and diseased tissue.
- Protein purification: SDS-PAGE can be used as a step in the purification of proteins, by allowing researchers to separate a protein of interest from other proteins in a sample.
- Overall, SDS-PAGE is a widely used and important technique for studying proteins and their roles in biological systems.

ELISA

ELISA (enzyme-linked immunosorbent assay) is a widely used and sensitive assay for detecting and quantifying proteins in a sample. It is based on the specific binding of an antibody to a protein or antigen of interest. In an ELISA assay, a specific protein or antigen is typically coated onto the surface of a 96-well plate, and the sample is then added to the wells. If the protein or antigen of interest is present in the sample, it will bind to the protein or antigen on the surface of the wells. A primary antibody specific for the protein or antigen is then added to the wells and will bind to the protein or antigen, if it is present in the sample. A secondary antibody conjugated to an enzyme is then added, which will bind to the primary antibody. The presence of the bound primary and secondary antibodies is then detected by adding a substrate for the enzyme, which will produce a detectable product, such as a color change. The amount of enzyme activity in each well is proportional to the amount of protein or antigen present in the sample. ELISA is a widely used and versatile assay that has many applications in molecular biology and biochemistry.

Types of ELISA-

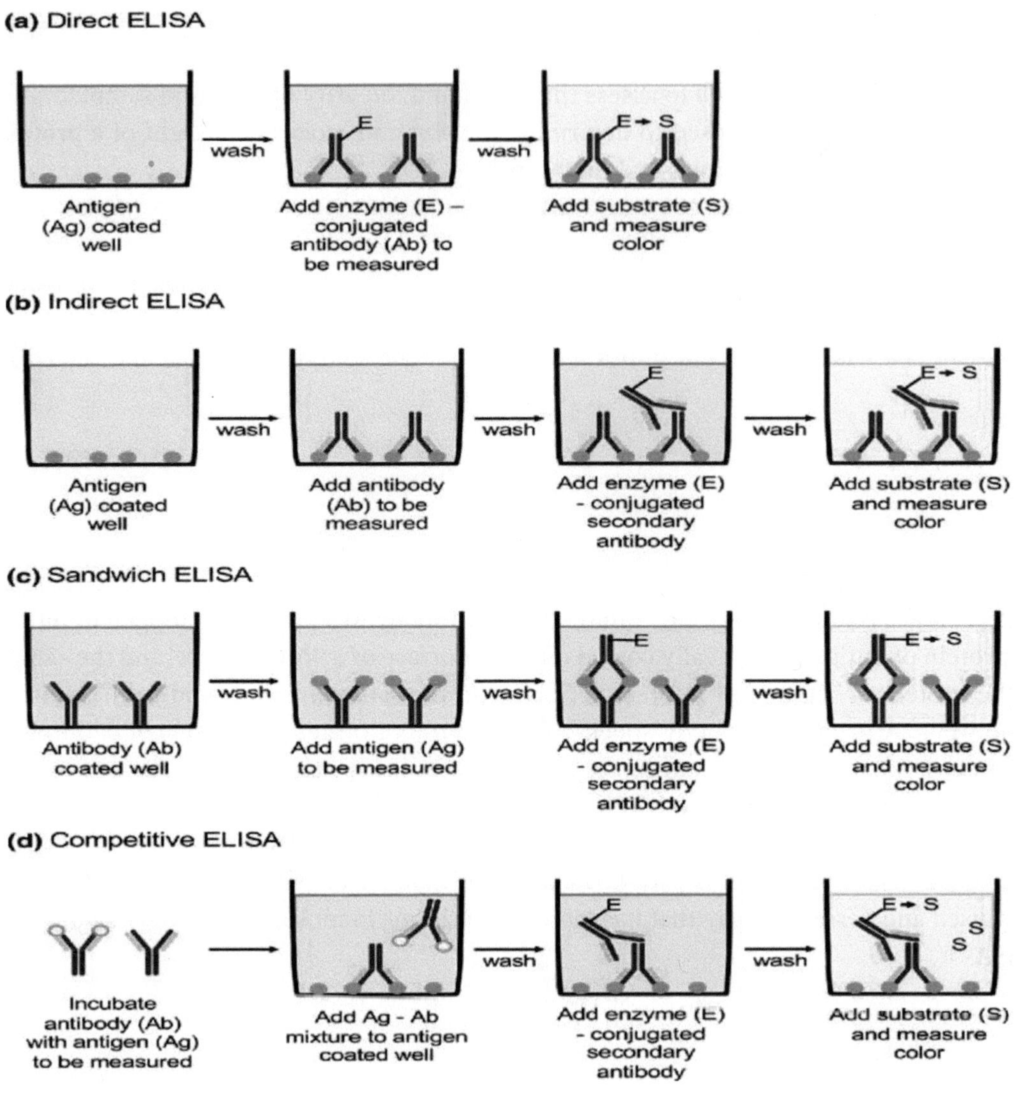

Fig 4.4:- types of ELISA [4]

Steps in ELISA

The steps in an ELISA assay typically include:

1. Coating the wells of a 96-well plate with a specific protein or antigen. This step typically involves incubating the wells with a solution containing the protein or antigen and allowing it to bind to the surface of the wells.
2. Blocking the wells to prevent nonspecific binding of proteins to the surface of the wells. This step typically involves incubating the wells with a solution containing a protein, such as milk or bovine serum albumin, that will coat the surface of the wells and block any remaining binding sites.
3. Adding the sample to the wells. This step involves adding the sample, which may contain the protein or antigen of interest, to the wells.
4. Adding a primary antibody specific for the protein or antigen of interest. This step involves adding a primary antibody that will bind to the protein or antigen of interest, if it is present in the sample.
5. Adding a secondary antibody conjugated to an enzyme. This step involves adding a secondary antibody that will bind to the primary antibody. The secondary antibody is typically conjugated to an enzyme, such as horseradish peroxidase (HRP), which will allow for the detection of the bound primary antibody.

6. Adding a substrate for the enzyme. This step involves adding a substrate that the enzyme can convert into a detectable product, such as a color change.
7. Reading the plate. This step involves measuring the amount of enzyme activity in each well, which is proportional to the amount of protein or antigen present in the sample. This is typically done using a plate reader, which measures the absorbance of the wells at a specific wavelength.

Overall, ELISA is a sensitive and specific assay that is widely used to detect and quantify proteins in a variety of sample types.

APPLICATIONS OF ELISA

ELISA is a widely used and versatile assay that has a variety of applications, including:

1. Detection and quantification of proteins in a sample: ELISA can be used to detect the presence of a specific protein in a sample and to measure the concentration of the protein.
2. Diagnostic testing: ELISA is often used in diagnostic testing to detect the presence of specific proteins or antibodies in bodily fluids, such as blood or urine. This can be useful for detecting infections, autoimmune disorders, and other conditions.
3. Monitoring protein levels in research: ELISA is frequently used in research to measure the expression levels of specific proteins in different samples, such as to compare protein levels between healthy and diseased tissue.
4. Assessing immune responses: ELISA can be used to measure the production of specific antibodies in response to an immune challenge, such as a vaccine or infection.

Overall, ELISA is a widely used and important technique that has many applications in molecular biology and biochemistry

Western blotting

Western blotting is a laboratory technique used to detect specific proteins in a sample of tissue homogenate or extract. It uses gel electrophoresis to separate the proteins by size, and then transfers them to a membrane, where they can be probed with antibodies specific to the protein of interest. The procedure is called a "Western" blot because it was developed by researchers at the Western General Hospital in Edinburgh, Scotland, who published the first description of the method in 1979.

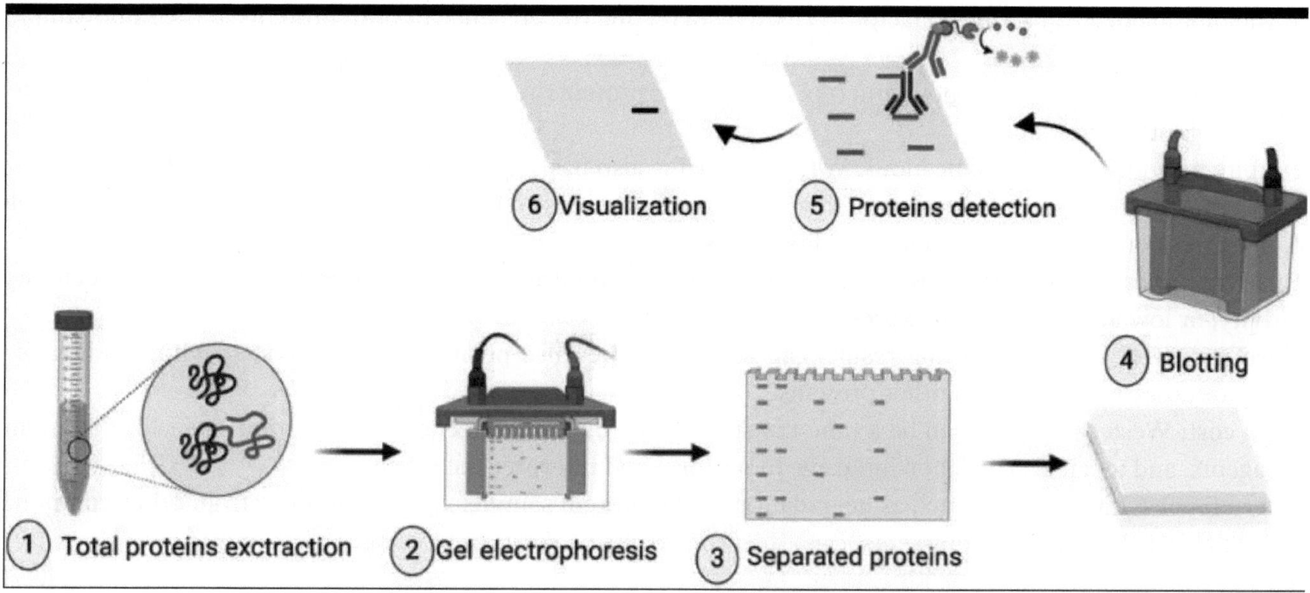

Fig 4.5:- western blotting [5]

The basic steps of a Western blot are:

1. Prepare the protein sample by denaturing it and separating the proteins by size using gel electrophoresis.
2. Transfer the separated proteins from the gel to a membrane using a process called electroblotting.
3. Block any non-specific binding sites on the membrane.
4. Add a primary antibody specific to the protein of interest, and incubate the membrane to allow the antibody to bind to the protein.
5. Wash the membrane to remove any unbound primary antibody.
6. Add a secondary antibody, which is conjugated to a detectable enzyme or fluorescent dye, and incubate the membrane to allow the secondary antibody to bind to the primary antibody.
7. Wash the membrane again to remove any unbound secondary antibody.
8. Develop the blot by adding a substrate that is converted by the detectable enzyme, or visualize the blot using a fluorescent scanner.

Western blotting is a widely used technique in molecular biology and biochemistry, and it is particularly useful for analyzing complex mixtures of proteins, such as those found in cell lysates or bodily fluids

Western blotting applicatios

Western blotting is a widely used technique in molecular biology and biochemistry, and it has a number of applications, including:

1. Identifying specific proteins in a sample: Western blotting can be used to detect and quantify specific proteins in a sample, such as enzymes, signaling proteins, and structural proteins.
2. Analyzing protein expression: Western blotting can be used to analyze changes in protein expression levels under different conditions, such as in response to a drug treatment or during the progression of a disease.
3. Detecting post-translational modifications: Western blotting can be used to detect post-translational modifications, such as phosphorylation, glycosylation, and acetylation, which can regulate protein function.
4. Diagnosing diseases: Western blotting can be used to diagnose certain diseases, such as HIV and Lyme disease, by detecting the presence of specific proteins in a patient's blood or other bodily fluids.
5. Monitoring protein-protein interactions: Western blotting can be used to study protein-protein interactions, such as the binding of a transcription factor to DNA, by detecting the presence of both proteins in the same sample.

Overall, Western blotting is a powerful tool for studying proteins and their functions in various biological systems.

Western blotting limitations

Despite its wide range of applications, Western blotting also has some limitations, including:

Low sensitivity: Western blotting can sometimes have low sensitivity, particularly when detecting low levels of protein expression or post-translational modifications.

False negatives: Western blotting results can sometimes be false negatives, due to poor antibody specificity or sensitivity, or low levels of protein expression.

False positives: Western blotting results can sometimes be false positives, due to non-specific binding of the antibody or cross-reactivity with other proteins.

High cost: Western blotting can be a time-consuming and expensive technique, requiring specialized equipment and reagents, and it can also be labor-intensive to perform and interpret the results.

Interferences: Interferences such as degradation of the protein sample, and interference from other components in the sample, such as salts or detergents, can affect the results of Western blotting.

In conclusion, Western blotting is a widely used technique with a range of applications, but it also has limitations that should be considered when selecting it as a method for a particular experiment.

Alternative techniques

There are several alternative techniques that can be used to study proteins, including:

ELISA (Enzyme-linked Immunosorbent Assay): ELISA is a sandwich-type assay that uses antibodies to detect specific proteins in a sample, similar to Western blotting. ELISA is more sensitive than Western blotting and can be used to quantitate protein levels, but it is limited to detecting only one protein at a time.

Immunoprecipitation: Immunoprecipitation is a technique that uses antibodies to selectively precipitate a specific protein from a sample, and it can be used to study protein-protein interactions, post-translational modifications, and protein localization.

Mass spectrometry: Mass spectrometry is a powerful technique for protein analysis that can be used to identify and quantify proteins in a sample, as well as to study post-translational modifications and protein-protein interactions. Mass spectrometry is highly sensitive and can be used to analyze complex mixtures of proteins, but it is also more complex and technically challenging than Western blotting or ELISA.

Flow cytometry: Flow cytometry is a high-throughput technique that uses fluorescence to measure the properties of individual cells, and it can be used to analyze the expression of cell surface and intracellular proteins.

These alternative techniques can complement Western blotting or be used instead of Western blotting, depending on the specific research question and the available resources.

Limitations of Western blotting

Western blotting is a powerful tool for studying proteins, but it also has several limitations, including:

Low sensitivity: Western blotting can have low sensitivity, especially for detecting low-abundance or weakly expressed proteins.

Interfering contaminants: Contaminants in the sample or the reagents used in the blot can interfere with the detection of the protein of interest, leading to false negative results.

Cross-reactivity: Antibodies used in Western blotting can sometimes cross-react with other proteins in the sample, leading to false positive results.

Time-consuming: Western blotting is a time-consuming technique, requiring several steps and multiple incubations to complete.

Technical variability: Western blotting is a technically demanding technique, and the results can be affected by variations in the preparation of the sample, the electrophoresis, the transfer, and the antibody incubations.

Despite these limitations, Western blotting is still widely used in molecular biology and biochemistry, and it remains an important tool for the study of proteins and their functions.

Recombinant DNA technology and gene therapy

Recombinant DNA technology is a set of techniques that allows scientists to manipulate and modify the DNA of an organism in a specific and controlled manner. It involves the cutting and pasting of DNA sequences from different sources and then inserting them into a host organism, such as bacteria or yeast cells. This technology has revolutionized many areas of biology and medicine, including gene therapy.

Gene therapy is a medical treatment that involves the use of genes to treat or prevent diseases. It involves the introduction of normal genes into cells in place of missing or defective ones in order to correct genetic disorders. Gene therapy has the potential to treat a wide range of diseases, including inherited disorders, cancer, and infectious diseases. There are several approaches to gene therapy, including the use of recombinant DNA technology to produce and deliver normal copies of a gene to cells.

Overall, recombinant DNA technology and gene therapy are powerful tools that have the potential to transform the way we treat and prevent diseases

Applications of recombinant DNA technology and gene therapy

Some examples of the applications of gene therapy include:

1. Treatment of genetic disorders: Gene therapy has the potential to treat genetic disorders, such as cystic fibrosis, sickle cell anemia, and muscular dystrophy, by introducing normal copies of a gene into cells to replace missing or defective ones.
2. Treatment of cancer: Gene therapy can be used to treat cancer by introducing genes that can kill cancer cells or make them more sensitive to chemotherapy and radiation therapy.
3. Treatment of infectious diseases: Gene therapy can be used to treat infectious diseases by introducing genes that can produce proteins that can inhibit the growth of the pathogen or stimulate the immune system to fight the infection.
4. Treatment of cardiovascular diseases: Gene therapy can be used to treat cardiovascular diseases by introducing genes that can stimulate the growth of new blood vessels or protect against heart muscle damage.
5. Treatment of neurodegenerative diseases: Gene therapy can be used to treat neurodegenerative diseases, such as Alzheimer's disease and Parkinson's disease, by introducing genes that can protect nerve cells or stimulate the growth of new ones.

Overall, gene therapy has the potential to treat a wide range of diseases and has the potential to transform the way we approach many health problems.

Recombinant DNA technology

The basic principles of recombinant DNA technology involve the manipulation and modification of DNA in a specific and controlled manner. This can be achieved through the use of several techniques, including:

1. DNA cloning: This involves the production of multiple copies of a specific DNA sequence. This can be achieved through the use of enzymes that can cut and paste DNA sequences and host cells, such as bacteria or yeast cells, which can replicate the introduced DNA.
2. DNA sequencing: This involves determining the order of the nucleotide bases (adenine, guanine, cytosine, and thymine) in a DNA molecule. This can be achieved through the use of automated sequencing machines and specialized software.
3. DNA amplification: This involves increasing the amount of a specific DNA sequence. This can be achieved through the use of the polymerase chain reaction (PCR), which allows for the rapid synthesis of large amounts of a specific DNA sequence.
4. DNA modification: This involves altering the sequence of a DNA molecule. This can be achieved through the use of enzymes that can cut and paste DNA sequences or through the use of chemical methods that can modify the structure of the DNA molecule.

Overall, these techniques allow scientists to manipulate and modify DNA in a specific and controlled manner, which has revolutionized many areas of biology and medicine.

The basic principles of recombinant DNA technology RESTRICTION ENZYMES

Recombinant DNA technology involves the manipulation of DNA molecules from different sources to create a new DNA molecule. One of the key tools used in this technology is restriction enzymes, which are enzymes that cut DNA at specific sequences called restriction sites. These restriction sites are typically short, specific sequences of nucleotides, and each restriction enzyme recognizes and cuts a specific restriction site. The resulting DNA fragments can then be manipulated and combined in various ways to create new DNA molecules.

Restriction enzymes are often used to cut DNA from different sources into fragments that can be easily manipulated. For example, if a researcher wants to insert a gene from one organism into the genome of another organism, they might use restriction enzymes to cut the DNA of both organisms into fragments. The desired gene can then be isolated from the fragments and inserted into the genome of the target organism using other techniques, such as ligase enzymes.

Restriction enzymes are an important tool in many areas of biology and biotechnology, including gene cloning, DNA sequencing, and the creation of genetically modified organisms. They are also used in forensic science and in the development of diagnostic tests

Various types of vectors

Vectors are used in recombinant DNA technology to transfer DNA fragments from one organism to another. There are several different types of vectors that can be used for this purpose, including:

1. Plasmids: Plasmids are small, circular pieces of DNA that are found in many bacteria. They can be easily isolated from bacterial cells and used as vectors because they can replicate independently of the bacterial chromosome.
2. Bacteriophages: Bacteriophages are viruses that infect bacteria. They can be used as vectors because they have the ability to insert their genetic material into the genome of a host cell.
3. Cosmids: Cosmids are hybrid vectors that combine features of plasmids and bacteriophages. They are able to carry larger DNA fragments than most plasmids and can be easily introduced into bacterial cells.
4. Yeast Artificial Chromosomes (YACs): YACs are large, circular pieces of DNA that are used as vectors in yeast cells. They can carry very large DNA fragments, making them useful for cloning large genes or even entire genomes.
5. Integrative Vectors: Integrative vectors are designed to insert the DNA they are carrying into the genome of the host cell. This can be useful for stable gene expression or for creating genetically modified organisms.
6. Transposons: Transposons are small pieces of DNA that can move from one location in the genome to another. They can be used as vectors for transferring DNA between cells.
7. Viral Vectors: Viral vectors are viruses that have been modified to carry foreign DNA. They can be used to introduce DNA into a host cell, where it can be expressed or used to create genetically modified organisms

Applications of recombinant DNA technology

Recombinant DNA technology has a wide range of applications in various fields, including medicine, agriculture, and industry. Some of the major applications of this technology are:

- Gene Cloning: Recombinant DNA technology is used to produce multiple copies of a specific gene or DNA fragment. This process, known as gene cloning, allows researchers to study the function of a particular gene or to produce large amounts of a specific protein.
- Gene Therapy: Recombinant DNA technology is used in the development of gene therapies, which are treatments that involve the introduction of a functional copy of a gene into cells to correct a genetic deficiency.
- Production of Recombinant Proteins: Recombinant DNA technology is used to produce proteins that are not normally produced by a particular organism. These proteins can be used for a variety of purposes, including medical treatments and research.
- Diagnostic Testing: Recombinant DNA technology is used to develop diagnostic tests for a variety of genetic disorders and diseases.
- Agricultural Applications: Recombinant DNA technology is used to produce genetically modified crops that are resistant to pests and diseases, have improved nutritional value, or are more drought-resistant.
- Industrial Applications: Recombinant DNA technology is used to produce a variety of products for industrial use, including enzymes for use in detergents and food processing, and hormones for use in livestock production.
- Environmental Applications: Recombinant DNA technology is also used in the development of genetically modified microorganisms that can be used to clean up environmental contaminants.

Gene Therapy

Gene therapy is a medical treatment that involves introducing genetic material into the cells of an individual to correct a genetic deficiency or disorder. The goal of gene therapy is to replace or repair a faulty gene with a healthy copy of the gene, or to introduce a new gene that can help the body fight a particular disease. Gene therapy can be used to treat a wide range of genetic disorders, including inherited disorders, cancer, and infectious diseases. There are several different approaches to gene therapy, including the use of viral vectors to deliver the therapeutic gene, the use of non-viral vectors such as liposomes or nanoparticles, and the use of gene-editing technologies such as CRISPR. While gene therapy holds great promise as a means of treating genetic disorders, it is still a relatively new and experimental field, and more research is needed to fully understand its potential and limitations.

Various types of gene transfer techniques

There are several different techniques that can be used to transfer genetic material to cells as part of gene therapy. Some of the most commonly used techniques include:

- Viral vectors: These are viruses that have been genetically modified to carry the therapeutic gene into the host cell. There are several types of viral vectors that can be used, including retroviruses, adenoviruses, and adeno-associated viruses (AAVs).
- Non-viral vectors: These are non-living carriers that can be used to deliver the therapeutic gene to cells. Examples of non-viral vectors include liposomes, nanoparticles, and plasmids.
- Gene-editing technologies: These are techniques that allow scientists to make precise changes to the genome of an organism. Examples of gene-editing technologies include CRISPR-Cas9, TALENs, and ZFNs.
- Ex vivo gene therapy: This involves removing cells from the body, modifying them genetically in the laboratory, and then returning them to the body.
- In vivo gene therapy: This involves administering the therapeutic gene directly to the patient, either through injection or inhalation.
- Each of these techniques has its own advantages and disadvantages, and the most appropriate technique will depend on the specific needs of the patient and the disease being treated

Clinical applications of gene therapy

- Gene therapy has the potential to be used to treat a wide range of genetic disorders and other diseases. Some of the conditions that are currently being explored as potential targets for gene therapy include:
- Inherited genetic disorders: Gene therapy can be used to replace or repair defective genes that are responsible for inherited disorders such as cystic fibrosis, hemophilia, and sickle cell anemia.
- Cancer: Gene therapy can be used to help the immune system recognize and attack cancer cells, or to introduce genes that can help kill cancer cells directly.
- Infectious diseases: Gene therapy has the potential to be used to treat viral infections such as HIV and hepatitis B and C by introducing genes that can help the body fight the virus.
- Neurological disorders: Gene therapy is being explored as a potential treatment for neurological conditions such as Parkinson's disease and Alzheimer's disease.
- Cardiovascular disease: Gene therapy is being studied as a potential treatment for conditions such as heart failure and arterial plaque buildup.
- Gene therapy is still an experimental field, and many of these applications are still in the early stages of development. More research is needed to fully understand the potential and limitations of gene therapy, and to

determine the most effective ways to use it to treat a variety of diseases.

Recent advances in gene therapy

Gene therapy has made significant progress in recent years, with a number of gene therapies being approved for use and many more in clinical trials. Some of the recent advances in gene therapy include:

- Approval of gene therapies: In 2017, the US Food and Drug Administration (FDA) approved the first gene therapy for use in the United States, a treatment for a rare genetic disorder called spinal muscular atrophy. Since then, several other gene therapies have been approved for use in the US and other countries, including treatments for rare genetic disorders such as hemophilia and sickle cell anemia.
- Development of gene-editing technologies: The development of gene-editing technologies such as CRISPR-Cas9 has revolutionized the field of gene therapy by making it possible to make precise changes to the genome. This has opened up new possibilities for treating genetic disorders and other diseases.
- Use of gene therapy to treat cancer: Gene therapy is being explored as a potential treatment for cancer, with several clinical trials underway to test the effectiveness of gene therapy in treating different types of cancer.
- Increased understanding of the potential and limitations of gene therapy: As more research is conducted, scientists are gaining a better understanding of the potential and limitations of gene therapy, which will help to guide the development of new treatments.

Overall, gene therapy has made significant progress in recent years, and it has the potential to be a powerful tool for treating a wide range of genetic disorders and other diseases.

Recent Updates:

Leaf senescence is a highly complex, genetically regulated and well-ordered process with multiple layers and pathways. Delaying leaf senescence would help increase in yields in rice over the past 15 years, more than 100 rice leaf-senescence genes have been cloned, greatly improving the understanding of leaf-senescence in rice[6].

Caseins in milk are similar in size and differ very little in net charge from each other. Also, in heated milk, κ-casein not only complexes with whey proteins but also undergoes self-polymerisation. These cause problems in the resolution of milk proteins and encouraged researchers to modify PAGE. Seven different types of PAGE, i.e., native-PAGE, urea-PAGE, reducing-sodium dodecyl sulphate (SDS)-PAGE, non-reducing-SDS-PAGE, urea-SDS-PAGE, tricine-PAGE, and two-dimensional electrophoresis (2DE) were developed by researchers(7).

Microarray technique has been used for very long time but in recent years there are new technologies developed for microarray analysis. Gene Expression Analysis Platform (GEAP) is a highly customizable, fast, versatile and ready-to-use and portable software developed for microarray analysis[8].

Genome sequencing is used in the diagnosis and developmentof disease treatment. Antimicrobial-resistant genes are causing restrictions on the treatment of microbial diseases and the efficacy of drugs. Rodrigues, Grazielle Lima, et al. have studied the frequency of antimicrobial resistance genes in Salmonella by in-silico Whole-Genome Sequencing Analysis[9].

In the last three decades, antivenom research has steadily been adopting methodologies from the field of biotechnology with the purpose of generating novel types of antivenoms with improved therapeutic benefits. In particular, recombinant DNA technology has enabled the application of monoclonal antibodies as an alternative to conventional antivenoms, which are based on polyclonal antibodies derived from the plasma of immunized animals[10].

The past few years have seen a renaissance in the field of gene and cell therapy and the first approved therapies following decades of efforts. This includes the first oligonucleotide-based therapies (Spinraza, Exondys 51, Vyondys

53), three cell therapies (Kymriah, Yescarta, Tescartus), and two in vivo gene therapies (Luxturna and Zolgensma), with more following close behind. These therapies treat diverse clinical indications and tissue targets, including neuromuscular disease, inherited blindness, and cancer.

Reference:

1. Magdeldin, S. ed., 2012. *Gel electrophoresis: Principles and basics*. BoD–Books on Demand.
2. Dr Tushar Chauhan, 2019 Reverse Transcription PCR: Principle, Procedure, Protocol, Advantages, Limitations, Applications. Genetic education.
3. Wangler, M.F. and Bellen, H.J., 2017. In Vivo Animal Modeling: Drosophila. In *Basic Science Methods for Clinical Researchers* (pp. 211-234). Academic Press.
4. Meftahi, G.H., Bahari, Z., Zarei Mahmoudabadi, A., Iman, M. and Jangravi, Z., 2021. Applications of western blot technique: From bench to bedside. *Biochemistry and Molecular Biology Education*, *49*(4), pp.509-517.
5. Xiong, E., Li, Z., Zhang, C., Zhang, J., Liu, Y., Peng, T., Chen, Z. and Zhao, Q., 2021. A study of leaf-senescence genes in rice based on a combination of genomics, proteomics and bioinformatics. *Briefings in Bioinformatics*, *22*(4), p.bbaa305.
6. Sharma, N., Sharma, R., Rajput, Y.S., Mann, B., Singh, R. and Gandhi, K., 2021. Separation methods for milk proteins on polyacrylamide gel electrophoresis: Critical analysis and options for better resolution. *International Dairy Journal*, *114*, p.104920.
7. Nunes, I.J.G., Recamonde-Mendoza, M. and Feltes, B.C., 2021. Gene Expression Analysis Platform (GEAP): A highly customizable, fast, versatile and ready-to-use microarray analysis platform. *Genetics and molecular biology*, *45*.
8. Rodrigues, G.L., Panzenhagen, P., Ferrari, R.G., Dos Santos, A., Paschoalin, V.M.F. and Conte-Junior, C.A., 2020. Frequency of antimicrobial resistance genes in Salmonella from Brazil by in silico whole-genome sequencing analysis: an overview of the last four decades. *Frontiers in Microbiology*, *11*, p.1864.
9. Laustsen, A.H., 2021. Antivenom in the Age of Recombinant DNA Technology. In *Handbook of Venoms and Toxins of Reptiles* (pp. 499-510). CRC Press.
10. Bulaklak, K. and Gersbach, C.A., 2020. The once and future gene therapy. *Nature communications*, *11*(1), pp.1-4.

CHAPTER FIVE

Pharmacogenomics

Miss Sayali Murkar, Mrs Ashwini Badhe and Dr Pravin Badhe

Introduction-

Pharmacogenomics is the study of how a person's genetic makeup can affect their response to medications. It is an emerging field that aims to use genetic information to tailor treatment to each individual, in order to improve the effectiveness and safety of medications.

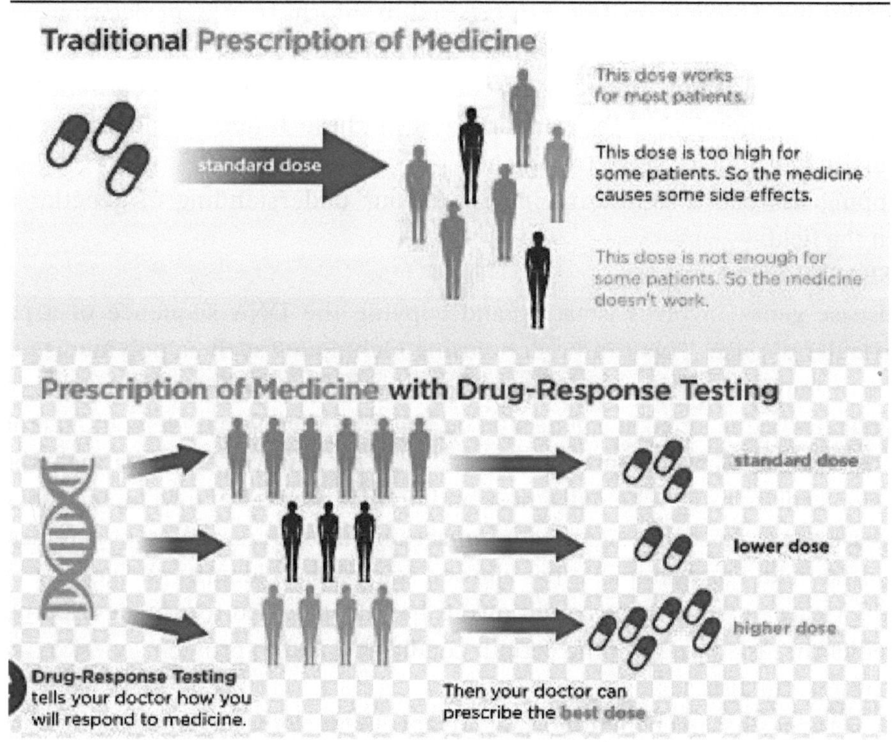

Figure 5.1: pharmacogenomics [1]

One way that pharmacogenomics can be used is to identify genetic variations that may cause a person to metabolize a drug differently than expected. For example, some people may have a variant in a gene that is involved in metabolizing a particular drug, which could cause them to have an increased or decreased response to the drug. This information can be used to adjust the dosage of the medication or to select a different treatment option that is more likely to be effective and safe for the individual.

Pharmacogenomics can also be used to predict the likelihood of side effects from a particular medication. For example, a person with a specific genetic variation may be more likely to experience a particular side effect from a drug, and this information can be used to inform treatment decisions.

Overall, pharmacogenomics has the potential to improve the effectiveness and safety of medications by helping to tailor treatment to the individual.

Gene mapping and cloning of disease gene

Gene mapping is the process of identifying the location of a particular gene on a chromosome. This can be done using a variety of techniques, including linkage analysis, which involves comparing the inheritance patterns of genetic markers in families affected by a particular disease to identify the location of the disease-associated gene.

Once the location of a disease-associated gene has been identified, it can be "cloned" by isolating and copying the DNA sequence of the gene. This can be done using techniques such as polymerase chain reaction (PCR), which allows scientists to amplify specific sequences of DNA.

Importance and application of gene mapping

Gene mapping is an important tool in the field of genetics, as it allows scientists to identify the location of particular genes on chromosomes. This information can be used to understand the genetic basis of various traits and conditions, and to develop new treatments and therapies for genetic diseases.

One important application of gene mapping is in the diagnosis and management of genetic diseases. By identifying the location of disease-associated genes, genetic tests can be developed to help diagnose and predict the risk of developing certain conditions. This information can be used to inform treatment decisions and to provide genetic counseling to individuals and families affected by genetic conditions.

Gene mapping can also be used in the study of complex traits, such as susceptibility to certain diseases or responses to medications. By identifying the genetic basis of these traits, scientists can better understand the underlying mechanisms and develop targeted treatments.

Overall, gene mapping has had a significant impact on our understanding of genetics and has led to many important advances in the field

CLONING OF DISEASED GENE

The cloning of disease genes involves isolating and copying the DNA sequence of a particular gene that is associated with a particular disease. This can be done using techniques such as polymerase chain reaction (PCR), which allows scientists to amplify specific sequences of DNA.

Once the disease gene has been cloned, it can be studied in greater detail to understand its role in the development and progression of the disease. This information can be used to develop new treatments and therapies for the condition, and to develop genetic tests to help diagnose and predict the risk of developing the disease.

The cloning of disease genes has had a significant impact on our understanding of genetics and has led to many important advances in the field. For example, it has allowed scientists to identify the genetic basis of many diseases and to develop targeted treatments for these conditions. It has also allowed for the development of genetic tests to help diagnose and predict the risk of developing certain conditions, and to provide genetic counseling to individuals and families affected by genetic diseases.

The cloning of disease genes has been an important advancement in the field of genetics, as it allows scientists to study the genetic basis of many diseases in greater detail. This information can be used to develop new treatments and therapies for these conditions, and to improve our understanding of how they develop and progress. It can also be used to develop genetic tests to help diagnose and predict the risk of developing certain diseases

There are several applications of the cloning of disease genes:

- Understanding the genetic basis of disease: By cloning disease genes, scientists can study the DNA sequence of the gene and understand how it contributes to the development and progression of the disease. This information can be used to develop new treatments and therapies for the condition.
- Developing genetic tests: The cloning of disease genes has allowed for the development of genetic tests to help diagnose and predict the risk of developing certain conditions. This can be useful for individuals with a family

history of a particular disease or for those who may be at increased risk due to certain genetic factors.

- Developing targeted treatments: By understanding the genetic basis of a disease, scientists can develop treatments that are specifically designed to target the underlying genetic causes of the condition. This can lead to more effective and personalized treatments for patients.
- Providing genetic counseling: Cloning disease genes can also be useful for providing genetic counseling to individuals and families affected by genetic conditions. This can help individuals understand their risk of developing a particular condition and make informed decisions about their healthcare.

Overall, the cloning of disease genes has had a significant impact on our understanding of genetics and has led to many important advances in the field of medicine.

With the help of gene cloning, researchers are able to better understand the genetic basis of many diseases, which in turn can lead to the development of more effective and personalized treatments. The cloning of disease genes also helps in the development of genetic tests, which can aid in early diagnosis and predict the risk of developing certain conditions. Additionally, genetic counseling becomes more informed with the help of cloning disease genes, allowing individuals and families to make informed decisions about their health. The applications of gene cloning are wide-ranging and continue to make a positive impact on the field of genetics and medicine.

Certainly! The cloning of disease genes is a crucial step in the process of understanding the genetic basis of various diseases. It provides researchers with the necessary information to study the function of the gene and how it contributes to the development and progression of a particular condition. This information can then be used to develop new treatments and therapies, as well as genetic tests for early diagnosis.

One of the key applications of gene cloning is the development of targeted treatments. By understanding the genetic basis of a disease, researchers can design treatments that specifically target the underlying genetic causes of the condition. This leads to more effective and personalized treatments for patients, as the treatments can be tailored to the individual's specific genetic make-up.

Another important application of gene cloning is the development of genetic tests. These tests can help diagnose a particular condition at an early stage, allowing for early intervention and treatment. They can also predict the risk of developing a particular condition, which can be useful for individuals with a family history of a particular disease or for those who may be at increased risk due to certain genetic factors.

Gene cloning also plays a crucial role in genetic counseling. By cloning disease genes, researchers can provide individuals and families with more accurate information about their risk of developing a particular condition. This can help individuals make informed decisions about their healthcare, including whether to undergo genetic testing, seek preventative measures, or pursue treatments.

In conclusion, the cloning of disease genes has had a profound impact on our understanding of genetics and has led to many important advances in the field of medicine. As technology and techniques continue to advance, the applications of gene cloning are likely to become even more widespread, leading to improved treatments and a better understanding of the genetic basis of disease.

Gene Mapping:

Linkage analysis: One of the main techniques used in gene mapping, linkage analysis involves comparing the inheritance patterns of genetic markers in families affected by a particular disease. This can help identify the location of the disease-associated gene on a chromosome.

Physical mapping: This involves using various techniques to create a detailed map of the DNA sequence of a particular chromosome, including restriction fragment length polymorphism (RFLP) analysis and fluorescence in situ hybridization (FISH).

Cytogenetic mapping: This involves the use of microscopy and staining techniques to visualize the physical location of genes on chromosomes and to identify any structural changes or abnormalities.

Cloning of Disease Genes:

Polymerase chain reaction (PCR): This is a widely used technique for amplifying specific sequences of DNA, and it is often used to clone disease genes. PCR allows scientists to isolate and copy the DNA sequence of a particular gene, making it easier to study the gene in greater detail.

Sequencing: Once a disease gene has been cloned, its DNA sequence can be determined using DNA sequencing techniques. This can help identify any mutations or changes in the gene that may be associated with the disease.

Model organisms: Scientists often use model organisms, such as mice or fruit flies, to study the effects of a particular disease gene. By creating transgenic animals that carry a mutated version of a disease gene, scientists can study the effects of the gene on the development and progression of the disease in a living organism.

In conclusion, gene mapping and cloning of disease genes are essential tools in the field of genetics, providing important insights into the genetic basis of various diseases and leading to the development of new treatments and therapies. With the continued advancements in genetics and biotechnology, we can expect to see even more breakthroughs in the field in the future.

Additionally, the cloning of disease genes can also aid in the development of gene therapy, which involves correcting or replacing defective genes with functional ones. Gene therapy has shown promise as a treatment for a variety of genetic conditions, including inherited disorders, some cancers, and some viral infections.

In summary, gene mapping and cloning of disease genes play a critical role in advancing our understanding of genetics and genetic disorders. These techniques provide important information about the location and function of disease-causing genes, which can be used to develop new treatments and therapies, genetic tests, and to provide genetic counseling to individuals and families affected by genetic conditions. The impact of these technologies is far-reaching and has the potential to significantly improve human health and well-being.

Furthermore, the study of disease genes can also provide insights into the evolution of species and the origins of diseases. By comparing the genetic sequences of different species, scientists can trace the evolutionary history of a particular gene and its role in the development of different diseases. This information can help to improve our understanding of the evolution of the human genome and the genetic factors that contribute to disease.

In addition to these applications, cloning disease genes can also be used in the study of drug development and personalized medicine. By understanding the genetic basis of a particular disease, scientists can design drugs that are targeted to specific genetic mutations, leading to more effective treatments with fewer side effects. Personalized medicine also aims to provide individualized treatment plans based on a patient's genetic profile, which can help to improve the effectiveness of treatments and reduce the risk of side effects.

Overall, gene mapping and cloning of disease genes continue to be an area of active research and development, with many exciting advancements and breakthroughs still to come. These technologies have the potential to revolutionize the field of medicine and improve human health and well-being in many ways.

Cloning disease genes can also be used in the development of gene therapy, which aims to treat genetic disorders by introducing functional copies of disease genes into affected individuals. This can be done through several methods, including:

Viral vectors: In this method, a functional copy of a disease gene is inserted into a viral vector, which is then delivered into the patient's cells. The viral vector carries the functional copy of the disease gene into the patient's cells, where it can replace the faulty gene and correct the genetic disorder.

Direct gene transfer: In this method, a functional copy of a disease gene is directly delivered into the patient's cells using various methods, including electroporation, ultrasound-mediated gene transfer, and nanoparticle-mediated gene transfer.

Gene editing: In this method, precise changes are made to the DNA sequence of a patient's cells to correct the disease-causing mutation. This can be done using tools such as CRISPR-Cas9, which can cut DNA at specific locations and introduce precise changes to the DNA sequence.

Gene therapy has the potential to cure genetic disorders and has already shown promising results in the treatment of several diseases, including genetic blood disorders, eye diseases, and cancer.

Moreover, cloning disease genes can also contribute to the development of preventive measures, such as vaccines and prophylactic treatments, to reduce the risk of developing certain genetic disorders.

Overall, gene mapping and cloning of disease genes continue to be a crucial area of research and development with numerous applications in medicine and biotechnology. These technologies hold great potential to improve human health and well-being and provide new solutions for the treatment of genetic disorders.

There are several ways in which gene mapping and cloning of disease genes have advanced the field of medicine and improved healthcare:

Improved Diagnosis: Gene mapping and cloning of disease genes have led to the development of genetic tests which can help diagnose diseases at an early stage. This allows for earlier treatment and management of the condition, which can improve patient outcomes.

Personalized Medicine: By understanding the genetic basis of a disease, scientists can develop treatments that are specifically designed to target the underlying genetic causes of the condition. This can lead to more effective and personalized treatments for patients, as treatments can be tailored to an individual's unique genetic profile.

Better Understanding of Diseases: Gene mapping and cloning of disease genes has allowed scientists to better understand the genetic basis of many diseases. This has improved our understanding of how diseases develop and progress, and has led to the development of new treatments and therapies.

Improved Genetic Counseling: Cloning disease genes can also be useful for providing genetic counseling to individuals and families affected by genetic conditions. This can help individuals understand their risk of developing a particular condition and make informed decisions about their healthcare.

Advancement in Research: Gene mapping and cloning of disease genes have greatly advanced the field of genetics and have paved the way for new discoveries and innovations in the field. This has led to the development of new treatments and therapies for a range of diseases, and has improved our overall understanding of genetics and the role of genetics in human health.

Overall, gene mapping and cloning of disease genes have had a significant impact on the field of medicine and have greatly improved healthcare.

As a language model, I can provide you with more details on gene mapping and cloning of disease genes. Here are a few additional details:

Gene mapping and linkage analysis: Gene mapping can be done using various techniques, including linkage analysis. Linkage analysis involves comparing the inheritance patterns of genetic markers in families affected by a particular disease to identify the location of the disease-associated gene. This process can be facilitated by the use of large families with multiple affected individuals, as well as the use of highly informative markers, such as single nucleotide polymorphisms (SNPs). The resulting linkage information can then be used to construct genetic linkage maps, which provide a visual representation of the relative positions of genes and markers on chromosomes.

Gene cloning: Gene cloning is the process of making multiple copies of a specific DNA sequence. The cloned DNA can then be used for a variety of purposes, such as DNA sequencing, expression analysis, and functional studies. The process of gene cloning typically involves three steps: (1) isolation of the target DNA, (2) insertion of the DNA into a suitable cloning vector, and (3) amplification of the cloned DNA. The most commonly used cloning vectors are plasmids and bacteriophages, which are small, circular DNA molecules that can be easily manipulated in bacteria.

Applications of gene cloning: Gene cloning has many practical applications, including the study of gene function, the identification of disease-causing genes, and the development of new therapies and treatments. For example, by cloning disease genes, researchers can study the DNA sequence of the gene and understand how it contributes to the development and progression of the disease. This information can then be used to develop new treatments and therapies for the condition. In addition, the cloning of disease genes has allowed for the development of genetic tests to help diagnose and predict the risk of developing certain conditions. This can be useful for individuals with a family history of a particular disease or for those who may be at increased risk due to certain genetic factors.

GENETIC VARIATION

Genetic variation refers to differences in an individual's DNA sequence. These differences can be caused by mutations, which are changes in the DNA sequence that can be inherited from a parent or that occur spontaneously during the development of an individual.

Genetic variation can occur at different levels, such as at the level of individual genes or at the level of the whole genome. Genetic variation can have a number of different effects on an individual's traits and characteristics, including their physical appearance, susceptibility to certain diseases, and response to medications. Genetic variation is an important factor in the evolution of species, as it allows for the emergence of new traits and characteristics and helps to increase the adaptability of a population to changing environments.

Overall, genetic variation is a key aspect of genetics that plays a significant role in the diversity of life on Earth and in the health and well-being of individuals.

Role of genetic variation in health /pharmacology

Genetic variation plays a significant role in health and pharmacology. For example, certain genetic variations can increase the risk of developing certain diseases or conditions, such as certain types of cancer or heart disease. These genetic variations can also affect an individual's response to medications, including their effectiveness and the likelihood of experiencing side effects.

In pharmacogenomics, the study of how genetic variation can affect an individual's response to medications, researchers use genetic information to tailor treatment to each individual. This can help to improve the effectiveness and safety of medications by helping to select the most appropriate treatment options for each individual.

For example, some people may have a variant in a gene that is involved in metabolizing a particular drug, which could cause them to have an increased or decreased response to the drug. This information can be used to adjust the dosage of the medication or to select a different treatment option that is more likely to be effective and safe for the individual.

Overall, understanding the role of genetic variation in health and pharmacology is an important area of research that has the potential to improve the effectiveness and safety of medications and to better understand the genetic basis of diseases.

It is also important to note that the role of genetic variation in health and pharmacology is complex and multifactorial, as many diseases and responses to medications are influenced by multiple genes and by environmental factors.

In addition, the study of genetic variation can also help to identify new targets for drug development and to understand why some individuals may have an increased risk of certain diseases.

Furthermore, genetic variation is a crucial aspect of personalized medicine, which aims to provide individualized healthcare based on an individual's genetic profile. By incorporating genetic information, personalized medicine has the potential to improve disease diagnosis, treatment, and prevention.

In conclusion, the role of genetic variation in health and pharmacology is critical for improving our understanding of the genetic basis of diseases and for developing more effective and personalized treatments. With advances in genetic technologies, this field is rapidly expanding and has the potential to revolutionize the way we approach healthcare.

Genetic testing: Genetic testing is a powerful tool for identifying genetic variations that can affect an individual's health and response to medications. The results of genetic testing can be used to determine an individual's risk of developing certain diseases, to select the most appropriate medications, and to monitor the effectiveness of treatment.

Genetic counsellingcounsellingcounsellors: Genetic counseling is an important aspect of personalized medicine, as it helps individuals understand the results of their genetic testing and the potential impact of genetic variations on their health. Genetic counselors can provide information and support to individuals and families, and help them make informed decisions about their health and treatment options.

Genome-wide association studies (GWAS): GWAS is a type of genetic study that aims to identify genetic variations that are associated with specific diseases or traits. This type of study can help to uncover new targets for drug development and to better understand the genetic basis of diseases.

Precision medicine: Precision medicine is an approach to healthcare that is based on an individual's genetic profile. By incorporating genetic information, precision medicine has the potential to improve disease diagnosis, treatment, and prevention. For example, precision medicine can be used to develop targeted treatments for diseases, such as cancer, that are more effective and have fewer side effects than traditional treatments.

Challenges and limitations: Despite the many benefits of genetic variation in health and pharmacology, there are also several challenges and limitations to this field. For example, the complex and multifactorial nature of many diseases and responses to medications means that genetic testing is not always a reliable predictor of disease risk or response to treatment. In addition, ethical and social considerations, such as privacy and discrimination, must also be taken into account when using genetic information for healthcare purposes.

Overall, genetic variation plays a significant role in health and pharmacology, and its study has the potential to revolutionize the way we approach healthcare. However, it is important to approach this field with caution and to consider the ethical and social implications of using genetic information for healthcare purposes.

Epigenetics: Epigenetics refers to changes in gene expression that are not due to changes in the DNA sequence itself. Environmental factors, such as diet, stress, and exposure to toxins, can cause epigenetic changes that affect the expression of genes and can have a lasting impact on health. The role of epigenetics in the development of diseases and in the response to medications is an active area of research that is helping to expand our understanding of the complex interplay between genetics and environment.

Gene-environment interactions: Gene-environment interactions refer to the complex relationship between genetic variations and environmental factors in the development of diseases and in the response to medications. For example, an individual may have a genetic variation that increases their risk of developing a disease, but the disease may only manifest if they are exposed to specific environmental factors, such as toxins or stress. Understanding the role of gene-environment interactions in health and pharmacology is critical for developing more personalized and effective treatments.

Ethical and social implications: The use of genetic information for healthcare purposes raises a number of ethical and social concerns, including privacy, discrimination, and stigma. For example, genetic testing can reveal sensitive information about an individual's health and ancestry, and there is a risk that this information could be used to discriminate against individuals in areas such as employment and insurance. In addition, the use of genetic information for healthcare purposes raises questions about access to and the affordability of genetic testing and personalized treatments.

Regulation: The use of genetic information for healthcare purposes is regulated by various laws and policies, including the Genetic Information Nondiscrimination Act (GINA) in the United States, which prohibits genetic discrimination in employment and insurance. However, regulation of this field is a rapidly evolving area, and there is ongoing debate about the appropriate level of regulation to ensure privacy and prevent discrimination while also allowing for the development and use of genetic technologies for healthcare purposes.

Overall, the study of genetic variation in health and pharmacology is a complex and rapidly evolving field with the potential to improve the effectiveness and safety of treatments and to better understand the genetic basis of diseases. However, it is important to approach this field with caution and to consider the ethical and social implications of using genetic information for healthcare purposes.

Individual variations: Genetic variations can occur at different levels, ranging from single nucleotide variations (SNVs) to larger structural variations such as deletions, duplications, and inversions. These variations can have different effects on an individual's health, depending on their location within the genome, their frequency in the population, and their interactions with other genetic and environmental factors. Understanding the individual variations that are most relevant to health and pharmacology is an important goal of genetics research.

Linkage disequilibrium: Linkage disequilibrium refers to the non-random association between variations at different loci within the genome. Linkage disequilibrium can affect the accuracy of genetic tests and the interpretation of genetic data, as it can cause certain genetic variations to be correlated with one another even if they are not directly causally related to a particular trait or disease. Understanding the patterns of linkage disequilibrium in populations is an important area of research in genetics.

Heritability: Heritability refers to the proportion of the variation in a particular trait or disease that is due to genetic factors. Heritability is influenced by a number of factors, including the number of genes involved in a particular trait, the environment in which an individual lives, and the age of onset and severity of the disease. Understanding the heritability of a particular trait or disease is important for developing effective treatments and for determining the best strategies for preventing and managing the condition.

Genetic counseling: Genetic counseling is a process in which individuals and families are provided with information and support regarding the implications of genetic test results for their health and well-being. Genetic counseling can help individuals and families to make informed decisions about genetic testing, to understand the risks and benefits of genetic information, and to cope with the emotional and psychological impact of genetic test results.

Personalized medicine: Personalized medicine, also known as precision medicine, is an approach to healthcare that takes into account an individual's unique genetic profile, environmental exposures, and lifestyle in order to develop personalized treatment plans. Personalized medicine has the potential to improve the effectiveness and safety of treatments by helping to select the most appropriate treatments for each individual.

Overall, the study of genetic variation in health and pharmacology is a complex and rapidly evolving field that has the potential to revolutionize healthcare. However, it is important to approach this field with caution and to consider the ethical and social implications of using genetic information for healthcare purposes.

Genome-wide association studies (GWAS): GWAS are a type of study that compares the genomes of individuals with a particular trait or disease to those of individuals without the trait or disease in order to identify genetic variations that are associated with the condition. GWAS have been used to identify many genetic variations that contribute to complex diseases such as cancer, heart disease, and mental illness. GWAS have also been used to identify genetic variations that influence individual responses to medications.

Exome and genome sequencing: Exome and genome sequencing are techniques that can be used to determine the complete DNA sequence of an individual. Exome sequencing focuses on the part of the genome that contains protein-coding genes, while genome sequencing determines the sequence of the entire genome. These techniques can provide a wealth of information about an individual's genetic variations, including rare and uncommon variations that might not be detected by other methods.

Epigenetics: Epigenetics refers to changes in the regulation of gene expression that occur in response to environmental and other factors, without altering the DNA sequence itself. Epigenetic changes can be influenced by a variety of factors, including diet, lifestyle, and environmental exposures. Understanding the role of epigenetics in health and pharmacology is an important area of research that has the potential to improve our understanding of the interplay between genetics and the environment in shaping health and disease.

Gene editing: Gene editing is a technique that allows for the precise modification of the DNA sequence. Gene editing has the potential to be used for the treatment of genetic disorders, by correcting the mutations that cause the disorder. Gene editing also has the potential to be used for the prevention of diseases, by introducing genetic variations that are associated with resistance to disease. However, gene editing also raises important ethical and safety concerns, as the long-term effects of these modifications on health and the environment are not yet fully understood.

Population genetics: Population genetics is the study of the distribution and evolution of genetic variation in populations. Understanding the patterns of genetic variation in populations can help to identify the genetic variations that are most relevant to health and pharmacology, as well as to identify populations that are at increased risk for certain diseases.

Overall, genetics is a rapidly evolving field that has the potential to revolutionize healthcare by providing new insights into the causes of disease and by developing more effective and personalized treatments. However, it is important to approach this field with caution and to consider the ethical and social implications of using genetic information for healthcare purposes.

Personalized medicine: Personalized medicine is a field of medicine that uses genetic information to tailor treatment to each individual. This approach to healthcare is based on the idea that each person's unique genetic makeup influences their health, including their response to medications, in different ways. By using genetic information to personalize treatment, healthcare providers can increase the chances of success and minimize the risk of side effects.

Precision medicine: Precision medicine is a term that is often used interchangeably with personalized medicine. Precision medicine refers to the use of genetic and other types of data to identify the most effective treatments for each individual, based on their unique characteristics. Precision medicine has the potential to improve the effectiveness and safety of treatments, by allowing healthcare providers to select treatments that are most likely to be effective for each individual.

Direct-to-consumer (DTC) genetic testing: Direct-to-consumer (DTC) genetic testing is a type of genetic testing that is marketed directly to consumers, without the involvement of a healthcare provider. DTC genetic testing companies offer tests that can be used to determine an individual's risk for certain diseases, based on their genetic variations. While DTC genetic testing can provide valuable information about an individual's health, it is important to understand that the results of these tests should be interpreted with caution, as they may not be accurate or complete.

Ethical and social implications: The use of genetic information for healthcare purposes raises a number of important ethical and social concerns. For example, some people may be concerned about the privacy of their genetic information, or about the potential for discrimination based on their genetic variations. Additionally, the use of genetic information for healthcare purposes raises questions about the allocation of resources and the accessibility of care, particularly for people who live in underserved communities.

Education and public engagement: Education and public engagement are crucial for ensuring that people have the knowledge and resources they need to make informed decisions about their health and their genetic information. This includes providing information about the benefits and limitations of genetic testing, as well as about the ethical and social implications of using genetic information for healthcare purposes. Additionally, it is important to engage with community groups and organizations to ensure that genetic information and technologies are used in ways that are equitable and accessible to all.

Overall, the use of genetic information for healthcare purposes has the potential to revolutionize the way that healthcare is delivered, by providing new insights into the causes of disease and by developing more effective and personalized treatments. However, it is important to approach this field with caution and to consider the ethical and social implications of using genetic information for healthcare purposes.

Polymorphism in Drug Metabolism

Drug polymorphism refers to the ability of a chemical compound, such as a drug, to exist in multiple different forms, or polymorphs. These different forms can have different physical and chemical properties, such as solubility, stability, and melting point.

Polymorphism can have significant impacts on the performance of a drug, including its bioavailability, pharmacokinetics, and manufacturing process. For example, if a drug exists in multiple polymorphic forms, the different forms may have different solubility and stability properties, which can impact how much of the drug is absorbed into the body and how long it remains active.

Understanding the polymorphic forms of a drug and their properties is important for optimizing the drug's effectiveness and minimizing the risk of side effects. This can involve identifying the most stable and bioavailable form of the drug, and developing manufacturing processes that can produce the drug in this form consistently.

Polymorphism affecting drug metabolism

Polymorphism can also refer to the ability of a chemical compound to exist in different forms, or polymorphs. In the context of drug metabolism, polymorphism can affect the bioavailability and pharmacokinetics of a drug.

For example, if a drug exists in multiple polymorphic forms, the different forms may have different solubility and stability properties, which can impact how much of the drug is absorbed into the body and how long it remains active. This can affect the drug's effectiveness and side effect profile.

In some cases, polymorphism can also affect the manufacturing process of a drug, as different polymorphic forms may have different processing requirements. It is important for drug developers to carefully characterize the polymorphic forms of a drug and consider their potential impacts on the drug's properties and performance.

There are several ways in which polymorphism can affect the bioavailability and pharmacokinetics of a drug:

1. Solubility: Different polymorphic forms of a drug may have different solubility properties, which can affect how much of the drug is absorbed into the body. For example, a more soluble form of the drug may be more readily absorbed than a less soluble form.
2. Stability: The stability of a drug can affect its shelf life and how long it remains active in the body. If a drug is unstable, it may break down or degrade over time, reducing its effectiveness.
3. Manufacturing process: Different polymorphic forms of a drug may have different processing requirements, which can impact the purity and consistency of the finished product.
4. Dosage form: The physical form of a drug, such as a tablet or capsule, can affect its bioavailability and pharmacokinetics. For example, a drug that is formulated as a sustained-release dosage form may be absorbed more slowly than a immediate-release form.
5. Drug-drug interactions: Polymorphism can also affect the way a drug interacts with other drugs or substances in the body, potentially altering its pharmacokinetics and bioavailability.

Understanding the potential impacts of polymorphism on the bioavailability and pharmacokinetics of a drug is important for optimizing its effectiveness and minimizing the risk of side effects.

Additionally, it is crucial for pharmaceutical companies to thoroughly evaluate the different polymorphic forms of a drug during the drug development process to ensure that the most stable, effective, and safe form is selected for commercialization. This can involve various characterization techniques, such as X-ray crystallography and thermal analysis, to identify the different forms and their properties. Furthermore, quality control measures must be implemented during the manufacturing process to ensure consistent production of the desired polymorphic form.

In conclusion, polymorphism in drug metabolism can have significant impacts on the performance of a drug, including its bioavailability, pharmacokinetics, and manufacturing process. Understanding and managing polymorphism is critical for ensuring the safe and effective use of drugs.

Different polymorphic forms can exhibit different pharmacokinetics, such as absorption, distribution, metabolism, and elimination (ADME) properties, which can affect the drug's bioavailability and overall effectiveness.

The choice of excipients, or inactive ingredients, used in the drug formulation can also impact the stability of different polymorphic forms and influence the formation of specific forms during the manufacturing process.

Different polymorphic forms can also exhibit different solubility, dissolution rate, and particle size, which can affect the drug's bioavailability and pharmacokinetics. For example, a more soluble form of the drug may be more rapidly absorbed into the bloodstream, while a less soluble form may exhibit slower and sustained release properties.

In some cases, different polymorphic forms can exhibit different crystal structures, which can affect the drug's physical properties, such as melting point and hardness, as well as its stability and shelf life.

Polymorphism can also affect the drug's efficacy and safety profile. For example, one form of the drug may exhibit higher potency than another form, or may have a lower risk of side effects.

In some cases, the formation of different polymorphic forms can be influenced by environmental factors, such as temperature, humidity, and light exposure, which can impact the drug's stability and shelf life.

To address these challenges, pharmaceutical companies must implement robust quality control measures to ensure consistent production of the desired polymorphic form and to minimize the risk of unwanted forms being present in the final product. This can involve the use of various characterization techniques, such as X-ray powder diffraction, differential scanning calorimetry, and Raman spectroscopy, to identify and track the different forms and their properties throughout the drug development and manufacturing process.

In conclusion, polymorphism in drug metabolism is a complex phenomenon that can significantly impact the performance and safety of a drug. A comprehensive understanding and management of polymorphism is crucial for ensuring the safe and effective use of drugs.

Polymorphism can have a significant impact on the drug's formulation and manufacturing process. For example, the process conditions used to produce the drug can influence the formation of different polymorphic forms, and the stability and shelf life of the drug can be affected by environmental factors such as temperature, humidity, and light exposure.

The different polymorphic forms can exhibit different physical properties, such as solubility, dissolution rate, and melting point, which can affect the drug's pharmacokinetics and overall effectiveness.

The selection of excipients, or inactive ingredients, used in the drug formulation can also impact the stability of different polymorphic forms and influence the formation of specific forms during the manufacturing process.

In some cases, the formation of different polymorphic forms can be influenced by the drug's interaction with other substances, such as excipients or other drugs, which can alter its pharmacokinetics and bioavailability.

Polymorphism can also affect the drug's stability, shelf life, and storage conditions, as different forms may have different stability and degradation profiles.

In some cases, different polymorphic forms may exhibit different toxicity profiles, which can affect the safety of the drug.

To address these challenges, pharmaceutical companies must implement robust quality control measures to ensure the consistent production of the desired polymorphic form and to minimize the risk of unwanted forms being present in the final product. This can involve the use of various characterization techniques, such as X-ray powder diffraction, differential scanning calorimetry, and Raman spectroscopy, to identify and track the different forms and their properties throughout the drug development and manufacturing process.

In conclusion, polymorphism in drug metabolism is a complex phenomenon that can significantly impact the performance and safety of a drug. A comprehensive understanding and management of polymorphism is crucial for ensuring the safe and effective use of drugs.

Genetic variation in drug transporters

Genetic variation in drug transporters can affect the pharmacokinetics of drugs, as drug transporters play a crucial role in the absorption, distribution, and elimination of drugs from the body.

Drug transporters are proteins that are expressed on the cell surface or within cells, and they facilitate the movement of drugs across cell membranes. There are several different types of drug transporters, including organic anion transporters (OATs), organic cation transporters (OCTs), and ATP-binding cassette (ABC) transporters, among others.

Drug transporters play a crucial role in the absorption, distribution, and elimination of drugs from the body by regulating the movement of drugs across cell membranes. For example, OATs and OCTs are responsible for the uptake of drugs into cells, while ABC transporters are involved in the efflux of drugs out of cells.

In the process of absorption, drug transporters in the gastrointestinal tract and liver can affect the amount of a drug that is absorbed into the bloodstream. In the process of distribution, drug transporters in the blood-brain barrier and other organs can affect the distribution of a drug to specific tissues. In the process of elimination, drug transporters in the liver and kidney can affect the metabolism and excretion of a drug.

Variation in the expression or activity of drug transporters can alter the pharmacokinetics of drugs, including their absorption, distribution, and elimination, and this can impact the effectiveness and side effect profile of the drugs

There are several different types of drug transporters, and they can vary in their expression levels and activity depending on genetic and environmental factors.

Variation in the genes encoding drug transporters can affect the activity and expression of these proteins, and this can alter the pharmacokinetics of drugs that are transported by these proteins. For example, a person with a genetic variant that results in reduced expression or activity of a particular drug transporter may have altered pharmacokinetics for drugs that are transported by that protein.

Genetic variation in drug transporters can also affect the effectiveness and side effect profile of drugs. For example, a person with a genetic variant that results in reduced activity of a particular drug transporter may be more susceptible to the side effects of a drug that is transported by that protein, or may require a higher or lower dose of the drug to achieve a therapeutic effect.

It is important to consider the potential impacts of genetic variation in drug transporters when prescribing and dosing drugs, as this can help to optimize their effectiveness and minimize the risk of side effects.

Genetic variation in drug transporters can also impact drug-drug interactions. Certain drugs may compete with each other for transport by the same transporter, and variation in transporter expression or activity can affect the balance between these drugs, leading to altered pharmacokinetics. This can be particularly important in situations where multiple drugs are prescribed, as altered pharmacokinetics can increase the risk of toxicity or reduce the effectiveness of the drugs.

Moreover, population-specific differences in drug transporter expression and activity have been observed, and these differences can impact the response to drugs across different populations. This highlights the importance of personalized medicine, where genetic information about drug transporters is considered in the prescription and dosing of drugs.

In conclusion, genetic variation in drug transporters plays a crucial role in the pharmacokinetics of drugs and can impact the effectiveness and side effect profile of drugs. It is important to consider these genetic factors in drug prescription and dosing to optimize therapeutic outcomes and minimize the risk of adverse effects.

Drug transporters are an important factor in pharmacogenomics, the study of how genetic variations affect a person's response to drugs. Genetic variations in drug transporter genes can result in changes in transporter expression, activity, localization, and substrate specificity, leading to altered pharmacokinetics of drugs.

One example is the ABCB1 gene, which encodes for P-glycoprotein, a well-known drug transporter that plays a role in the efflux of drugs from cells. Variations in this gene have been associated with altered pharmacokinetics of many drugs, including anticancer drugs, immunosuppressants, and HIV medications.

Another example is the SLC22A1 gene, which encodes for the organic cation transporter 1 (OCT1). Variations in this gene have been associated with altered pharmacokinetics of drugs, including antipsychotics, anti-inflammatory drugs, and antineoplastic agents.

Pharmacogenetic testing can identify genetic variations in drug transporter genes and provide valuable information for personalized medicine. With this information, healthcare providers can make informed decisions on drug choice, dosing, and treatment strategy based on a person's unique genetic makeup, leading to improved therapeutic outcomes and reduced adverse drug reactions.

In conclusion, genetic variation in drug transporters can greatly impact the pharmacokinetics of drugs and is an important consideration in personalized medicine. It is crucial to understand the role of drug transporters and the potential impact of genetic variations in drug transporter genes in order to optimize therapeutic outcomes and minimize adverse drug reactions.

Additionally, the role of drug transporters can also vary depending on the stage of a person's life, such as during pregnancy or aging. During pregnancy, changes in drug transporter expression and activity can occur, leading to altered pharmacokinetics of drugs and increased risk of adverse effects in both the mother and the fetus. In the elderly, changes in drug transporter expression and activity can also occur, leading to altered pharmacokinetics and increased risk of adverse drug reactions.

Drug interactions can also occur due to changes in drug transporter expression and activity. For example, drugs that are inhibitors or inducers of drug transporters can alter the pharmacokinetics of other drugs that are transported by the same transporter. This can result in changes in drug efficacy and toxicity.

In the context of drug development, understanding the role of drug transporters is important for optimizing drug efficacy and reducing the risk of adverse effects. In vitro and in vivo studies can be used to evaluate the impact of drug transporters on drug pharmacokinetics, and pharmacogenetic testing can be used to predict individualized responses to drugs.

In conclusion, genetic variation in drug transporters plays a complex role in determining the pharmacokinetics of drugs, and a thorough understanding of this relationship is important for personalized medicine, drug development, and the optimization of therapeutic outcomes and safety.

It is also important to note that genetic variations in drug transporter genes are not the only factor that can affect drug transport. Other factors such as age, sex, disease state, diet, and the use of concomitant medications can also impact drug transporter expression and activity.

In addition to pharmacogenetic testing, other approaches such as physiologically-based pharmacokinetic (PBPK) modeling can be used to predict the impact of drug transporters on drug pharmacokinetics in individuals with varying genetic backgrounds and in different physiological conditions. PBPK modeling takes into account multiple factors, including genetic variation, age, body weight, and other demographic variables to predict drug pharmacokinetics.

The use of drug transporters as therapeutic targets is also an area of ongoing research. For example, the inhibition of efflux transporters such as P-glycoprotein can enhance the efficacy of anticancer drugs, while the inhibition of uptake transporters such as OATs can reduce the toxicity of drugs.

In conclusion, genetic variations in drug transporter genes, combined with other factors such as age, sex, disease state, diet, and concomitant medications, can greatly impact the pharmacokinetics of drugs. The use of pharmacogenetic testing and PBPK modeling can help to predict individualized responses to drugs and optimize therapeutic outcomes and safety. The exploration of drug transporters as therapeutic targets holds promise for the development of new and more effective treatments for various diseases.

It is also important to consider the potential for drug-drug interactions when prescribing medications in individuals with genetic variations in drug transporter genes. For example, drugs that are inhibitors or inducers of specific transporters can affect the pharmacokinetics of other drugs that are transported by the same transporter, leading to changes in drug efficacy and toxicity.

In order to optimize therapeutic outcomes and minimize the risk of adverse effects, it is essential for healthcare providers to have access to accurate and up-to-date information about the pharmacogenetics of drug transporters and the potential impact of genetic variations on drug pharmacokinetics.

Pharmacogenetic testing can be used to identify individuals with genetic variations in drug transporter genes and to predict the potential impact of these variations on drug pharmacokinetics. This information can then be used to guide personalized medication dosing and to help healthcare providers make informed decisions about medication use.

The use of electronic health records and other health information technologies can also play an important role in facilitating the integration of pharmacogenetic information into clinical practice. By allowing healthcare providers to quickly access and review pharmacogenetic information, these technologies can help to optimize the use of medications and improve patient outcomes.

In conclusion, genetic variations in drug transporter genes can greatly impact the pharmacokinetics of drugs, and it is important for healthcare providers to consider this information when prescribing and dosing medications. The use of pharmacogenetic testing and health information technologies can help to improve the integration of pharmacogenetic information into clinical practice and to optimize therapeutic outcomes for patients.

In addition to the genetic variation in drug transporters, the impact of environmental factors such as diet, disease state, and other medications should also be considered when evaluating the pharmacokinetics of drugs. For example, certain foods and medications can alter the expression or activity of drug transporters, leading to changes in drug pharmacokinetics.

In some cases, drugs can compete for the same transporter and alter the pharmacokinetics of each other. For example, a drug that is a substrate for a particular transporter may be displaced by another drug that is also a substrate for the same transporter, leading to changes in the pharmacokinetics of both drugs.

To further complicate the situation, some drugs can also act as inhibitors or inducers of drug transporters. For example, a drug may inhibit the function of a transporter, leading to changes in the pharmacokinetics of other drugs that are substrates for that transporter.

Additionally, it is important to consider the role of polymorphisms, or genetic variations, in drug metabolizing enzymes, which can also impact the pharmacokinetics of drugs by altering their metabolism.

Therefore, a comprehensive evaluation of an individual's drug pharmacokinetics should consider not only genetic variations in drug transporters, but also environmental factors and genetic variations in drug metabolizing enzymes. This can help to optimize the dosing and use of medications and to minimize the risk of adverse effects.

In summary, genetic variation in drug transporters, environmental factors, and polymorphisms in drug metabolizing enzymes should all be considered when evaluating the pharmacokinetics of drugs and making decisions about medication use. The integration of pharmacogenetic information into clinical practice through the use of pharmacogenetic testing and health information technologies can greatly improve the outcomes of medication therapy.

Pharmacogenetic testing, also known as genetic testing for drug response, is a rapidly growing field that aims to improve patient outcomes by utilizing genetic information to guide personalized medication therapy.

Pharmacogenetic testing can involve the analysis of genetic variations in drug transporters, drug metabolizing enzymes, and other genes that can impact drug response. By determining an individual's specific genetic profile, healthcare providers can make more informed decisions about medication selection, dosing, and monitoring, which can help to optimize the efficacy of drugs and minimize the risk of adverse effects.

Incorporating pharmacogenetic information into clinical practice can also lead to improved patient outcomes by reducing the risk of medication-related adverse events, improving drug efficacy, and reducing healthcare costs associated with ineffective or harmful medications.

Despite the potential benefits of pharmacogenetic testing, its integration into clinical practice has been slow due to a number of barriers, including the high cost of testing, limited access to testing, and the lack of education and training for healthcare providers.

In order to overcome these barriers and to maximize the potential benefits of pharmacogenetics, it is important to increase the availability of pharmacogenetic testing, improve access to testing, and provide education and training to healthcare providers to ensure that they are equipped to interpret and utilize pharmacogenetic information in their clinical practice.

In conclusion, genetic variation in drug transporters can significantly impact the pharmacokinetics of drugs and lead to differences in drug response between individuals. Utilizing pharmacogenetic information through pharmacogenetic testing and incorporating this information into clinical practice can help to optimize medication therapy and improve patient outcomes.

The field of pharmacogenetics is rapidly evolving, and new genetic markers for drug response are being discovered at a rapid pace. As a result, it is important to stay up-to-date on the latest developments in this field, as well as the availability of pharmacogenetic tests for specific drugs and conditions.

It is also important to consider the limitations and challenges of pharmacogenetic testing. For example, genetic variations are only one of many factors that can impact drug response, and the effects of genetic variations may not always be predictable or consistent. In addition, the complexity of pharmacogenetics can make it difficult to accurately interpret test results and to translate this information into meaningful clinical recommendations.

In order to maximize the potential benefits of pharmacogenetics, it is important to approach pharmacogenetic testing with caution and to consider a range of factors, including an individual's clinical history, medication history, and other relevant medical information, when making decisions about medication therapy.

In conclusion, while pharmacogenetics has the potential to significantly improve patient outcomes by guiding personalized medication therapy, it is important to approach this field with caution and to stay up-to-date on the latest developments and challenges in this field.

It is also important to consider the ethical and social implications of pharmacogenetics, such as access to genetic testing and equal treatment for all individuals, regardless of their genetic makeup. The availability of genetic information about an individual can raise privacy and discrimination concerns, and it is important to have appropriate regulations and guidelines in place to protect the rights and privacy of individuals.

In addition, the integration of pharmacogenetics into routine clinical practice can pose challenges, such as the need for healthcare providers to receive adequate training in pharmacogenetics, the development of evidence-based clinical guidelines, and the need for appropriate reimbursement for pharmacogenetic testing.

Despite these challenges, pharmacogenetics has the potential to greatly improve patient outcomes and to transform the way that drugs are prescribed and used. By leveraging the power of genetic information, healthcare providers can optimize treatment regimens for individual patients, reducing the risk of adverse reactions and improving the overall efficacy of drug therapy.

In conclusion, pharmacogenetics has the potential to revolutionize the field of medicine by enabling personalized, precision-based treatment strategies, but it is important to approach this field with caution and to consider the ethical, social, and practical implications of this rapidly evolving field.

Another important aspect to consider in pharmacogenetics is the need for large-scale, well-designed clinical trials to validate and confirm the findings of pharmacogenetic studies. These trials are critical for establishing the clinical utility and relevance of pharmacogenetic testing, and they help to determine the optimal way to use pharmacogenetic information in routine clinical practice.

It is also important to consider the role of pharmacogenetic information in the drug development process. By incorporating pharmacogenetic information into the development and testing of new drugs, researchers and pharmaceutical companies can optimize the design and development of new drugs to better target specific patient populations and reduce the risk of adverse reactions.

Another important consideration in pharmacogenetics is the need for robust and accurate pharmacogenetic databases that can be used to support clinical decision making. These databases should include information on the frequency and clinical significance of different genetic variants, as well as information on the pharmacokinetics and pharmacodynamics of drugs in specific patient populations.

In conclusion, pharmacogenetics is a rapidly evolving field with the potential to greatly improve patient outcomes and transform the way that drugs are prescribed and used. However, it is important to approach this field with caution, considering the ethical, social, and practical implications of pharmacogenetics, and to support continued research and development in this field to fully realize its potential.

Finally, it is also important to consider the role of pharmacogenetics in promoting patient engagement and empowerment. By providing patients with information about their genetic predisposition to certain drug responses, patients can be more informed and proactive about their own health and treatment decisions. This can help to foster greater trust in the healthcare system, and can also lead to more effective and personalized care.

In order to effectively integrate pharmacogenetics into routine clinical practice, it is also important to have robust infrastructure in place to support the use of pharmacogenetic information. This includes electronic health records (EHRs) that can capture and store pharmacogenetic information, as well as decision support systems that can provide clinicians with relevant pharmacogenetic information at the point of care.

Finally, it is important to consider the cost-effectiveness of pharmacogenetic testing, and to ensure that patients have access to testing and interpretation of results, regardless of their ability to pay.

In conclusion, pharmacogenetics is a rapidly evolving field with the potential to greatly improve patient outcomes and to transform the way that drugs are prescribed and used. By considering the ethical, social, practical, and economic implications of pharmacogenetics, and by continuing to support research and development in this field, we can fully realize the potential of pharmacogenetics to improve patient care and outcomes.

To sum up, the role of genetic variation in drug transporters is important for the pharmacokinetics of drugs, as it can impact the absorption, distribution, and elimination of drugs from the body. This can result in altered pharmacokinetics and impact the effectiveness and side effect profile of drugs. To optimize the use of pharmacogenetics in clinical practice, it is important to consider the following factors:

Clinical validation: It is important to validate pharmacogenetic tests and to ensure that they provide reliable and clinically meaningful information.

Patient engagement: Providing patients with information about their genetic predisposition to certain drug responses can help to foster greater trust in the healthcare system and can lead to more informed and personalized care.

Infrastructural support: Robust infrastructural support, such as electronic health records (EHRs) and decision support systems, is crucial for the effective integration of pharmacogenetics into clinical practice.

Cost-effectiveness: The cost-effectiveness of pharmacogenetic testing needs to be considered and access to testing needs to be ensured regardless of the patient's ability to pay.

Ethical and social implications: The ethical and social implications of pharmacogenetics also need to be considered, such as privacy concerns and potential discrimination based on genetic information.

Continued research and development in the field of pharmacogenetics will be crucial in realizing its full potential to improve patient care and outcomes.

Additionally, it is important to note that pharmacogenetics is still an evolving field, and more research is needed to fully understand the impact of genetic variation on drug response. The use of pharmacogenetics in clinical practice is also subject to some limitations, including:

Polymorphism: The majority of drug transporters are subject to genetic polymorphism, meaning that there are multiple variations in the same gene. These variations can result in different levels of expression or activity of the drug transporter, leading to differing drug responses.

Interactions: The impact of genetic variation on drug response can also be influenced by other factors, such as environmental factors, lifestyle choices, and other medications being taken.

Complexity: The relationship between genetic variation and drug response can be complex, and it is often difficult to predict the impact of a specific genetic variant on drug response.

Limited knowledge: Our understanding of the impact of genetic variation on drug response is still limited, and more research is needed to fully understand the relationship between genetic variation and drug response.

Despite these limitations, pharmacogenetics has the potential to revolutionize the way drugs are prescribed and dosed, leading to improved patient outcomes and a reduction in adverse drug reactions. The integration of pharmacogenetics into clinical practice will require the collaboration of healthcare providers, researchers, and patients to ensure that the full potential of this field is realized.

In conclusion, genetic variation in drug transporters can significantly impact the pharmacokinetics of drugs, including their absorption, distribution, and elimination. This variation can also affect the effectiveness and side effect profile of drugs, making it important to consider pharmacogenetics when prescribing and dosing drugs.

Pharmacogenetics can also help healthcare providers to identify patients who are at increased risk of adverse drug reactions, allowing for more personalized and effective treatment strategies. By considering the impact of genetic variation on drug response, healthcare providers can improve patient outcomes and minimize the risk of adverse drug reactions.

However, it is important to keep in mind that pharmacogenetics is still an evolving field, and more research is needed to fully understand the impact of genetic variation on drug response. The use of pharmacogenetics in clinical practice is also subject to some limitations, including the complexity of the relationship between genetic variation and drug response, and the limited knowledge about the impact of genetic variation on drug response.

Despite these limitations, pharmacogenetics has the potential to revolutionize the way drugs are prescribed and dosed, leading to improved patient outcomes and a reduction in adverse drug reactions. The integration of pharmacogenetics into clinical practice will require the collaboration of healthcare providers, researchers, and patients to ensure that the full potential of this field is realized.

Genetic variation in G protein coupled receptors

Genetic variation in G protein-coupled receptors (GPCRs) can affect the pharmacodynamics and pharmacokinetics of drugs that act on these receptors.

GPCRs are a large family of transmembrane proteins that are involved in a wide range of physiological processes. Many drugs, including neurotransmitter agonists and antagonists, hormones, and others, act on GPCRs to produce their therapeutic effects.

Variation in the genes encoding GPCRs can affect the activity and expression of these receptors, and this can alter the pharmacodynamics and pharmacokinetics of drugs that act on these receptors. For example, a person with a genetic variant that results in reduced expression or activity of a particular GPCR may have altered pharmacodynamics for drugs that act on that receptor, or may have altered pharmacokinetics for drugs that are metabolized by enzymes regulated by that receptor.

Genetic variation in GPCRs can also affect the effectiveness and side effect profile of drugs. For example, a person with a genetic variant that results in increased activity of a particular GPCR may be more sensitive to the effects of a drug that acts on that receptor, or may be more susceptible to the side effects of the drug.

It is important to consider the potential impacts of genetic variation in GPCRs when prescribing and dosing drugs, as this can help to optimize their effectiveness and minimize the risk of side effects.

Genetic variation in G protein-coupled receptors (GPCRs) can affect the pharmacodynamics and pharmacokinetics of drugs that act on these receptors in several ways:

1. Pharmacodynamics: Variation in the genes encoding GPCRs can affect the activity and expression of these receptors, and this can alter the pharmacodynamics of drugs that act on these receptors. For example, a person with a genetic variant that results in reduced expression or activity of a particular GPCR may have altered pharmacodynamics for drugs that act on that receptor.
2. Pharmacokinetics: Genetic variation in GPCRs can also affect the pharmacokinetics of drugs. For example, a person with a genetic variant that results in altered activity of a particular GPCR may have altered pharmacokinetics for drugs that are metabolized by enzymes regulated by that receptor.
3. Effectiveness and side effect profile: Genetic variation in GPCRs can also affect the effectiveness and side effect profile of drugs. For example, a person with a genetic variant that results in increased activity of a particular GPCR may be more sensitive to the effects of a drug that acts on that receptor, or may be more susceptible to the side effects of the drug.

It is important to consider the potential impacts of genetic variation in GPCRs when prescribing and dosing drugs, as this can help to optimize their effectiveness and minimize the risk of side effects.

Additionally, genetic testing can provide important information on the patient's GPCR genotype, allowing for personalized medicine and tailored drug treatment. This can lead to improved therapeutic outcomes and reduced adverse effects, as well as improved overall health outcomes. However, it is important to note that genetic testing is still in its early stages and not all genetic variants have a clear impact on drug response, and more research is needed to fully understand the relationship between genetic variation and drug response. Nevertheless, considering genetic variation in GPCRs is a promising step towards precision medicine and improved patient outcomes.

Polymorphisms: One way genetic variation can affect GPCRs is through the presence of polymorphisms, or genetic differences that occur in more than 1% of the population. These polymorphisms can change the structure, function, or expression of the receptor, leading to altered drug response.

Gene duplication and deletion: Another type of genetic variation that can affect GPCRs is gene duplication or deletion. In these cases, a person may have an extra copy of the gene encoding a GPCR, leading to increased receptor expression, or may have a missing copy, leading to decreased expression. This can result in altered drug response, as drugs that act on the receptor will have a different target.

Post-transcriptional modifications: Gene expression can also be regulated by post-transcriptional modifications, such as alternative splicing or protein modification. These modifications can result in different variants of the same receptor, each with distinct properties and functions. Variation in these modifications can affect drug response, as drugs may target specific variants of the receptor.

It is important to note that the relationship between genetic variation and drug response can be complex, as multiple genes and pathways are often involved in drug action. Nevertheless, genetic testing and the consideration of genetic variation in GPCRs is becoming increasingly important in personalized medicine and improving patient outcomes.

Additionally, genetic testing for GPCR variants can provide important information for pharmacogenomics, the study of how genetics affects an individual's response to drugs. This information can inform clinical decision making, including choosing the most appropriate drug, determining the optimal dose, and predicting potential adverse effects.

For example, genetic testing can identify individuals who are carriers of a genetic variant associated with reduced drug metabolism, which can lead to increased drug exposure and increased risk of adverse effects. In these cases, a lower dose or alternative drug may be prescribed to minimize the risk of adverse effects.

Similarly, genetic testing can identify individuals who are carriers of a genetic variant associated with reduced drug efficacy. In these cases, a different drug or higher dose may be prescribed to optimize therapeutic effect.

Overall, considering genetic variation in GPCRs can improve the safety and efficacy of drug treatment, leading to improved health outcomes for patients. However, it is important to remember that genetics is only one factor that contributes to drug response, and other factors such as age, sex, liver and kidney function, and drug-drug interactions should also be considered.

Furthermore, the impact of genetic variation in GPCRs on drug response can vary depending on the specific drug and GPCR involved. For example, genetic variations in the GPCR that is targeted by beta-blockers, a class of drugs used to treat heart disease, can result in altered drug response, including reduced efficacy and increased adverse effects. Similarly, genetic variations in the GPCR targeted by opioids, a class of drugs used to treat pain, can result in altered drug response, including reduced efficacy and increased risk of addiction.

Moreover, advances in genomic technologies have made it possible to identify large numbers of genetic variants associated with altered drug response, and this information is being incorporated into large pharmacogenomics databases. This information can be used to inform clinical decision making and improve the safety and efficacy of drug treatment.

Finally, it is important to recognize that genetic testing for GPCR variants is still a rapidly evolving field, and not all variants have been thoroughly characterized or validated. Additionally, the clinical implications of many genetic variants remain uncertain, and further research is needed to fully understand the impact of genetic variation on drug response. However, as our understanding of the genetic basis of drug response continues to grow, the use of genetic testing to inform personalized medicine is likely to become increasingly common.

In conclusion, genetic variation in G protein-coupled receptors (GPCRs) plays a significant role in determining an individual's response to drugs that act on these receptors. Understanding the impact of genetic variation in GPCRs can inform clinical decision making and improve the safety and efficacy of drug treatment. However, it is important to consider multiple factors that contribute to drug response, including genetics, age, sex, liver and kidney function, and drug-drug interactions. Additionally, genetic testing for GPCR variants is a rapidly evolving field, and further research is needed to fully understand the impact of genetic variation on drug response. Nevertheless, the integration of genetic information into clinical practice is likely to become increasingly common as our understanding of the genetic basis of drug response continues to advance.

It's also worth noting that pharmacogenetics, the study of the role of genetics in determining drug response, is a rapidly growing field and is becoming increasingly important in personalized medicine. By considering a patient's genetic background, healthcare providers can select the most appropriate drug and dose for that individual, reducing the risk of ineffective treatment or adverse effects. This can lead to improved health outcomes, reduced healthcare costs, and improved patient satisfaction.

Additionally, pharmacogenetics can also inform drug development. By understanding the genetic basis of drug response, pharmaceutical companies can develop drugs that are more effective and have a reduced risk of adverse effects, leading to improved outcomes for patients.

In conclusion, genetic variation in GPCRs plays a significant role in determining an individual's response to drugs, and understanding this variation is crucial for optimizing drug treatment and improving patient outcomes. The integration of pharmacogenetics into clinical practice is likely to become increasingly common, and will play a vital role in the future of personalized medicine.

It's also worth mentioning that there are ongoing efforts to establish pharmacogenetic guidelines for certain drugs and genetic variants. For example, the US Food and Drug Administration (FDA) has approved labeling for certain drugs that includes information on genetic variants that affect drug response. The FDA also has a pharmacogenomic data submission program that allows companies to submit pharmacogenomic information for review and potential inclusion in drug labeling.

Moreover, there are also initiatives underway to incorporate pharmacogenetic testing into routine clinical practice. For example, some healthcare systems have implemented pharmacogenetic testing as a part of their electronic health records, allowing healthcare providers to easily access this information when making treatment decisions.

In summary, genetic variation in GPCRs plays a significant role in determining an individual's response to drugs, and understanding this variation is crucial for optimizing drug treatment and improving patient outcomes. There are ongoing efforts to establish pharmacogenetic guidelines, incorporate pharmacogenetic testing into routine clinical practice, and integrate pharmacogenetics into drug development. These efforts are likely to lead to improved patient outcomes and reduced healthcare costs in the future.

It's also important to note that pharmacogenetics is not the only factor that affects drug response. Other factors, such as age, weight, liver and kidney function, and drug interactions, can also play a role in determining an individual's response to a particular drug. Therefore, it is important to consider multiple factors, including pharmacogenetics, when making treatment decisions.

Additionally, it is important to keep in mind that not all drugs have pharmacogenetic information available. There is still much to be learned about the genetic basis of drug response, and ongoing research is needed to expand our understanding of the role of genetics in determining drug response.

In conclusion, pharmacogenetics is an important tool in personalized medicine, but it is not the only factor that affects drug response. It is important to consider multiple factors, including pharmacogenetics, when making treatment decisions, and ongoing research is needed to expand our understanding of the genetic basis of drug response. The integration of pharmacogenetics into clinical practice is likely to play an increasingly important role in the future of personalized medicine.

It's also worth mentioning that the field of pharmacogenetics is rapidly advancing, and new information is constantly being discovered. As our understanding of pharmacogenetics continues to expand, it is likely that the use of pharmacogenetics in clinical practice will become more widespread.

Pharmacogenetics has the potential to improve patient outcomes by helping healthcare providers make more informed treatment decisions. By considering an individual's genetic background, healthcare providers can choose the most effective and safe drugs for each patient, reducing the risk of adverse drug reactions and improving patient outcomes.

Moreover, pharmacogenetics can also help to reduce healthcare costs by reducing the use of ineffective or unsafe drugs and by reducing the need for dose adjustments and additional tests. By optimizing drug treatment and improving patient outcomes, pharmacogenetics has the potential to improve the overall efficiency of the healthcare system.

In conclusion, pharmacogenetics is a rapidly advancing field with the potential to improve patient outcomes and reduce healthcare costs. The integration of pharmacogenetics into clinical practice is likely to become increasingly important in the future, as our understanding of the genetic basis of drug response continues to expand.

It's also worth mentioning that pharmacogenetic testing is becoming increasingly accessible and affordable. There are a number of commercially available pharmacogenetic tests that can be used to determine an individual's genetic predisposition to certain drug responses. This information can then be used by healthcare providers to make more informed treatment decisions.

However, it is important to keep in mind that not all pharmacogenetic tests are created equal. Some tests may have limited evidence to support their use, and some may provide results that are not directly relevant to an individual's drug response. Therefore, it is important to use pharmacogenetic tests that are supported by robust scientific evidence and that are relevant to the individual's specific medical history and treatment plan.

Additionally, it is important to interpret pharmacogenetic test results in the context of an individual's overall medical history and other factors that can affect drug response. This information can then be used to make informed treatment decisions that are tailored to each individual patient.

In conclusion, pharmacogenetic testing is becoming increasingly accessible and affordable, and it has the potential to improve patient outcomes and reduce healthcare costs. However, it is important to use pharmacogenetic tests that are supported by robust scientific evidence and to interpret test results in the context of an individual's overall medical history and other factors that can affect drug response.

It's also important to note that while pharmacogenetic testing can provide useful information about an individual's genetic predisposition to certain drug responses, it is not the only factor that determines an individual's response to a drug. Other factors, such as age, weight, diet, other medications, and underlying health conditions, can also play a role in an individual's drug response. Therefore, pharmacogenetic testing should be used in conjunction with other patient-specific information to make informed treatment decisions.

Another important consideration is that pharmacogenetic testing can reveal information that may impact an individual's insurance coverage and employment opportunities. In some cases, individuals may be denied insurance coverage or employment based on their pharmacogenetic test results. Therefore, it is important for individuals to understand the potential consequences of pharmacogenetic testing before undergoing the test.

It is also important for healthcare providers to be knowledgeable about pharmacogenetic testing and to use this information in a responsible and ethical manner. This includes obtaining informed consent from patients, providing accurate and understandable information about the test results, and using this information to make informed treatment decisions that are in the best interest of the patient.

Finally, it is important to note that the field of pharmacogenetics is rapidly evolving, and new information is constantly being added to our understanding of how genetic variation affects drug response. Therefore, it is important to keep up-to-date with the latest developments in this field and to use the most current and relevant information when making treatment decisions.

Additionally, the relationship between genetic variation and drug response can be complex and multifaceted. There may be multiple genetic variants that influence a particular drug response, and these variants may interact with each other and with environmental factors in unpredictable ways. This complexity makes it challenging to predict individual drug responses with certainty and highlights the need for ongoing research in this field.

Pharmacogenetic testing can be performed using a variety of techniques, including polymerase chain reaction (PCR), restriction fragment length polymorphism (RFLP), and DNA sequencing. The specific technique used will depend on the type of genetic variant being tested for and the availability of testing resources.

In conclusion, genetic variation in G protein-coupled receptors (GPCRs) can significantly impact the effectiveness and safety of drugs that act on these receptors. Understanding the potential effects of genetic variation on drug response is critical for making informed treatment decisions and optimizing patient outcomes. Ongoing research in this field will continue to advance our understanding of the complex relationships between genetic variation, drug response, and health outcomes.

Applications of proteomics science

Genomics

Genomics is the study of the genome, which is the complete set of genetic material (DNA) of an organism. It is a rapidly growing field that encompasses a wide range of subdisciplines, including DNA sequencing, gene expression analysis, and genetic variation analysis.

The genome contains the instructions for building and maintaining an organism, and it is composed of DNA molecules that are organized into chromosomes. The genome includes both coding and non-coding DNA, and it is responsible for the inherited characteristics of an organism.

Genomics has a wide range of applications, including the identification of genetic risk factors for diseases, the development of personalized medicine, the improvement of crop yields and disease resistance in agriculture, and the study of evolution and population genetics.

Genomics research often involves the use of high-throughput DNA sequencing technologies and computational analysis to study the structure and function of the genome. It has led to many important discoveries and has had a significant impact on our understanding of biology and the treatment of human diseases.

Applications of genomics

Genomics has a wide range of applications in various fields, including:

1. Medicine: Genomics can be used to identify genetic risk factors for diseases and to develop personalized medical treatments based on an individual's genetic profile.
2. Agriculture: Genomics can be used to improve crop yields and disease resistance by identifying and manipulating genes that control important traits in plants.
3. Environmental science: Genomics can be used to study the impacts of environmental factors on organisms, including the effects of pollution or other stressors on the genome.
4. Evolution and population genetics: Genomics can be used to study the evolution of species and to understand the genetic basis of variations within and between populations.
5. Drug development: Genomics can be used to identify and characterize drug targets and to evaluate the effects of drugs on the genome.
6. Diagnostics: Genomics can be used to develop diagnostic tests for a variety of diseases by identifying characteristic genetic signatures in tissues or body fluids.
7. Biomarker discovery: Genomics can be used to identify biomarkers, which are genetic variations that are associated with specific diseases or conditions, for use in diagnosis and prognosis.
8. Forensics: Genomics can be used in forensic science to identify individuals based on their DNA profile.
9. Wildlife conservation: Genomics can be used to study the genetic diversity and relationships of different populations of wildlife, which can inform conservation efforts.
10. Industrial biotechnology: Genomics can be used to improve industrial processes, such as the production of biofuels and bioplastics, by optimizing the genomes of microorganisms used in these processes.

Overall, genomics plays a critical role in advancing our understanding of the biological world and improving various fields including medicine, agriculture, environmental science, and more. The use of genomics continues to expand as new technologies and methods are developed, leading to new and exciting discoveries in the field.

DNA sequencing: DNA sequencing is the process of determining the exact order of nucleotides (A, C, G, T) in a DNA molecule. This is a critical component of genomics as it enables the analysis of the complete genome of an organism.

Gene expression analysis: Gene expression analysis refers to the study of the process by which a gene's coded information is converted into a functional product, such as a protein. This involves measuring the amount of mRNA (messenger RNA) produced from a gene and the level of protein expression.

Genetic variation analysis: Genetic variation analysis involves the study of variations in the DNA sequence between individuals or populations. This includes single nucleotide polymorphisms (SNPs), which are variations in a single nucleotide, as well as larger structural variations such as deletions, insertions, and duplications.

High-throughput DNA sequencing technologies: High-throughput DNA sequencing technologies refer to methods that allow for the rapid sequencing of large amounts of DNA. This has revolutionized the field of genomics, enabling the sequencing of entire genomes in a relatively short amount of time and at a relatively low cost.

Computational analysis: Computational analysis plays a critical role in genomics research, as it is often used to analyze and interpret the vast amounts of data generated from DNA sequencing and other genomics experiments. This includes the use of algorithms and software tools to analyze DNA sequence data, gene expression data, and genetic variation data.

Personalized medicine: Personalized medicine is a medical approach that takes into account an individual's unique genetic profile in the diagnosis, treatment, and prevention of diseases. This allows for the development of targeted, effective treatments that are customized to an individual's specific needs.

In conclusion, genomics is a rapidly growing field with a wide range of applications in many different areas. The development of new technologies and techniques continues to push the boundaries of what is possible in the field, leading to new discoveries and advancements in our understanding of the biological world.

Identification of genetic risk factors for diseases: By analyzing the genomes of individuals with and without a particular disease, it is possible to identify genetic variations that are associated with an increased risk of developing the disease. This information can then be used to develop screening tests, risk assessment tools, and personalized medical treatments.

Crop improvement in agriculture: By analyzing the genomes of crops, it is possible to identify genes that control important traits such as yield, disease resistance, and stress tolerance. This information can then be used to improve crop varieties through traditional breeding or genetic engineering.

Environmental genomics: Environmental genomics involves the study of the impacts of environmental factors on the genomes of organisms. This can include the effects of pollutants, climate change, or other stressors on the genome. The goal of environmental genomics is to understand how the environment influences the biology of organisms and to develop strategies for mitigating negative impacts.

Evolution and population genetics: By analyzing the genomes of different species, it is possible to understand the evolutionary relationships between species and to reconstruct the evolutionary history of life on Earth. Additionally, by analyzing the genomes of populations within a species, it is possible to understand the genetic basis of variations within and between populations.

Drug development: By analyzing the genomes of diseases, it is possible to identify genetic targets for drug development. This can include the identification of genes that are associated with the disease or the identification of genetic variations that contribute to drug resistance. Additionally, genomics can be used to evaluate the effects of drugs on the genome and to optimize drug delivery and dosing.

Biomarker discovery: Biomarkers are genetic variations that are associated with specific diseases or conditions. By identifying biomarkers, it is possible to develop diagnostic tests and to monitor the progression of diseases. Additionally, biomarkers can be used for prognosis, predicting the likelihood of disease progression or treatment response.

These are just a few of the many applications of genomics. The field continues to expand and evolve as new technologies and techniques are developed, leading to new and exciting discoveries in the field.

Predictive medicine: Predictive medicine uses genomics information to predict an individual's likelihood of developing certain diseases, allowing for early intervention and prevention. This includes genetic risk assessments, genetic counseling, and personalized medical treatments based on an individual's genomic profile.

Genetic testing: Genetic testing is used to diagnose genetic disorders, to predict an individual's likelihood of developing a disease, and to screen for genetic predisposition to certain conditions. This can include prenatal genetic testing, carrier testing, and predictive testing for genetic disorders.

Development of gene therapies: Gene therapies are a type of medical treatment that involve the delivery of therapeutic genes to treat genetic disorders. By understanding the genomic basis of a disease, it is possible to develop targeted gene therapies to treat specific genetic disorders.

Personalized nutrition: Personalized nutrition uses genomics information to develop personalized dietary recommendations based on an individual's genetic profile. This can include recommendations for nutrient intake, recommendations for specific foods, and personalized recommendations for weight management.

Development of new drugs: The study of genomics is leading to the development of new drugs to treat a wide range of diseases. This includes the identification of new drug targets, the development of new drugs based on genomic information, and the optimization of drug delivery and dosing based on an individual's genomic profile.

Wildlife conservation: Wildlife conservation uses genomics information to understand the evolutionary relationships between species and to identify genetic diversity within species. This information is then used to develop conservation strategies, to understand the impact of environmental factors on wildlife populations, and to monitor the health of wildlife populations.

Understanding the microbiome: The microbiome is the collection of microorganisms that live in and on our bodies. By studying the genomes of these microorganisms, it is possible to understand the role that the microbiome plays in health and disease, and to develop strategies for manipulating the microbiome for therapeutic purposes.

These are just a few of the many applications of genomics. The field continues to evolve and expand, leading to new and exciting discoveries and advancements in the field.

Genome sequencing: The process of determining the complete DNA sequence of an organism's genome is known as genome sequencing. This information can be used to identify genetic variations, to understand the function of genes, and to study the evolution of species. The development of high-throughput DNA sequencing technologies has revolutionized the field of genomics and has led to many important discoveries.

Comparative genomics: Comparative genomics involves the comparison of genomes from different organisms to understand the similarities and differences between genomes. This information can be used to study the evolution of species, to identify genes involved in specific biological processes, and to understand the genomic basis of diseases.

Functional genomics: Functional genomics is the study of the function of genes and their interactions within the genome. This information can be used to understand the role of specific genes in disease, to identify new drug targets, and to understand the mechanisms underlying complex biological processes.

Epigenomics: Epigenomics is the study of changes in gene expression that occur without changes in the DNA sequence. This includes changes in the way that genes are regulated, including changes in the way that DNA is packaged, changes in the way that genes are turned on and off, and changes in the way that RNA is processed.

Systems biology: Systems biology is the study of the interactions between different components of biological systems, including genes, proteins, and metabolites. By integrating genomic, transcriptomic, proteomic, and metabolomic data, it is possible to understand the complex relationships between these components and to study the biological systems that they comprise.

Metagenomics: Metagenomics is the study of the genomes of microorganisms in environmental samples, such as soil, water, and air. This information can be used to understand the diversity of microorganisms in the environment, to study the role of microorganisms in environmental processes, and to identify new microorganisms and their potential applications.

Synthetic biology: Synthetic biology is the design and construction of new biological systems or the modification of existing systems. By integrating genomic, transcriptomic, and proteomic data, it is possible to design and build new biological systems, to engineer existing systems for specific purposes, and to study the interactions between components of biological systems.

These are a few examples of the different areas of study within the field of genomics. By integrating data from a wide range of technologies and disciplines, it is possible to gain a comprehensive understanding of the genome and its role in biology and disease.

Personalized medicine: One of the most exciting applications of genomics is personalized medicine, which is the tailoring of medical treatment to the specific genetic characteristics of an individual. By identifying genetic variations that contribute to disease, it is possible to develop more effective treatments for a wide range of conditions, including cancer, cardiovascular disease, and neurodegenerative disorders.

Precision agriculture: Precision agriculture is the use of genomics and other technologies to improve crop yields and quality. By understanding the genetic basis of important agronomic traits, such as disease resistance and stress tolerance, it is possible to develop crops that are better adapted to changing environmental conditions and to improve food security.

Microbial genomics: Microbial genomics is the study of the genomes of microorganisms, including bacteria, viruses, fungi, and parasites. This information can be used to understand the biology of microorganisms, to develop new treatments for infectious diseases, and to study the interactions between microorganisms and their environment.

Transcriptomics: Transcriptomics is the study of the transcriptome, which is the complete set of RNA molecules produced by an organism. This information can be used to understand gene expression, to identify new genes, and to study the regulation of gene expression.

Proteomics: Proteomics is the study of the proteome, which is the complete set of proteins produced by an organism. This information can be used to understand the function of proteins, to identify new proteins, and to study the interactions between proteins.

Metabolomics: Metabolomics is the study of the metabolome, which is the complete set of small molecules produced by an organism. This information can be used to understand metabolic pathways, to identify new metabolic pathways, and to study the relationships between metabolism and disease.

Genome editing: Genome editing is the process of making specific, targeted changes to the genome. This can be done using a variety of techniques, including CRISPR/Cas9 and other genome editing tools. By making specific changes to the genome, it is possible to cure genetic diseases, to develop new treatments for cancer, and to improve the production of crops and other biological systems.

These are a few examples of the many applications of genomics and related fields. The rapid advancement of genomics technologies is leading to many exciting new discoveries and to new ways of thinking about biology, health, and the environment.

Next-Generation Sequencing (NGS): NGS is a powerful and widely used technology for DNA sequencing. It allows researchers to sequence large portions of the genome in a relatively short amount of time and at a relatively low cost. NGS has revolutionized genomics research and has led to many important discoveries in fields such as medicine, agriculture, and environmental science.

Bioinformatics: Bioinformatics is the field of computer science and statistics that deals with the analysis of biological data, including DNA sequences, gene expression data, and protein interactions. Bioinformatics plays a critical role in genomics research, as it provides the tools and methods needed to analyze and interpret the vast amounts of data generated by DNA sequencing and other genomics technologies.

Epigenetics: Epigenetics is the study of changes in gene expression that are not caused by changes to the DNA sequence. These changes can be influenced by a wide range of factors, including environmental factors, such as diet, stress, and toxins, and they can play a critical role in the development of diseases, such as cancer and neurodegenerative disorders.

Synthetic Biology: Synthetic biology is the field of engineering that deals with the design and construction of new biological systems, including genomes and other genetic elements. Synthetic biology has the potential to revolutionize a wide range of fields, including medicine, agriculture, and energy production, by allowing researchers to create new organisms with specific desired characteristics.

Genetic Privacy: As genomics research continues to advance, it is important to consider the ethical, legal, and social implications of this work. One of the key concerns is genetic privacy, which refers to the right of individuals to control who has access to their genetic information and how that information is used. Ensuring genetic privacy is a critical issue, as genetic information can be used to make decisions about employment, insurance, and other important aspects of life.

These are a few additional areas of genomics and related fields that might be of interest. The rapid growth and expansion of genomics research is leading to many exciting new discoveries and to new ways of thinking about biology, health, and the environment.

Personalized Medicine: Personalized medicine is a growing field that uses an individual's genetic information to guide medical treatment. By identifying genetic variations that influence disease risk, treatment response, or drug metabolism, doctors can choose treatments that are more likely to be effective and have fewer side effects. Personalized medicine has the potential to revolutionize the way that diseases are treated and has already led to important advances in fields such as cancer and cardiovascular disease.

Genome Editing: Genome editing is a technique that allows researchers to make precise changes to the DNA of an organism. This can be used to correct genetic mutations that cause disease, or to introduce new traits that might be beneficial. There are several different genome editing technologies available, including CRISPR/Cas9, TALENs, and ZFNs, and these technologies have the potential to be used for a wide range of applications, including agriculture, animal breeding, and human medicine.

Functional Genomics: Functional genomics is the study of the functions of genes and other elements of the genome. This includes the study of gene expression, the regulation of gene expression, and the interactions between genes and other components of the cell. By understanding the functions of the genome, researchers can gain insights into the underlying mechanisms of disease and the ways in which cells and organisms respond to changes in their environment.

Comparative Genomics: Comparative genomics is the study of the differences and similarities between the genomes of different species. By comparing genomes, researchers can learn about the evolution of species, the functions of genes, and the mechanisms of genetic adaptation. Comparative genomics has been used to study the genomes of a wide range of organisms, including humans, mice, fruit flies, and plants, and has led to many important discoveries about the mechanisms of evolution and the genetic basis of traits.

Structural Genomics: Structural genomics is the study of the three-dimensional structure of proteins and other biological molecules. By determining the structures of proteins and other molecules, researchers can gain insights into their functions, the ways in which they interact with other molecules, and the ways in which they are regulated. Structural genomics has been used to study a wide range of proteins, including those involved in disease processes, and has led to important advances in fields such as drug development and protein engineering.

These are a few additional areas of genomics and related fields that might be of interest. As the field continues to grow and evolve, researchers are likely to make many more exciting discoveries in the coming years.

Epigenomics: Epigenomics is the study of changes in gene expression that are not due to changes in the DNA sequence itself, but rather to modifications of the DNA and associated proteins that regulate gene expression. Epigenetic changes can be influenced by a wide range of factors, including environmental factors such as diet, toxins, and stress, and they have been implicated in the development of a wide range of diseases, including cancer, heart disease, and mental illness.

Transcriptomics: Transcriptomics is the study of the transcriptome, which is the complete set of RNA molecules that are produced in a cell or tissue in response to a particular set of conditions. By studying the transcriptome, researchers can learn about the genes that are being expressed in a particular cell or tissue, and the ways in which gene expression is regulated in response to different stimuli. Transcriptomics has been used to study a wide range of biological systems, including developing embryos, cancer cells, and the brain.

Proteomics: Proteomics is the study of the proteome, which is the complete set of proteins that are produced in a cell or tissue. By studying the proteome, researchers can learn about the proteins that are being produced in a particular cell or tissue, and the ways in which protein expression is regulated in response to different stimuli. Proteomics has been used to study a wide range of biological systems, including cancer cells, the brain, and the immune system.

Metabolomics: Metabolomics is the study of the metabolome, which is the complete set of small molecules (metabolites) that are produced by an organism in response to a particular set of conditions. By studying the metabolome, researchers can learn about the metabolic pathways that are active in a particular cell or tissue, and the ways in which metabolism is regulated in response to different stimuli. Metabolomics has been used to study a wide range of biological systems, including developing embryos, cancer cells, and the gut microbiome.

Synthetic Genomics: Synthetic genomics is the design and construction of new genetic systems, including artificial chromosomes, synthetic genomes, and modified organisms. By synthesizing new genetic systems, researchers can study the functions of individual genes and other elements of the genome, and they can create new organisms with desirable traits, such as improved disease resistance or enhanced metabolic pathways. Synthetic genomics has the potential to revolutionize fields such as agriculture, biotechnology, and medicine.

These are a few additional areas of genomics and related fields that may be of interest. The field of genomics is growing rapidly, and new discoveries and technologies are being developed all the time, so this is certainly not an exhaustive list.

Genome editing: Genome editing is a technique that allows researchers to make precise changes to the DNA sequence of an organism, such as adding, deleting, or modifying specific genes. This technology has a wide range of applications, including the treatment of genetic diseases, the development of new crops with improved traits, and the creation of new animal models for studying diseases. There are several methods of genome editing, including CRISPR/Cas9, TALENs, and zinc-finger nucleases.

Personalized medicine: Personalized medicine is a field of medicine that uses genomics and other technologies to tailor medical treatments to the specific needs of each patient. By using genomic information to identify genetic risk factors for disease, to predict which treatments will be most effective, and to monitor the progression of disease, personalized medicine has the potential to improve patient outcomes and to reduce the cost of healthcare. Personalized medicine has been used to treat a wide range of diseases, including cancer, heart disease, and mental illness.

Comparative genomics: Comparative genomics is the study of the similarities and differences in the genomes of different species, including both closely related and distantly related species. By comparing the genomes of different species, researchers can learn about the evolution of specific genes and pathways, and they can identify the genetic basis of important traits such as disease resistance, improved agricultural yields, and enhanced metabolism.

Epigenetic inheritance: Epigenetic inheritance is the transmission of epigenetic changes from one generation to the next. Epigenetic changes are modifications to the DNA or associated proteins that regulate gene expression, and they can be influenced by a wide range of environmental factors, such as diet, toxins, and stress. By studying epigenetic inheritance, researchers can learn about the ways in which environmental factors can affect gene expression and contribute to the development of diseases, and they can explore the potential for environmental interventions to improve health outcomes.

Systems biology: Systems biology is a field of biology that aims to understand the complex interactions between different components of biological systems, including genes, proteins, metabolic pathways, and signaling networks. By using computational and experimental approaches, systems biology has the potential to provide a more comprehensive understanding of the underlying mechanisms of diseases, and it can be used to identify new therapeutic targets and to optimize the use of existing treatments.

These are a few additional areas of genomics and related fields that may be of interest. The field of genomics continues to evolve, and new discoveries and technologies are being developed all the time, so this is not an exhaustive list.

Proteomics

Proteomics is a branch of biotechnology that involves the study of the proteome, which is the complete set of proteins produced by an organism. Proteomics involves the identification, characterisation, and quantification of proteins, as well as the study of their function and regulation.

Proteomics can be used to study a wide range of biological processes, including cell signaling, metabolism, and gene expression. It can also be used to identify and characterize drug targets and to evaluate the effects of drugs on the proteome.

Proteomics research often involves the use of high-throughput techniques such as mass spectrometry to analyze large numbers of proteins simultaneously. It has led to many important discoveries and has had a significant impact on our understanding of biology and the treatment of human diseases.

Applications of proteomics

Proteomics has a wide range of applications in various fields, including:

1. Drug development: Proteomics can be used to identify and characterize drug targets and to evaluate the effects of drugs on the proteome.
2. Diagnostics: Proteomics can be used to develop diagnostic tests for a variety of diseases by identifying characteristic protein signatures in tissues or body fluids.
3. Biomarker discovery: Proteomics can be used to identify biomarkers, which are proteins that are associated with specific diseases or conditions, for use in diagnosis and prognosis.
4. Environmental monitoring: Proteomics can be used to study the effects of environmental factors on organisms, including the impact of pollution or other stressors on the proteome.

5. Food science: Proteomics can be used to study the protein content and composition of food products and to develop new food products.
6. Plant biology: Proteomics can be used to study the proteomes of plants and to identify proteins involved in important plant processes such as growth and development.
7. Personalized medicine: Proteomics can be used to determine an individual's unique protein profile, which can inform personalized treatment and diagnosis.
8. Neuroscience: Proteomics can be used to study the proteomes of the brain and nervous system, leading to a better understanding of neurological disorders and the development of new treatments.
9. Cancer research: Proteomics can be used to study the proteomes of cancer cells and to identify proteins involved in cancer progression and drug resistance, leading to the development of new cancer treatments.
10. Immunology: Proteomics can be used to study the proteomes of the immune system, leading to a better understanding of immune responses and the development of new immunotherapies.

In summary, proteomics plays a crucial role in many fields and has the potential to greatly improve our understanding of biology and human health.

Proteomics is a rapidly developing field that uses cutting-edge technologies to study the complete set of proteins in an organism or system. The goal of proteomics is to understand the structure, function, and regulation of proteins and how they interact with each other and with other cellular components.

One of the key technologies used in proteomics is mass spectrometry, which allows for the precise identification and quantification of proteins. Other important technologies include gel electrophoresis, which separates proteins based on their size and charge, and protein microarrays, which can be used to study protein-protein interactions.

In addition to its applications in drug development and diagnostics, proteomics also has many other important uses. For example, it can be used to study the proteomes of organisms in the environment, leading to a better understanding of how pollutants and other stressors impact their health. Proteomics can also be used to study the proteomes of food products, allowing for the development of new and improved food products.

In the field of personalized medicine, proteomics can be used to determine an individual's unique protein profile, which can inform the selection of personalized treatments and improve the accuracy of diagnosis. In cancer research, proteomics can be used to identify proteins involved in cancer progression and drug resistance, leading to the development of new cancer treatments.

In summary, proteomics is a rapidly developing field with many exciting applications. As our understanding of the proteome continues to grow, it has the potential to revolutionize our understanding of biology and human health.

Proteomics research is typically conducted in a multi-disciplinary environment, involving collaboration between biologists, chemists, physicists, computer scientists, and medical experts. The study of the proteome involves several key steps, including protein extraction, separation, identification, and characterization.

Protein extraction is the process of obtaining proteins from a biological sample, such as a tissue or fluid. This step is critical, as the quality and quantity of proteins obtained can have a significant impact on the accuracy of the proteomics analysis.

Separation is the process of separating proteins from one another based on physical or chemical properties, such as size, charge, or hydrophobicity. This step is important because it allows for the precise characterization and quantification of individual proteins.

Identification is the process of determining the identity of a protein based on its mass and other characteristics. This is typically done using mass spectrometry, which provides precise and detailed information about the protein.

Characterization involves the study of the structure, function, and regulation of a protein. This may include determining its amino acid sequence, post-translational modifications, and interaction with other proteins.

Proteomics research is highly data-intensive, and the analysis of the data generated is a critical aspect of the field. This may involve the use of bioinformatics tools and databases, such as the Human Protein Atlas and UniProt, to help interpret and make sense of the large amounts of data generated.

Overall, proteomics is a rapidly evolving field with many exciting developments. It has the potential to greatly improve our understanding of biology and human health and to inform the development of new and improved treatments for a wide range of diseases.

One of the challenges in proteomics research is the large size and complexity of the proteome. The human proteome is estimated to contain over 20,000 different proteins, making it difficult to study all of them in detail.

Another challenge is the dynamic nature of the proteome. Proteins are constantly being produced, degraded, and modified, and their levels can vary greatly in response to different biological conditions and stimuli. This makes it difficult to obtain an accurate snapshot of the proteome at any given time.

To overcome these challenges, proteomics researchers have developed a range of innovative techniques and approaches. For example, they have developed new mass spectrometry methods that allow for the rapid and sensitive analysis of large numbers of proteins simultaneously. They have also developed new approaches for protein separation, such as multidimensional chromatography, which allow for the more effective separation and analysis of complex protein mixtures.

In addition, proteomics researchers are working to develop new methods for protein characterization and analysis. For example, they are developing new techniques for identifying protein modifications, such as phosphorylation and glycosylation, and for characterizing protein-protein interactions.

Finally, proteomics researchers are working to develop new bioinformatics tools and approaches for data analysis, such as machine learning and artificial intelligence algorithms, to help make sense of the vast amounts of data generated by proteomics experiments.

Overall, the field of proteomics is facing many challenges, but researchers are making great progress in developing new and innovative approaches to address these challenges. As our understanding of the proteome continues to grow, it has the potential to greatly impact our understanding of biology and human health.

One of the key areas of application of proteomics is in the development of new drugs and therapies. By analyzing the proteome of diseased tissues or cells, researchers can identify new drug targets and better understand the molecular mechanisms underlying disease. This can inform the development of new and improved treatments.

Proteomics is also increasingly being used in diagnostics and personalized medicine. By analyzing the proteome of a patient's blood or other body fluid, researchers can identify unique protein signatures that are associated with specific diseases. This information can be used to develop diagnostic tests that are more sensitive and specific than current methods.

In addition, proteomics is being used to identify biomarkers for disease. Biomarkers are proteins or other molecules that are indicative of the presence of a disease or condition. The identification of biomarkers can greatly improve the early diagnosis and treatment of diseases, as well as the development of new drugs and therapies.

Another important application of proteomics is in the study of the impact of environmental factors on living organisms. By analyzing the proteome of organisms exposed to different environmental conditions, researchers can better understand how pollution, stress, and other factors affect the function and regulation of proteins.

Proteomics is also having a major impact on our understanding of plant biology. By analyzing the proteome of different plant species, researchers can identify key proteins involved in growth, development, and stress responses. This information can be used to improve the yield and quality of crops, as well as to develop new methods for sustainable agriculture.

Overall, proteomics is a rapidly growing field with a wide range of applications in various areas of biology and medicine. As our understanding of the proteome continues to grow, it has the potential to greatly impact our understanding of human health and the environment.

Another important application of proteomics is in the field of neuroscience. By analyzing the proteome of the brain, researchers can gain insights into the molecular mechanisms underlying various neurological disorders, such as Alzheimer's disease, Parkinson's disease, and depression. This information can be used to develop new and more effective treatments for these conditions.

Proteomics is also being used to study the immune system and to develop new immunotherapies. By analyzing the proteome of immune cells, researchers can better understand how the immune system responds to different pathogens and how it can be activated to fight disease.

In addition, proteomics is being used to study the interaction between bacteria and their host. By analyzing the proteome of both the bacteria and host, researchers can gain insights into the molecular mechanisms underlying infectious diseases and how bacteria can evade the host immune response.

Another important area of application of proteomics is in the study of cancer. By analyzing the proteome of cancer cells, researchers can gain insights into the molecular changes that occur during tumor development and progression. This information can be used to develop new and more effective treatments for cancer, as well as to identify new targets for therapy.

Overall, the applications of proteomics are diverse and far-reaching, and it has the potential to greatly impact our understanding of human health and disease. As our understanding of the proteome continues to grow, it will continue to inform the development of new and innovative treatments and therapies.

One of the key challenges in proteomics is the complexity of the proteome. The human proteome, for example, consists of tens of thousands of different proteins, each with its own unique properties and functions. This makes it difficult to study the proteome as a whole and to understand the complex interactions between proteins that occur within the cell.

Another challenge in proteomics is the difficulty in detecting and quantifying proteins. The majority of proteins are present at low levels in cells and tissues, making them difficult to detect and analyze. This is particularly challenging in the study of diseases, where the changes in protein levels or function can be subtle.

Despite these challenges, proteomics has made tremendous advances in recent years, largely due to the development of new and improved technologies for protein analysis. For example, mass spectrometry has become a powerful tool for the analysis of complex protein mixtures, and the development of high-throughput sequencing technologies has greatly improved our ability to identify and quantify proteins.

Additionally, new bioinformatics tools and computational approaches are being developed to analyze the large amounts of data generated by proteomics experiments. These tools allow researchers to perform large-scale, data-driven analyses of the proteome and to identify patterns and relationships between proteins that were previously difficult to detect.

Overall, proteomics is a rapidly evolving field that is making significant contributions to our understanding of human health and disease. As new technologies and techniques continue to be developed, it will continue to provide insights into the complex world of proteins and to inform the development of new and innovative treatments and therapies.

Another important aspect of proteomics is the study of protein modifications, such as post-translational modifications (PTMs). PTMs are chemical modifications to proteins that occur after protein synthesis and can significantly impact protein function. For example, PTMs such as phosphorylation and glycosylation can affect protein localization, stability, and activity, and are often involved in signaling pathways and regulation of gene expression.

Proteomics has the ability to study these PTMs at a large scale and to identify their specific sites of occurrence on proteins. This information is important for understanding the complex regulation of proteins and can inform the development of new drugs that target specific PTMs to treat diseases.

Furthermore, proteomics can also be used to study protein interactions and networks. By analyzing the interactions between proteins, researchers can gain insights into the molecular pathways that underlie cellular processes and can identify potential drug targets.

In addition, proteomics is also being used to study the evolution of proteins. By comparing the proteomes of different species, researchers can gain insights into the molecular changes that have occurred over time and the evolution of specific functions and processes.

Finally, it is also worth mentioning that proteomics has the potential to revolutionize personalized medicine. By analyzing the individual proteomes of patients, researchers can identify unique protein signatures that are associated with specific diseases or conditions. This information can be used to develop customized treatments that are tailored to the individual needs of each patient.

Overall, proteomics is a rapidly expanding field that is making significant contributions to our understanding of biology and human health. As our understanding of the proteome continues to grow, it will continue to inform the development of new and innovative treatments and therapies.

One of the key areas of proteomics is the study of disease-specific proteomes. By comparing the proteomes of healthy individuals to those of individuals with specific diseases, researchers can identify proteins that are differentially expressed or modified in disease states. These proteins can then be further studied to determine their role in the disease process and to identify potential drug targets.

In addition, proteomics can also be used to monitor the effectiveness of treatments and to determine the mechanisms by which treatments are working. For example, proteomics can be used to track changes in protein expression and modification in response to treatment, providing important insights into the underlying biology of the disease and the mechanism of action of treatments.

Proteomics is also being used in the study of infectious diseases. By analyzing the proteomes of pathogenic microorganisms, researchers can gain insights into the molecular mechanisms that allow these organisms to cause disease and can identify potential drug targets.

Furthermore, proteomics is being used in the study of cancer. By analyzing the proteomes of cancer cells, researchers can identify proteins that are involved in the development and progression of cancer, and can identify potential drug targets for the treatment of cancer.

Overall, proteomics is playing a critical role in the study of human diseases, providing important insights into the underlying molecular mechanisms of disease and informing the development of new and innovative treatments.

In conclusion, proteomics is a rapidly growing field that is making significant contributions to our understanding of biology and human health. With the continued development of new and improved technologies, proteomics has the potential to revolutionize our understanding of the proteome and to inform the development of new and innovative treatments and therapies.

Another application of proteomics is in the field of toxicology and environmental science. By analyzing the proteomes of organisms exposed to environmental stressors, such as pollution, researchers can identify proteins that are affected by these stressors and gain insights into the molecular mechanisms of toxicity. This information can then be used to develop new strategies for the mitigation of environmental stressors and to protect the health of both human and wildlife populations.

Proteomics is also being used in the field of food science, where it is being applied to study the protein content and composition of food products. This information can be used to develop new and improved food products and to monitor the quality of food products for human consumption.

Furthermore, proteomics is being used in the study of aging and age-related diseases. By analyzing the proteomes of elderly individuals and comparing them to the proteomes of younger individuals, researchers can identify proteins that are involved in the aging process and gain insights into the molecular mechanisms of age-related diseases.

Finally, it is worth mentioning that proteomics is also being used in the study of human nutrition. By analyzing the proteomes of individuals on different diets, researchers can gain insights into the effects of diet on the proteome and can inform the development of new and innovative nutritional strategies.

In summary, proteomics is a rapidly growing field with a wide range of applications in various fields, including drug development, diagnostics, biomarker discovery, environmental monitoring, food science, plant biology, and more. With the continued development of new and improved technologies, proteomics has the potential to revolutionize our understanding of biology and human health.

One area of proteomics that has gained significant attention in recent years is the study of post-translational modifications (PTMs) of proteins. PTMs are modifications that occur to proteins after they have been translated from their corresponding messenger RNA. Examples of PTMs include phosphorylation, ubiquitination, and sumoylation, among others. These modifications play crucial roles in regulating the activity, localization, and stability of proteins, and they are often involved in the regulation of cellular processes such as cell signaling, metabolism, and gene expression.

The study of PTMs has been facilitated by the development of mass spectrometry-based techniques that allow for the sensitive and quantitative analysis of PTMs at the proteome-wide level. By analyzing the PTMs of proteins in different cellular states or under different conditions, researchers can gain insights into the molecular mechanisms underlying cellular processes and disease states.

Another area of proteomics that is being actively researched is the study of protein-protein interactions (PPIs). PPIs are interactions between two or more proteins that play a crucial role in regulating cellular processes. By analyzing the PPIs of proteins in different cellular states or under different conditions, researchers can gain insights into the molecular mechanisms underlying cellular processes and disease states.

Proteomics has also been applied in the study of immunology, where it is being used to study the proteomes of immune cells and to identify proteins involved in the regulation of the immune response. This information can be used to develop new strategies for the treatment of immune-related diseases, such as autoimmune diseases and cancer.

In conclusion, proteomics is a rapidly evolving field that has the potential to revolutionize our understanding of biology and human health. With the continued development of new and improved technologies, it is likely that we will see even more exciting breakthroughs in the future.

One of the key challenges in proteomics is the identification and characterization of proteins. The large number of proteins produced by an organism, combined with their complex structures and functions, makes the task of identifying and characterizing proteins a challenging one.

To address this challenge, researchers often use a combination of different methods and technologies, including separation techniques such as 2D gel electrophoresis and liquid chromatography, as well as mass spectrometry-based techniques.

In mass spectrometry-based approaches, proteins are first separated into their individual components and then subjected to mass spectrometry analysis to determine their mass and sequence. The resulting data is then compared to databases of known protein sequences to identify the proteins that were analyzed.

In addition to identifying and characterizing proteins, proteomics also involves the study of their function and regulation. This often involves the study of post-translational modifications (PTMs) of proteins, such as phosphorylation, ubiquitination, and sumoylation, as well as the study of protein-protein interactions.

In order to fully understand the functions and regulation of proteins, it is also important to study them in the context of their cellular and biological environments. To this end, researchers often use high-throughput approaches such as quantitative proteomics and imaging-based proteomics to analyze large numbers of proteins simultaneously in different cellular states or under different conditions.

Finally, it is worth mentioning that proteomics is a highly interdisciplinary field that draws on expertise from many different areas, including biology, chemistry, physics, computer science, and engineering. As a result, proteomics often involves close collaborations between researchers from different fields, which can lead to a more complete understanding of the complex processes underlying biology and human health.

Proteomics has made significant contributions to our understanding of many important biological processes, including cell signaling, gene expression, and metabolism. For example, proteomics studies have helped to identify many key signaling pathways involved in regulating cell growth, differentiation, and death. These pathways play critical roles in many biological processes and are often dysregulated in diseases such as cancer, making them important targets for drug development.

Proteomics has also been used to study the effects of drugs on the proteome. For example, researchers have used proteomics to study the effects of chemotherapy drugs on cancer cells. This has helped to identify new drug targets and to better understand the mechanisms by which chemotherapy drugs exert their effects on cancer cells.

In the field of diagnostics, proteomics has been used to develop diagnostic tests for a variety of diseases by identifying characteristic protein signatures in tissues or body fluids. For example, proteomics has been used to develop tests for the early detection of cancer and for the diagnosis of Alzheimer's disease.

Proteomics has also been used to identify biomarkers for use in diagnosis and prognosis. Biomarkers are proteins that are associated with specific diseases or conditions and can be used to monitor the progression of the disease or to evaluate the effectiveness of treatment.

In addition to its contributions to our understanding of biology and human health, proteomics has also had a significant impact on many other fields, including food science, environmental monitoring, and plant biology. For example, proteomics has been used to study the protein content and composition of food products and to develop new food products with improved nutritional and functional properties.

Overall, proteomics is a rapidly growing field with significant potential to improve our understanding of biology and to lead to the development of new and improved diagnostic tests, drugs, and other biotechnology products.

Proteomics research requires the use of sophisticated technologies and methods, including mass spectrometry, protein separation techniques, and bioinformatics. One of the major challenges of proteomics research is the complexity of the proteome, which can contain hundreds of thousands of different proteins. To overcome this challenge, researchers often use high-throughput techniques such as mass spectrometry to analyze large numbers of proteins simultaneously.

In mass spectrometry-based proteomics, proteins are first separated and then fragmented into smaller peptides, which are then analyzed using a mass spectrometer. The mass spectrometer provides information about the masses of the peptides, which can then be used to identify the corresponding proteins. This information can then be used to quantify the levels of individual proteins in a sample, to study the interactions between proteins, and to identify post-translational modifications, such as phosphorylation, which can have important regulatory functions.

Proteomics research often involves the use of bioinformatics tools to analyze the large amounts of data generated by mass spectrometry and other high-throughput techniques. These tools are used to identify proteins, to annotate their functions, and to compare proteomes from different samples.

In conclusion, proteomics is a complex and rapidly evolving field that requires interdisciplinary expertise in areas such as biochemistry, biology, and computer science. Despite the challenges, the field has made significant contributions to our understanding of biology and human health and has great potential for continued growth and impact.

Metabolomics

Metabolomics is the study of the metabolites in a biological system, which are the small molecules (such as sugars, amino acids, and lipids) that are involved in metabolism. It is a rapidly growing field that involves the identification, characterisation, and quantification of metabolites in order to understand their roles in biological processes.

Metabolomics can be used to study a wide range of biological processes, including metabolism, gene expression, and environmental responses. It can also be used to identify and characterize drug targets and to evaluate the effects of drugs on the metabolome.

Metabolomics research often involves the use of high-throughput techniques such as mass spectrometry to analyze large numbers of metabolites simultaneously. It has led to many important discoveries and has had a significant impact on our understanding of biology and the treatment of human diseases.

Applications of metabolomics

Metabolomics has a wide range of applications in various fields, including:

1. Drug development: Metabolomics can be used to identify and characterize drug targets and to evaluate the effects of drugs on the metabolome.
2. Diagnostics: Metabolomics can be used to develop diagnostic tests for a variety of diseases by identifying characteristic metabolite signatures in tissues or body fluids.
3. Biomarker discovery: Metabolomics can be used to identify biomarkers, which are metabolites that are associated with specific diseases or conditions, for use in diagnosis and prognosis.
4. Environmental monitoring: Metabolomics can be used to study the effects of environmental factors on organisms, including the impact of pollution or other stressors on the metabolome.
5. Food science: Metabolomics can be used to study the metabolite content and composition of food products and to develop new food products.

6. Plant biology: Metabolomics can be used to study the metabolomes of plants and to identify metabolites involved in important plant processes such as growth and development.
7. Clinical research: Metabolomics can be used to understand the metabolic changes that occur in human diseases, and to develop new treatments based on these findings.
8. Personalized medicine: By analyzing an individual's unique metabolite profile, metabolomics can be used to provide personalized health recommendations and treatments.
9. Nutritional research: Metabolomics can be used to study the effects of dietary interventions and to understand the relationship between nutrition and health.
10. Toxicity testing: Metabolomics can be used to assess the toxicity of chemicals and drugs, and to understand how they affect the metabolome.

In conclusion, metabolomics is a rapidly growing field that has the potential to greatly impact our understanding of biology and medicine. By analyzing the metabolites in biological systems, metabolomics can provide important insights into a wide range of biological processes and has the potential to inform the development of new treatments for various diseases.

Sample preparation: In order to perform a metabolomics analysis, the first step is to obtain a sample, which can be anything from a tissue sample to a fluid sample like blood or urine. The sample must then be prepared for analysis, which typically involves extraction of the metabolites and preparation of the extract for analysis.

Analytical methods: There are several analytical methods used in metabolomics, including NMR spectroscopy, mass spectrometry (MS), and gas chromatography-mass spectrometry (GC-MS). The choice of method will depend on the type of sample, the metabolites of interest, and the goals of the analysis.

Data analysis: Once the data is generated from the analytical method, the next step is to analyze the data. This can involve several steps, such as peak picking, alignment, and normalization, in order to correct for differences in the sample preparation and measurement conditions. The data can then be analyzed using various statistical techniques to identify significant changes in the metabolome and to understand the biological significance of these changes.

Limitations: While metabolomics has many potential applications, there are also some limitations to the field. One of the biggest limitations is the complexity of the metabolome, which makes it challenging to accurately identify and quantify all of the metabolites in a sample. Additionally, metabolomics studies are often limited by the sensitivity and specificity of the analytical methods used, and by the need for large amounts of sample in order to obtain meaningful results.

Despite these limitations, metabolomics continues to be a rapidly growing field, and new techniques and technologies are being developed all the time to address these limitations and to make the field more accessible and useful to researchers.

Collaboration with other omics: Metabolomics often works in conjunction with other 'omics' fields, such as genomics, proteomics, and transcriptomics, in order to provide a more comprehensive understanding of the biological system being studied. By integrating data from multiple 'omics' fields, researchers can gain a more holistic understanding of the relationships between different biological processes and can identify key metabolic pathways and enzymes that are involved in various diseases.

Integration with clinical data: In addition to working with other 'omics' fields, metabolomics can also be integrated with clinical data to provide a more complete picture of human health and disease. For example, by comparing metabolite profiles from patients with a particular disease to those from healthy individuals, researchers can identify metabolites that are associated with the disease and can use this information to develop new diagnostic tests and treatments.

Impact on human health: One of the most exciting potential applications of metabolomics is its impact on human health. By understanding the metabolic changes that occur in disease, researchers can develop new treatments that target specific metabolic pathways or enzymes. Additionally, by identifying biomarkers of disease, metabolomics has the potential to revolutionize the way diseases are diagnosed and monitored, allowing for earlier and more accurate diagnosis and improved patient outcomes.

In conclusion, metabolomics is a rapidly growing field that has the potential to greatly impact our understanding of biology and medicine. With its ability to provide insights into the metabolic changes that occur in a wide range of biological processes, metabolomics has the potential to inform the development of new treatments for various diseases and to improve human health.

Types of metabolites: The metabolome is composed of a wide variety of small molecules, including sugars, amino acids, lipids, nucleotides, and others. Each of these types of metabolites has a unique set of properties and functions that make it important for understanding biological processes. For example, sugars and amino acids are involved in energy metabolism, while lipids play a role in cell membrane structure and function.

Metabolic pathways: Metabolites are involved in a complex network of metabolic pathways that regulate the flow of energy and materials within a biological system. These pathways can be disrupted by genetic mutations, environmental factors, or other disturbances, leading to changes in the metabolome that are indicative of disease or other biological processes. By studying these metabolic pathways and the metabolites that participate in them, researchers can gain insights into the underlying biological mechanisms that drive disease and health.

Clinical metabolomics: Clinical metabolomics is the application of metabolomics to the study of human health and disease. It involves the analysis of metabolites in various body fluids, including blood, urine, and cerebrospinal fluid, in order to identify metabolite changes that are associated with disease. Clinical metabolomics has the potential to provide valuable information for the diagnosis, prognosis, and treatment of various diseases, including cancer, neurological disorders, and metabolic diseases.

Emerging technologies: The field of metabolomics is constantly evolving, with new technologies and methods being developed all the time. For example, there are now high-throughput methods available for the analysis of large numbers of metabolites, as well as new techniques for the identification and quantification of low-abundance metabolites. Additionally, advances in computational biology and data analysis are allowing researchers to make sense of the large amounts of data generated by metabolomics studies.

In summary, the field of metabolomics is a rapidly evolving area of research that has the potential to greatly impact our understanding of biology and medicine. With its ability to provide insights into the metabolic changes that occur in a wide range of biological processes, metabolomics has the potential to inform the development of new treatments for various diseases and to improve human health.

Limitations of metabolomics: While metabolomics has many potential applications, there are also some limitations that need to be taken into account. For example, the field is still relatively new and many aspects of metabolomics are still being developed and refined. Additionally, the techniques used for metabolomics can be complex and time-consuming, and the results of metabolomics studies can be difficult to interpret.

Standardization: Standardization is an important issue in metabolomics, as different laboratories can use different techniques and methods to analyze metabolites. This can lead to inconsistencies in the results obtained from different studies, which can make it difficult to compare findings across different studies. In order to overcome these limitations, there is an ongoing effort to establish standardized protocols and methods for metabolomics analysis.

Interdisciplinary approach: Metabolomics is a highly interdisciplinary field that draws on expertise from a range of disciplines, including biochemistry, analytical chemistry, biology, and computer science. This interdisciplinary approach allows researchers to address complex questions that cannot be tackled by any single discipline alone.

Ethics: The analysis of metabolites can reveal sensitive information about a person's health and well-being, which raises important ethical considerations. For example, the use of metabolomics in clinical research raises questions about patient privacy and the confidentiality of medical information. It is important for researchers to consider these ethical issues when designing and conducting metabolomics studies.

In conclusion, the field of metabolomics is a rapidly growing and exciting area of research that has the potential to greatly impact our understanding of biology and medicine. While there are still many challenges to overcome, the potential benefits of metabolomics are numerous, and the field holds great promise for improving human health in the future.

Data analysis: One of the biggest challenges in metabolomics is the analysis of the large amounts of data generated by the techniques used to study metabolites. This requires the use of specialized software and algorithms to process and interpret the data, which can be a complex and time-consuming task. In recent years, there has been a growing focus on developing new algorithms and methods for the analysis of metabolomics data, with the goal of improving the accuracy and reliability of the results obtained from these studies.

Quality control: Quality control is an important issue in metabolomics, as it is crucial to ensure that the results obtained from metabolomics studies are accurate and reliable. This requires the use of strict quality control measures, such as the use of internal standards and control samples, to monitor the performance of the methods used to analyze metabolites.

Integration with other omics: Metabolomics is one of the "omics" sciences, which also includes genomics, transcriptomics, and proteomics. The integration of metabolomics with these other omics disciplines can provide a more complete picture of biological processes and improve our understanding of the relationship between genetics, gene expression, and metabolism.

Collaboration: Collaboration is key to the success of metabolomics research, as it often requires the use of specialized techniques and expertise from a range of disciplines. This can lead to the development of new and more powerful methods for the analysis of metabolites, and to new discoveries about the role of metabolites in biology and medicine.

Future developments: The field of metabolomics is rapidly evolving, and there are many exciting new developments on the horizon. For example, there is growing interest in developing new techniques for the analysis of metabolites, such as new mass spectrometry methods or imaging techniques, that can provide even more detailed information about metabolites. Additionally, there is a growing focus on using metabolomics to develop new diagnostic tests for a wide range of diseases, as well as to improve our understanding of the role of metabolites in health and disease.

In conclusion, the field of metabolomics is an exciting and rapidly growing area of research with the potential to greatly impact our understanding of biology and medicine. With the continued development of new techniques and methods, the future of metabolomics is bright, and the field holds great promise for improving human health in the coming years.

Technological advances: Technological advances have played a major role in the growth of the field of metabolomics, as they have enabled the development of new and more powerful methods for the analysis of metabolites. For example, the development of high-throughput mass spectrometry methods has greatly improved our ability to study metabolites on a large scale, and has led to many important discoveries about the role of metabolites in biology and medicine.

Cost: One of the challenges facing the field of metabolomics is the cost of the techniques used to analyze metabolites. Many of the methods used in metabolomics are highly specialized and can be expensive, which can limit their use in some settings. However, the cost of metabolomics techniques is rapidly decreasing, and it is expected that the field will become more accessible and widely used in the coming years.

Sample preparation: Sample preparation is an important step in the process of metabolomics, as it can greatly impact the quality and accuracy of the results obtained from metabolomics studies. This requires the use of specialized techniques, such as liquid chromatography or solid-phase extraction, to isolate and purify metabolites from biological samples.

Quality of data: The quality of the data obtained from metabolomics studies is critical to the accuracy and reliability of the results. This requires the use of high-quality samples, appropriate controls, and strict quality control measures to ensure that the results obtained are accurate and reproducible.

Personalized medicine: Metabolomics has the potential to play a major role in the development of personalized medicine, as it can be used to study the metabolome of individual patients and to identify metabolite signatures that are associated with specific diseases or conditions. This information can then be used to develop customized treatments that are tailored to the unique needs of each patient.

Network analysis: Network analysis is a powerful tool in metabolomics, as it can be used to study the interactions between metabolites and to identify the pathways and processes involved in metabolism. This information can then be used to develop new insights into the role of metabolites in biology and to identify new targets for drug development.

In conclusion, metabolomics is a rapidly growing field that holds great promise for improving our understanding of biology and medicine. With the continued development of new techniques and methods, the future of metabolomics is bright, and the field is poised to make many important contributions to the advancement of science and medicine in the years to come.

Functionomics

Functionomics is a field of biology that focuses on understanding the functions of genes and their products, including proteins and RNA molecules, in a biological system. It aims to identify and characterize the functions of genes and gene products in order to understand their roles in biological processes and diseases.

Functionomics can be used to study a wide range of biological processes, including gene expression, metabolism, and cellular signaling. It can also be used to identify and characterize drug targets and to evaluate the effects of drugs on gene and protein function.

Functionomics research often involves the use of high-throughput techniques such as microarray analysis and RNA sequencing to study gene expression and the functions of RNA molecules. It has led to many important discoveries and has had a significant impact on our understanding of biology and the treatment of human diseases.

Applicatins of functionomics

Functionomics has a wide range of applications in various fields, including:

1. Drug development: Functionomics can be used to identify and characterize drug targets and to evaluate the effects of drugs on gene and protein function.
2. Diagnostics: Functionomics can be used to develop diagnostic tests for a variety of diseases by identifying characteristic changes in gene expression or protein function.
3. Biomarker discovery: Functionomics can be used to identify biomarkers, which are changes in gene expression or protein function that are associated with specific diseases or conditions, for use in diagnosis and prognosis.
4. Environmental monitoring: Functionomics can be used to study the effects of environmental factors on organisms, including the impact of pollution or other stressors on gene and protein function.
5. Plant biology: Functionomics can be used to study the functions of genes and gene products in plants and to identify their roles in important plant processes such as growth and development.
6. Evolutionary biology: Functionomics can be used to study the evolution of gene and protein function and to understand the genetic basis of adaptations in different organisms.
7. Personalized medicine: Functionomics can be used to tailor treatments to individual patients based on their unique genetic makeup and the functions of their genes and gene products.
8. Agricultural biotechnology: Functionomics can be used to improve crop productivity and resistance to pests and diseases by identifying and manipulating the functions of genes in crops.
9. Microbiology: Functionomics can be used to study the functions of genes and gene products in microorganisms and to understand their roles in processes such as antibiotic resistance and pathogenesis.
10. Neuroscience: Functionomics can be used to study the functions of genes and gene products in the nervous system and to understand their roles in neurological disorders and brain function.

Functionomics is a highly interdisciplinary field that combines knowledge and techniques from molecular biology, genetics, biochemistry, and computational biology. The goal of functionomics is to understand the relationship between a gene's DNA sequence and its function, as well as the relationships between genes and the biological processes in which they participate. This knowledge can then be used to develop new treatments for diseases, improve agricultural productivity, and understand the effects of environmental stressors on living organisms.

One of the key techniques used in functionomics is high-throughput molecular biology, which allows for the simultaneous analysis of thousands of genes and their products. This includes methods such as microarray analysis, RNA sequencing, and proteomics. These techniques allow researchers to study gene expression patterns and the functions of RNA and protein molecules on a large scale, providing a comprehensive understanding of the gene functions in a particular biological system.

Functionomics research has led to many important discoveries, including the identification of novel drug targets, the development of new diagnostic tests, and the discovery of biomarkers for various diseases. In personalized medicine, functionomics can be used to tailor treatments to individual patients based on their genetic makeup and the functions of their genes, resulting in more effective and efficient treatment. In agriculture, functionomics can be used to improve crop productivity and resistance to pests and diseases by manipulating the functions of genes in crops. In microbiology, functionomics can be used to study the functions of genes in microorganisms and understand their roles in processes such as antibiotic resistance and pathogenesis. In neuroscience, functionomics can be used to study the functions of genes in the nervous system and understand their roles in neurological disorders and brain function.

In conclusion, functionomics is a rapidly evolving field with broad applications in various fields of biology. Its goal is to understand the functions of genes and their products in biological systems and use that knowledge to improve human health and the environment.

Functionomics is a key aspect of systems biology, which is the study of biological systems at a holistic and integrated level. In systems biology, the goal is to understand how different biological components interact and work together to perform specific functions. Functionomics contributes to this by providing insights into the functions of individual genes and their products.

In functionomics research, bioinformatics plays a critical role in the analysis and interpretation of large amounts of data generated from high-throughput techniques. Bioinformatics tools and algorithms are used to identify patterns and correlations in the data, which can then be used to make predictions about gene function and biological processes.

Another important aspect of functionomics is the study of gene regulation, which is the process by which genes are turned on or off in response to different signals. Gene regulation is essential for the proper functioning of cells and tissues, and disruptions in gene regulation can result in disease. Functionomics research can provide insights into the mechanisms of gene regulation, including the role of regulatory proteins, non-coding RNA molecules, and epigenetic changes, and how these mechanisms can be disrupted in disease.

Functionomics also plays a crucial role in the development of new drugs and therapies. By understanding the functions of genes and their products, researchers can identify potential drug targets and evaluate the effects of drugs on gene and protein function. This information can then be used to design more effective and targeted drugs.

In summary, functionomics is a critical field of biology that provides important insights into the functions of genes and their products and how they interact in biological systems. Its findings have significant implications for the diagnosis and treatment of diseases, the development of new drugs and therapies, and the understanding of biological processes.

Functionomics is an important area of research in the field of genetics and genomics. By studying the functions of genes and their products, functionomics provides a deeper understanding of the underlying causes of genetic diseases and how they can be treated.

In addition to identifying potential drug targets, functionomics can also be used to study the effects of genetic variations on gene and protein function. This includes understanding how mutations in genes can lead to disease and how these mutations can be targeted for treatment.

Functionomics can also be used to study the evolution of genes and their functions. This includes understanding how gene functions have changed over time and how different organisms have adapted to their environment. This information can also be used to design better agricultural crops and improve our understanding of the relationships between different species.

Another application of functionomics is in the study of epigenetics, which refers to changes in gene expression and function that are not due to changes in the DNA sequence. Epigenetic changes can have a profound impact on gene function and are important in the development of diseases such as cancer. Functionomics can provide important insights into the molecular mechanisms of epigenetic changes and how they can be targeted for treatment.

Finally, functionomics has important implications for the development of synthetic biology, which is the design and construction of new biological systems and components. By understanding the functions of genes and their products, researchers can design new biological systems with specific functions and applications, such as the production of biofuels or the creation of new medicines.

In conclusion, functionomics is a rapidly evolving field with broad applications in genetics, genomics, medicine, and the environment. Its goal is to understand the functions of genes and their products in biological systems and use that knowledge to improve human health and the environment.

Nutrigenomics

Nutrigenomics is a branch of nutritional sciences that studies the interaction between an individual's genetic makeup and their response to nutrients. It aims to understand how the individual's genetic variations affect the way they metabolize and utilize different nutrients and how that information can be used to optimize their diet and improve health outcomes. The goal of nutrigenomics is to develop personalized nutrition plans based on an individual's unique genetic profile to achieve optimal health and prevent or manage chronic diseases.

Sure! Nutrigenomics is an interdisciplinary field that draws on knowledge from genetics, biochemistry, nutrition, and other related fields to explore the impact of diet on gene expression and health outcomes. The field is still in its infancy, but research so far has shown that the nutrient composition and timing of meals can alter the expression of genes involved in metabolism, inflammation, and other biological processes.

One example of how nutrigenomics can be applied is in the identification of individuals who are carriers of specific genetic variants that increase their risk for certain health conditions, such as cardiovascular disease or type 2 diabetes. For these individuals, nutrigenomic tests can be used to assess their metabolic responses to different nutrients and to provide tailored dietary recommendations to help manage their risk.

It is important to note that while nutrigenomics holds promise for the development of personalized nutrition strategies, it is not a one-size-fits-all approach. Genetic testing is just one part of the larger picture and other factors such as an individual's lifestyle, environment, and medical history also play important roles in health outcomes.

Overall, nutrigenomics is an exciting and rapidly evolving field with the potential to revolutionize the way we approach nutrition and health.

Additionally, nutrigenomics has the potential to impact various industries, such as the food and beverage industry, by allowing them to develop and market foods that are specifically designed for individuals with specific genetic profiles. This can lead to the development of functional foods, which are foods that have additional health benefits beyond their basic nutritional value.

Research in nutrigenomics is also helping to clarify the role of specific nutrients in health and disease. For example, studies have shown that the relationship between nutrients and health outcomes can be complex and depend on multiple factors, such as the individual's genetics and overall diet.

However, it is important to understand that while nutrigenomics has the potential to improve our understanding of nutrition and health, it is not a substitute for a balanced diet and a healthy lifestyle. Eating a diet rich in fruits, vegetables, whole grains, and lean protein, and engaging in regular physical activity are still the cornerstone of a healthy lifestyle.

In conclusion, nutrigenomics is a rapidly evolving field that holds great promise for the development of personalized nutrition strategies and the prevention and management of chronic diseases. However, further research is needed to fully understand the complex relationships between genetics, nutrition, and health, and to ensure that nutrigenomics is used in a responsible and ethical manner.

Moreover, nutrigenomics is also playing a crucial role in advancing our understanding of the molecular mechanisms underlying various health conditions. For example, research has shown that certain genetic variants can affect the way an individual metabolizes certain nutrients and increase their risk of certain health problems. This knowledge can help researchers develop targeted interventions, such as dietary recommendations or specific nutrient supplements, to address these risk factors and improve health outcomes.

It is also worth noting that nutrigenomics is not just about genetics. The field also takes into consideration other factors, such as the microbiome, which refers to the collection of bacteria, viruses, fungi, and other microorganisms that live in and on our bodies. The microbiome can have a significant impact on our health, and research has shown that it can be influenced by diet, lifestyle, and other environmental factors.

In terms of limitations, it is important to understand that nutrigenomics is a complex field and there is still much that is unknown. For example, while certain genetic variants have been linked to specific health outcomes, the strength of these associations can vary greatly and there is still much that is unknown about the underlying mechanisms.

Additionally, the interpretation of nutrigenomic test results can be challenging, and it is important to have a trained professional involved in the process to ensure that the results are properly interpreted and applied. Finally, nutrigenomic testing is still relatively new, and there is a need for further research to validate the results and ensure that the tests are accurate, reliable, and relevant.

In summary, nutrigenomics is a rapidly evolving field that has the potential to revolutionize the way we approach nutrition and health. However, it is important to approach nutrigenomics with caution, understand its limitations, and seek the advice of a trained professional before undergoing any nutrigenomic testing or making changes to your diet or lifestyle based on the results.

Another aspect of nutrigenomics is the impact of epigenetics on health outcomes. Epigenetics refers to the study of changes in gene expression that are not caused by changes to the underlying DNA sequence but rather by modifications to the DNA or its associated proteins. These modifications can be influenced by various environmental factors, such as diet, stress, and toxins.

Research in epigenetics has shown that these modifications can have a lasting impact on health and that they can be passed down from one generation to the next. This has important implications for nutrigenomics, as it suggests that the impact of diet on health outcomes may be mediated, at least in part, through epigenetic mechanisms.

In terms of practical applications, nutrigenomics has the potential to inform public health policies and to guide the development of new food products that are optimized for specific health outcomes. For example, nutrigenomics could be used to identify populations at high risk for certain health problems and to develop targeted interventions, such as specific nutrient supplements or functional foods, to address these risk factors.

Additionally, nutrigenomics could also be used to optimize the treatment of various medical conditions, such as cancer. For example, research has shown that certain chemotherapy drugs are more effective in individuals with specific genetic profiles. By using nutrigenomic tests to identify these individuals, doctors could optimize the treatment and improve outcomes for these patients.

In conclusion, nutrigenomics is a rapidly evolving field that has the potential to improve our understanding of nutrition and health and to inform the development of new and effective interventions for the prevention and management of various health problems. However, it is important to approach nutrigenomics with caution and to seek the advice of a trained professional before undergoing any nutrigenomic testing or making changes to your diet or lifestyle based on the results.

Furthermore, nutrigenomics is also helping to bridge the gap between nutrition and other related fields, such as pharmacology and toxicology. For example, nutrigenomics can be used to study the interaction between nutrients and drugs and to understand how certain genetic variations can affect drug metabolism and toxicity.

This information can then be used to optimize drug treatment and minimize side effects, by selecting drugs that are well-tolerated by a specific patient population and tailoring dosing regimens to the individual's genetic profile.

In terms of the future of nutrigenomics, there are many exciting developments on the horizon. For example, advances in sequencing technologies are making it possible to obtain large amounts of genomic data at an affordable cost, and this is likely to drive further progress in the field.

In addition, there is growing interest in the development of nutrigenomic-based mobile applications and online platforms, which would make nutrigenomic information more accessible to the general public. These applications could provide personalized nutrition recommendations based on an individual's genetic profile and other health information.

However, it is also important to be aware of the potential ethical, legal, and social implications of nutrigenomics. For example, there is a need to ensure that nutrigenomic information is used in a responsible and ethical manner, and that individuals have control over how their genetic information is used and shared.

In conclusion, nutrigenomics is a rapidly evolving field that has the potential to revolutionize the way we approach nutrition and health. While there are many exciting developments on the horizon, it is important to approach nutrigenomics with caution and to be aware of the potential ethical, legal, and social implications of this emerging field.

Another important aspect of nutrigenomics is its potential impact on personalized nutrition. Personalized nutrition refers to the use of genetic, metabolic, and other individualized information to develop specific dietary recommendations that are tailored to meet the unique needs of each individual.

Research in nutrigenomics has shown that individuals can respond differently to the same diet due to genetic differences, and that certain genetic variations can affect the way the body processes and utilizes certain nutrients. By using nutrigenomic information, it may be possible to identify specific nutritional needs and to develop personalized dietary recommendations that are optimized for a person's unique genetic profile.

However, it is important to note that nutrigenomics is still a relatively new field and that much more research is needed to fully understand its potential for personalized nutrition. Additionally, it is also important to consider other factors that can affect nutrient metabolism, such as the gut microbiome and environmental factors, and to incorporate these into personalized nutrition recommendations.

In terms of implementation, there are several challenges that need to be addressed in order to make personalized nutrition a reality. For example, there is a need for standardization of nutrigenomic testing methods, as well as for validated and accurate nutrigenomic databases to be established.

In addition, there is also a need for increased public awareness and education about nutrigenomics and personalized nutrition, as well as for effective communication of nutrigenomic information to individuals and healthcare providers.

In conclusion, nutrigenomics has the potential to play a key role in personalized nutrition and to revolutionize the way we approach dietary recommendations. However, there are many challenges that need to be addressed in order to make personalized nutrition a reality, and it is important to approach nutrigenomics with caution and to seek the advice of a trained professional.

Another application of nutrigenomics is in the area of precision agriculture. Precision agriculture refers to the use of advanced technologies, such as remote sensing, geospatial analysis, and robotics, to optimize agricultural production and to improve the efficiency and sustainability of food production.

Nutrigenomics can play a key role in precision agriculture by providing information on the genetic basis of plant responses to various environmental and nutritional factors. For example, nutrigenomic approaches can be used to identify specific genetic variations that confer tolerance to environmental stress, such as drought or salinity, or that increase the efficiency of nutrient uptake and utilization by plants.

This information can then be used to develop improved crop varieties that are better adapted to specific environmental conditions and to optimize crop management practices, such as nutrient application and pest control, to improve agricultural productivity and sustainability.

In addition, nutrigenomics can also be used to study the impact of environmental and agricultural practices on the nutritional quality of crops. For example, research has shown that environmental stress can alter the levels of certain nutrients in crops, such as vitamins and minerals, and that this can have a significant impact on human health.

By using nutrigenomic approaches to study these interactions, it may be possible to develop agricultural practices that maintain or improve the nutritional quality of crops and to optimize food production to meet the nutritional needs of the global population.

In conclusion, nutrigenomics has the potential to play a key role in precision agriculture and to improve the efficiency and sustainability of food production. Additionally, it has the potential to enhance the nutritional quality of crops and to provide a more secure and nutritious food supply for the global population.

Finally, nutrigenomics also has applications in the food industry. Food companies are increasingly using nutrigenomic approaches to develop new food products that are tailored to the unique needs of specific consumer groups.

For example, nutrigenomic research can be used to develop functional foods that are enriched with specific nutrients or bioactive compounds, based on the genetic profiles of targeted consumer groups. This can help to address specific health concerns, such as cardiovascular disease or type 2 diabetes, and to provide consumers with more targeted and effective nutritional solutions.

In addition, nutrigenomics can also be used to improve food safety by identifying genetic variations that affect the metabolism of toxic compounds, such as mycotoxins or heavy metals. This information can then be used to develop new food products that are safer for consumers and to minimize the risk of food-borne illness.

Moreover, nutrigenomics can also play a role in the development of precision nutrition, which refers to the use of individualized nutrition information, such as genomics data, to develop customized food and beverage products. Precision nutrition has the potential to improve health outcomes and to provide consumers with more personalized and effective dietary solutions.

In conclusion, nutrigenomics has the potential to revolutionize the food industry by providing new and innovative solutions for food safety, food product development, and personalized nutrition. By leveraging nutrigenomic information, the food industry can better meet the needs of consumers and provide more targeted and effective dietary solutions.

It is also worth noting that nutrigenomics is not without its challenges and controversies. One of the main challenges is the need for robust and validated nutrigenomic databases, which are essential for the interpretation of nutrigenomic information and for the development of personalized nutrition recommendations.

In addition, there is also a need for increased regulation and standardization of nutrigenomic testing, as well as for effective communication of nutrigenomic information to consumers and healthcare providers. This is important to ensure that nutrigenomic information is accurate, reliable, and properly understood, and to minimize the risk of miscommunication or misinterpretation of nutrigenomic data.

Another issue that is often raised in the context of nutrigenomics is the potential for discrimination or unequal access to health services, based on genetic information. For example, there is a risk that individuals with certain genetic variations could be denied health insurance or employment opportunities, based on the perception that they have an increased risk of disease.

Therefore, it is important to address these ethical and social concerns as nutrigenomics continues to develop and to ensure that nutrigenomic information is used in an ethical and responsible manner.

In conclusion, nutrigenomics has the potential to revolutionize our understanding of the relationships between nutrition, genetics, and health, and to provide new and innovative solutions for personalized nutrition and food product development. However, it is important to approach nutrigenomics with caution, to seek the advice of a trained professional, and to address the challenges and controversies that arise as this field continues to develop.

One of the key directions for future research in nutrigenomics is the integration of multi-omics data, such as genomics, transcriptomics, proteomics, and metabolomics. The integration of multi-omics data provides a more comprehensive understanding of the complex interactions between nutrition, genetics, and health, and can help to identify new targets for personalized nutrition and disease prevention.

Another area of active research in nutrigenomics is the development of predictive models for health outcomes, such as risk of chronic diseases, based on nutrigenomic and other lifestyle factors. These models have the potential to provide personalized nutrition recommendations, based on an individual's genetic profile and lifestyle habits, and to help to prevent or manage chronic diseases.

In addition, there is also growing interest in the use of nutrigenomics to improve the nutritional quality of food crops, such as fruits and vegetables, to enhance the health benefits of these foods for consumers. This includes research on the impact of environmental and agricultural practices on the nutritional quality of crops, as well as the development of new crops with improved nutritional content.

Finally, nutrigenomics is also being applied to the study of gut microbiome, the microorganisms that live in the human gut, and their interaction with nutrition and health. The gut microbiome has been shown to play a key role in health and disease, and nutrigenomics is being used to study the genetic and nutritional factors that influence the composition and function of the gut microbiome.

In conclusion, nutrigenomics is a rapidly evolving field with numerous avenues for future research and applications. The integration of multi-omics data, the development of predictive models for health outcomes, the improvement of food crops, and the study of gut microbiome are just a few of the many exciting areas of research in nutrigenomics. As this field continues to develop, it has the potential to revolutionize our understanding of the relationships between nutrition, genetics, and health, and to provide new and innovative solutions for personalized nutrition and disease prevention.

Another promising application of nutrigenomics is in the field of sports nutrition. Nutrigenomics can help to identify the genetic factors that influence athletic performance, such as muscle strength and endurance, and can provide personalized nutrition recommendations for athletes, based on their genetic profile.

For example, nutrigenomics can help to identify genetic variations that affect the way that an athlete metabolizes certain nutrients, such as carbohydrates or fats, which can have a significant impact on athletic performance. Based on this information, nutrigenomics can provide personalized nutrition recommendations to optimize energy metabolism and improve athletic performance.

Nutrigenomics is also being used to study the impact of nutrition on muscle recovery and injury prevention in athletes. For example, research has shown that certain nutrients, such as antioxidants and anti-inflammatory agents, can play a role in reducing muscle damage and promoting recovery after exercise. Nutrigenomics can help to identify the genetic factors that influence the response to these nutrients and can provide personalized nutrition recommendations to optimize muscle recovery and reduce the risk of injury.

In addition, nutrigenomics is also being used to study the impact of nutrition on the health and well-being of athletes, such as the risk of chronic diseases, such as cardiovascular disease, and the impact of nutrition on mental health and cognitive function.

In conclusion, nutrigenomics has the potential to revolutionize sports nutrition and to provide new and innovative solutions for optimizing athletic performance, reducing the risk of injury, and improving the health and well-being of athletes. As nutrigenomics continues to develop, it will be an increasingly valuable tool for athletes, coaches, and sports medicine professionals.

The field of nutrigenomics is also expanding into the development of new and improved dietary supplements and functional foods. For example, nutrigenomics is being used to identify genetic factors that influence the effectiveness of certain dietary supplements, such as vitamins, minerals, and phytochemicals. Based on this information, nutrigenomics can help to develop more effective and personalized dietary supplements, tailored to the genetic needs of individual consumers.

In addition, nutrigenomics is also being used to study the impact of food processing and preparation on the nutritional quality of foods. For example, research has shown that cooking and processing can alter the bioavailability of certain nutrients, such as vitamins and minerals, and can also generate new compounds with potential health benefits. Nutrigenomics can help to identify the genetic factors that influence the response to these food processing and preparation methods and can provide personalized nutrition recommendations to optimize the health benefits of food.

Another application of nutrigenomics is in the development of new and improved functional foods, such as probiotics and prebiotics, that can provide health benefits beyond basic nutrition. For example, nutrigenomics is being used to identify the genetic factors that influence the efficacy of probiotics and prebiotics, and to develop new strains of probiotics with improved health benefits.

In conclusion, nutrigenomics is playing an increasingly important role in the development of new and improved dietary supplements and functional foods, with the potential to provide new and innovative solutions for personalized nutrition and health. As nutrigenomics continues to develop, it will be an increasingly valuable tool for the food and dietary supplement industries, and will play a key role in improving the nutritional quality and health benefits of the foods that we consume.

However, despite its promise, the field of nutrigenomics is still in its early stages, and there are several challenges that need to be addressed before it can be widely adopted and fully realized.

One of the main challenges is the complexity of the human genome and the vast number of genetic variations that exist. This makes it difficult to understand the specific genetic factors that influence nutrient metabolism and response to food and dietary supplements, and to develop accurate and personalized nutrition recommendations based on genetic information.

Another challenge is the lack of standardization in the field of nutrigenomics. There is currently no standardization of the genetic tests used to assess nutrient metabolism and response to food and dietary supplements, and the interpretation of genetic data can be difficult and subject to interpretation.

In addition, there is also a need for more rigorous scientific evidence to support the claims made by nutrigenomics, and to establish the validity and reliability of the genetic tests used. While there is some evidence to support the benefits of nutrigenomics, much of it is still preliminary, and more research is needed to fully understand the impact of genetics on nutrient metabolism and response to food and dietary supplements.

Another challenge is the cost of genetic testing and the lack of insurance coverage for nutrigenomics. Currently, genetic tests for nutrigenomics can be expensive, and there is limited insurance coverage for these tests, which can make it difficult for many consumers to access this information.

Finally, there are also ethical and privacy concerns associated with the use of genetic information for nutritional purposes, and there is a need for clear guidelines and regulations to protect consumer privacy and ensure that genetic information is used responsibly.

In conclusion, while nutrigenomics has the potential to revolutionize the field of nutrition and to provide new and innovative solutions for personalized nutrition, there are still many challenges that need to be addressed before it can be widely adopted and fully realized. The field of nutrigenomics is rapidly evolving, and as more research is conducted and more evidence is gathered, it will be an increasingly valuable tool for improving health and nutrition.

In recent years, there has been a growing interest in the potential applications of nutrigenomics in the prevention and treatment of chronic diseases. Many chronic diseases, such as obesity, type 2 diabetes, cardiovascular disease, and certain cancers, have been shown to have a significant genetic component, and nutrigenomics can provide new insights into the genetic basis of these conditions.

For example, nutrigenomics can help to identify genetic variants that are associated with an increased risk of developing certain chronic diseases, and can also help to identify genetic factors that influence the response to dietary interventions and treatments. This information can be used to develop personalized nutrition plans and dietary interventions that are tailored to the genetic needs of individual patients, and that can help to prevent or manage chronic diseases.

In addition, nutrigenomics is also being used to study the impact of nutrients and dietary compounds on the epigenome, which is the system of chemical modifications that regulate gene expression. Epigenetic changes can be influenced by a variety of environmental factors, including diet, and can have a lasting impact on gene expression and health. Nutrigenomics can help to identify the specific nutrients and dietary compounds that have the greatest impact on the epigenome, and can provide new insights into the mechanisms by which diet affects health.

Another application of nutrigenomics is in the development of new and improved dietary interventions for the treatment of chronic diseases. For example, nutrigenomics can help to identify genetic factors that influence the response to dietary interventions for obesity, type 2 diabetes, and cardiovascular disease, and can be used to develop more effective and personalized dietary interventions for these conditions.

In conclusion, nutrigenomics has the potential to play a significant role in the prevention and treatment of chronic diseases, and is providing new and innovative solutions for personalized nutrition and health. As nutrigenomics continues to develop, it will become an increasingly important tool for the healthcare industry, and will play a key role in improving the health outcomes of patients with chronic diseases.

As the field of nutrigenomics continues to advance, new and innovative applications are being developed, and there is increasing interest in the potential of nutrigenomics to improve food production and agriculture.

One application of nutrigenomics in agriculture is the development of crops that are better adapted to specific climates and growing conditions, and that are more resistant to disease and pests. For example, nutrigenomics can be used to identify genetic factors that influence the response of crops to environmental stress, such as drought, and to develop new crop varieties that are more resistant to these stresses.

Another application of nutrigenomics in agriculture is the development of crops that are more nutritious, and that can provide essential nutrients to populations in need. For example, nutrigenomics can be used to identify genetic factors that influence the production of essential nutrients in crops, and to develop new crop varieties that are more nutritious and that can help to address micronutrient deficiencies in populations around the world.

In addition, nutrigenomics can also be used to improve the quality and safety of food products, and to identify new and innovative food ingredients that can provide health benefits. For example, nutrigenomics can be used to identify genetic factors that influence the production of bioactive compounds in food crops, such as antioxidants and anti-inflammatory compounds, and to develop new food ingredients that are rich in these compounds and that can improve health and prevent disease.

In conclusion, nutrigenomics has the potential to play a significant role in food production and agriculture, and is providing new and innovative solutions for improving the quality, safety, and nutritional value of food products. As nutrigenomics continues to develop, it will become an increasingly important tool for the food and agriculture industries, and will play a key role in improving the health outcomes of populations around the world.

The development of nutrigenomics is still in its early stages, and there are many challenges that need to be addressed before the full potential of nutrigenomics can be realized. Some of the major challenges facing the field of nutrigenomics include:

Data integration and management: The large amount of data generated by nutrigenomics studies is a challenge for data integration and management, and requires the development of new and innovative methods for data analysis and interpretation.

Standardization and validation of methods: The field of nutrigenomics requires standardized and validated methods for gene expression analysis, functional genomics, and other technologies, in order to ensure that results are reliable and comparable across different studies.

Integration with other disciplines: Nutrigenomics is a multidisciplinary field that requires close collaboration with other disciplines, including genetics, nutrition, and biochemistry, in order to fully understand the complex interactions between genes, nutrition, and health.

Ethical, legal, and social implications: The development of nutrigenomics raises important ethical, legal, and social questions, including privacy, discrimination, and access to health care, and requires careful consideration of these issues in order to ensure that the benefits of nutrigenomics are maximized and its risks minimized.

Cost and access: The cost of genetic testing and personalized nutrition services remains a barrier for many people, and efforts are needed to ensure that nutrigenomics is accessible to all who need it.

Despite these challenges, the field of nutrigenomics is advancing rapidly, and new and innovative solutions are being developed to address these challenges. As the field continues to mature, it is likely that nutrigenomics will become an increasingly important tool for improving health and preventing disease, and will play a key role in the future of personalized medicine and health care.

One of the key areas where nutrigenomics is having an impact is in the development of personalized nutrition plans. Personalized nutrition plans are designed to take into account an individual's unique genetic profile, along with factors such as their age, gender, lifestyle, and health status, in order to provide tailored recommendations for their diet and nutrition.

For example, nutrigenomics can be used to determine an individual's genetic susceptibility to certain diseases, such as obesity, type 2 diabetes, or cardiovascular disease, and to provide recommendations for diet and lifestyle changes that can reduce their risk of developing these conditions.

In addition, nutrigenomics can also be used to determine an individual's ability to metabolize certain nutrients, such as vitamins and minerals, and to provide recommendations for dietary supplements or fortified foods that can help to address any deficiencies.

Another important application of nutrigenomics is in the development of functional foods and dietary supplements. Nutrigenomics can be used to identify genetic factors that influence the production and bioavailability of certain nutrients, such as antioxidants and anti-inflammatory compounds, and to develop functional foods and dietary supplements that are rich in these nutrients and that can improve health and prevent disease.

Finally, nutrigenomics is also having an impact on the food industry, as food companies are using nutrigenomics to develop healthier and more nutritious products. For example, nutrigenomics can be used to identify genetic factors that influence the production of bioactive compounds in food crops, such as flavonoids and anthocyanins, and to develop new food ingredients that are rich in these compounds and that can improve health and prevent disease.

In conclusion, nutrigenomics is a rapidly developing field with numerous applications in the areas of personalized nutrition, functional foods and dietary supplements, and food production. As nutrigenomics continues to advance, it has the potential to revolutionize the way we approach nutrition and health, and to provide new and innovative solutions for improving health outcomes and preventing disease.

There are also some potential limitations and criticisms of nutrigenomics that need to be considered. Some of the major limitations and criticisms include:

Lack of robust evidence: While there is a growing body of research in the field of nutrigenomics, many of the findings are still preliminary, and more robust evidence is needed to fully understand the role of genes and nutrition in health and disease.

Interaction with the environment: The interaction between genes and the environment is complex and dynamic, and it is difficult to determine the relative contributions of genes and environment to health outcomes.

Limited genetic testing: Currently, only a limited number of genetic variations can be tested, and it is unclear how much of an individual's health outcomes are influenced by these genetic variations, as opposed to other factors such as lifestyle and environment.

Potential for over-interpretation of results: The results of nutrigenomic tests can be difficult to interpret, and there is a risk of over-interpretation or misuse of the results, leading to incorrect conclusions and recommendations.

Ethical and legal considerations: The use of nutrigenomics raises important ethical and legal considerations, such as privacy, discrimination, and access to health care, and requires careful consideration of these issues in order to ensure that the benefits of nutrigenomics are maximized and its risks minimized.

Despite these limitations and criticisms, the field of nutrigenomics continues to advance, and new and innovative solutions are being developed to address these challenges. As the field continues to mature, it is likely that nutrigenomics will become an increasingly important tool for improving health and preventing disease, and will play a key role in the future of personalized medicine and health care.

It is important to keep in mind that nutrigenomics is just one part of a larger picture, and that the ultimate goal of nutrigenomics is to improve health and prevent disease through a combination of genetic testing, personalized nutrition recommendations, and lifestyle modifications. The potential benefits of nutrigenomics are substantial, but it is essential that nutrigenomics be used in a responsible and ethical manner, and that the limitations and criticisms of the field be carefully considered and addressed.

In addition to the limitations and criticisms mentioned above, there are also some challenges that need to be addressed in order to fully realize the potential of nutrigenomics. Some of the key challenges include:

Integration with traditional medicine: Nutrigenomics is still a relatively new field, and it needs to be integrated with traditional medicine in order to be effectively applied in clinical practice. This requires close collaboration between nutritionists, geneticists, and healthcare providers.

Education and training: There is a need for education and training of healthcare providers, nutritionists, and other professionals in the field of nutrigenomics in order to ensure that nutrigenomics is used effectively and responsibly.

Standardization of genetic testing: Currently, there is a lack of standardization in genetic testing, and there is a need for standardized methods for genetic testing and interpretation of results in order to ensure the reliability and accuracy of nutrigenomic testing.

Cost-effectiveness: Currently, nutrigenomic testing can be expensive, and there is a need for cost-effective and accessible genetic testing in order to make nutrigenomics widely available to the general population.

Evidence-based recommendations: There is a need for evidence-based recommendations for personalized nutrition plans, based on the latest research in the field of nutrigenomics, in order to ensure that nutrigenomics is used effectively and responsibly.

In conclusion, nutrigenomics has the potential to revolutionize the way we approach nutrition and health, and to provide new and innovative solutions for improving health outcomes and preventing disease. However, in order to fully realize the potential of nutrigenomics, it is essential to address the limitations, criticisms, and challenges facing the field, and to use nutrigenomics in a responsible and ethical manner.

Nutrigenomics is still a relatively new field, and there is a need for continued research and development in order to fully understand the complex interactions between genes, nutrition, and health. Some of the areas of research that are currently being explored in nutrigenomics include:

Personalized nutrition: The development of personalized nutrition plans based on genetic information, which take into account an individual's unique genetic variations and nutritional needs.

Gene-diet interactions: The study of how different dietary patterns and nutrients interact with specific genetic variations to influence health outcomes.

Nutrigenetic testing: The development of new and more sophisticated methods for genetic testing, which can provide more comprehensive and accurate information about an individual's genetic variations.

Functional genomics: The study of how different genes and genetic pathways interact with each other to influence health outcomes, with a focus on identifying new targets for the development of personalized nutrition plans.

Epigenetics: The study of how the environment, including diet, can affect gene expression and influence health outcomes, and how this information can be used to develop personalized nutrition plans.

Clinical trials: The use of clinical trials to evaluate the effectiveness of personalized nutrition plans based on nutrigenomic information, and to determine the optimal combination of genetic testing and personalized nutrition for different health outcomes.

By continuing to advance the field of nutrigenomics through research and development, we can gain a deeper understanding of the complex interactions between genes, nutrition, and health, and use this information to improve health outcomes and prevent disease.

The impact of nutrigenomics is already being felt in several areas of healthcare, including disease prevention and management, personalized nutrition, and personalized medicine. Some of the key ways in which nutrigenomics is being used and applied in these areas include:

Disease prevention and management: By understanding the genetic factors that influence an individual's risk for certain diseases, such as heart disease, cancer, and obesity, nutrigenomics can be used to develop targeted nutrition and lifestyle interventions to prevent or manage these diseases.

Personalized nutrition: By using genetic information to tailor dietary recommendations to an individual's unique genetic variations and nutritional needs, nutrigenomics can help to improve the effectiveness of dietary interventions and support optimal health outcomes.

Personalized medicine: By using nutrigenomic information to identify an individual's genetic variations, healthcare providers can better understand an individual's risk for certain diseases and tailor treatments and medications to best meet their specific needs.

Sports nutrition: Nutrigenomics can be used to understand the genetic factors that influence an individual's response to exercise and physical activity, and to develop personalized nutrition plans that support optimal athletic performance.

Food industry: Nutrigenomics can be used by the food industry to develop more targeted and personalized food products, such as functional foods and nutraceuticals, that are designed to meet the unique nutritional needs of different populations.

In conclusion, nutrigenomics is already having a significant impact in several areas of healthcare and is likely to continue to play an important role in improving health outcomes and preventing disease in the future. By leveraging the latest advances in genetics and nutrigenomics, we can better understand the complex interactions between genes, nutrition, and health, and use this information to develop more effective and personalized solutions for improving health and preventing disease.

While nutrigenomics offers many potential benefits for improving health and preventing disease, there are also some challenges and limitations that must be addressed in order to fully realize its potential. Some of these challenges include:

Lack of standardization: There is currently a lack of standardization in the field of nutrigenomics, with different methods and technologies being used to determine genetic variations and predict nutritional needs. This makes it difficult to compare results across different studies and to develop evidence-based guidelines for nutrigenomic testing and personalized nutrition.

Cost: Nutrigenomic testing and personalized nutrition can be expensive and may not be accessible to all individuals. In addition, the cost of genetic testing and interpretation is likely to decrease over time as the technology continues to advance and become more widely available.

Regulation: The regulation of nutrigenomic testing and personalized nutrition is still evolving, and there is a need for clear and consistent regulations to ensure that these technologies are used appropriately and to protect consumer safety.

Limited evidence base: While there is a growing body of evidence to support the use of nutrigenomics in healthcare, much of this evidence is still in the early stages of development and more research is needed to fully understand the impact of nutrigenomic testing and personalized nutrition on health outcomes.

Complexity: The field of nutrigenomics is complex, and it can be difficult for healthcare providers and consumers to understand and interpret the results of nutrigenomic testing and to use this information to make informed decisions about nutrition and lifestyle.

Despite these challenges, nutrigenomics has the potential to significantly impact healthcare and improve health outcomes in the future. By addressing these challenges and continuing to advance the field of nutrigenomics through research and development, we can help to ensure that nutrigenomic testing and personalized nutrition are used effectively and safely to improve health and prevent disease.

Immunotherapeutics

Immunotherapeutics is a field of medicine that involves the use of the immune system to prevent or treat diseases. It includes a wide range of approaches, including vaccines, which are designed to stimulate the immune system to protect against infections, and immunotherapies, which are designed to enhance or suppress the immune response to specific diseases.

Immunotherapeutics can be used to treat a wide range of diseases, including infections, cancer, and autoimmune disorders. They can also be used to prevent or reduce the severity of certain diseases, such as by providing immunity against infectious agents or by modulating the immune response to reduce inflammation.

Immunotherapeutics research involves the development of new and improved vaccines and immunotherapies, as well as the study of the immune system and its functions. It has led to many important discoveries and has had a significant impact on the treatment of diseases.

Types of Immunotherapeutics

There are several types of immunotherapeutics, including:

1. Vaccines: Vaccines are designed to stimulate the immune system to protect against infections. They contain a weakened or inactivated form of a pathogen, such as a virus or bacterium, or a fragment of the pathogen's genetic material. When a vaccine is administered, the immune system mounts a response against the pathogen, producing antibodies and activating immune cells. If the individual is later exposed to the pathogen, the immune system will recognize it and mount a rapid and effective response to protect against infection.
2. Antibodies: Antibodies are proteins produced by the immune system that bind to specific pathogens or toxins and help to neutralize them. Immunotherapies that use antibodies can be used to target specific pathogens or toxins, or to alter the immune response to a specific disease.
3. T cells: T cells are a type of immune cell that play a central role in the immune response to infections and cancer. Immunotherapies that use T cells can be used to enhance or suppress the immune response to specific diseases.

4. Interferons: Interferons are proteins produced by the immune system that help to control the immune response and inhibit the growth of certain pathogens. Immunotherapies that use interferons can be used to treat a variety of diseases, including infections and cancer.
5. Immune adjuvants: Immune adjuvants are substances that are added to vaccines to enhance the immune response to the vaccine. They can help to increase the effectiveness of vaccines and reduce the amount of vaccine needed to achieve immunity
6. Checkpoint inhibitors: Checkpoint inhibitors are immunotherapies that target specific proteins on immune cells, known as checkpoint proteins, which can limit the immune response to cancer cells. By blocking these checkpoint proteins, checkpoint inhibitors can enhance the immune response to cancer and help to fight the disease.
7. CAR-T cell therapy: CAR-T cell therapy is a type of immunotherapy that involves the genetic modification of T cells to express a chimeric antigen receptor (CAR). This allows the T cells to recognize and target specific cancer cells, leading to an enhanced immune response to the cancer.
8. Oncolytic viruses: Oncolytic viruses are viruses that are designed to specifically target and destroy cancer cells, while sparing normal cells. They can be used to boost the immune response to cancer and help to fight the disease.

Overall, immunotherapeutics is a rapidly growing and evolving field that offers new and innovative approaches for the treatment and prevention of diseases. It has the potential to transform the way we treat and manage a wide range of diseases, and will likely continue to play a key role in the development of new and improved therapies in the years to come.

Advantages of Immunotherapeutics

Specificity: One of the main advantages of immunotherapies is their specificity, as they can be designed to target specific diseases, pathogens, or cancer cells. This helps to minimize side effects and improve the efficacy of the treatment.

Long-lasting effect: Unlike traditional treatments, such as chemotherapy, which have a limited duration of effect, many immunotherapies have the potential to produce a long-lasting response. This is because they can train the immune system to recognize and respond to specific pathogens or cancer cells, leading to a persistent immune response.

Fewer side effects: Many immunotherapies have fewer side effects compared to traditional treatments, such as chemotherapy or radiation therapy. This is because they can target specific diseases or cancer cells without affecting normal cells, reducing the risk of toxicity and side effects.

Effective against multiple diseases: Some immunotherapies, such as vaccines, can provide protection against multiple diseases, making them a cost-effective and efficient way to prevent disease.

Complementary to other treatments: Immunotherapies can also be used in combination with other treatments, such as chemotherapy, to improve the overall effectiveness of the treatment and reduce the risk of side effects.

Challenges in Immunotherapeutics

Cost: One of the main challenges in the field of immunotherapeutics is the high cost of these treatments, which can make them inaccessible to many patients.

Limited efficacy: While immunotherapies have shown promising results in many diseases, they are not effective in all patients, and their efficacy can vary depending on the specific disease and patient population.

Side effects: Some immunotherapies can have side effects, such as severe allergic reactions, and there is a need for better ways to predict and manage these side effects.

Lack of standardization: There is a need for better standardization in the production and administration of immunotherapies, to ensure consistent and reliable results across different patients and populations.

Regulatory hurdles: There are also regulatory hurdles that need to be overcome to ensure that new and innovative immunotherapies can be rapidly and effectively developed and brought to market.

In conclusion, immunotherapeutics is a rapidly growing and evolving field that offers new and innovative approaches for the treatment and prevention of diseases. While there are still many challenges to be overcome, the potential benefits of these therapies make them a promising area of research and development, and they are likely to play an increasingly important role in the future of medicine.

Recent Advances in Immunotherapeutics

Cancer immunotherapy: One of the most promising areas of research in immunotherapeutics is the development of immunotherapies for cancer. Cancer immunotherapies aim to harness the power of the immune system to target and eliminate cancer cells, either by stimulating the immune system to recognize and attack cancer cells, or by blocking the mechanisms that allow cancer cells to evade the immune response.

Checkpoint inhibitors: Checkpoint inhibitors are a type of immunotherapy that block the mechanisms that allow cancer cells to evade the immune response. These therapies have shown remarkable efficacy in the treatment of several types of cancer, including melanoma, lung cancer, and kidney cancer.

CAR-T cell therapy: CAR-T cell therapy is a type of immunotherapy that involves genetically engineering a patient's T cells to express a chimeric antigen receptor (CAR) that recognizes specific cancer cells. These engineered T cells are then infused back into the patient, where they can target and eliminate cancer cells.

Cancer vaccines: Cancer vaccines aim to stimulate the immune system to recognize and attack cancer cells. While cancer vaccines are still in the early stages of development, they show great promise as a way to prevent or treat cancer.

Autoimmune disorder immunotherapy: Another area of research in immunotherapeutics is the development of immunotherapies for autoimmune disorders, such as rheumatoid arthritis, lupus, and multiple sclerosis. These therapies aim to modulate the immune response to reduce inflammation and protect against tissue damage in affected patients.

Conclusion

Immunotherapeutics is a rapidly evolving field with the potential to revolutionize the treatment and prevention of a wide range of diseases. Despite some challenges, such as the high cost and limited efficacy of some treatments, the recent advances in the field demonstrate the potential for immunotherapies to offer new and innovative approaches to the treatment of cancer, autoimmune disorders, and other diseases. As research continues, it is likely that new and improved immunotherapies will emerge, offering better outcomes for patients and improving public health.

Future of Immunotherapeutics

The future of immunotherapeutics is bright, with many exciting new treatments and approaches in development. New advances in the field of immunology, such as the discovery of new immune checkpoint inhibitors and the development of personalized immunotherapies, are expanding the possibilities for the treatment of cancer and other diseases. Additionally, the rapid growth of the field of synthetic biology is providing new tools for the engineering and design of immunotherapies, and is expected to lead to new and innovative treatments in the coming years.

Overall, the future of immunotherapeutics holds great promise, as these treatments offer the potential to transform the way that diseases are treated and prevented. By harnessing the power of the immune system, immunotherapies have the potential to offer new and effective solutions to some of the most challenging diseases facing our world today.

Humanisation antibody therapy

Humanization of antibody therapy refers to the process of modifying an antibody to make it more similar to a naturally occurring human antibody. This can be done in several ways, including:

CDR grafting: CDR grafting involves replacing the complementarity-determining regions (CDRs) of a non-human antibody with the CDRs of a human antibody. This can be done to create a hybrid antibody that has improved affinity and specificity for its target.Humanization by gene synthesis: Humanization by gene synthesis involves synthesizing a human antibody gene from scratch, based on the amino acid sequence of a non-human antibody. This allows the creation of a completely human antibody with improved affinity and specificity for its target.

Humanization by transgenic animals: Humanization by transgenic animals involves genetically engineering animals, such as mice or rabbits, to produce human antibodies. This allows the production of large quantities of human antibodies with improved affinity and specificity for their targets.Humanization of antibody therapy can improve the safety and effectiveness of these therapies by reducing the risk of immune reactions and increasing the specificity of the antibody for its target. It has led to the development of many important therapies for a variety of diseases.

Additionally, humanized antibodies have better pharmacokinetics (how the body processes the drug), which can result in longer-lasting and more effective treatments. They are also less likely to bind to normal human tissues, reducing the risk of side effects. Humanized antibodies are widely used in the treatment of cancer, autoimmune disorders, and infectious diseases. They are also being researched for their potential in the treatment of a range of other medical conditions. Overall, the humanization of antibody therapy has greatly advanced the field of immunotherapy and has improved the lives of countless individuals.

Humanization of antibody therapy is an important step in the development of monoclonal antibody-based drugs. Monoclonal antibodies are laboratory-made molecules that mimic the immune system's ability to fight off harmful invaders such as viruses, bacteria and cancer cells. They are designed to specifically target and neutralize a specific molecule or antigen, making them a powerful tool in the treatment of diseases.

However, early generations of monoclonal antibodies were often derived from non-human sources, such as mice, and had limited efficacy due to the presence of non-human sequences that could trigger an immune response. This led to the development of humanization techniques, which aim to reduce the non-human sequences in the antibody while preserving its potency and specificity.

Humanized antibodies have shown tremendous success in the treatment of various diseases, including cancer, autoimmune diseases, and infectious diseases. For example, Rituximab, a humanized monoclonal antibody that targets the CD20 antigen on B-cells, has revolutionized the treatment of non-Hodgkin's lymphoma and rheumatoid arthritis.

The humanization of antibody therapy continues to be an active area of research and development, as scientists strive to create more effective and safer treatments for a range of medical conditions. With ongoing advancements in biotechnology and genetic engineering, the future of humanized antibody therapy holds great promise for improving patient outcomes and quality of life.

The process of humanizing an antibody can be time-consuming and complex, requiring a detailed understanding of antibody structure and function. The goal of humanization is to retain the binding specificity of the original non-human antibody while minimizing the presence of non-human sequences that could trigger an immune response.

One of the key challenges in humanizing an antibody is preserving the structure of the antigen-binding site, which is responsible for the antibody's specificity and affinity for its target. This requires careful selection of human complementarity determining regions (CDRs) that will be grafted onto the non-human antibody.

In addition to CDR grafting, humanization can also be achieved through other methods such as transgenic animal production, phage display, and ribosome display. These methods differ in terms of the specific techniques used, but they all aim to create a humanized antibody that is highly specific and effective in targeting its intended antigen.

Humanized antibodies have proven to be highly effective in treating a range of medical conditions, including cancer, autoimmune diseases, and infectious diseases. They are also being researched for their potential in the treatment of other medical conditions such as Alzheimer's disease, cardiovascular disease, and neurological disorders.

In conclusion, the humanization of antibody therapy has revolutionized the field of immunotherapy and has led to the development of many important therapies for a range of medical conditions. With ongoing advancements in biotechnology, the future of humanized antibody therapy holds great promise for improving patient outcomes and quality of life.

Another important aspect of humanized antibody therapy is the manufacturing process. Humanized antibodies must be produced in a highly controlled and sterile environment to ensure their safety and efficacy.

The production of humanized antibodies typically involves growing large quantities of cells, such as Chinese hamster ovary (CHO) cells or transgenic animals, that have been genetically engineered to produce the desired antibody. The cells are then harvested and purified to remove any contaminants, and the antibody is purified and formulated into a final product.

The quality of the final product is critically important, and rigorous testing is performed to ensure that the antibody meets strict quality standards. This includes testing for purity, potency, and stability, as well as for the presence of any impurities or contaminants.

In addition to the production of humanized antibodies, there is also ongoing research into the design and engineering of next-generation antibodies. This includes the development of bispecific and multispecific antibodies, which can target multiple antigens, and the use of nanobodies, which are smaller and more versatile than traditional antibodies.

The humanization of antibody therapy has greatly advanced the field of immunotherapy and has improved the lives of countless individuals. With ongoing advancements in biotechnology and genetic engineering, the future of humanized antibody therapy holds great promise for the development of even more effective and safe treatments for a range of medical conditions.

Another important aspect of humanized antibody therapy is their administration. Humanized antibodies are typically administered intravenously, either as a single dose or as a series of doses over a period of time.

The dose and frequency of administration depend on the specific antibody and the medical condition being treated. For example, a single high-dose of a humanized antibody may be sufficient to treat a cancer patient, while a lower dose may be required for the treatment of a chronic autoimmune disease.

In addition to intravenous administration, there is ongoing research into alternative routes of administration, such as subcutaneous, intradermal, and oral administration. These alternative routes of administration offer the potential for greater patient convenience and improved outcomes.

The safety and efficacy of humanized antibodies are closely monitored in clinical trials, and once a humanized antibody is approved by regulatory agencies such as the US Food and Drug Administration (FDA) or the European Medicines Agency (EMA), it can be prescribed to patients.

In conclusion, humanized antibody therapy is a rapidly advancing field that holds great promise for the treatment of a wide range of medical conditions. With ongoing research and development, the future of humanized antibody therapy is bright, and we can expect to see continued advancements in their production, administration, and efficacy in the coming years.

One important aspect of humanized antibody therapy is their mechanism of action. Humanized antibodies work by binding to specific antigens or proteins in the body and either blocking or neutralizing their function.

For example, in the case of cancer, humanized antibodies may bind to and neutralize growth factors or receptors that are involved in the growth and spread of cancer cells. In the case of autoimmune diseases, humanized antibodies may bind to and neutralize cytokines or other proteins that are involved in the immune response.

The specificity of humanized antibodies is one of their key advantages over other forms of therapy, as they are designed to target only specific proteins or antigens, reducing the risk of unwanted side effects.

Another important aspect of humanized antibody therapy is their ability to recruit and activate the immune system. Humanized antibodies can serve as "flags" for the immune system, marking specific antigens for destruction. This can lead to the activation of immune cells such as T cells and natural killer cells, which can then help to eliminate the targeted cells.

In addition to their direct therapeutic effects, humanized antibodies also have the potential to be used in combination with other therapies, such as chemotherapy or radiotherapy. This combination approach can lead to improved outcomes and greater efficacy compared to monotherapy.

In conclusion, humanized antibody therapy is a highly targeted and effective form of therapy that offers many advantages over traditional treatments. With their mechanism of action, specificity, and ability to activate the immune system, humanized antibodies hold great promise for the treatment of a wide range of medical conditions.

The cost of humanized antibody therapy can vary widely depending on several factors, including the specific antibody, the medical condition being treated, and the location of the patient.

In general, humanized antibody therapy is considered a high-cost therapy, due to the cost of production, research and development, and clinical trials. However, many insurance providers cover the cost of these therapies, and financial assistance programs are available for patients who are unable to pay for their treatment.

Another important aspect of humanized antibody therapy is the availability of these treatments. While many humanized antibodies have been approved by regulatory agencies such as the US Food and Drug Administration (FDA) and the European Medicines Agency (EMA), access to these treatments can be limited in some regions of the world, due to factors such as cost, regulatory approval, and distribution networks.

In conclusion, the cost and availability of humanized antibody therapy can be significant challenges for some patients and healthcare systems. However, with ongoing advancements in biotechnology and genetic engineering, and with increasing investment in the development of new therapies, we can expect to see continued improvements in the cost-effectiveness and availability of these treatments in the coming years.

One important aspect of humanized antibody therapy is the potential for side effects and adverse reactions. Like all forms of therapy, humanized antibodies can cause side effects, although these are typically mild and short-lived.

The most common side effects of humanized antibody therapy include:

Infusion reactions: Infusion reactions can occur during the administration of humanized antibodies and may include symptoms such as fever, chills, headache, and low blood pressure. These reactions are typically short-lived and can be managed with medications.

Allergic reactions: Allergic reactions to humanized antibodies can occur, although they are rare. Symptoms may include itching, hives, shortness of breath, and swelling of the face and lips.

Immune reactions: In rare cases, humanized antibodies can trigger an immune reaction, leading to the formation of antibodies against the treatment. This can reduce the effectiveness of the therapy and may require the patient to switch to a different treatment.

In addition to these side effects, humanized antibodies can also interact with other medications and treatments, so it is important for patients to inform their healthcare provider of all medications and treatments they are taking before starting humanized antibody therapy.

In conclusion, the potential for side effects and adverse reactions is an important consideration for patients who are considering humanized antibody therapy. However, with close monitoring and proper management, the majority of patients can safely and effectively receive these treatments.

Another important aspect of humanized antibody therapy is the duration of treatment. The length of treatment with humanized antibodies can vary widely depending on the specific antibody and the medical condition being treated.

For some medical conditions, humanized antibody therapy may be given as a single treatment, while for others, it may be given over a period of several weeks or months. In some cases, humanized antibody therapy may be given for several years to maintain the therapeutic effect.

The duration of treatment is determined by several factors, including the specific medical condition, the stage of the disease, the patient's overall health, and the response to the treatment.

In addition, the duration of treatment with humanized antibodies may change as new research and developments in biotechnology emerge. For example, new humanized antibodies may be developed that are more effective and have longer durations of action, reducing the need for repeated treatments.

In conclusion, the duration of treatment with humanized antibody therapy can vary widely depending on several factors. Patients should discuss their individual treatment plan with their healthcare provider, including the length of treatment, the frequency of treatments, and the potential for changes to the treatment plan.

Another important aspect of humanized antibody therapy is the administration method. Humanized antibodies can be administered in a variety of ways, including intravenous infusion, subcutaneous injection, and intramuscular injection.

Intravenous infusion is the most common method of administration for humanized antibodies, as it allows for the rapid delivery of the treatment to the patient's bloodstream. This method is typically performed in a clinical setting, such as a hospital or clinic, and may take several hours to complete.

Subcutaneous injection is another method of administration for humanized antibodies, which involves injecting the treatment just below the skin. This method is typically less invasive than intravenous infusion and may be performed at home by the patient or a caregiver.

Intramuscular injection is a less common method of administration for humanized antibodies, which involves injecting the treatment directly into a muscle. This method is typically used for treatments that require a slow and steady release of the medication into the bloodstream.

In conclusion, the method of administration for humanized antibody therapy can vary depending on the specific treatment and the patient's individual needs. Patients should discuss the administration method with their healthcare provider, including the benefits and risks of each method, to determine the best approach for their individual treatment plan.

One final aspect of humanized antibody therapy is the cost. The cost of humanized antibody therapy can be substantial, as these treatments are typically expensive to produce and require specialized administration.

The cost of humanized antibody therapy will vary depending on the specific treatment, the patient's insurance coverage, and the location of the treatment. Some insurance plans may cover the cost of humanized antibody therapy, while others may require the patient to pay for some or all of the treatment out-of-pocket.

In addition, the cost of humanized antibody therapy may be impacted by several factors, including the length of treatment, the frequency of treatments, and the method of administration. For example, a treatment that requires frequent intravenous infusions may be more expensive than a treatment that can be administered at home via subcutaneous injection.

Patients should discuss the cost of humanized antibody therapy with their healthcare provider, including their insurance coverage and any potential out-of-pocket expenses. In some cases, financial assistance programs may be available to help patients pay for their treatment.

In conclusion, the cost of humanized antibody therapy can be substantial and will vary depending on several factors. Patients should discuss the cost of their treatment with their healthcare provider to determine the best approach for their individual treatment plan.

Another important aspect of humanized antibody therapy is the potential side effects. Like any medical treatment, humanized antibody therapy can cause side effects, although the exact nature and severity of these side effects will vary depending on the specific treatment and the patient's individual health status.

Some common side effects of humanized antibody therapy include:

Infusion reactions: These can occur during or shortly after an intravenous infusion and may cause symptoms such as fever, chills, hives, and low blood pressure.

Allergic reactions: Some patients may experience an allergic reaction to the humanized antibody treatment, which can cause symptoms such as itching, swelling, difficulty breathing, and low blood pressure.

Infections: Humanized antibody therapy can suppress the immune system, making patients more susceptible to infections. Patients should be cautious and seek medical attention if they develop symptoms of an infection, such as fever, chills, and fatigue.

Tumor lysis syndrome: This can occur in patients with cancer who are receiving humanized antibody therapy and can cause symptoms such as nausea, vomiting, muscle cramps, and kidney failure.

Other side effects: Other potential side effects of humanized antibody therapy can include fatigue, headache, joint pain, and muscle pain.

In conclusion, humanized antibody therapy can cause side effects, although the risk and severity of these side effects will vary depending on the specific treatment and the patient's individual health status. Patients should discuss the potential side effects of humanized antibody therapy with their healthcare provider, and seek medical attention if they experience any unusual symptoms or reactions. It's important to carefully monitor any side effects and to report them promptly to the healthcare provider to ensure the best possible outcome.

In terms of monitoring and follow-up, humanized antibody therapy typically requires close monitoring by a healthcare provider. This may include regular check-ups, blood tests, imaging studies, and other tests to assess the patient's response to the treatment and to monitor for any side effects.

Patients should also be aware of the importance of adhering to their treatment plan, including taking all medications as prescribed, avoiding missed doses, and keeping all scheduled appointments.

In addition, patients should be aware of the importance of staying informed about their condition and the latest developments in humanized antibody therapy. This may involve reading relevant literature, attending patient support groups, and talking to healthcare providers, other patients, and advocacy organizations.

Finally, patients should be aware of the importance of working with a healthcare provider to develop a comprehensive, individualized treatment plan that takes into account their unique needs and goals. This may involve working with a team of healthcare providers, including primary care doctors, specialists, and other healthcare professionals, to ensure the best possible outcome.

In conclusion, close monitoring, adherence to the treatment plan, staying informed, and working with a healthcare provider to develop a comprehensive, individualized treatment plan are all important aspects of humanized antibody therapy. Patients should be aware of these important considerations and take an active role in their own care.

The development of humanized antibody therapy has been a major advance in the treatment of many diseases. This type of therapy has shown great promise in the treatment of cancer, autoimmune disorders, infectious diseases, and other conditions, and continues to be an area of active research and development.

One of the benefits of humanized antibody therapy is its ability to target specific molecules or cells involved in disease, thereby reducing the risk of side effects and improving the overall efficacy of the treatment.

Another advantage of humanized antibody therapy is its versatility, as it can be used to treat a wide range of diseases and conditions. For example, humanized antibodies can be used to block the activity of harmful proteins, to stimulate the immune system to fight disease, or to deliver drugs directly to diseased cells.

Humanized antibody therapy also has the potential to be personalized, as it can be tailored to each patient's unique genetic and health status. This can help to ensure the best possible outcome and to reduce the risk of side effects.

In conclusion, humanized antibody therapy offers a number of benefits over traditional therapies, including improved specificity, versatility, and the potential for personalization. This makes humanized antibody therapy an important area of research and development, with the potential to significantly improve the treatment of many diseases and conditions.

Recent update :

1.Single-cell proteomics [2]:

Single-cell proteomics typically focuses on either the absolute quantification of a small number of proteins or highly multiplexed protein measurements. Single-cell proteomics holds the potential to create a mechanistic understanding of how the products of many genes interact to produce a cellular phenotype. The recent growth in single-cell profiling has been focused primarily on nucleic acid measurement. There is now a pressing need for more comprehensive protein measurements of single cells, particularly in absolute quantification and multiplexed measurements.

2.Single-Cell Genomics and Transcriptomics By Imaging [3]:

Genome-scale imaging has enabled single-cell omics analysis in a spatially resolved manner in intact cells and tissues. These advances allow gene expression profling of individual cells, and hence in situ identifcation and spatial mapping of cell types, in complex tissues. The high spatial resolution of these approaches further allows determination of the spatial organizations of the genome and transcriptome inside cells, both of which are key regulatory mechanisms for gene expression.

a. Imaging-based single-cell genomics and transcriptomics methods:

Two classes of methods have been reported for imaging-based single-cell transcriptomics and genomics, based on in situ sequencing or multiplexed fluorescence in situ hybridization (FISH).

b. Multiplexed FISH:

FISH has long been used to image genomic loci and RNA transcripts. FISH at the single-molecule level allows highly accurate localization and counting of RNA molecules in cells. Single-molecule FISH with combinatorial color schemes has been used for single-cell gene expression profiling — for example, simultaneously imaging more than ten genes. Endogenous cellular RNAs and DNAs, the ability of these multiplexed imaging methods to identify a large number of artificial nucleic acid barcodes introduced into cells has also led to other important applications.

3. Mol* Viewer [4]:

The web-native Mol* Viewer enables 3D visualization and streaming of macromolecular coordinate and experimental data, together with capabilities for displaying structure quality, functional, or biological context annotations. High-performance graphics and data management allows users to simultaneously visualise up to hundreds of (superimposed) protein structures, stream molecular dynamics simulation trajectories, render cell-level models, or display huge I/HM structures. It is the primary 3D structure viewer used by PDBe and RCSB PDB.

4. Chromatin Tracing [5]:

Recent advances in image-based 3D genomics techniques have enabled direct tracing of chromatin folding and multiplexed imaging of nucleome architectures in single cells of several important biological systems. Chromatin tracing pinpoints the 3D positions of numerous genomic loci along the same chromosome, and links the 3D positions based on their genomic identities to reveal the chromatin folding path. Chromatin tracing uses a sequential imaging and reconstruction procedure which follows;

1. First, a library of primary FISH probes is hybridized to all genomic loci of interest.
2. Next, fluorescently labelled secondary FISH probes are sequentially hybridized to the unique overhang regions on the primary probes associated with individual genomic loci.
3. This way each genomic locus is visualized as a diffraction-limited spot in 3D, which allows fitting of its center position with nanoscale accuracy.

5. Multiomics and deep learning in cancer research:

Multi-omics profiling shows promise for cancer research and precision oncology, due to the high-throughput nature of the generated data. The inherent high dimensionality of multiomics datasets, combined with the heterogeneity of the collected data necessitates the application of specialized machine learning and deep learning methods [6].

6 . Spatial Genomics [7]:

Slide-DNA-seq, a method for capturing spatially resolved DNA sequences from intact tissue sections. Through integration with spatial transcriptomics, distinct sets of genes that are associated with clone-specific genetic aberrations. Together, this multi-modal spatial genomics approach provides a versatile platform for quantifying how cell-intrinsic and cell-extrinsic factors contribute to gene expression, protein abundance and other cellular phenotypes.

Reference:

1.https://researchbank.kaiserpermanente.org/newsletter/pharmacogenomics-using-genetic-data-to-improve-prescribing/

2.Vistain, L.F. and Tay, S., 2021. Single-cell proteomics. Trends in biochemical sciences, 46(8), pp.661-672.

3.Zhuang, X., 2021. Spatially resolved single-cell genomics and transcriptomics by imaging. Nature methods, 18(1), pp.18-22.

4.Sehnal, D., Bittrich, S., Deshpande, M., Svobodová, R., Berka, K., Bazgier, V., Velankar, S., Burley, S.K., Koča, J. and Rose, A.S., 2021. Mol* Viewer: modern web app for 3D visualization and analysis of large biomolecular structures. Nucleic Acids Research, 49(W1), pp.W431-W437.

5.Hu, M. and Wang, S., 2021. Chromatin tracing: imaging 3D genome and nucleome. Trends in cell biology, 31(1), pp.5-8.

6.Tarazona, S., Arzalluz-Luque, A. and Conesa, A., 2021. Undisclosed, unmet and neglected challenges in multi-omics studies. Nature Computational Science, 1(6), pp.395-402.

7.Zhao, T., Chiang, Z.D., Morriss, J.W., LaFave, L.M., Murray, E.M., Del Priore, I., Meli, K., Lareau, C.A., Nadaf, N.M., Li, J. and Earl, A.S., 2022. Spatial genomics enables multi-modal study of clonal heterogeneity in tissues. Nature, 601(7891), pp.85-91.

CHAPTER SIX

Cell culture techniques

Miss Snehal Veer, Mrs Ashwini Badhe and Dr Pravin Badhe

Introduction-

Cell culture is the process of growing cells in the laboratory, typically in a dish or flask that is specifically designed for this purpose. It is a commonly used technique in biology and biotechnology, and it allows researchers to study the growth and behavior of cells under controlled conditions.

Cell culture can be used to study a wide range of biological processes, including cell division, gene expression, and metabolism. It is also used to produce proteins and other biomolecules for use in research and industry.

Cell culture requires the use of specialized equipment, including incubators, cell culture flasks, and laminar flow hoods, as well as cell culture media, which is a nutrient-rich liquid that supports the growth of cells in the laboratory.

There are several types of cells that can be cultured, including primary cells, which are isolated directly from an organism, and cell lines, which are cells that have been immortalized and can be grown indefinitely in the laboratory.

Cell culture techniques

There are several techniques that are commonly used in cell culture, including:

- Suspension culture: Suspension culture is a technique in which cells are grown in a liquid medium without the use of a solid support. This allows the cells to grow as a free-floating suspension.
- Monolayer culture: Monolayer culture is a technique in which cells are grown on a solid surface, such as a tissue culture dish or flask. The cells are grown in a layer, or monolayer, that covers the surface of the dish or flask.
- Spheroid culture: Spheroid culture is a technique in which cells are grown in a three-dimensional structure that resembles a ball, or spheroid. This allows the cells to grow in a more physiological environment that more closely resembles the tissue in which they would normally be found in the body.
- Primary cell culture: Primary cell culture is a technique in which cells are isolated directly from an organism and grown in the laboratory. These cells are typically more difficult to grow and maintain than cell lines, but they can provide important information about the function and behavior of cells in their native environment.
- Cell line culture: Cell line culture is a technique in which cells are grown from a cell line, which is a population of cells that has been immortalized and can be grown indefinitely in the laboratory. Cell lines are commonly used in cell culture because they are easier to grow and maintain than primary cells.

Basic equipments used in cell culture lab

There are several basic pieces of equipment that are commonly used in a cell culture laboratory:

- Incubator: An incubator is a device that is used to maintain a controlled environment for cells. It is used to maintain a constant temperature, humidity, and carbon dioxide level, as well as to provide an appropriate amount of oxygen.
- Microscopes: Microscopes are used to observe cells and other small structures. There are several types of microscopes that are commonly used in a cell culture laboratory, including light microscopes, fluorescence microscopes, and electron microscopes.
- Cell culture flasks: Cell culture flasks are used to grow cells in the laboratory. They are typically made of glass or plastic and are available in a variety of sizes and shapes.
- Cell culture media: Cell culture media is a nutrient-rich liquid that is used to support the growth of cells in the laboratory. It typically contains a combination of nutrients, such as amino acids, sugars, and vitamins, as well as growth factors and other factors that are essential for cell growth.
- Autoclave: An autoclave is a device that is used to sterilize equipment and materials using high pressure steam. It is an important tool in a cell culture laboratory to prevent contamination of cell cultures.
- Laminar flow hood: A laminar flow hood is a device that is used to create a sterile environment for handling cells and other materials. It uses a flow of filtered air to create a clean area where cells can be handled without the risk of contamination.

Cell culture media

Cell culture media is a nutrient-rich liquid that is used to support the growth of cells in the laboratory. It typically contains a combination of nutrients, such as amino acids, sugars, and vitamins, as well as growth factors and other factors that are essential for cell growth.

There are several types of cell culture media that are used for different purposes, including:

1. Basal media: Basal media is a simple medium that contains the minimum nutrients required for cell growth. It is often used as a starting point for the development of more complex media formulations.
2. Serum-containing media: Serum-containing media is a medium that contains serum, which is a component of blood that contains a variety of growth factors and other nutrients. Serum-containing media is often used to support the growth of cells that require these factors for optimal growth.
3. Specialized media: Specialized media is a medium that is formulated for a specific cell type or purpose. It may contain specialized ingredients, such as hormones or other growth factors, that are required for the growth or differentiation of specific cell types.
4. Defined media: Defined media is a medium that contains all of the necessary nutrients in known concentrations. It is often used to study the effects of specific nutrients on cell growth and function.
5. Chemically defined media: Chemically defined media is a medium that is composed of pure, chemically defined molecules. It does not contain any undefined components, such as serum, and is often used to study the effects of specific molecules on cell growth and function.

Various types of cell culture

There are several types of cell culture, including:

1. **Primary cell culture-**

Primary cell culture is a type of cell culture in which cells are isolated directly from an organism and grown in the laboratory. These cells are typically more difficult to grow and maintain than cell lines, which are cells that have been immortalized and can be grown indefinitely in the laboratory.

Primary cells are often used in cell culture because they are more representative of the cells found in the body and because they can provide important information about the function and behavior of cells in their native environment.

There are several steps involved in primary cell culture, including:

- Isolation: The first step in primary cell culture is to isolate the cells from the tissue of interest. This typically involves mechanically dissociating the tissue and then separating the cells from other tissue components using techniques such as centrifugation or filtration.
- Plating: After the cells have been isolated, they are usually plated in a cell culture dish or flask that has been coated with a substance such as collagen or fibronectin to promote cell attachment.
- Incubation: The cells are then incubated in an incubator, which is a device that is used to maintain a controlled environment for cells. The incubator is used to maintain a constant temperature, humidity, and carbon dioxide level, as well as to provide an appropriate amount of oxygen.
- Passaging: As the cells grow and divide, they will eventually become confluent, which means that they will cover the entire surface of the dish or flask. At this point, the cells can be harvested and replated in a fresh dish or flask, a process known as passaging. This allows the cells to continue to grow and divide in the laboratory.

2. Cell line culture

Cell line culture refers to the process of growing and maintaining cells in a laboratory setting. Cell lines are a type of immortalized cell that can be maintained in culture indefinitely, as long as the conditions are appropriate. They can be derived from a variety of sources, such as cancer cells, primary cells, or embryonic cells. Cell lines are used in a wide range of research applications, including drug development, genetic engineering, and the study of cellular processes.

The process of cell line culture typically begins with the isolation and propagation of cells from a primary source. The cells are then grown in a culture medium, which provides the nutrients and growth factors necessary for cell growth and division. The cells are typically grown in flasks or dishes that are kept in an incubator, which maintains the appropriate temperature, humidity, and carbon dioxide levels for optimal cell growth.

As the cells divide and grow, they may need to be passaged, or transferred to a new dish or flask, to prevent overcrowding and to maintain optimal conditions for cell growth. When cells are passaged, they are typically trypsinized, or treated with an enzyme that breaks down the connections between cells, allowing them to be more easily removed from the dish or flask.

It's important to keep in mind that it's not always easy to create a cell line, and keeping it alive. There are many potential pitfalls that can arise during the culture process, such as contamination with bacteria or other cells, changes in the genetic makeup of the cells, or changes in the cells' sensitivity to drugs or other agents. Because of this, it's important to maintain strict aseptic technique when working with cell cultures, and to monitor the cells regularly to ensure that they are healthy and growing properly.

In summary, Cell line culture refers to the process of growing and maintaining cells in a laboratory setting. It is an important tool for various research applications, but needs proper care, attention and standard protocols to maintain the optimal growth conditions and keep the cells healthy.

3. **Suspension culture**

Suspension culture is a method of growing cells in which the cells are suspended in a liquid culture medium, rather than being grown on a solid surface. This type of culture is often used for cells that do not adhere well to a solid surface, such as stem cells, or for cells that are grown in large quantities, such as for the production of biologics or other products.

In suspension culture, cells are typically grown in a vessel such as a flask or a bioreactor, and the culture medium is agitated to keep the cells in suspension. This allows for the efficient transfer of oxygen, nutrients, and other factors necessary for cell growth and division.

Suspension culture can be divided into two main types: Shake Flask culture and Stirred Tank culture.

1. Shake Flask culture: Shake flasks are used for growing small amounts of cells. They are relatively inexpensive, easy to use and can be used for a wide range of cell types. The culture medium is agitated by shaking the flask, which helps to keep the cells in suspension and promotes oxygenation. However, due to the limited capacity of the shake flask, they are not suitable for large-scale cell cultivation.
2. Stirred Tank culture: They are known as bioreactors and are used for growing large amounts of cells, such as for the production of biologics or other products. Stirred-tank bioreactors are equipped with an impeller or other device that agitates the culture medium, providing optimal oxygenation and mixing of the cells. Bioreactors come in different sizes and designs, and can be used for both batch and continuous cultivation.

In addition to the method of agitation, the culture conditions such as temperature, pH, dissolved oxygen, and the concentration of nutrients can be precisely controlled in these bioreactors, which gives more control over the growth of the cells and make it possible to scale up the production of the cells.

Suspension culture has its own advantages and disadvantages, but it's an efficient way to grow cells, specially when it is difficult to grow them in monolayer. It's especially useful when you want to grow cells in large quantities or when you want to grow cells that do not adhere to a solid surface.

4. **Monolayer culture**

Monolayer culture is a method of growing cells in which the cells are grown on a solid surface, typically in a dish or a flask. In this type of culture, cells are typically grown in a single layer, hence the name "monolayer."

The cells are usually grown in a culture medium that contains all the necessary nutrients and growth factors for cell growth and division. The culture dish is then placed in an incubator, which maintains the appropriate temperature, humidity, and carbon dioxide levels for optimal cell growth.

One of the main advantages of monolayer culture is that it allows for the easy manipulation and observation of the cells. Since the cells are grown on a solid surface, they can be easily examined under a microscope and can be manipulated with a variety of tools, such as pipettes and cell scrapers. This type of culture is also relatively easy to set up, and is well suited for a wide range of cell types.

However, this method has its own limitations too. Some cells, such as stem cells, do not adhere well to a solid surface and are better suited to suspension culture. Additionally, as cells grow and divide, they can become crowded and begin to pile up on one another, which can impede proper growth and division. This can be solved by subculturing or passaging the cells, which involves transferring them to a new dish or flask.

The monolayer culture is widely used in cellular biology and medicine, since it allows for an easy manipulation and observation of the cells. It's relatively easy to set up, and is well suited for a wide range of cell types. However, for certain types of cells, the suspension culture is more suitable due to the cell's adherence preference and growth pattern.

5. **Spheroid culture**

Spheroid culture, also known as 3D culture, is a method of growing cells in which the cells are grown in a spherical shape, rather than in a monolayer or suspension. Spheroids mimic the microenvironment of in vivo tumors and provide a more physiologically relevant model to study cell-cell interactions and the effects of drugs or other agents on the cells.

There are a few different methods that can be used to create spheroids, including:

Self-assembling spheroids: This method is based on the natural tendency of certain cell types to aggregate and form spheroids. This method typically uses a low attachment surface, such as a microplate, to grow the cells. As the cells grow and divide, they naturally form into spheroids.

Aggregate spheroids: Cells are mixed with a gel-like substance such as agarose, and then the mixture is poured into a dish or well. The cells will aggregate together to form spheroids.

Hanging droplet method: A droplet of cell suspension is suspended over a culture dish or well, and allowed to form a spheroid.

Spheroid culture can be an efficient way to grow cells in 3D, and is useful for the study of certain cell types such as cancer cells, stem cells, or cells that are part of organoids. Also, it can provide a more realistic model for studying cell-cell interactions, drug uptake, resistance and response to treatments, as well as for screening drug candidates.

It's important to note that spheroid culture has its own specific requirements, and it's not always easy to create spheroids and keeping them alive. The growth conditions, including the temperature, humidity, and the composition of the culture medium, have to be optimized for each cell type. Additionally, the maintenance of 3D architecture and the homogeneity of the spheroids throughout the culture period, need to be carefully monitored.

In summary, Spheroid culture, also known as 3D culture, is a method of growing cells in which the cells are grown in a spherical shape, rather than in a monolayer or suspension. Spheroid culture can provide a more physiologically relevant model to study cell-cell interactions and the effects of drugs or other agents on the cells. It's an efficient way to grow cells in 3D, but has its own specific requirements that need to be considered.

General procedure for cell culture

The general procedure for cell culture can vary depending on the type of cells being cultured, the type of culture (monolayer or suspension), and the specific goals of the experiment.

However, there are some basic steps that are common to most cell culture protocols.

- Cell isolation: The first step in cell culture is to isolate the cells from their primary source, which could be an animal or human tissue, or a cell line. The cells can be isolated using mechanical methods such as scraping or cutting, or using enzymes such as trypsin or collagenase to break down the connections between the cells.
- Cell counting and viability: After isolation, it's important to determine the number of cells present and the percentage of live cells, dead cells, and cell debris. This can be done using a cell counter or by counting cells under a microscope, or using a assay for determining cell viability.
- Cell culture: The isolated cells are then placed in a culture dish, flask or a bioreactor, depending on the type of culture. They are then incubated in a suitable growth medium that contains the necessary nutrients and growth factors for the cells to grow and divide. Depending on the type of cells and the experiment, the culture medium might also include supplements such as antibiotics, to prevent contamination, or growth factors to promote cell growth.
- Incubation: The culture dish, flask or bioreactor is then placed in an incubator, which maintains the appropriate temperature, humidity, and carbon dioxide levels for optimal cell growth. The length of time that the cells are incubated will depend on the specific goals of the experiment and the rate of cell growth.
- Subculturing/Passaging: As the cells grow and divide, they may need to be passaged, or transferred to a new dish or flask, to prevent overcrowding and to maintain optimal conditions for cell growth. The cells are typically trypsinized, or treated with an enzyme that breaks down the connections between cells, allowing them to be more easily removed from the dish or flask.
- Maintenance and Monitoring: Regular monitoring of the cells is crucial to ensure that they are healthy and growing properly. This includes monitoring the growth rate, cell morphology, and the pH and the oxygen levels of the culture medium. It is also important to maintain strict aseptic technique when working with cell cultures, to prevent contamination.
- It's important to note that this general procedure applies to many cell culture protocols, but specific protocols can vary depending on the type of cells, the type of culture, and the specific goals of the experiment. Cell culture protocols should be read carefully and strictly followed to ensure optimal growth conditions and to obtain

reproducible results.

Cryopreservation

Cryopreservation is the process of freezing living tissue or cells at very low temperatures in order to preserve them for long periods of time. The idea behind cryopreservation is that if the cells or tissue are frozen quickly enough and stored at a low enough temperature, the metabolic processes that would normally lead to their deterioration will be slowed or stopped completely, allowing them to be preserved in a "suspended animation" state.

There are a number of different methods that can be used for cryopreservation, depending on the type of tissue or cells being preserved and the intended use. Some common methods include:

- Slow freezing: This method involves gradually lowering the temperature of the cells or tissue over a period of time, typically at a rate of 1-2 degrees Celsius per minute. This helps to prevent the formation of ice crystals within the cells that can cause damage.
- Vitrification: This method involves freezing the cells or tissue at a very rapid rate, typically at a rate of several hundred degrees Celsius per minute. This helps to prevent the formation of ice crystals and allows the cells or tissue to be stored at temperatures below the freezing point.
- Chemical preservation: This method involves adding chemicals such as dimethyl sulfoxide (DMSO) or ethylene glycol to the cells or tissue to protect them from freezing damage. The cells or tissue can then be stored at a temperature below the freezing point.

Cryopreservation is used in a variety of applications, including preserving sperm and eggs for fertility treatments, preserving embryos for in vitro fertilization, preserving cells for research and medical treatments, and preserving organs and other tissue for transplantation. Additionally, it is used in the long-term preservation of valuable biological samples like stem cells, viruses and bacteria for future research and analysis.

It is important to note that there are still many challenges to overcome with cryopreservation, particularly when it comes to preserving complex structures like organs and tissues. While significant progress has been made in recent years, much more research is needed before cryopreservation can be used to preserve organs and tissues for transplantation.

Characterization of cells and their application

Characterization of cells refers to the process of identifying and measuring the various physical, biochemical, and functional properties of cells. This can include identifying the type of cells (such as stem cells, cancer cells, immune cells, etc.), determining their size and shape, measuring their metabolism, and analyzing their gene expression and epigenetic status.

Cell characterization is an important step in understanding the biology of cells and how they work. It is also critical for applications such as drug discovery, stem cell therapy, cancer research, and regenerative medicine.

Some of the techniques used for cell characterization include:

Light microscopy: This method allows for the visual observation of cells and can be used to identify different cell types, measure cell size and shape, and observe cell movement and behaviour.

Flow cytometry: This method uses a laser to analyze cells as they flow through a small nozzle. It can be used to count cells, measure cell size and shape, and detect and analyze specific cell surface markers and intracellular molecules.

Immunofluorescence: This method uses fluorescently labelled antibodies to detect specific proteins on the surface or inside of cells. It can be used to identify different cell types, measure cell signalling and responses, and analyze the localization of proteins within cells.

Western blot: This method uses antibodies to detect specific proteins in cell extracts. It can be used to quantify the amount of a protein present in a sample, or to compare the protein expression levels between different cell types or under different conditions.

PCR and qPCR : This method allows the quantification and analysis of specific gene expression in cells by amplification of a specific DNA region and later on quantify it.

Cell culture and differentiation: Cell culture refers to the growth and maintenance of cells in the laboratory, while differentiation refers to the process by which cells acquire specialized properties and functions. These techniques are used to study the behavior and characteristics of different cell types, and to generate specific cell types for research and therapeutic applications.

Overall, cell characterization is a critical step in understanding the biology of cells and developing new treatments and therapies. It's a multi-disciplinary field that requires knowledge and expertise in various areas such as cell biology, genetics, biochemistry, and bioinformatics.

Principle and application of cell viability assay

Cell viability assays are techniques used to determine the number of live or viable cells in a culture or sample. These assays are important for a wide range of applications, including cell culture, drug discovery, and toxicology.

The principle of a cell viability assay is based on the ability of living cells to take up and metabolize a specific probe or dye. These probes or dyes can be either membrane-permeable or membrane-impermeable, depending on the assay. The dye or probes are then used to distinguish live cells from dead cells by measuring a specific cellular activity or parameter.

Here are a few examples of commonly used cell viability assays:

- Trypan blue exclusion assay: This assay uses a membrane-impermeable dye called trypan blue. Live cells are unable to take up the dye and appear blue, while dead cells are able to take up the dye and appear colourless. The number of live cells is then calculated by counting the number of blue cells in the sample.
- MTT assay: This assay uses a membrane-permeable dye called MTT (3-(4,5-dimethylthiazol-2-yl)-2,5-diphenyltetrazolium bromide). The live cells convert MTT into a coloured formazan product which can be quantified.
- Alamar Blue assay: This assay uses a redox dye called Alamar Blue, which changes colour from blue to pink when it is reduced by the metabolic activity of living cells.
- Caspase-Glo assay: This assay is based on the activity of caspase enzymes that is activated after apoptotic signalling. It measures the active caspase enzyme activity in live and apoptotic cells.
- LDH assay: This assay measures the lactate dehydrogenase (LDH) enzyme that is released from cells when they are damaged or dying.
- Cell viability assays are widely used in laboratory research and the pharmaceutical industry to evaluate the effects of drugs and chemicals on cells. They are also used to monitor the health and growth of cell cultures, and to assess the effectiveness of cell-based therapies.

It's important to note that, depending on the application, cell viability assays can be designed to measure both, the number of dead and alive cells or specifically the number of viable cells. Additionally, many assays may not distinguish between live and necrotic cells, therefore it is important to be aware of the assay's specificity and select the most suitable assay for the research question.

Principle and application of glucose uptake assay

The glucose uptake assay is a technique used to measure the ability of cells to take up glucose, which is a primary energy source for many cells. The assay is based on the principle that when cells take up glucose, the glucose is metabolized and converted into energy, which can be measured as an increase in the intracellular level of glucose.

There are different ways of measuring glucose uptake, but one common method is based on using a glucose-specific substrate called 2-deoxyglucose (2-DG) or 3-O-methylglucose (3-OG). These are glucose analogs that are taken up by cells through glucose transporters, but cannot be further metabolized by the cells. Thus, the intracellular accumulation of these glucose analogs reflects the rate of glucose uptake by the cells.

The 2-DG uptake assay is a widely used method which is based on the principle of competitive inhibition: 2-DG is added to the cells together with a known amount of regular glucose, and the uptake of 2-DG competes with the uptake of glucose. The amount of 2-DG taken up by the cells reflects the rate of glucose uptake. This method can be measured using radioactive labeled 2-DG or using fluorescence-based methods using non-radioactive labeled 2-DG.

Another method to measure glucose uptake is the utilization of a fluorescence-based assay using 3-OG. This assay is based on the principle of measuring the accumulation of the non-metabolizable glucose analog 3-OG after adding it to the cells.

Glucose uptake assays are widely used in a number of research areas including:

- Metabolism and diabetes research : glucose uptake is closely linked to insulin signaling and resistance, thus these assays can help to understand glucose metabolism disorder
- Cancer research: cancer cells typically have a higher rate of glucose uptake, so these assays can be used to study the metabolic characteristics of cancer cells and to identify potential therapeutic targets.
- Cell biology : these assays can help to understand the cellular mechanism of glucose uptake and glucose transport system.
- Drug development : these assays can be used to evaluate the effect of potential drugs on glucose uptake by cells and to identify potential therapeutic targets.

It's important to note that glucose uptake assays are designed to measure specifically glucose uptake, thus it's important to consider the glucose uptake inhibitors and activators which could be present in the culture medium and/or used drugs. Also, glucose uptake may not be the only or primary energy source for all cells, thus it's important to be aware of the cell type used in the assay and interpret the results accordingly.

Principle and application of calcium influx assay

Calcium influx assay is a technique used to measure the influx of calcium ions (Ca2+) into cells. Calcium ions play an important role in many cellular processes such as muscle contraction, nerve impulse transmission, and cell signaling. Therefore, measuring the influx of calcium ions can provide insight into the physiology of cells, and the regulation of those processes.

The principle of a calcium influx assay is based on the ability of calcium ions to cross the cell membrane when certain signaling molecules bind to their receptors on the cell membrane. The influx of calcium ions can be measured using a variety of techniques, but one common method is to use a fluorescent calcium-sensitive dye that binds to and is excited by calcium ions.

The most common method is the use of a fluorescent calcium-sensitive dye such as Fura-2 or Fluo-3, which are membrane-permeable dyes that are able to bind calcium ions. They change their fluorescence intensity when they bind to the calcium ions, thus the fluorescence intensity of the cells can be used as an indicator of the influx of calcium ions into cells

The assay can be performed by loading the cells with the calcium sensitive dyes and then measuring the changes in the fluorescence intensity after adding the signaling molecules that are known to induce calcium influx, such as neurotransmitters, hormones or others.

Calcium influx assay is widely used in various areas of research such as:

- Cell signaling research: to study the signaling pathways involved in cell signaling and the regulation of intracellular calcium levels.
- Neurotransmitter research: to study the release and reuptake of neurotransmitters and their effects on cell signaling.
- Cardiology: to study the effects of signaling molecules on the contraction and relaxation of heart muscles.
- Cancer research: to study the role of calcium in cell proliferation and cell death, and to identify potential therapeutic targets.

It's important to note that, The results of a calcium influx assay may depend on the cell type, the experimental conditions, and the signaling molecules used. Therefore, the results should be interpreted in the context of the specific experimental conditions, and the physiology of the cells being studied. Additionally, measuring calcium influx alone might not give a complete understanding of the physiology of the cells. Calcium imaging may be used along with other techniques such as other imaging techniques like electron microscopy or electrophysiology, or downstream cellular readout such as gene expression to get a complete understanding of the phenomenon.

Principles and application of flowcytometry

Flow cytometry is a powerful technique used to analyze the physical and chemical properties of cells and particles suspended in fluid. It is widely used in research and clinical settings to analyze a variety of biological samples, including blood, bone marrow, and other body fluids.

The basic principle of flow cytometry is that cells or particles suspended in a fluid are passed through a beam of light, typically from a laser. As the cells or particles pass through the beam, they scatter the light in different directions and at different intensities, depending on their size, shape, and internal structure. In addition, fluorescence from dyes or antibodies that are bound to specific cell surface or intracellular molecules can be excited by the laser, providing additional information about the cells or particles.

In order to analyze the scattered light and fluorescence, the cells or particles are typically passed through a series of optical filters and detectors. These filters and detectors are used to separate the scattered light and fluorescence into different channels, each of which corresponds to a specific wavelength range or fluorescence emission. The data from each channel is then collected and analyzed by a computer, typically using specialized software.

Flow cytometry can be used to perform a wide range of assays, including cell counting, cell sorting, cell proliferation assays, and measurement of cell surface and intracellular markers. It also widely used to analyze the immune cells population such as T cells, B cells, Natural Killer cells etc.

In clinical setting it's used to help diagnose and monitor many diseases such as blood cancer, autoimmune disorders, and to monitor the progress of transplant patients and it also used in many fields like biotechnology, microbiology and stem cell research.

It should be noted that for obtaining accurate results sample preparation is crucial and proper instrument settings, calibration and quality control measures also necessary.

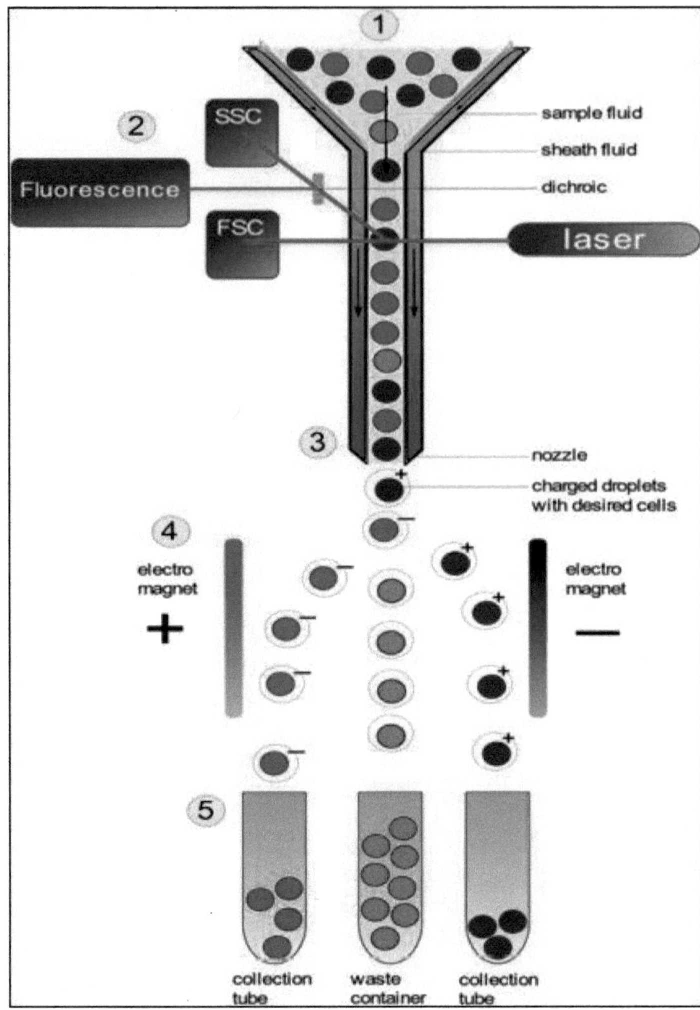

Figure 6.1 :- flow cytometry(1)

Application of flowcytomerty

Flow cytometry is a highly versatile technique that can be used for a wide range of applications, both in research and in the clinical setting.

Some of the key applications of flow cytometry include:

- Cell counting and analysis: Flow cytometry is widely used to count and analyze cells in a variety of biological samples, including blood, bone marrow, and other body fluids. It can be used to identify and quantify different cell types, including red blood cells, white blood cells, and platelets. It can also be used to analyze the size and shape of cells, as well as their surface markers and intracellular proteins.
- Cell sorting: Flow cytometry can also be used to sort cells based on their physical and chemical properties. This is done by passing cells through a laser beam and detecting the scattered light and fluorescence from dyes or antibodies that are bound to specific cell surface or intracellular molecules. Cells can then be separated based on the intensity of their scattered light or fluorescence, and collected for further analysis.
- Cell proliferation assays: Flow cytometry can also be used to measure the proliferation of cells by analyzing the DNA content of cells. This can be done by staining cells with a DNA-specific dye, and then measuring the intensity

of fluorescence using a flow cytometer.

- Measurement of cell surface and intracellular markers: Flow cytometry is also used to measure the expression of cell surface and intracellular markers, such as proteins and antigens, on the cells. This can be done by using fluorescently-labeled antibodies to bind to specific markers on the cells, and then measuring the intensity of fluorescence using a flow cytometer.
- Immune cell analysis: Flow cytometry is a powerful tool for analyzing the immune cells in blood and other body fluids. It can be used to identify and quantify different types of immune cells, such as T cells, B cells, and natural killer cells, as well as to analyze the expression of surface markers and intracellular proteins on these cells.
- Infectious disease research and diagnosis: Flow cytometry can be used in many ways to study the spread of diseases and to detect the presence of pathogens. It also used to identify and quantify different subpopulations of leukocytes, in order to understand how the immune system responds to infection.
- Cancer diagnosis and monitoring: In the clinical setting, flow cytometry is used to diagnose and monitor many types of cancer, such as lymphoma and leukemia, by analyzing the physical and chemical properties of cancer cells in the blood or bone marrow.

These are some of the main ways that flow cytometry is used, but the technique is highly adaptable and new applications are being developed all the time.

Biosimilars

Biosimilars, also known as follow-on biologics, are biologic medical products that are highly similar to, but not identical to, an already approved reference product. Biosimilars are intended to be used as a substitute for the reference product, with the goal of providing the same clinical benefit at a lower cost.

Biosimilars are different from generics, which are copies of small-molecule drugs that have the same active ingredient as the original brand-name product. Because biologics are large and complex molecules, they cannot be exactly replicated like small-molecule drugs. Instead, biosimilars are required to demonstrate that they are highly similar to the reference product, but may have small differences in the manufacturing process or other properties.

The process of approving biosimilars is different from that of approving traditional small-molecule generics. In the United States, biosimilars are regulated by the Food and Drug Administration (FDA) under the Biologics Price Competition and Innovation Act (BPCIA). The FDA evaluates data from preclinical studies, animal studies, and clinical trials to determine whether a biosimilar is highly similar to the reference product, and whether it is safe and effective for its intended use.

Biosimilars have the potential to increase access to expensive biologic therapies and reduce healthcare costs. They are already used in many countries to treat a range of conditions such as cancer, autoimmune disorders, and hormonal disorders.

In order to use biosimilars effectively, it's important to ensure proper communication and education of healthcare providers, patients, and payers. So that they can be used to the fullest potential and without any confusion.

Importance of biosimilar

- Biosimilars, also known as follow-on biologics, are becoming increasingly important in healthcare due to their potential to increase access to expensive biologic therapies and reduce healthcare costs. Here are a few reasons why biosimilars are important:
- Cost-effectiveness: Biosimilars are typically sold at a lower cost than the reference product, making them more affordable for patients, healthcare systems, and payers. This can help to increase access to expensive biologic therapies, particularly for patients who may not have been able to afford the reference product.
- Improved access to treatment: Due to the potential cost savings from biosimilars, healthcare systems may be able to provide these treatments to more patients than would be possible with the reference product. This can result in improved patient outcomes, particularly for those with chronic or life-threatening conditions who may not have

had access to treatment before.

- Competition: The availability of biosimilars can promote competition in the market for biologic therapies, which can further drive down prices and improve access to treatment. This can also encourage innovation and R&D within the pharmaceutical industry.
- Reduced healthcare costs: The reduced costs associated with biosimilars can help to reduce the overall cost of healthcare and make it more sustainable in the long run.
- Environmental sustainability: The usage of biosimilars can also decrease the demand for reference products, this may in turn could lead to a decrease in resource consumption, pollution and CO2 emissions during the production process.

Establishing biosimilars can also be an important measure in addressing the issue of drug shortages which is becoming a serious problem in recent years.

It's important to note that biosimilars are thoroughly evaluated and tested before being made available to patients, to ensure that they are safe, effective, and highly similar to the reference product. Health care providers, patients, and payers all play an important role in ensuring that biosimilars are used in a safe and effective manner.

Importance of biosimilars

• Improved patient outcomes: Biosimilars have the potential to provide patients with access to the same effective treatment as the reference product, at a lower cost. This can lead to improved patient outcomes and quality of life, particularly for those with chronic or life-threatening conditions.

• Increased choice for patients: With the availability of biosimilars, patients may have a wider range of treatment options, which can be especially important for those who have not responded well to the reference product.

• Encouragement of R&D in the biologic industry: The market competition created by the availability of biosimilars can encourage further R&D and innovation in the biologic industry, leading to the development of new and better treatments for patients.

• Improved sustainability of healthcare systems: The reduced costs associated with biosimilars can help to ensure the long-term sustainability of healthcare systems, making it possible to provide access to life-saving treatments to more people.

In conclusion, the importance of biosimilars lies in their potential to increase access to expensive biologic therapies, reduce healthcare costs, and improve patient outcomes. Proper communication and education are important to ensure that biosimilars are used effectively and to their fullest potential.

It's worth noting that despite their potential benefits, there have been some concerns raised about the use of biosimilars, including questions about their safety and efficacy compared to the reference product. However, rigorous scientific evaluation and testing by regulatory agencies, such as the FDA, have demonstrated that biosimilars are highly similar to the reference product and can provide the same clinical benefit.

Additionally, there have been concerns raised about interchangeability, which is a designation given to biosimilars that can be substituted for the reference product without the intervention of a healthcare provider. Currently, only a limited number of biosimilars have been designated as interchangeable by the FDA.

Healthcare providers, patients, and payers all play an important role in ensuring that biosimilars are used effectively. Healthcare providers need to be well-informed about the different biosimilars available and their properties, so they can make informed decisions about treatment options for their patients. Patients need to be informed about the different treatment options available to them, including biosimilars, so they can make informed decisions about their care. And payers need to support access to biosimilars and help to educate patients about these treatments.

In conclusion, biosimilars have the potential to revolutionize the biological industry by increasing access to expensive treatments, reducing healthcare costs, and improving patient outcomes. It is important to continue to support their development and use, while also addressing any concerns and ensuring proper education and communication about their use.

There are also efforts underway to standardize the naming and labelling of biosimilars to help minimize confusion and promote safe use. This is particularly important because biosimilars, despite being highly similar to the reference product, may have differences in their manufacturing processes, formulation, or other properties that could potentially impact their safety and efficacy.

It is also important to continue to monitor the long-term safety and efficacy of biosimilars. Post-marketing surveillance is an important tool for ensuring that any potential issues with biosimilars are identified and addressed quickly. This helps to ensure that patients continue to receive safe and effective treatments, and can also provide valuable data that can be used to further improve the development and use of biosimilars.

In some countries, there are also ongoing debates about how to price and reimburse biosimilars, and how to ensure that they are used appropriately and fairly within the healthcare system. These debates are important to address as they can have a significant impact on patient access to these treatments and the overall sustainability of healthcare systems.

In conclusion, the use of biosimilars is a rapidly evolving field that presents both opportunities and challenges. It is important to continue to support and promote the development and use of biosimilars, while also addressing any concerns and ensuring that they are used in a safe, effective, and equitable manner. Through continued education and communication, as well as ongoing monitoring and evaluation, we can help to ensure that biosimilars reach their full potential to improve patient outcomes and reduce healthcare costs.

Another important aspect of the use of biosimilars is the role of pharmacovigilance. This refers to the ongoing monitoring of the safety of a medicine, including biosimilars, once they have been approved and are in use. This includes the collection, analysis, and dissemination of information about adverse events or side effects associated with the use of the medicine. This information is used to help identify any potential safety issues and to ensure that patients receive the safest and most effective treatments possible.

Pharmacovigilance is an important tool for ensuring the long-term safety of biosimilars and helps to ensure that any potential issues are identified and addressed quickly. It also provides valuable data that can be used to further improve the development and use of biosimilars and to help support informed decision-making about their use.

Another key aspect of the use of biosimilars is the role of prescribing information and labelling. This information is designed to help healthcare providers, patients, and payers understand the benefits, risks, and limitations of biosimilars, as well as how to use them appropriately and effectively. The labelling should provide important information such as the name of the reference product, the indication for use, dosing, administration, and storage information.

Finally, it's important to note that, although biosimilars are intended to be used as substitutes for the reference product, they may not be appropriate for all patients. For example, some patients may have had a previous adverse reaction to the reference product, or they may have certain medical conditions that make it unsafe for them to take a biosimilar. In these cases, the reference product may be the only appropriate treatment option.

In conclusion, the use of biosimilars is an important aspect of the effort to improve access to affordable, high-quality biologic therapies. However, it is important to ensure that biosimilars are used appropriately and safely, and that their benefits are fully realized. This requires ongoing education, communication, and collaboration between healthcare providers, patients, payers, and regulatory agencies.

It's also important to monitor the long-term safety and efficacy of biosimilars, especially since some biologic drugs have been used for many years and their long-term effects may not yet be fully understood. To ensure that biosimilars are safe and effective for long-term use, it's important for regulatory agencies to continue monitoring and gathering data on their use.

Another important factor to consider is the potential for interchangeability between biosimilars and reference products. Interchangeability means that a biosimilar can be substituted for the reference product without the need for a new prescription or additional monitoring. Currently, not all biosimilars are considered interchangeable with their reference products. Interchangeability is a complex issue and it is up to the regulatory agencies to make a determination on a case-by-case basis.

Finally, it's important to consider the impact of biosimilars on the biopharmaceutical industry, including the potential for job losses, the effect on innovation, and the impact on R&D investments. While biosimilars have the potential to reduce costs and increase access to treatment, they may also have unintended consequences for the industry as a whole. It's important for policy makers and stakeholders to consider these factors and take steps to mitigate any potential negative impact.

In conclusion, the use of biosimilars is an important aspect of the effort to improve access to affordable, high-quality biologic therapies. However, it is important to ensure that biosimilars are used appropriately and safely, and that their benefits are fully realized. Ongoing monitoring, education, and collaboration among healthcare providers, patients, payers, and regulatory agencies are key to ensuring the long-term success of the biosimilar industry.

In addition to the benefits and challenges mentioned above, it's also important to consider the impact of biosimilars on the development of new biologic drugs. Biosimilars can reduce the costs of existing biologic drugs, which can increase access to these treatments for patients. However, the reduced revenue from these existing drugs can also make it more difficult for biopharmaceutical companies to invest in the research and development of new drugs. This can potentially limit the development of new treatments for serious and life-threatening diseases.

Another important factor to consider is the potential for intellectual property issues with biosimilars. The reference product and the biosimilar both contain the same active ingredient, but the biosimilar may have small differences in the manufacturing process or other properties. This can raise questions about whether the reference product's patent and intellectual property rights extend to the biosimilar.

Another challenge to the widespread adoption of biosimilars is the need for education and awareness among healthcare providers, patients, and payers. Healthcare providers need to be aware of the availability of biosimilars, as well as their safety and efficacy. Patients also need to be informed about the potential benefits and limitations of biosimilars, so that they can make informed decisions about their care. And payers need to understand the potential cost savings associated with biosimilars, so that they can make decisions about coverage and reimbursement.

In conclusion, the use of biosimilars is a complex issue that requires ongoing monitoring and collaboration among a wide range of stakeholders, including healthcare providers, patients, payers, regulatory agencies, and the biopharmaceutical industry. To ensure the long-term success of the biosimilar industry, it's important to consider the benefits and challenges associated with biosimilars, and to work together to ensure that these drugs are used in a safe and effective manner to improve access to affordable, high-quality biologic therapies.

It's important to note that while biosimilars have the potential to greatly benefit patients and the healthcare system as a whole, there may still be some challenges in the adoption and usage of these products. One of the biggest challenges is a lack of awareness and education about biosimilars among healthcare providers, patients, and payers. There may also be concerns about the interchangeability and substitution of biosimilars for reference products.

To address these challenges, it is important for healthcare providers to be well-informed about the safety and efficacy of biosimilars, and for patients and payers to be educated about the potential benefits of these products. Additionally, regulatory bodies such as the FDA in the United States and their equivalents in other countries play an important role in monitoring the safety and efficacy of biosimilars and ensuring that they are properly labeled and marketed.

Overall, the development and adoption of biosimilars is a promising step forward in the effort to increase access to effective and affordable biologic therapies and reduce the overall cost of healthcare.

In addition, it's important to maintain a transparent and open dialogue between healthcare providers, patients, and regulators to address any concerns and to promote the safe and effective use of biosimilars. This can be done through public education campaigns, educational resources for healthcare providers, and collaboration between stakeholders in the healthcare industry.

Another important aspect to consider is the monitoring and tracking of biosimilar usage and outcomes. This can help to ensure the safe and effective use of these products, and to continuously evaluate and improve their impact on the healthcare system.

It's also worth mentioning that the development and adoption of biosimilars is still a relatively new phenomenon, and more research is needed to fully understand the long-term benefits and potential challenges of these products.

Nevertheless, the potential benefits of biosimilars are significant, and it is important for healthcare providers, patients, and regulators to continue to work together to promote the safe and effective use of these products.

In conclusion, the development and adoption of biosimilars have the potential to greatly improve access to effective and affordable biologic therapies and reduce the overall cost of healthcare. However, it's important to maintain open communication, collaboration, and education to ensure their safe and effective use.

One other aspect worth mentioning is the importance of ensuring patient access to biosimilars in a timely manner. This requires a collaborative effort between healthcare providers, patients, regulators, and payers to ensure that these products are available and affordable to those who need them.

In some countries, there may be barriers to access such as reimbursement policies or limited availability. It is important to address these barriers and work towards making biosimilars more accessible to patients in need.

Moreover, ongoing monitoring and surveillance of the safety and efficacy of biosimilars is important, even after they have been approved and made available for use. This can be done through post-marketing surveillance programs, registry studies, and ongoing clinical trials.

Additionally, it is also crucial to understand and address any potential immunogenicity issues with biosimilars, which refers to the potential for the body to mount an immune response to the product. This is important to ensure the long-term safety of these products.

In conclusion, ensuring patient access to biosimilars, ongoing monitoring and surveillance of their safety and efficacy, and addressing any potential barriers to access are all important factors in promoting the safe and effective use of these products.

Another important aspect to consider is the role of pharmacovigilance in biosimilars. Pharmacovigilance refers to the scientific and regulatory activities related to the detection, assessment, understanding, and prevention of adverse effects or any other drug-related problems.

In the case of biosimilars, it is important to have a robust pharmacovigilance program in place to ensure the continued safety of these products. This can involve monitoring for adverse effects through spontaneous reporting systems, clinical trials, and registry studies.

In addition, it is important to educate healthcare providers, patients, and payers on the importance of reporting any adverse effects or problems they may experience while using biosimilars. This information can then be used to improve the safety profile of these products and ensure their long-term safe use.

In some countries, regulatory agencies may also require that biosimilar manufacturers have a pharmacovigilance plan in place, which outlines the measures they will take to monitor and address any potential safety concerns.

In conclusion, a robust pharmacovigilance program is an important component of ensuring the safe and effective use of biosimilars and should be carefully considered and implemented by regulatory agencies, manufacturers, and healthcare providers.

Another important aspect to consider when it comes to biosimilars is their impact on the healthcare system. Biosimilars have the potential to significantly impact the healthcare system in a number of ways, including:

- Increased patient access to treatment: By reducing the cost of biologic treatments, biosimilars can increase patient access to these therapies, particularly for those who may have previously been unable to afford them. This can result in improved patient outcomes and quality of life.

- Reduced healthcare costs: Biosimilars are typically sold at a lower cost than the reference product, which can help to reduce the overall cost of healthcare. This can be particularly important for healthcare systems that are facing increasing financial pressures.

- Increased competition: The availability of biosimilars can promote competition in the market for biologic therapies, which can further drive down prices and improve access to treatment.

- Improved innovation: By promoting competition and reducing the cost of biologic treatments, biosimilars can encourage further innovation and R&D within the pharmaceutical industry.

- Increased sustainability: By reducing the demand for reference products, the use of biosimilars can also lead to a decrease in resource consumption, pollution and CO_2 emissions during the production process.

It is important to consider the impact of biosimilars on the healthcare system as a whole, and to work towards implementing policies and initiatives that promote their safe and effective use, while also ensuring that patients have access to the treatments they need.

In addition, as the use of biosimilars continues to grow, it will be important to continue monitoring their impact on the healthcare system and to make any necessary adjustments to ensure that they are being used in the most effective and safe manner possible.

RECENT UPDATE-

Three-dimensional (3D) cell culture-

Cell culture is an important and necessary process in drug discovery, cancer research, as well as stem cell study. Most cells are currently cultured using two-dimensional (2D) methods but new and improved methods that implement three-dimensional (3D) cell culturing techniques suggest compelling evidence that much more advanced experiments can be performed yielding valuable insights. When performing 3D cell culture experiments, the cell environment can be manipulated to mimic that of a cell in vivo and provide more accurate data about cell-to-cell interactions, tumour characteristics, drug discovery, metabolic profiling, stem cell research, and other types of diseases. Scaffold-based techniques such as hydrogel-based support, polymeric hard material-based support, hydrophilic glass fibre, and organoids are employed, and each provides its own advantages and applications. Likewise, there are also scaffold-free techniques used such as hanging drop microplates, magnetic levitation, and spheroid microplates with ultra-low attachment coating. 3D cell culture has the potential to provide alternative ways to study organ behaviour via the use of organoids and is expected to eventually bridge the gap between 2D cell culture and animal models (2).

Rotary Cell Cultures

One of the methods of obtaining spheroids is cell culture in a bottle with an agitator. In these conditions, cells cannot attach to the substrate, and start aggregating and self-assembling. It is one of the simplest methods to produce spheroids on a large scale. This method has certain disadvantages e.g., longevity of cultures, variation in spheroid size, and mechanical damages of cells. One variation of this method is a system with a flask rotating around a horizontal axis. Simulation of microgravity with minimal hydrodynamic forces does not destroy cells, such that this method allows the formation of bigger spheroids than in a bottle with an agitator. Morphological differences between spheroids are also smaller than in the first method (3).

Microfluidic Systems-

The non-microfluidic environment causes a reduction of oxygen and nutrients and an increase of osmolality and level of metabolites. To overcome those limitations microfluidics systems are created. The device with the microfluidic flow is made of microwells which are connected by microfluidic channels, from simple to more sophisticated arrays of microchannels. Microchannels are prepared through etching or forming on the surface using neutral materials, e.g., silicon, glass or polydimethylsiloxane (PDMS). The cells are cultured above layers made of the matrix-coated porous membrane and with direct contact with endothelial cells. Additionally, immune cells and tumour cells flow through the microchannels.

Very important advantages of microfluidic systems are controlled mixing, chemical concentration gradients, lower consumption of reagents, control of shear stress and pressure on cells, and also constant perfusion. Microfluidic chips provide a dynamic environment for better reflection of the tissue environment. The sizes of spheroids are homogenous. The viability of hepatocytes cultured in spheroids inflow conditions is higher than in the static model. Cancer spheroids cultured in a microwell plate in dynamic conditions exhibit higher resistance to drugs than in no-flow conditions (4).

Bioprinting-

Simple structure and low vascularization potential are the main limits of using current 3D culture models. The lack of vascularization limits the spheroid's size and probably does not mimic the later stages of tumours very well. In most of the models of 3D cultures, the spatial distribution of cancer cells and ECM composition is not well arranged. The solution to the lack of vascularization and designing scaffolds for better reflection of tumour microenvironment and heterogeneity could be bioprinting technology. Bioprinting includes a variety of approaches consisting of distributing of biological materials and cells in a spatially defined way. In other words, the bioprinting technique could be defined as a technology in which cell layers and supporting biological materials are positioned precisely to mimic the functions of the tissue or organ. There are few strategies of bioprinting: inkjet printing, extrusion-based printing, laser-assisted printing and stereolithography. In inkjet bioprinting, the droplets made of bioink (cell-laden) filling the cartridge are generated and deposited on a scaffold precisely. A computer program controls the deposition of the droplets and it leads to the creation of 3D structures. This method is relatively fast and not expensive and provides high viability of cells. In the extrusion-based bioprinting the bioink is moved through the nozzle with pneumatic or mechanical pressure. This method is also quite cheap and fast. In laser-assisted bioprinting laser stimulation leads to a response of the donor layer which absorbs energy and generates a high-pressure bubble that leads to pushing a droplet of the bioink onto the substrate. Some disadvantages of this method are expensive equipment and poor choice of bioinks. In the stereolithography, an array of programmed mirrors generates a digital mask, which is projected to the reservoir with bioink to photo-crosslink patterns layer by layer. This method is characterized by high resolution and fast speed (4,5).

EZMTT Assay-

EZMTT is a novel mono-sulfonated tetrazolium salt, 2-(3-(2- methoxy-4-nitrophenyl)-2-(4-nitrophenyl)-2H-tetrazol-3-ium-5-yl) benzenesulfonate sodium salt that synthesized earlier. As shown in Fig. 1F, the NAD(P)H in viable cells reduce EZMTT to the soluble yellow formazan in the presence of an electron coupling agent (EC), which has strong absorbance at 450 nm. Using the EZMTT assay, precisely measured the dehydrogenase activity, IC50 values and compound efficacy of mammalian cells (6).

EdU Incorporation To Assess Cell Proliferation-

Alternative methods to assess cell proliferation that are commonly used for other cell types and develop a novel drug screening assay to evaluate drug efficacy. EdU (5-ethynyl-2′-deoxyuridine) is a pyrimidine analog of thymidine that can be used as a quantitative endpoint for cell proliferation. EdU incorporation is detected via a copper catalyzed click reaction with an Alexa Fluor-linked azide. EdU incorporation in replicating cells was validated using fluorescence microscopy, and quantitative methods for assessing EdU incorporation were developed by using an imaging flow cytometer (7).

Unlabeled image analysis-based cell viability assay with intracellular movement monitoring-

It is a phase-contrast microscopy-based imaging technique to monitor cell viability or compound cytotoxicity. The technique involves high-resolution motion vector analysis based on a block-matching algorithm to compare sequential time-lapse images, enabling theoretical detection of movement at sub-micrometre resolution. Cells transport intracellular granules and consume energy in the process, leading to changes in the morphology of the cells and their organelles. This technique can measure the movement of phase-contrast-visible intracellular granules, consequently enabling the monitoring of cell viability.

Motion vectors of the movement of intracellular granules were calculated with the Cell Motion Imaging System SI8000R. Briefly, each frame was divided into square blocks of 16 × 16 pixels. Then, the current pixel block was matched to the corresponding block at the same coordinates in the previous frame within a square window of 24 pixels. Motion vectors were calculated for every 4 × 4 pixels in the frame of 2448 × 2050 pixels. The average spatial speed was calculated by dividing the average motion vector length in the whole field of view or the region of interest with every five-frame interval. Finally, the average spatiotemporal speed was calculated over 50 frames (8,9).

Reference-

1. Bleichrodt, R.J. and Read, N.D., 2019. Flow cytometry and FACS applied to filamentous fungi. Fungal Biology Reviews, 33(1), pp.1-15.

2. Jensen, C. and Teng, Y., 2020. Is it time to start transitioning from 2D to 3D cell culture?. Frontiers in molecular biosciences, 7, p.33.
3. Białkowska, K., Komorowski, P., Bryszewska, M. and Miłowska, K., 2020. Spheroids as a type of three-dimensional cell cultures—examples of methods of preparation and the most important application. International Journal of Molecular Sciences, 21(17), p.6225.
4. Hoarau-Véchot, J., Rafii, A., Touboul, C. and Pasquier, J., 2018. Halfway between 2D and animal models: are 3D cultures the ideal tool to study cancer-microenvironment interactions?. International journal of molecular sciences, 19(1), p.181.
5. Aughton, K., Shahidipour, H., Djirackor, L., Coupland, S.E. and Kalirai, H., 2020. Characterization of uveal melanoma cell lines and primary tumor samples in 3D culture. Translational Vision Science & Technology, 9(7), pp.39-39.
6. Rui, J., Xu, N., Yin, J., Yu, Y., Bai, R., Su, W. and Ruan, B., 2020. The EZMTT cell proliferation assay provides precise measurement for drug combinations and better correlation between in vitro and in vivo efficacy. Bioorganic & Medicinal Chemistry Letters, 30(11), p.127134.
7. Troth, E.V. and Kyle, D.E., 2021. EdU incorporation to assess cell proliferation and drug susceptibility in Naegleria fowleri. Antimicrobial agents and chemotherapy, 65(7), pp.e00017-21.
8. Nakagawa, K. and Kishimoto, T., 2019. Unlabeled image analysis-based cell viability assay with intracellular movement monitoring. Biotechniques, 66(3), pp.128-133.
9. Abebe, F.A., Hopkins, M.D., Vodnala, S.N., Sheaff, R.J. and Lamar, A.A., 2021. Development of a Rapid In Vitro Screening Assay Using Metabolic Inhibitors to Detect Highly Selective Anticancer Agents. ACS omega, 6(28), pp.18333-18343.

Printed by Libri Plureos GmbH in Hamburg,
Germany